SPY TRADER

SPY TRADER

GERMANY'S DEVIL'S ADVOCATE AND THE
DARKEST SECRETS OF THE COLD WAR

CRAIG R. WHITNEY

TIMES **T** BOOKS

RANDOM HOUSE

Library of Congress Cataloging-in-Publication Data

Whitney, Craig R.
  Spy trader: Germany's devil's advocate and the darkest secrets
of the cold war/by Craig R. Whitney.—1st ed.
      p.   cm.
      Includes index.
    ISBN 0-8129-2221-2
    1. Vogel, Wolfgang, 1925–   . 2. Diplomats—Germany (East)—
Biography. 3. Germany (East)—Foreign relations—Germany (West)
4. Germany (West)—Foreign relations—Germany (East) 5. Espionage—
Germany. 6. Lawyers—Germany (East) 7. Espionage, East German.
I. Title.
DD287.7.V64W48   1993
327.2′092—dc20
[B]

Manufactured in the United States of America
98765432
First Edition

DESIGN BY GLEN M. EDELSTEIN

To Heidi
And for Alexandra and Stefan

FAUST: *Nun gut, wer bist du denn?*
MEPHISTOPHELES: *Ein Teil von jener Kraft,*
Die stets das Böse will und stets das Gute schafft.
(Goethe: Faust, *Part I, 1335–1336)*

FAUST: *Very well, who are you, then?*
MEPHISTOPHELES: *Part of a power that would*
Everywhere work evil, but nonetheless does good.

FOREWORD

Fifteen years before this book was written, when I was a correspondent of *The New York Times* in Moscow, Robert Gottlieb of the William Morris Agency wrote asking whether I would consider writing a spy novel. To make a long story short, this book, though not a spy novel at all, is the answer to Robert's question. To him, my agent, my thanks for asking.

It was Peter Osnos, publisher of Times Books at Random House, who had the idea that this should be not a novel but a work of journalism. Peter, a true friend of many years' standing, suffered through the various drafts and, with Ken Gellman, associate editor, helped push them closer toward coherence. Follin Armfield sensitively edited the final version. Whatever faults remain are mine alone.

The book would never have been possible unless Wolfgang and Helga Vogel had been willing to open their lives and answer my many questions over a period of nearly two years, despite the many more pressing problems they faced. I am equally grateful to their lawyers, Dr. Friederike Schulenburg and Wolfgang Schomburg, for their unstinting and trusting cooperation.

But this is no authorized biography. Dr. Vogel patiently looked up facts and data from hundreds of his files, and did his best to recall distant events, but he did not give me uncontrolled access to his archives. Some of these were seized by German prosecutors investigating allegations against him, and as to many others, Vogel is still bound to respect the privacy of his clients.

To try to get at the truth despite all the obstacles, I have attempted, wherever possible, to verify Vogel's account of his activities with other people who witnessed or took part in them.

Nevertheless, it would be foolish to pretend that this is a complete record of some of the most secret chapters of the entire Cold War. I hope it is a useful first draft of history. Wolfgang Vogel, like some of the other actors in his story, may not always agree with the portrait of him and his activities that I have drawn. But I hope he will recognize it as the critical but fair account I assured him I would try to make it.

To all those who have helped by so generously sharing their recollections, I express my gratitude, most of all to John Mapother, who first got me interested in Vogel's story. There is a full list of the interviewees at the end of the book. I owe a particular debt to Francis J. Meehan, Jeffrey H. Smith, Harvey A. Silverglate, Frederic L. Pryor, and Ronnie Greenwald for their extensive help in the research, and for reviewing parts of the drafts of the manuscript. Ludwig Rehlinger, Klaus Bölling, Richard A. Barkley, and Carl Gustaf Svingel were all extraordinarily generous with their time and observations; and Volker Heinz, Heinz Felfe, Martina Kischke, and Richard D. Copaken stand out among the many others who especially enriched this story by being willing to tell me their own.

For their equally invaluable assistance and cheerful cooperation in other ways, I thank my colleagues at *The New York Times:* Marion Underhill, R. A. Beard, and Suzanne Cassidy of the London Bureau; Victor Homola of the Berlin Bureau; Kerstin Witt and Adele Riepe of the Bonn Bureau; and Nikolai Khalip of the Moscow Bureau. Leslie Susser, a journalist in Jerusalem, was also helpful in research there.

I am grateful to my editors at *The New York Times* for assigning me to Germany in the early 1970s, giving me my life's work then, and sending me back over the decades since. To Arthur O. Sulzberger, chairman of *The New York Times,* and Carol Sulzberger go my thanks for providing me with the congenial setting in which almost all of the writing was done.

But most of all, my thanks go to my wife and hardest-working helper, Heidi Whitney, for preparing transcripts of many hours of interviews in both English and German, for retyping large sections of the manuscript after the computer ate them, and for being there and sustaining me in the work all the while. I hope she finds the result worth the sacrifice.

Craig R. Whitney
London—New York City—Bonn

CONTENTS

GLOSSARY OF NAMES AND GERMAN ABBREVIATIONS

Abel, Rudolf Ivanovich 1903–1971. Soviet spy, born as William H. Fisher to Russian émigré parents in Britain and infiltrated into the United States after World War II. Tried in New York City in 1957 and sentenced to thirty years' imprisonment. Swapped, with Vogel's help, at the Glienicke Bridge on February 10, 1962, for Francis Gary Powers, the captured American U-2 pilot. Later taught at the KGB's "Higher School" in Moscow.

Barkley, Richard C. 1932–. American career diplomat, political counselor, U.S. Embassy in Bonn, 1982–1985; deputy chief of mission in Pretoria, 1985–1988, and ambassador to East Germany, 1988–1990.

Benjamin, Hilde 1902–1989. Communist lawyer who restructured East German justice system after the war, becoming justice minister after the anti-Soviet riots of 1953. She purged the ministry and dismissed Vogel from his position as a junior official. Retired 1967. Widow of a Jewish Communist who perished in Mauthausen concentration camp in 1942, she was known for her harsh sentences.

Bölling, Klaus 1928–. Journalist and Social Democratic Party official, spokesman for Chancellor Helmut Schmidt's government, 1974–1981, and second West German "ambassador" to East Berlin, 1981–1982.

Brandt, Willy 1913–1992. German anti-Nazi resistance fighter, Social Democrat, mayor of West Berlin, foreign minister and chancellor of West Germany, 1969–1974. Initiated the *Ostpolitik* by which West Germany normalized its relations with the Soviet Union and the other Communist countries, including East Germany, and won the 1971 Nobel Peace Prize.

Bräutigam, Hans Otto 1931–. West German "ambassador" to East Berlin, 1982–1988.

Copaken, Richard D. 1941–. Washington lawyer who represented Ewa Shadrin, the wife of a Soviet defector who disappeared mysteriously in Vienna in 1975 while working for the CIA.

Donovan, James B. 1916–1970. American lawyer, chosen by the New York bar to defend Rudolf I. Abel in his espionage trial in 1957. Donovan had been general counsel to the Office of Strategic Services during World War II and associate American prosecutor at the International Military Tribunal in Nuremberg.

Falin, Valentin Mikhailovich 1926–. Soviet Communist party official, German expert, and ambassador to West Germany, 1971–1978. Mikhail S. Gorbachev's chief adviser on Germany in the CPSU Central Committee in Moscow, 1986–1991.

Felfe, Heinz 1918–. East German spy for the Soviet Union. In the Nazi secret service during the war, Felfe studied law in Bonn and was recruited by Soviet intelligence to penetrate the Gehlen Organization, the CIA-sponsored network that later became the BND. Arrested in 1961, he was freed in one of Vogel's spy exchanges in 1969 and later taught at the Humboldt University in East Berlin.

Fischer, Oskar 1923–. Communist party functionary and East German foreign minister, 1975–1989.

Flatto-Sharon, Samuel 1930–. Israeli politician and businessman, immigrated from France in 1971, held a seat in the Knesset, 1977–1981, accused of election fraud and massive embezzlement from French banks. His aide Shabtai Kalmanovich, who frequently negotiated with Vogel over the years to try to obtain the release of Anatoly Shcharansky from Soviet prison camps, was later arrested as a Communist spy.

Franke, Egon 1913–. Social Democratic politician, minister for Inner-German Relations, 1969–1982, and instrumental in approving payments for the prisoner releases negotiated by Vogel. Accused and acquitted in 1986 of negligence in administering the funds.

Gaus, Günter 1929–. Journalist, Social Democrat, adviser to Chancellor Willy Brandt who became first West German "ambassador" to East Berlin, 1974–1981.

Greenwald, Ronnie 1934–. New York rabbi and commodities trader, active in Republican party politics on behalf of Rep. Benjamin Gilman of New York City. Had frequent dealings with Vogel during the long negotiations for freedom for Anatoly Shcharansky.

Guillaume, Günter 1927–. East German spy, infiltrated with his wife Christel into West Germany as refugees in 1956 to become Social Democratic party worker in Frankfurt and later in Bonn, where he became Chancellor Willy Brandt's party liaison aide. His discovery and arrest in the spring of 1974 led to Brandt's resignation. Vogel arranged his release in October 1981 in exchange for eight agents captured by the West Germans.

Gysi, Gregor 1948–. Lawyer who defended dissidents under the Communist regime; elected as Egon Krenz's successor as leader of the East German Communist party, renamed party of Democratic Socialism in 1990. Elected to the German Federal Parliament in 1991.

Hirt, Edgar 1937–. Social Democrat, official of Intra-German Ministry who effectively ran the Bonn end of the prisoner-release program, 1969–1982, and negotiated with Vogel. Convicted of negligence in administering funds in 1986.

Honecker, Erich 1912–. East German Communist party leader, 1971–1989, and the source of much of Vogel's authority and influence. Built the Wall, fled to Moscow in March 1991, sought refuge in the Chilean Embassy there, and returned in July 1992 to face trial in Berlin for manslaughter in the deaths of scores of people killed trying to flee the country while he ruled it. Released in January 1993 because of terminal illness.

Kalmanovich, Shabtai 1947–. Russian immigrant to Israel, aide to legislator Samuel Flatto-Sharon, who used him to negotiate with Vogel on Anatoly Shcharansky and related cases. Arrested in Israel December 23, 1987, on suspicion of being a KGB agent, though never publicly charged. Sentenced after a closed trial in 1989 to a nine-year prison term; released March 10, 1993.

Kaul, Friedrich Karl 1916–1981. The most famous and flamboyant East German trial lawyer of the 1960s, son of a Jewish father, exiled to South America and interned by the United States during World War II; Communist party member and resident of East Germany from 1946 until his death. He also wrote crime novels.

Kischke, Martina 1935–. West German journalist for the *Frankfurter Rundschau* arrested by the Soviets in Alma-Ata as a spy in August 1966 and freed through Vogel, who picked her up at the Lubyanka prison in Moscow just before Christmas in an exchange for Alfred Frenzel, West German member of Parliament convicted of spying for Czechoslovakia in 1961.

Krenz, Egon 1937–. Erich Honecker's "Crown Prince," head of the Free German Youth organization until he was forty-six years old, responsible for security questions from 1983 until he succeeded in replacing Honecker as East German Communist leader in October 1989. Presided over opening of the Berlin Wall and resigned in December.

Kunst, Hermann 1907–. Lutheran bishop, represented the church in Bonn, 1949–1977, and authorized the church's financial channels to be used for West German government payments to East Germany for the release of political prisoners.

Meehan, Francis J. 1924–. American diplomat, educated at University of Glasgow, a foreign service officer from 1951 until retirement in 1988, served in Moscow and met Vogel while stationed in Berlin between 1961 and 1966; godfather of Vogel's daughter, served in important U.S. diplomatic posts in Bonn, Vienna, and Washington before becoming ambassador to Czechoslovakia and, from 1985 to 1988, to East Germany.

Mende, Erich 1916–. West German minister for All-German Questions, 1963–1966, when arrangements for the Bonn government to purchase the release of political prisoners from East Germany were made.

Mielke, Erich 1907–. German Communist, fled to Moscow in 1933 after being accused of being one of the two killers of two Berlin policemen the previous year. Returned after the war to become a policeman, later building the Stasi; was minister for State Security, 1957–1989, making it one of the largest and most ruthless secret police organizations in the world.

Modrow, Hans 1928–. Communist party leader in Dresden and last East German prime minister before democratic elections of March 1990.

New, Ricey S., Jr. 1916–. Washington immigration lawyer, worked with Vogel in the mid-1960s on cases of Americans arrested in East Berlin.

Niebling, Gerhard 1932–. Stasi lieutenant-general who coordinated with Vogel on prisoner releases, spy swaps, and emigration cases, 1986–1989. Successor to Heinz Volpert.

Powers, Francis Gary 1929–1977. American pilot of the CIA U-2 spy plane shot down by the Soviets over Sverdlovsk on May 1, 1960, exchanged with Vogel's help for Col. Rudolf Ivanovich Abel in February 1962.

Priesnitz, Walter 1932–. Ludwig Rehlinger's successor as state secretary in the Ministry for Intra-German Questions, 1988–1989, Vogel's principal West German negotiating counterpart in Bonn during this period.

Pryor, Frederic L. 1933–. American Ph.D. student arrested in 1961 for alleged economic espionage, represented by Vogel and freed in February 1962 as part of the Abel-Powers exchange. Later professor of economics at Swarthmore College.

Rehlinger, Ludwig 1927–. West German lawyer, civil servant, and Christian Democratic politician, and one of the principal figures behind the secret Bonn government payments to East Germany for the release of political prisoners between 1964 and 1989. Official of the Ministry for All-German Questions (later Inner-German Relations), 1957–1969, and again, October 1982–May 1988, as state secretary, or junior minister.

Reinartz, Rudolf 1913–1972. Communist jurist, and Vogel's immediate superior in the East German Ministry of Justice until his defection to the West four months after the anti-Communist demonstrations of June 17, 1953. Arrested in East Germany in February 1955, convicted of espionage, and sentenced to life imprisonment. Released to West Germany in 1965 and died in West Berlin in 1972.

Schalck-Golodkowski, Alexander 1932–. Undercover Stasi officer, ostensibly an official of the East German Foreign Trade Ministry and later state secretary who masterminded an empire of Communist-controlled foreign currency businesses and institutions known as "Commercial Coordination" (CoCo), established in 1966; handled the Bonn government payments for the releases of East German political prisoners negotiated by Vogel.

Scharf, Kurt 1902–1990. Lutheran Bishop in East Germany until his expulsion in 1961; spent much of his life trying to preserve ties between the two branches of the Church in East and West.

Schmidt, Helmut 1918–. Social Democrat, Willy Brandt's successor as West German chancellor, 1974–1982.

Seidel, Manfred 1928–. Stasi major and Schalck-Golodkowski's deputy in the CoCo hard-currency empire.

Shadrin, Nicholas (Nikolai F. Artamonov) 1928–. Soviet Navy captain who defected in 1959, became an American citizen, and then worked as a double agent in Washington before disappearing on a trip to meet a Soviet contact in Vienna in December 1975. Vogel's attempt to become involved was cut short by Moscow.

Shcharansky, Anatoly (Natan Sharansky) 1947–. Soviet computer specialist accused of espionage for the United States after becoming active in the human rights movement and applying to emigrate to Israel; released as part of an exchange with agents arranged by Vogel in February 1986.

Silverglate, Harvey 1942–. Boston lawyer who represented Alfred Zehe, an East German physicist accused by the United States of espionage in 1983.

Smith, Jeffrey H. 1944–. U.S. Army officer and later State Department lawyer who negotiated the technical details of spy swaps for the United States with Vogel from 1978 to 1984 before going into private law practice in Washington.

Stange, Jürgen 1928–. Vogel's counterpart in West Germany, a lawyer who worked with him in West Berlin on political prisoner and spy exchange cases and did liaison with the Bonn government from the early 1960s until 1983.

Stolpe, Manfred 1936–. Lawyer, leading Lutheran layman in East Germany from 1959; negotiated for the Church with Vogel and also with the Stasi on political prisoner cases under the Communists; elected as Social Democratic governor of the state of Brandenburg in 1990.

Stoph, Willi 1914–. Prime minister of East German Communist government, 1964–1989, and member of Communist party Politburo, 1953–1989.

Strauss, Franz Josef 1915–1988–. Conservative Bavarian politician and West German national leader, Defense minister, governor of Bavaria, and head of the Bavarian Christian Social Union party. Fiercely anti-Communist for most of his career, he astonished the country by supporting a billion-mark credit to East Germany in 1983. Documents published after his death revealed his extensive and extraordinarily friendly secret negotiations with Schalck-Golodkowski.

Streit, Josef 1911–1987. Communist party official, born in Czechoslovakia and held in Nazi concentration camps, 1938–1945; key figure in restructuring of the East German legal system after the war and, as head of the Justice Section of the Politburo and prosecutor-general of the GDR, 1962–1986, launched Vogel on his career.

Svingel, Carl Gustaf 1917–. Swedish ex-opera singer who settled in West Berlin in 1958 to run a home, Haus Victoria, for old-age refugees from East Germany for the Swedish Lutheran Church. Friend of Herbert Wehner and Wolfgang Vogel, who often used the house to meet secretly.

Thompson, Robert Glenn 1935–. American, possibly born in Germany, convicted of spying for the Soviet Union while serving in the U.S. Air Force; later, in 1965, sentenced to thirty years' imprisonment and released as part of a three-way exchange of agents arranged by Vogel in 1978.

Ulbricht, Walter 1893–1973. German Communist who returned from exile in Moscow after World War II to build Communism in the Soviet Occupation Zone. East German Communist leader, 1953–1971.

Volpert, Heinz 1932–1986. Stasi officer who was Vogel's principal contact in the organization until his death, operating directly under Minister of State Security Erich Mielke, on prisoner releases and spy exchanges. He was also Schalck-Golodkowski's control officer.

von Wedel, Reymar 1926–. West German lawyer for the Lutheran Church in West Berlin, instrumental in negotiating with Vogel the foundations for the release of political prisoners for money paid by the West German government through the Church.

Wehner, Herbert 1906–1990. German politician born in Dresden, Communist party official in exile in Moscow and elsewhere after 1933; imprisoned by the Swedes during the war, left the party, and became the key figure in the West German Social Democratic party's abandonment of Marxist platform in 1959 and in its later assumption of government responsibilities from 1966 until 1982, during most of which Wehner was party leader in the Bundestag. Met Vogel as All-German minister, 1966–1969; became one of Vogel's principal contacts and closest West German friends.

Wolf, Markus 1923–. Chief of the East German foreign espionage service, 1953–1987. Son of the dramatist Friedrich Wolf, a Communist and a Jew, Wolf grew up in Moscow and returned to Germany in 1945. He fled Berlin for Central Europe and the Soviet Union just before unification in 1990, but returned in late 1991 to face charges of espionage.

Zehe, Alfred 1939–. East German physicist arrested and accused by the United States of espionage in 1983, exchanged through Vogel's efforts in June 1985, and returned to East Germany.

ABBREVIATIONS

BND. Bundesnachrichtendienst, or Federal Intelligence Service, the West German equivalent of the CIA.

CoCo. The Area of Commercial Coordination (Bereich kommerzieller Koordinierung, KoKo in German), the secret East German hard-currency empire run for the Stasi, through a web of front companies, by Alexander Schalck-Golodkowski.

DDR. Deutsche Demokratische Republik, the German Democratic Republic, also abbreviated as GDR.

MfS. Ministerium für Staatssicherheit, the East German Ministry of State Security (Stasi).

SED. Sozialistische Einheitspartei Deutschlands, or Socialist Unity Party of Germany, the official name for the Communist party created by the forced merger of the Social Democrats and the old Communist party of Germany, the KPD, in the Soviet zone in 1946, and the ruling party of East Germany throughout its existence.

SPD. Sozialdemokratische Partei Deutschlands, or Social Democratic party of Germany, the party of Willy Brandt and Helmut Schmidt.

Stasi. The East German Staatssicherheit, or State Security, known for most of its existence as Ministry of State Security, or MfS, in German.

INTRODUCTION

T he Berlin Wall went up on August 13, 1961, for the same reason it came down on the night of November 9, 1989: to keep the people of East Germany from running away from Communism.[1] Only a year later, almost all signs of the Wall were gone. Here and there, a few pieces remained to remind the people of the once-divided city what twenty-eight years of their past had been like. These sections also served as memorials to the two hundred people killed trying to cross from one side of Germany to the other over the forty-year life of the late, largely unlamented German Democratic Republic.

At the southwest entrance to Berlin, the Wall enfolded the Communist side of the Glienicke Bridge, a graceful structure of green steel girders that crosses the Havel River at the point where it begins to widen toward the Wannsee. The bridge stands in the birch, pine, and hardwood forest park surrounding the Glienicke hunting lodge, a fantasy castle that was built by the Prussian royal family in the late seventeenth century and enlarged in the early eighteenth. The bridge dates only from the early part of the twentieth century, but it, too, has been witness to many historical events. In a villa a few thousand yards to the northeast, the Nazi elite plotted its "final solution" in 1942. In the Cäcilienhof Palace in Potsdam, within walking distance of the western side of the bridge, the leaders of the Allied coalition that won World War II divided the spoils of eastern Europe in the summer of 1945.

Before the war, the Glienicke Bridge had been the main entrance to the city from Potsdam, along the main east–west road of prewar Germany, the B 1 highway from Aachen on the Belgian border to Berlin, and beyond to Königsberg in faraway East Prussia. The span had been blown up by the German defenders at the end of April 1945 in a last-ditch attempt to keep the Red Army from rolling across into the capital. Four years later, it was rebuilt and renamed—at a time when the Communist authorities were paying lip service to German unification—as the "Bridge of Unity."

As long as German unity was impossible, the sign bearing the name hung like a taunt from one of the supporting towers. On the Potsdam (the East German) side, after 1961, the Wall slashed along the riverbank right through the stone colonnade, disfiguring it and provoking angry West Berliners to post a sign at their end: GLIE-NICKE BRIDGE—THOSE WHO CALL IT THE "BRIDGE OF UNITY" ALSO BUILT THE WALL, STRUNG UP BARBED WIRE, AND CLEARED DEATH STRIPS, AND THUS STAND IN THE WAY OF UNITY. Next to this sign stood another: YOU ARE LEAVING THE AMERICAN SECTOR, a warning given in English, Russian, French, and German.

West Berliners could stroll up to the sign and peer across to Potsdam, but they could not cross the bridge. East Germans could not even approach the bridge from their side. Between Potsdam and the river stood the Wall, a reinforced concrete structure about twelve feet tall topped by an impassable round concrete tube too wide for a man to encircle with his arms. But no human being could get that far in any case, for the hundred-yard strip in front of the Wall was indeed a no-man's land, a lethal zone patrolled by guards and dogs and separated from the city by a smaller concrete barrier and a barricade of barbed wire. At other points along the border, from the early 1970s until the mid-1980s, the Communists main-tained automatic devices mounted in the fence poles and connected to each other by straight-line electric-eye beams. These SM-70 de-vices were set to shoot along the beam the instant contact was interrupted, killing any human being or animal trying to cross. If by some miracle someone made it over the Wall to the riverbank, more barbed wire and mines awaited in the shallows on the East German side, where spotlights swept the shore and guards on motor launches patrolled the water.

A Soviet military sentry controlled the little traffic that was allowed to cross. This traffic was limited mainly to spies. Most did not like to acknowledge their calling; they were "military attachés"—officially sanctioned spies in uniform—whom treaties allowed each of the victorious Allied powers to send between West Berlin and Potsdam. There, the Soviet military headquarters was located, and the Western military liaison offices accredited to it. So nearly every day, trucks and jeeps bearing the markings of the American, British, French, or Soviet armies used the Glienicke Bridge to cross between east and west.

But real cloak-and-dagger spies also used the bridge, in rare and dramatic exchanges of captured Western and Communist agents for which the out-of-the-way location seemed made to order. On these occasions, all traffic halted, and a hush descended on the scene. Then, in a Mercedes limousine that was the color of gold, the impresario of these secret trades, an East German lawyer named Wolfgang Heinrich Vogel was driven up by his wife. Vogel was always immaculately dressed in formal double-breasted suits cut of Western cloth. He looked like a diplomat and he moved with confident ease. He warmly greeted American and West German officials by name, and seemed just as relaxed with the East German secret police in plain clothes who also hovered around the scene. His wife, Helga, a former client from West Germany who had fallen in love with him in 1968 while he was defending a friend against charges of espionage, was on first-name terms with many of them as well.

Vogel never lacked for clients. The best-known ones made the bridge famous. Soviet guards released American Francis Gary Powers from the Potsdam side in February 1962, two years after his U-2 spy plane had been shot down over Sverdlovsk and brought down with it most of the world's hopes for peace. Colonel Rudolf Ivanovich Abel passed Powers in the opposite direction, five years after his conviction in a spectacular espionage trial in New York City. Twenty-five imprisoned Western spies and four Communist ones were released here under Vogel's auspices in 1985. Chartered buses brought them up to the barriers, television cameras focused in on their faces for a brief moment, and then they disappeared back into the secret world—but into freedom, on their own side, after months or years of imprisonment by their adversaries. In February 1986, Vogel had proudly presided over the biggest triumph of his career, the release of Anatoly B. Shcharansky, Soviet prisoner of conscience, for whose liberation Vogel had worked for more than six years.

The heavily guarded Iron Curtain held no terrors for Vogel. He was as familiar with Checkpoint Charlie as with the Glienicke Bridge. East and West German guards at the crossing point in Herleshausen, in the mountains near Eisenach, knew him well enough to let him pass without checking his papers. Vogel visited Herleshausen once every two weeks for twenty-five years, to oversee the release of more than thirty thousand East German political prisoners who were also, in a sense, his clients. He bartered for their freedom with the West German government, which paid the Communists billions of marks to release the prisoners and their families. The number of people who owed their freedom to Vogel's unique practice eventually reached nearly a quarter of a million.

What could motivate a man like this, I wondered: a peculiar German kind of guilt, or simple ambition? Was it humanitarianism, as he claimed, or humbug? My experience in Communist countries over the years had taught me that human character under Communism could be every bit as rich, complex, and contradictory as it was in freedom. People who seemed to be heroes often turned out to be cowards; sinners often proved to be saints. Which sort was Wolfgang Vogel? The answer might tell a great deal about the meaning of the cold war, itself the murkiest of conflicts.

I first met Vogel in East Berlin in 1975, late on an autumn evening so dense with pungent East German soft-coal smog that I lost my way and nearly missed my appointment. His office lay in an out-of-the-way neighborhood in the Friedrichsfelde district, far from the center, in a neighborhood of small garden plots and fruit trees, on a cinder lane—later paved—called the Reilerstrasse. As the darkness grew deeper, I kept imagining East German Stasi secret police agents tracking me from the rapid transit station a quarter of a mile away and I began walking faster and faster before I finally found the little street and made my way, apparently unobserved, to the three-story stucco house he used as his office. For all I knew, Vogel himself was a Stasi agent.

I relaxed somewhat as a secretary showed me into the waiting room, a large, mostly barren chamber with battered black leather couch chairs along the walls. The Honoré Daumier prints that decorated them reminded me of those in the West Berlin offices of the lawyer who had been his principal legal contact on the West Berlin side over the years, a jovial man named Jürgen Stange, whom I had seen earlier the same day. *"Mes amis, mes bons amis, vous me recompensez trop dignement de mes travaux,"* the caricatured Daumier lawyer in one of the prints was protesting, aptly enough, since Vogel was one of the Communist world's few millionaires.

The calm, well-dressed, father-confessor figure I met a few moments later neither looked nor talked much like an agent. He had been a strikingly handsome figure in his younger years, and now, with his thinning grey hair and a trim and athletic build he carried with dignity on a frame of medium height, Professor Dr. (h.c.) Vogel looked more like an attorney for a rich West German company like Siemens than a mouthpiece for captured spies.

There was reserve and a certain mystery about his manner. By the way his alert blue eyes sized me up from behind a stylish pair of West German eyeglasses, I supposed that he was hiding many secrets within himself, secrets locked up in his precise mind and in his files in the vault beneath the house. He fenced with me about his work in the spy trade, winking that with some of his clients, he had not pressed very hard to find out who was paying the bills. In the middle of the cold war, in the capital of the most exposed and paranoid state in the Communist bloc, his oblique answers were as direct as I could expect to get.

His study, which looked out through a large picture window at the back onto a garden of fir trees, was neither cold nor forbidding, but reassuringly middle class. The office might have belonged to George Smiley, I imagined, with its heavy and dignified dark-wood furniture, laden with sentimental kitsch and bric-a-brac. Vogel seemed neither a Communist functionary nor an austere intellectual mandarin, but a typically German figure—a man who dressed properly because that was the way he had been taught to behave, a man with a ponderous but engaging German sense of humor, as the embroidered slogan just outside his study also seemed to show: RULES. (1) THE BOSS IS ALWAYS RIGHT. (2) IF SOME DAY THE BOSS SHOULD NOT BE RIGHT, RULE (1) AUTOMATICALLY ENTERS INTO FORCE. There was a clock on the mantelpiece that chimed, in awkward imitation, the tones of Big Ben. Antique watches from Vogel's collection hung on the walls over his desk, in a niche near a side window, close to the door. "A watch is witness to many lives," he would say, when offering one of these timepieces as a gift to a client he especially liked.

By the time of my next visit to his office just after the Wall had fallen in November 1989, the world had changed. Far from being a man of power and influence in the Communist empire, Vogel had lost most of his leverage a month after the fall of his protector, the East German Communist leader Erich Honecker. The more than sixteen million East Germans were seething with anger and resentment at anything and anyone associated with the old system. They demanded freedom as a right, not as a privilege to be negotiated by a rich lawyer, and many of them now bitterly turned against Vogel. He had just turned sixty-four in 1989 and was ready to retire. But instead of being honored for moderating the worst excesses of the Communist regime over a period of a quarter century, he was insulted and accused of having been part of it and having profited handsomely besides. East Germans no longer saw him as an angel of deliverance from the Stasi; now he was an agent of Stasi repression.

As John le Carré kept telling us, the cold war had seldom been the black-and-white, good-versus-evil confrontation it seemed. More often, it was gray. Vogel had worked in the mists with intelligence services on both sides of the Iron Curtain, and none of his East German clients or his Western negotiating partners had questioned his sincerity as long as they had needed him. Because he could get not only the Stasi but the KGB to deliver, the West was willing to pay a high price in return. He seemed able to speak not only for East Berlin and Moscow but for Prague, Warsaw, and Budapest—and even Angola, Mozambique, Cuba, and many other states in the Soviet orbit. In turn, his Communist clients could count on him to get Washington, Bonn, and the other Western allies to come across in circumstances where diplomats and official government envoys were either ineffective or indiscreet.

Vogel was useful to both sides because he provided them with a way of dealing indirectly with each other on matters that were either too delicate or too distasteful to talk about directly. Neither American diplomats nor West German officials wanted to negotiate with Erich Mielke, the hardbitten, slit-eyed chief of the Stasi, who had built the organization into the most ruthlessly efficient secret service in the world. But Vogel was clearly authorized to negotiate in the Stasi's name and, by the mid-1970s, in Erich Honecker's as well. Vogel's connections earned him not just a comfortable living, but the trust and confidence of the Western officials and lawyers who negotiated with him. His charm, his pragmatic, nonideological way of approaching problems and his touching concern for the wives and children of his negotiating partners won them over. One of them, American diplomat Francis J. Meehan, had borne witness at the confirmation of Vogel's daughter, Lilo, in East Berlin in 1964, and become his lifelong friend. Chancellor Helmut Schmidt and other West German officials who had frequent contact with Vogel over the years found that he could always be trusted to make good on his promises.

Vogel was not even a Communist party member until 1982, joining then only because of an accident provoked unintentionally by Schmidt at the East–West German summit meeting that had taken place in East Germany the previous December. During the preceding summer, Vogel had made several secret trips to Schmidt's modest cottage on the Brahmsee, a lake in Schleswig-Holstein, to work out the agenda. At one point, Schmidt had asked Vogel offhandedly if he belonged to the party.

"No, *Herr Bundeskanzler*," Vogel answered.

"But how is this possible?" Schmidt asked. In East Germany, as in the Soviet Union, the Communist party ran everything; one in six people in the country held membership cards. Why was Vogel not among them?

Vogel had shrugged. In December, when Honecker and Schmidt had begun their private talks, man to man, Vogel had served as East German notetaker, and after several hours Schmidt observed that the preparations for the meetings had been handled with exceptional skill and diplomacy.

Honecker agreed. "Yes, we should give Comrade Vogel our thanks." Schmidt's eyebrows shot up. "Comrade Vogel?" he asked, looking over at the lawyer. "But I thought you told me you weren't in the party."

In the presence of the West German chancellor, Honecker had treated this as an amusing moment. But as the four men walked to the negotiating chamber to rejoin their delegations, he had taken Vogel by the arm and hissed, "We're going to fix that right away."[2]

And Vogel did not resist or protest. He passively accepted what seemed to him then to be an honor. His membership in the party did not bother Schmidt, who wrote years later that he trusted Vogel "without reservation," both for his discretion and for his scrupulous accuracy in conveying messages, in both directions.[3]

There was something quintessentially German about Vogel's story, with its underlying moral and ethical dilemma of collaboration with evil. Part of it was a uniquely German kind of passivity in moral conflict, a willingness church leaders since Martin Luther had shown to submit to evil and corrupt rulers for a greater good. Perhaps it had been born in the Thirty Years' War, a conflict that had left many lasting marks on the German character and divided the German people, Protestant and Catholic, centuries before the Berlin Wall. There was more than a little of Faust in Dr. Vogel, too—he had sold his soul to the Communists, thinking that he could somehow outwit the devil. Was it vanity that led him to think he had preserved his honor, or self-delusion? Or was it cynical deception?

Vogel had always been blind to an iniquity at the heart of all his bargains. The Wall had not crumbled all at once; Vogel had opened cracks in it, at first for hundreds, then for thousands of people every year. What he had done was every bit as dangerous as boring holes in a dike, yet all the while, he and the Communist leaders he worked for thought they were simply opening a safety valve that would preserve the ideological division of the country for a century.

They were fatally wrong in one sense. Germany, even in its exhausted 1945 state of devastation and partial dismemberment, had not split neatly into two new, independent organisms, like living cells. Historical, linguistic, and even many cultural differences existed between the provinces in the Soviet zone and those in the three Western zones. But economic and family ties had grown up across them over centuries. Germans remained recognizably German in both East and West. In Bonn no less than in East Berlin, they ate freshly baked bread rolls for breakfast, liked the same comfortable Sunday afternoon rituals of coffee and cakes, and stopped at crosswalks when the light was against them even if no traffic was in sight. They preserved their family rituals, celebrating birthdays, weddings, and funerals despite the barriers between them. Families in the East sent their children to grow up with uncles and cousins in the West, and nieces and nephews and grandchildren came back to visit their uncles and aunts and grandparents in the

East, despite the hardships. The country kept roughly the same religious division as in the seventeenth century: Capitalist Rhineland and much of Communist Saxony were as Catholic in the 1960s as they had been two hundred years before; and the political boundary did not make Hamburg, in the West, or Rostock, a hundred miles or so to the East, any less Protestant. What had been unnaturally divided seemed to want naturally to come together, as former Chancellor Willy Brandt later put it.

Insisting that unification was an irrevocable national goal, the West Germans at first refused to recognize East Germany at all. And under the "Hallstein Doctrine," Bonn even refused to have diplomatic relations with other countries that did. The Western allies did not recognize East German sovereignty in East Berlin; the United States, the Soviet Union, Britain, and France shared sovereignty over the whole of the city. So vehemently were the West Germans opposed to conceding that the Communists ruled part of Germany that they even had a ministry, the Ministry for All-German Questions, to speak to the interests of the Germans in the Soviet zone. The West German constitution of 1949—the Basic Law—proclaimed the right of the Federal Republic to represent and speak for all Germans, and it recognized only one German citizenship. Therefore, citizens of the German Democratic Republic who managed to make their way to the West were instantly granted all the benefits of West German citizenship, including passports and rights to state pensions, welfare, and social security.

Millions of East Germans fled to the West in the 1950s. But while Bonn publicly welcomed Easterners, it secretly wished that most of them would stay where they were and await the day of reunification. Depopulating the East German countryside would make unification even more difficult, and the burden of millions of refugees would create intolerable economic and social strains on West German society. So while officially Bonn scorned the German Democratic Republic, it had also had a real interest in seeking ways of making the lives of the people who lived there more bearable, on the Communists' terms, if necessary.

The central paradox of the entire era was, then, that while professing to want nothing at all to do with one another, each of these German fragments needed the other. Formally, for more than twenty years, they had no relations. But practically, they needed to find ways of allowing people to pass back and forth across the divide, of trading with each other, of preventing political tensions from building into explosive pressures. And they succeeded—with the help of unofficial intermediaries such as Vogel.

The contradictions came to a head in 1961 with the construction of the Wall. The East Germans built it to show their Soviet patrons that their country could survive and they could stem the hemorrhage of people by themselves, even with West Berlin in the midst of their country. For fifteen years, the Soviet Union had been trying to drive the Allies out of Berlin. Josef Stalin had imposed a blockade on the Western zones of the city in 1948–1949, and the United States had responded with the greatest airlift the world had ever known to keep West Berlin alive. Nikita Khrushchev blustered, threatening to use military force to get the allies to leave, and they had responded with demonstrations of firm resolve. Still, East Germans were fleeing through the capital, and finally Khrushchev allowed the Communist leadership under Walter Ulbricht to build a wall to keep them in.[4]

The Western world reacted with a storm of outrage at the "anti-Fascist protective rampart," so called by the Communists as if they had built it to keep the Allies from invading rather than to prevent their own discontented population from leaving. Outrage faded; the Wall remained. The impotence of his American Allies to prevent the division of his city in August 1961 had shaken Willy Brandt, the governing mayor of West Berlin, to his core. The Western response to the construction of the Wall had been confused, hesitant, blustering, and entirely ineffectual. Brandt concluded that, in any situation short of an outright Soviet invasion and military takeover, the Germans would be on their own—and in this confrontation, West Berlin would likely be ground zero. There was, therefore, really only one way to overcome the Wall and all it stood for, and that was by political dialogue that would move the focus of West German policy from confrontation to accommodation, with the aim of making partition "more bearable," as Brandt put it in his memoirs.[5]

So began the policy of "small steps" that Brandt applied in earnest after he became West German chancellor in 1969. For the first few years after the Wall had gone up, the separation of the two parts of Germany and the division of Berlin had been nearly absolute. In the capital, East Germans could not go West, and West Berliners could not travel into East Berlin at all. Gradually, the rules were relaxed. East German pensioners, retired people older than sixty-five who were of no productive economic interest to the

East German state, were permitted to move west. Later, younger members of families—though never all of them at once—were allowed to join relatives on the other side for funerals, birthdays, and other important occasions. After 1971, as Brandt's *Ostpolitik* brought a rapprochement between West Germany and the Communist countries, East Germany began to emerge from its diplomatic isolation, and at the end of 1972 Bonn and East Berlin agreed to recognize each other, setting up "permanent missions" in both capitals that were almost but not quite embassies. By this time, millions of East German pensioners were being permitted to take trips to the West every year.

But most other East Germans could not even visit the West. The Stasi saw to that. Its vast headquarters on the Normannenstrasse in East Berlin directed formidable and far-reaching operations both at home and abroad. But by far the majority of them were concentrated on keeping close watch over the domestic scene, and keeping the Communist party in control. Rigid enforcement of laws that defined free expression as a political crime kept East German jails full of thousands of prisoners, most of them guilty of nothing more than trying to leave the country.

When the West Germans had declared themselves ready to pay for political prisoners, the East Germans had eagerly grasped the opportunity to earn hard currency. This trade had begun in 1963, when Bonn bought the freedom of a handful of prisoners in exchange for a few hundred thousand marks. By Christmas 1989, when the last three political captives left Bautzen prison, Wolfgang Vogel had negotiated freedom for 33,755 human beings, and family reunifications for another 215,019. And the total price he had succeeded in getting the West German government to pay for them over the years was 3,464,900,000 deutsche marks, all of it paid through the German Protestant Church.[6]

The church had been key to the entire arrangement. Both the Roman Catholic and the Lutheran churches had been able to maintain a footing in East Germany under the Communists, who used them to command social stability and moral authority just as Stalin had used the Russian Orthodox Church.[7] With stealth, blackmail, and bribery, the Stasi had infiltrated the church leadership, with considerable success. It had winked more than once at the questionable and even illegal financial methods church leaders had used to get money across the Iron Curtain. The Stasi clearly wielded more leverage over church money channels than the Bonn politicians who agreed to use the channels or the bishops who had made them available knew about.

Without the moral blessing that church involvement had provided, the government in Bonn would have found it much more difficult to agree to the human trade. Church support made it unassailable. As long as the trade continued, the West German government never came under serious fire for agreeing to it. What could be wrong with using money to buy a higher good—human freedom? From the beginning, the trade enjoyed the complete backing of all the West German political parties. Begun under the Christian Democrats, it continued under the Social Democrats after they came to power in 1969.

That same year, the East German prosecutor-general, Josef Streit, gave Vogel a written power of attorney (which Vogel deposited in the chancellor's office in Bonn) naming him "standing legal adviser and in special cases legal representative" of the German Democratic Republic "until cancellation in writing." The power of attorney—and the exchanges—continued, despite occasional hitches caused by international or intra-German tensions, after the Christian Democrats took over in Bonn again under Chancellor Helmut Kohl in 1982.[8]

Vogel's spy trades also filled an essential requirement of both adversaries in the cold war. Each needed spies, or thought it did, but spies often got caught. The choice between publicly acknowledging and disavowing a spy was not one that any government liked to be forced to make. Leaving spies in limbo to die was hardly conducive to good morale or high motivation in the espionage services, and it was certainly not calculated to ensure continued recruitment of new agents.

To avoid such an impasse and try to arrange the release of Colonel Abel, one of its most senior and valuable agents, the Soviet Union asked the East Germans to provide an unofficial middleman. Thus Vogel embarked upon an unusual career that soon completely captivated his imagination. Over the years, he became a sort of sophisticated ambulance chaser who cruised the darker and more secretive back alleys of the cold war looking for potential clients. *Neues Deutschland,* the East German Communist party newspaper, did not often run news stories about spies, but West German newspapers did; Vogel, who was allowed to subscribe to them, clipped out articles about the arrests and trials of agents, using them to sound out Western diplomatic contacts later about the interest their governments might have in arranging swaps. He began to keep lists.

There were others like him—American, German, and Israeli lawyers who enjoyed handling such cases, or were so outraged by the behavior of their own intelligence services in entrapping foreign spies that they took on these spies as clients, out of principle. Vogel soon came to sense which "colleagues" had connections and influence, and cultivated them, keeping in touch by phone and flattering them by calling them his secret channels. He was appalled by suggestions of sensationalism. "I am no James Bond," he would sniff, drawing himself up and flapping his jowls, when confronted with exaggerated accounts of his own activities.

But gradually, he amassed a record of success that brought welcome recognition to his government. Political espionage was a booming business throughout the cold war for both the East and the West Germans; spying was one of the few ways Germans could satisfy their unrequited passion for one another.

Faust made his bargain with the devil. Vogel made his with the Stasi. He could not have obtained the release of so many spies, or of so many East German political prisoners, without maintaining close ties to the Stasi. But he vigorously disputed assertions that he, too, was merely an agent. Vogel was a prominent servant of a regime whose methods, if not its socialist ideals, were often abhorrent to him. He freely acknowledged that every one of his thousands of files contained a human tragedy, and some of them, he claimed, had brought tears to his eyes. Yet he willingly served the system that inflicted such pain. In more courageous moments, he complained to his protectors within the party and the Stasi about excesses. Usually, he was warned to keep quiet lest he follow his clients into jail. In a man more prone than Vogel to being troubled by moral dilemmas, such moments might have led to a break with the regime. But Vogel was, he said himself, a man whose greatest talent had always been the art of compromise.[9]

He was slow to see how the regime's internal contradictions—and his own work—undermined the system. The moral grounding of the spy trade was precarious: The secret channels that Vogel had negotiated opened fissures that ultimately brought the whole repressive structure tumbling down.

By the 1980s, the crumbling of the system was impossible to overlook. And by 1989, the trickle of resettlements of divided East

German families and prisoners that Vogel had been arranging quietly for years had turned into a turbulent flood. *Glasnost* in the Soviet Union and revolutionary changes taking place in Poland and Hungary left East Germany's aging Communist leaders baffled and defensive. In May, when Hungary decided to cut the barbed wire on its border to Austria and to let anybody who wanted go across, thousands of East Germans joyfully surged through. Thousands, then tens of thousands, began flocking to Hungary and Czechoslovakia and demanding the right to follow these lucky ones. Vogel, called in to try to persuade them to change their minds and return home, was finally overwhelmed.

Vogel had spent the preceding three decades arranging exceptional ways for his clients to reach West Germany, while all other East German citizens had been prosecuted or shot for even trying. But, by late summer of 1989, Vogel could see that East German citizens who wanted to go West would no longer need an influential lawyer with connections. And with the collapse of Communism in East Germany, Eastern Europe, and eventually in the Soviet Union, the master of the spy trades on the Glienicke Bridge had lost his mystique, just as the bridge itself was now no longer a mysterious passage to freedom but simply a way to get from one side of the Havel to the other.

The artificial ideological barriers were gone. What remained were the real cultural and mental barriers that had grown up in people's minds on both sides of the border over the previous forty years. These soon turned out to be far sturdier than anybody had imagined. East Germans, angry that they had ever needed to ask for indulgences from intercessories like Vogel, turned against him; the reforming zealots from West Germany who swept into the prosecutor's office in Berlin were determined to punish him as a corrupt relic of the Communist regime.

The infallible holy writ of these rites of retribution became the Stasi's voluminous files. These, people on both sides came to believe, would unmask the secret agents and informers who had riddled East German society and expose the truth about their rulers. There was a frenzy to storm the files and discover who the traitors had been. But there was also self-deception. No totalitarian regime, however efficient, can hold power for long if the majority of the people it rules actively reject it. Most East Germans had been as guilty as Vogel of passive acceptance of the Communist dictatorship, if not of active collaboration; this, they told themselves, was how they had survived. Having lived in their vast prison for forty years, the last thing they wanted to do now was to admit that they had been locking themselves in every night. Still less did West Germans want to acknowledge that they had helped make the institution more impenetrable by paying money to the jailkeepers all those years. Indeed, they furiously denied it.

At first, Vogel had thought that the joy of reunification would overpower the urge to settle accounts. He was wrong. The obsession with punishing the Communists continued, but the task proved more difficult than expected. Erich Honecker, who had been welcomed to Bonn as a visiting head of state in 1987, fled Germany in 1990 to avoid prosecution, by withdrawing first to a Soviet military hospital and then to the apparent safety of Moscow. Erich Mielke, imprisoned, withdrew into senility, whether genuine or feigned was hard to tell. Markus Wolf, the legendary East German spymaster who had provided so many clients for Vogel's services over the years, quietly slipped across the border through Czechoslovakia into Austria a few days before unification day, October 3, 1990, and later continued to Moscow.

Wolfgang Vogel stayed where he was, and quickly found himself a prime target for state prosecutors who seemed determined to prove that his whole life's work had been a gigantic swindle perpetrated on gullible East German prisoners and innocent West German politicians by his real masters in the Stasi. A few of the tens of thousands of his former East German clients who had asked Vogel to dispose of their property, as Communist regulations required them to do before they could leave the country, accused him of swindling them. Unification meant that their former homes and garden plots had suddenly acquired a value they had never had under Communism, and they blamed Vogel for depriving them of the windfall.

Vogel protested in vain to the investigators that he had been only doing his duty as a lawyer, bound by the rules and regulations of a Communist dictatorship. It was absurd to prosecute him for not acting as if East Germany had been a democracy, he said. But if Vogel was guilty of complicity, so too were the West Germans. A major grievance against Vogel was his wealth. But the source of much of his fortune had been the annual retainer the Bonn government had paid him—360,000 West German marks by 1989—and hundreds of thousands more in individual clients' fees also paid by the West German government. This was now held against him, as if he had somehow taken unfair advantage of the gullible good will of decent West German politicians. There seemed little he could do to defend himself.

Though he had steadfastly remained in a lakeside retreat in Teupitz, an hour's drive south of Berlin, that he and Helga had made over the years into a comfortable escape from the pressures of his work, zealous prosecutors briefly persuaded a judge that he might flee to Switzerland to be with the bank accounts he had allegedly secreted away. In mid-March 1992, Vogel spent two weeks in a cell in the Moabit jail, the West Berlin prison he had visited so often to receive captured Communist spies. Released on bail, he was left to try to salvage what was left of his reputation.

By this time, Erich Honecker had also returned for a trial that began in November 1992, on charges of the manslaughter of some of the two hundred victims of the Wall. Honecker's trial was cut short the following January because he was terminally ill with cancer of the liver, and he flew off to spend his last days with his wife and daughter in Chile. Vogel remained in Berlin, while prosecutors continued investigating charges of blackmail raised by clients who had previously thanked him for his help.

There are few villains in the story that follows, and few heroes. Readers can judge for themselves who the victims were.

The full truth about Vogel may lie tightly wrapped inside deeper layers of the onion than my investigations and conversations with him and others associated with him over the years have been able to peel away. I have had only selective access to his own vast archives. His Stasi file is incomplete, and like all Stasi files it is a compound of truth and lies, intending deception and suggesting self-deception. The German prosecutors were still investigating Vogel's life in early 1993. Among the few people in the East and West who had knowledge of the events described in this book, memories were becoming more selective and more defensive with every passing month. Those who remember them at all become fewer with every passing year.

If there is one thing I hope I have succeeding in doing it is to describe the complexity of what it meant to be German while the country was divided, and the still greater complexity of what it means to be German now that it is united. That, in a sense, is the meaning of Wolfgang Vogel's story.

PART ONE

EARLY YEARS

CHAPTER ONE

EAST GERMANY CREATES
A SPY LAWYER

"I see that you would like to have a law practice."

Wolfgang Heinrich Vogel was born on October 30, 1925, in Lower Silesia, the region between Czechoslovakia and Poland that Germany lost forever at the end of World War II. He grew up in a strictly Roman Catholic household in the village of Wilhelmsthal, at the base of a four-thousand-foot mountain. The village was twenty miles southeast of Glatz, a middle-sized market town of about seventy thousand where almost all of the people were German, but there was a strong Slavic influence in the region.

Vogel was almost twenty when he saw his native city for the last time. At the end of September 1945, after the Red Army had swept through, Glatz and the surrounding region had become Polish territory. The Poles, their nation torn apart and devastated by the war, expelled all ethnic Germans back to what remained of Germany as retribution for the Nazi crimes committed during the brutal occupation. Thus ended centuries of peaceful coexistence between Germans and Slavs not only in Upper and Lower Silesia, but also in Pomerania, the Sudetenland, and East Prussia. Few

Poles, Czechs, or Russians shed any tears over the abrupt end of German history and tradition in these areas.

Nor could the young Wolfgang Vogel feel bitterness, as he stood with his seventeen-year-old sister Gisela, awaiting deportation near the Graf Götzen School where he had studied before the war. Vogel realized that a whole way of life was disappearing, along with Glatz itself, which the Poles called Klodzko. The Poles forced the Vogel family and the other Germans of the town into cattle cars, just as the Germans had done to millions of Poles and Jews before them. For the Jews, these had been one-way journeys to the gas chambers. For the Silesian Germans, the trips ended in German cities to the west where they could try to build new lives—in the Vogels' case, the university town of Jena in the Soviet occupation zone, two hundred miles away. But as he took a last look around the market square, before the march to the railway station, Vogel felt that he would never again cross the cobblestoned square.

Still fresh in mind was the shock he had experienced after his return to Wilhelmsthal to see how one of his high school friends, Lilo Nebler, a blond daughter of a physician, had come through the war. As a boy, Vogel had often carried her schoolbooks to her lyceum. This had made him late for his own classes at the former Jesuit priory so often that the teachers had reprimanded him to keep his mind on his own schoolwork. Now, coming back over the hill from a distance, he saw that where the house had stood, only black, burned-out rubble remained. Dr. Nebler had poisoned the family—Lilo, her two sisters and her mother—a few weeks earlier. He had then taken poison himself after dousing the living room with gasoline and lighting a match. Various stories were circulating among the neighbors, attempts at explanation: Dr. Nebler had worked for the SS; his wife had been raped by Soviet soldiers. But Vogel would never know exactly what the truth had been.[1]

Such things were nearly incomprehensible in the closed, Roman Catholic world of Lower Silesia, but the war had turned the world upside down. Vogel's father, Walther, had raised him, his older brother, and his two sisters to go to church faithfully every Sunday. Wilhelmsthal was the kind of rural community where the neighbors would look askance if a family failed to attend regularly. The Vogel children grew up under even stricter parental control than most; at the village school, their father was also their teacher. Walther Vogel stood lower down in the German academic hierarchy than professors at a *gymnasium,* which prepared students for university studies. But like the village lawyer, notary, and priest, he was a figure of respect. Every Sunday after Mass, people would find their way to the family's modest home near the school and ask for counsel. Sometimes Walther was asked to write letters for farmers who did not trust their own ability to correspond with the local bureaucracy. The letters mirrored the cares of small-town life everywhere: alimony, debt payments, marital quarrels, and taxes. The boy Wolfgang was soon put to work as a messenger during and after these sessions. As payment for his services, he was rewarded with coins, apples, or candy. But it was the assignment itself that he found most challenging. The responsibility of carrying important messages from a respected authority figure to people who depended on his advice was important, even vital to those who were waiting for the letters. Discharging this responsibility made Vogel feel, in his own words, "very important indeed."[2]

The boy was only eight years old when in 1933 the Nazis came to power. The event was not welcomed by the Vogel family. Throughout the 1930s, the Nazi presence gradually made itself felt in the town and in the family's life. At first only the Nazi loyalists, who were numerous enough, greeted Walther Vogel on the street with the German salute, hand raised stiffly high, and the words, "Heil Hitler." Later this greeting would become obligatory. But the teacher stubbornly raised his hat and answered back with a traditional *"Grüss Gott."* Wolfgang's siblings were among the last in Wilhelmsthal to join the Hitler Youth, their parents preferring to keep them in a Catholic youth fellowship called "New Germany," until Nazi pressures grew too strong. Vogel himself never belonged to the Nazi youth organization and remained a member of the Catholic group until 1942, after it became officially forbidden. One of Vogel's aunts, his mother Elfriede's sister, had married a man with a Jewish background, and Walther Vogel helped them get across the Czech border; eventually they reached the United States.

Explaining his political background later to the East German Communist authorities, Vogel wrote, "It may seem surprising that I did not belong to the Hitler Youth, the Nazi Party or any of its organizations . . . [but] I am honest enough to admit that this did not mean I was in active opposition. For this, at that time, I would not have been politically aware enough, though since early childhood I enjoyed a strict Catholic upbringing."[3]

Indeed, when Vogel, approaching age eleven, had outgrown the village school, his parents sent him away to the former Catholic higher school in Glatz, renamed under the Nazis as the Graf Götzen School. There Vogel boarded and began to prepare for university studies. Because his birthday came so late in the year, Vogel found himself the oldest in his class. He concentrated in the classics and, by dint of taking private tutorials in Greek and Latin from his father at home, he was able to skip a year. But Vogel was no dull grind. A handsome youth, with a head full of dark blond hair, blue eyes, regular features, and a dignified carriage, he caught the eyes of many of his female classmates in dance evenings (among the last events the Nazis permitted after the war had begun). Like many of his contemporaries, he acquired a pair of wooden skis and leather lace-up boots. After school and during the winter holidays, he skied with considerable skill on the slopes of the Glatzer Schneeberg.[4]

The outbreak of the war, with Hitler's 1939 blitzkrieg into Poland, brought new pressures on the family. Vogel's elder brother Hans was drafted into the army almost immediately. Wolfgang was drafted into the civilian labor corps and lived with an uncle in Breslau for the first part of 1944, but in March he, too, was called to arms in the Luftwaffe. But his military physical revealed a stomach disorder that put off active duty long enough for Vogel to earn his school diploma in Glatz at the end of May, with honors. As an airman in the Luftwaffe, Vogel was trained as a navigation instructor, and served in Toul, in Lorraine, in Breslau, and finally, in early 1945, in Danzig. By then, with the Red Army rolling in from the east, flight training had become a joke, because there was no fuel for the planes. Because of his stomach disorder, Vogel was discharged as an airman first class at the end of January and assigned to the "homeland reserve" for the possible last-ditch defense of the Reich. Vogel's medical problems kept him in a clinic and spared him further combat until the Nazi surrender in early May.[5]

Even these banal facts later became surrounded by a mystery that followed Vogel for most of his life. When he had stood on the market square in Glatz with his sister in September 1945, he had still been wearing a dogtag, an oval metal plate with no name but a personal number, 283, and a unit, the 92d Flight Regiment, 10th Company. But four hundred miles to the south, in one of the last battles between German and American forces in northern Italy the previous year, a German soldier wearing the dogtag that Vogel should have been given had been killed. This man was buried in a vast cemetery for more than thirty thousand German soldiers near the Futa Pass. Years later, a gravestone with Vogel's name and his birthdate was placed over the remains. When the mistake was discovered, the grave turned out to be the resting place of a Luftwaffe soldier who had been one of the millions of German soldiers listed as missing at the end of the war. At the time, these had included Vogel's own brother, who had last been seen on the eastern front. But in those days, the world cared little about the fate of German soldiers. It was more concerned about the suffering and the destruction they had helped to cause.[6]

Neither did it care much about the fate of the millions of Germans driven from their ancestral lands in Silesia, East Prussia, Pomerania, and the Sudetenland after the war, one of the greatest forced migrations of modern-day Europe. Whatever happened to these Germans was no more than they deserved, most of their neighbors and erstwhile victims thought. And if thousands perished along the way, the survivors would understand a little better what the Nazis had done to the millions they had exterminated in the concentration camps or the millions more they had driven out of their homes.

Jena, the Vogel family's new home, was an ancient German university town in hills much like those in Silesia. The Schiller University, the first one in the Soviet zone to be reopened, had begun operating amid the ruins in October 1945. Vogel had wanted to study dentistry, but the course was filled. The professor in charge of the department had advised him to register for something else, it didn't matter what, and attend the dental courses anyway if he liked. So Vogel signed up as a law student. The law that was taught at the university just after the war was that of the Weimar Republic, with many of the same textbooks being used across the border in West German universities. Communism affected the students' routines only insofar as they had to spend a certain amount of time every week at construction tasks, laying bricks and setting concrete, and have the numbers of hours they had worked recorded in their student workbooks.

Vogel was immediately fascinated by criminal law. This fact, combined with his Catholic upbringing, made Vogel sometimes wonder if he should have studied for the priesthood. But in the Soviet occupation zone, this would have required renouncing all worldly ambitions, and this was not Vogel's intention. He had joined one of the non-Communist political parties permitted in the Soviet zone, a small group called the Liberal Democrats, "to openly make a break with what lay behind us," Vogel later wrote.[7] And he had also fallen in love—with Eva Anlauf, a young kindergarten teacher from Leipzig whom he married in April 1946. Her father owned and operated a small window-cleaning business in the city, and Vogel took a job as his office manager and moved there to be with his wife, transferring and continuing his law studies at Leipzig's Karl Marx University. In August of the following year, their first child, a son, was born.

The move to Leipzig was crucial for another reason. It set in train a series of events that led to Vogel's first brush with the world of espionage, which came soon after he passed his first state law examination in early 1949 and began climbing the legal ladder.

In May 1949 Vogel was sworn in for his preliminary legal training, as an assistant to a senior judge named Rudolf Reinartz at the district court in Waldheim. This small town was the site of a Soviet internment camp where, in 1950, at mass trials the Communists had indiscriminately convicted more than thirty-three hundred people of Nazi crimes and executed twenty-four of them. The cases Vogel worked on at the district court were far more routine, but Waldheim was a good forty miles southeast of Leipzig, too far to commute, and he collected a family separation allowance of 127 marks a month. The hardship did not last long; Vogel completed his training with Reinartz at the end of November. But their association continued long beyond in a way that would mark Vogel's life forever, shaping not only his view of the law but his entire future career.

Reinartz, a Communist party member, was twelve years older than Vogel. He had lost both his legs to frostbite during the battle of Stalingrad, and had acquired a tolerance for the failings of people faced with the smaller tragedies of life that reinforced Vogel's own pastoral leanings.

Vogel's duties consisted of processing legal papers for the judge, doing research, and drafting his opinions. Occasionally Reinartz even let Vogel sit in for him on the bench. In one instance, Vogel was called upon to arraign a man accused of stealing a goat. He discovered that the defendant had been without work and unable to feed his seven children and that he had slaughtered the goat to keep them alive. After hearing and deciding the case, Vogel had reported to Reinartz, who had asked, "Well, will there be an appeal?"

"If there is, it'll be the prosecution," Vogel had replied. "I set him free."

"Are you out of your mind?" Reinartz exploded.

The accused had been in a desperate situation, Vogel explained. Considering all the circumstances, the young lawyer had thought to himself, "There but for the grace of God . . ." and had released the prisoner. Reinartz had gone away shaking his head, but after a few hours, he returned and put his arm around his young apprentice. "I guess I'd have ruled the same way," Reinartz told Vogel, who told and retold this story to friends in the West over the next four decades.[8] The tale reflects the way Vogel saw himself and wished to be seen: as a humanitarian willing to bend the rigid rules imposed by Communist justice for humanitarian ends, even at risk to his career.

Reinartz was impressed with Vogel's talents. "Vogel is a talented jurist. He has a very good ability to absorb facts, and he thinks clearly and logically," he wrote in his final evaluation. "Vogel has good theoretical and practical knowledge of the law, especially in the area of economic planning law and economic criminal law," the evaluation noted, and Vogel had worked diligently into the late evening hours every day.[9]

Vogel continued his practical legal training in Leipzig until Reinartz called him to his side again in Berlin in mid-1952. By then, Reinartz had moved to an important post in the criminal law division of the Justice Ministry in Berlin. His job was to help the Communists make over justice in the Marxist image, and he wanted Vogel to be his assistant. The prospect of a higher salary in the capital appealed to Vogel's ambition. By now, he had two children to support. When their daughter had been born earlier that year, Vogel had named her Lilo—the same name as the girl he had found burned to death in Glatz in 1945. Eva, sharing the same sentimental streak, had persuaded Vogel to name their son Manfred after one of her childhood friends who had died in action on the German Eastern front during the war.

So Vogel accepted Reinartz's call and joined the Justice Ministry on August 1, 1952. At first, the housing shortage in the shattered German capital forced Vogel to live in the ministry itself and leave his family behind in Leipzig. His colleagues in the ministry found him eager, competent, and hard working. On September 18, he

passed his second state examination, allowing him to pursue life-
time work as a lawyer, judge, or prosecutor. The following year he
found an apartment on the eastern outskirts of the city, where Eva,
Manfred, and Lilo joined him.[10]

These were difficult times in East Germany. While West Berlin,
like most of West Germany, was beginning to work its way back
toward prosperity, East Berlin and the rest of East Germany still
looked like a war zone. And the people were growing impatient.
Stalin's death in March 1953 signaled a time of uncertainty and
turbulence throughout the Communist world, and nowhere were
the effects felt more directly than in East Germany. A period of
national mourning was declared throughout the whole country,
and East Germans respected it on pain of punishment; two workers
in Leipzig who had mocked the dead Soviet leader were sentenced
to four and six years' imprisonment in April, as an example to the
rest. Political uncertainty brought the threat of even greater economic chaos. Black marketeering was rife because there had been
no meaningful increase in production to offset the strict government price limits on consumer goods. East German wages were also
kept artificially low—too low for most people to afford the goods
black marketeers were selling. The disparity in living standards
between the Germanies increased resentment against the Communists, and ten thousand people a week simply packed up and left for
the West.

This volatile, uncontrollable mix ignited a wave of strikes and
violent protests that culminated in mass uprisings throughout East
Germany on June 17, a date immediately commemorated in the
West as a national holiday of remorse and reflection. The deaths of
Stalin and of Lavrentii Beria, the hated chief of the Soviet secret
police, kindled a mood of daring and revolt that surprised those
who were convinced that Germans would follow orders no matter
where they came from.

The Communist authorities in East Germany undertook "reforms" to prevent the economy from collapsing, but instead of
bringing forth popularity, these moves sharpened the internal contradictions to the point of endangering the regime's political foundations. The measures began with drastic increases in the state-
controlled prices for meat, meat products, and sugar in April. In
mid-May, the party's central committee "recommended" a rise of
at least 10 percent in all production quotas by the end of June. This

was to be a key part of what was called a "new course," which would put the country on the road to greater prosperity. Instead, it brought the crisis to a head. When the recommendations were put into effect on May 28, the workers laid down their tools in the coal mines, the steel works, and the factories of Berlin, Leipzig, Dresden, Magdeburg, and Rostock. On June 16, construction workers in the heart of East Berlin, on the Stalinallee, went on strike. Thousands marched on the government, calling on ministers to resign and demanding the withdrawal of the new production quotas.

A general strike then began on June 17, and it brought a brutal Soviet response. Soviet armored scout vehicles moved onto the Alexanderplatz, the vast, cleared square in what had been the center of the prewar working-class quarter of Berlin, provoking protest that soon turned into mass revolt. Demonstrators tore down the red flag from the Brandenburg Gate and ripped it up shortly after 11 A.M., when the first machine-gun salvoes ripped through the city and Soviet T-34 tanks began rumbling toward the crowds, who fought back with stones and sticks.

How many people the guns and rocks and riots killed that day is still not known. Figures ranged from the official count of 19 demonstrators and 4 policemen, up to the hundreds, as rioting spread to 272 other places in the country. The pathetic scenes of men and boys throwing stones at Soviet tanks in East Berlin, while the Western allies stood powerless to prevent the inevitable repression, caused intense frustration and outrage throughout West Germany. The Soviet tanks achieved their aim and crushed the uprising.

The East German justice machine went into overdrive. Vogel, only a few months on the job, found himself at the center of events, for Rudolf Reinartz had become the right arm of Max Fechner, the East German justice minister. Fechner was one of the few former Social Democrats the Soviets had allowed to hold government positions after his party, which had a long and distinguished democratic tradition, had been forced to amalgamate with the Communists in 1946 to form the SED or Socialist Unity Party. Fechner had become a deputy chairman of the new party. In this position, he held the same ostensible rank as Walter Ulbricht, the leading figure among the prewar German Communists whom the Soviets had brought back with them from exile in Moscow to build the new regime. But by 1953 Ulbricht had become SED first secretary, and as Soviet military tribunals and East German courts cracked down brutally on the estimated nine thousand arrested rioters, Fechner's loyalties were put to the test. The party's central committee met a week after the uprising and declared that the riots had been a "fascist provocation" by "Western agent centers" and called upon the organs of justice to deal with the perpetrators accordingly.

The state's retribution had been swift, even before the party provided any ideological justification. On the 18th, the Soviet military commandants of East Berlin and Jena announced the sentencing and execution of two workers. On the 19th, nine more people were sentenced to execution by Soviet firing squads in Leipzig, Magdeburg, Stralsund, Görlitz, and Apolda; eight of the sentences were summarily carried out. On the 20th a district court in Rostock sentenced a "ringleader" to twenty-five years' imprisonment, and on the 22nd a court in Potsdam sentenced another worker to death.[11]

The uprising gave the state the impetus to make the Stasi a vast apparatus of hundreds of thousands of people, including tens of thousands of "informal collaborators," undercover agents, and information networks—an all-pervasive instrument of political coercion that propped up Communist rule by instilling fear. Blackmail, coercion, and distrust were the basic methods of control, with neighbors informing on neighbors, friends on friends, children on their parents, husbands on their wives.

The entire apparatus, eventually far larger than anything the Nazis had needed to ensure their own political control, was founded on a basic insecurity: the inability of Communists to command the loyalty of the people except at the point of a bayonet. And after the 17th of June, the Communists were teetering on the brink of political failure. Behind the scenes, a power struggle was under way in the Central Committee, between those who felt that previous repression and overambitious economic plans had precipitated the riots, and those who felt that to show weakness by admitting error could bring down all that the Communists had worked for since 1945.

As the contradictions intensified, the signals emanating from the regime became confused. On the 25th of June, the government reversed the increase in production quotas that had sparked the violence. Five days later, in an interview published in the official Communist newspaper, *Neues Deutschland,* Fechner moved to reassure the disaffected masses that justice would be discriminate:

"Only those persons who made themselves guilty of a serious crime will be punished. Others will not be punished," he said.

At the height of the cold war, when secrecy prevailed in the Communist world, it was difficult for the West Germans or their American, British, and French allies to assess the political significance of these shifts of course. Nevertheless, the West Germans had concluded before the events of June that Fechner's position as a former leading Social Democrat ultimately would make his political position in the Communist regime untenable. Now, in early July, Fechner seemed to raise the pistol to his own temple and squeeze the trigger, adding a "correction" on July 2 to the interview in *Neues Deutschland:* "The right to strike is guaranteed in the constitution. The members of strike committees will not be punished for their activity as strike leaders," Fechner said.

This was too much for the hardliners, and apparently for their Soviet patrons. Here a member of the East German government had publicly implied that the riots' ringleaders could get off on a technicality. Walter Ulbricht used the crisis to begin a purge and thus consolidate his own power. On July 15, a few days before Wilhelm Zaisser was dismissed as minister for state security, the hardliners struck against Fechner, dismissing him as justice minister and announcing his arrest for "activities hostile to the republic." Ulbricht replaced him with Hilde Benjamin—"Red Hilde," or "Red Guillotine" as she was known in the West, the vice-president of the East German High Court. She was a fearsome figure with a legendary Communist past.

A trained lawyer from an upper-middle-class family, she had married Georg Benjamin, a Communist doctor, in 1926. As a Jew, he had been one of the first to be arrested by the Nazis. Hilde, who had joined the party herself in 1927, never again saw her husband. He perished in the Mauthausen concentration camp in 1942. After the war, she had led the Communists' purge of Nazis from the justice system in the Soviet zone. She had been a judge since 1949 and had become famous for her harsh sentences against "enemies of the state" and "saboteurs." Often she had been caricatured, with her severe, tight braids, as the epitome of heartless Soviet-inspired repression.

Less than a week after taking office, and in the best Stalinist fashion, the new justice minister declared on July 21 in *Neues Deutschland* that even inside the East German system of justice, there had been sabotage—a tendency to protect provocateurs and allow them to carry on their destructive work. "This found astonishing expression in the well-known Fechner interview," Hilde Benjamin said. "This interview justly called forth outrage and protest among our population, because it committed the fundamental error of justifying an attempted coup and fascist Putsch as a strike."[12]

Benjamin's intervention meant the end of Rudolf Reinartz's political career. Reinartz was swept out in the purge and pressured to denounce Fechner to save his own skin. The pressure drove Reinartz to his breaking point, and he turned his back on the system rather than give in. On October 24, he fled to West Berlin with his family.[13] In those days before the Wall, tens of thousands of people could cross back and forth between the Soviet and Western zones of the city every day to work or visit relatives, and thousands were fleeing every day. So Reinartz's crossing attracted no attention at the time. But at the Justice Ministry, the department he had headed was left in a condition of utter panic.

Two weeks later Reinartz did two things that changed the course of Vogel's life.

On Monday, November 9, at a public hearing held in West Berlin by an anti-Communist Central Intelligence Agency (CIA)–front organization, the Committee of Free Jurists, Reinartz denounced the East German Justice Ministry and Benjamin as willing tools of repression in the hands of the Soviet and East German Communist authorities who had crushed the June rebellion. The testimony that Reinartz and other witnesses gave before the group demolished any pretense that Hilde Benjamin's ministry served justice. The Communist party told prosecutors and courts what to do. To serve "class justice," the GDR had revised its criminal laws to make judges replaceable. It had suited standards of evidence and proof to the ideological purposes of Communism rather than the principles of pre-Hitler bourgeois German law. In the June uprisings, Reinartz testified, Benjamin, then a vice-president of the highest East German court, had worked hand-in-glove with prosecutors to put the troublemakers behind bars. "A permanent night service was established in the building of the high court," he testified. "The investigating magistrates would call in from the 'Zone' and ask for decisions. Mrs. Benjamin would decide the sentences if the cases were complicated, and the investigating magistrates would then inform the judges."[14]

Reinartz's testimony before the Committee of Free Jurists, whose connections to the CIA and to West German intelligence were well known to the Stasi, was a major propaganda coup for the West Germans. Moreover, his defection was a major intelligence victory. As head of the criminal justice section of the Justice Ministry, Reinartz was a source of inside information about the political intentions of the East German leadership and, by implication, of the Soviet authorities. In the eyes of the East German regime, Reinartz had betrayed himself to the same Western intelligence agencies the Communists accused of having fomented the uprising.

Five days earlier Reinartz had sent a letter to Wolfgang Vogel. The envelope bore a stamp, but someone besides the mailman had dropped it into the mailbox, Eva Vogel told him when he had arrived at their apartment in Neuenhagen, far out on the eastern outskirts of Berlin. Inside the envelope was a handwritten message from Reinartz, urging Vogel to follow him to West Berlin and giving him a rendezvous that Sunday at Hartke's, a popular pub off the Kurfürstendamm. In a back room, Reinartz wrote, he would be waiting, with some Americans whom he had told about Vogel and who would be eager to work with him. Communism was not the way of the future; Vogel should come over to the right side while he could.[15]

Vogel had just turned twenty-eight years old and was father of a six-year-old son and an infant daughter. The Stasi, he knew, would take the letter as incriminating evidence of his own involvement in a Western espionage ring. Eva was terrified. The only possible course, she insisted, was for Vogel to turn in the letter to the ministry the first thing in the morning.

Vogel knew his wife was right. The day after he received the letter, when he showed his building pass at the ministry's gate, Vogel was told to report immediately to room 120 instead of going to his office. Two Stasi officers were waiting for him there; the worst had come to pass. They would be sure to find the letter, and unless he turned it over right away, he too would come under suspicion of working for American intelligence. There was only one thing to do to save himself, even if it meant sacrificing Reinartz. So Vogel did what he thought any loyal East German citizen would do—he handed over the letter.[16]

What the Stasi did with the information in the letter is not known, though not hard to imagine. The two officers interrogated

Vogel for hours. They grilled him about where Reinartz had gone, who his friends had been, and what contacts he had had in West Berlin. Vogel was aware of the danger that almost anything he said could bring to his friend. In 1953, secret services of both sides regularly abducted on both sides of the Wall. If the Stasi could locate Reinartz, it was perfectly capable of trying to kidnap him to bring him back to the Eastern side.

It would have been easy for the Stasi to force Vogel to answer the letter, have him appear at the rendezvous as suggested, find out where Reinartz lived, and then snatch him back to East Berlin. But, Vogel insisted later, he prevaricated. "They wanted me to answer the letter, to say that I would go to meet Reinartz in West Berlin," he recalled. "They were insistent. They wanted to use me to get at him. I can't guarantee that I didn't promise to talk to Reinartz, or to go see him. What is important is that I never did it."[17]

The Stasi file on Vogel's interrogation, signed by a Captain Werner Johde and dated November 11, seems to bear him out. "During the conversation with Vogel we talked about the letter," Johde wrote. "Vogel stated that he could not understand why Reinartz would write to him, because he was not on good terms with Reinartz. I told him that he could expect to be written to by Reinartz again. At this point Vogel stated, 'He can write to me ten times; I still won't go to West Berlin.' "[18]

If Reinartz did write or call, the Stasi man told Vogel, he was to report the contact immediately. If he heard that Reinartz had written to his colleagues in the ministry, Vogel was to report that, too. Captain Johde's file continued: "I asked him if he would be prepared to help the security agencies. Vogel agreed without reservations and said that he, too, was interested in seeing to it that elements who made themselves available to enemy agencies and harmed our government and working people received their just punishment."

Vogel now had two choices: He could cooperate with the Stasi, or he could try to follow Reinartz to West Berlin. But with a nervous wife and two small children at home, and menacing-looking men in leather overcoats lurking on the sidewalk outside, Vogel felt he had no real choice at all. When Captain Johde asked Vogel if he would prove his loyalty by working for the Stasi as a "secret informant," he knew that the moment of truth had arrived. A "secret informant" was in a category slightly below that of "chief informant" or "secret collaborator," but the job would mean snitching all the same. If he signed, Vogel would have sold his soul. Should he give his signature? Vogel's mind raced.

The Stasi had had Vogel in its sights for a long time. It had been investigating him for more than a year and, as if banking on his agreement to collaborate, it had prepared a four-page personnel file, with Vogel's picture attached and his personal data already typed in. But the secret police work was sloppy and the file was misleading. The Stasi branch office in Frankfurt-on-the-Oder had correctly confirmed that he lived in Neuenhagen, and that he appeared to be politically reliable, but it reported—wrongly—that he had been a member of the Communist party since 1952. The section on Vogel's relatives included a sister named Elli, born the year after Vogel, who did not even exist. On the line for his signature was typed, "signed, Wolfgang Vogel," with the date, September 19, 1952. A report on his work within the Justice Ministry had also gone into the file, describing Vogel's legal research on such questions as war reparations, foreign currency law, property held by foreigners, and payments systems between the two German states.

On August 31, 1953, Captain Johde had obtained official approval from his deputy department head to make the next move—a formal recruitment approach to Vogel. As justification for bringing the young lawyer into the Stasi's network, Johde reported that Vogel could provide reports on people in the Justice Ministry. This suggestion apparently was made by the ministry's undercover Stasi officer, to whom Vogel had once unwittingly complained that someone had been going through his desk.[19]

The files say that a first approach to Vogel was made in October, either on the 10th or the 19th of the month, well before Reinartz had defected to West Berlin.

But the crucial moment came on November 10, 1953, after Reinartz's defection had changed Vogel's situation utterly. And in room 120 of the ministry, Captain Johde had the upper hand, pressing Vogel to sign the contract that would make him a Stasi "secret informant."[20]

Vogel took a deep breath. He would agree to do as the Stasi asked. But he did not want to sign.

"The agreement was dictated to Vogel, who took it down calmly and convincingly," Captain Johde wrote in the typewritten report he filed the next day. But in the Stasi files, a single ink line was drawn through that sentence. The following one, which was not crossed out, read: "He chose the code name 'Eva' and pledged to sign all his reports with this name." What seems clear is this: Signature or no signature, in the Stasi's eyes Vogel had agreed to collaborate.[21]

At first, Vogel felt more like a Stasi prisoner than a Stasi informant. Two plainclothes agents remained outside his door virtually twenty-four hours a day, and followed him and Eva everywhere, perhaps suspecting that if allowed out of sight, he would try to follow his mentor to West Berlin. His career in the Justice Ministry was over, though to save face he was allowed to resign "for health reasons," effective the end of January 1954.[22] Hilde Benjamin, the new justice minister, wanted Vogel out, along with all the others who had been associated with Reinartz and Fechner, and insisted that Vogel should be packed back to the provinces in Thuringia to work as a judge. Vogel was saved from that obscurity by an important new protector: Josef Streit, the Communist Party Central Committee official in charge of affairs of justice.

Streit, like Vogel, had lost his homeland. He had grown up in the German-speaking territory of Czechoslovakia, become an activist in the printers' union, and joined the Communist party of Czechoslovakia at the age of nineteen. Arrested by the Nazis after Hitler's occupation of the Sudetenland in 1938, Streit had spent seven years in the concentration camps of Dachau and Mauthausen and then had returned to the Soviet zone of occupied Germany after the war. His years in the camps and in Nazi forced-labor battalions had made him determined to shape the East German legal system to serve the purposes of "people's justice." Now the Stasi and Hilde Benjamin had thrown Vogel's fate into his hands.

It is inconceivable that Streit would not have been aware of at least the outlines of the Stasi's approaches to Vogel; the Stasi served the party apparatus, and while it might well have kept such things from the Justice Ministry, it would not have left Streit, the key party Central Committee official responsible for Vogel's field, in the dark.

Streit summoned Vogel into his office in November 1953 for a discussion of his future. Vogel complained that a move to the provinces would be too costly, and protested that he could not live on a judge's salary in the remote town of Suhl after having grown accustomed to 1,200 East German marks a month, a princely salary, in Berlin. "I don't see why I should be punished for cooperating and turning in Reinartz's letter," he insisted.[23]

Streit relieved Vogel's concern in this matter. He and Benjamin had never been on the best of terms, and in any case Streit had no intention of making Vogel a judge. Reading Vogel's Justice Ministry file, Streit saw that Vogel had resigned his membership in the Liberal Democratic Party in March. "Since studying Marxism-Leninism, I can no longer identify myself with the goals of the LDP. At the appropriate time, I will try for membership in the SED [the Communist Party]," Vogel had explained.[24]

"I've read your records," Streit told Vogel, "and I see that when you finished your studies in Leipzig you said that you would like to have a law practice."[25] This kind of work, even under the Communist rules that forced most lawyers to work in collaboratives, was the most lucrative an East German lawyer could hope for. The fees the state set were low, but since there were so few lawyers—even by 1990, there were only nine hundred in a country of sixteen and a half million people—a few went a long way. The connection between Streit's support of Vogel's ambition and Vogel's agreement to cooperate with the Stasi is obvious: Instead of being punished for his lack of "watchfulness" before his superior's defection to the West, as the Communist rules demanded, Vogel was being offered a substantial reward. Small wonder that he seized it eagerly.

With Streit's support, Vogel was accepted by the Greater Berlin Lawyers' Collaborative at the beginning of March 1954, and assigned to its branch in Lichtenberg—well out from the center of East Berlin on a street called Alt-Friedrichsfelde, at No. 113. The office was in a square stucco building that looked like a garage, set back from the street, and up a narrow, dingy flight of wooden stairs on the first floor, and a long way from the Vogels' home in Neuenhagen, but it was a start. Vogel was welcomed into the collaborative with a letter that reminded him that he was to pay all the income from the practice to its account every ten days. The collaborative would pay his own fees.[26]

Vogel was bothered by the need to lead a double life. "I am not proud of what I did in those days, but I was in an impossible position," he acknowledged later.[27] Like any other loyal East German citizen, he believed he owed allegiance to the state, but a lawyer also had obligations to his clients. To be true to these and yet also satisfy the Stasi would require all the skills of the tightrope artist Vogel later proved himself to be.

All that he actually did in these early years as a secret informant or "SI" in Stasi jargon may never be clear. Vogel's later recollections were incomplete and selective. The files the Stasi kept on him are partly misleading, probably incomplete, and certainly cryptic. "The SI is very conscientious in his work and provides materials on prisoners with whom he has dealings as a lawyer," an evaluation report in early 1955 testified. It added that through him the Stasi had recruited a secret collaborator. "The SI does not receive financial support," the report asserted,[28] but the report also gave a hint of the Stasi's hopes for "Eva" in the future: "Prospectively, the SI has the possibility of representing clients in West Berlin and then providing us with information about Western courts."[29]

As "Eva," between the end of 1953 and late 1955, Vogel met his Stasi contacts at least once a month, according to the files—occasionally in Stasi safe houses or apartments, but more often in public restaurants and bars or in the law office where he worked.[30] The Stasi constantly pressed him to reveal everything he knew about Reinartz and his association with the Committee of Free Jurists in West Berlin, a subject on which Vogel professed to know little more than he did the day he had received Reinartz's letter. But he did give the Stasi the names of Reinartz's closest friends and associates in the Justice Ministry and in the East Berlin legal community.[31]

Vogel had not been the only one of his friends in East Berlin to whom Reinartz had written from the West, nor had Reinartz been particularly careful about his own security. Indeed, he had sneaked back across the border into the Soviet sector several times after his defection, during 1954 and early 1955.[32]

Reinartz had been prone to depression and instability ever since he had come back from the war, in poor health, unable to walk except with the aid of double prostheses. In West Berlin, his defection apparently began to weigh heavily on his mind. By early 1955, Reinartz had become so irritable and quarrelsome with his wife that they had separated. Though she did not know it, he had been negotiating with the East German authorities to return and tell all he knew about his work for the West Germans and the American Counter-Intelligence Corps in West Berlin. On February 4, he left for East Berlin with a briefcase full of documents. Instead of welcoming him, the Stasi took him under arrest. That summer, far from the prying eyes of the Western press, he was put on trial for the capital crime of espionage in the East German Baltic seaport of Rostock, 120 miles north of Berlin.[33]

Vogel was never called as a witness in the secret trial that followed and if he had been, he would have been unable to testify about any of his former associate's alleged espionage activities, he insisted.[34]

Reinartz, also accused of having kept his wartime Nazi Party membership a secret, was lucky to escape with his life. After the inevitable guilty verdict, the sentence, on August 22, was life imprisonment.[35]

By this time, the Stasi was ready to promote secret informant Vogel to a new and closer stage of collaboration. Also, apparently because the code name "Eva" caused confusion on the telephone in the Vogel household, he was given a new code to use—"Georg," German for George. He had demonstrated his loyalty in many ways, large and small—and without compromising his Stasi obligations, he had also used Stasi contacts to work on behalf of law clients. Vogel's Stasi file reveals, for example, that he pleaded with his contacts to help rehabilitate prisoners released after serving their sentences. Many of them were leaving for the West simply because as ex-convicts, they could not get jobs in the Communist sector, he reported.[36] He passed on information that he believed would help clients, relaying requests from West German citizens for information about relatives and friends held in East German prisons. He also passed on to the Stasi the names of lawyers in the West whom he believed to be agents for what would later become the Federal Intelligence Service (BND), and of East German colleagues he believed to have suspiciously close relationships with their Western counterparts.[37] Tipoffs such as these could have dire consequences for those involved. But few individual names are mentioned in the reports that have survived in Vogel's Stasi file. Asked to file an assessment of what people thought of Soviet policy in the middle of 1955, for example, Vogel did not name names and thus bring individuals under suspicion, but reported this: "Nobody knows what to think any more. The headlines of our newspapers say that Adenauer has been invited. A few lines later he is denounced as a warmonger. Politically indifferent people, mainly housewives, express this opinion."[38]

It was not for such innocuous services that the Stasi wished to spin Vogel even more tightly into its web. The Stasi was attracted by Vogel's contacts in West Berlin, which were beginning to look far more promising than even the secret police had ever imagined.

Vogel's success was not due solely to his sponsors in the East

German secret service. Indeed, the West German authorities had as much interest as the East Germans in bringing Vogel to work in West Berlin.

On January 12 of 1955, Vogel had told the Stasi, a friend had called him with the news that a lawyer from West Berlin was offering Vogel a thousand deutsche marks to take on the case of a prisoner in Potsdam. The fee, Vogel's friend had been told, would be paid by the West German Ministry for All-German Questions in Bonn, but Vogel was not supposed to know this. In the following months, Vogel found himself being intensively courted by a West German lawyer with powerful connections, a man named Werner Commichau. At first, the contact was cautious; Commichau was sounding out Vogel, trying to determine whether he would be able to represent prisoners the West German authorities had an interest in. Vogel would be asked to do only legal work, the West German lawyer assured him; he would not be "misused" for "political activities." "I told him that our organs [the usual euphemism for the Stasi] would have nothing against purely professional contact, lawyer to lawyer," Vogel reported. "Neither one of us would be doing anything wrong."[39] By April, Commichau was openly suggesting clients to Vogel, including one from Denmark. "How should I respond?" Vogel asked his Stasi contacts.[40]

The Stasi was interested in finding out more about just where Commichau's connections led, and Vogel persisted. In a handwritten report to the Stasi on April 16, he reported that three days earlier, he had been approached by a man and a woman who wanted him to take on the defense of an accused West German spy. "At first both clients refused to answer my questions about who had sent them to me," Vogel reported. "To find out, I flirted with Frau Newitzki, a pretty young woman. She played along," and told Vogel that it had been Commichau.[41]

With this information, the Stasi was close to positively identifying Werner Commichau as a West German secret agent. Meanwhile, Commichau and his colleagues were working hard on Vogel, suggesting that he apply for admission to the bar in West Berlin—not because he could not practice there without being a member, but because the courts and judges would be more inclined to trust him if he were.[42] In June, the West Berlin lawyer was actively pushing Vogel: "[He told me] I should apply officially to the board of the lawyers' collective and the ministry [in East Berlin] and ask whether there would be any objection to my being accredited in

West Berlin. I should say that I wanted above all to represent peace activists who had been arrested in West Berlin," he reported. "I should do everything to push through my application, because he was afraid that my connections in West Berlin would otherwise arouse suspicions sooner or later. . . . Commichau made clear to me that he was playing a dual role, working as a lawyer on one hand and, on all matters that concerned the East, for the Foreign Office and the (All-German) Ministry. . . . I have the impression that lawyers in West Berlin are not supposed to know anything about Commichau's real activities."[43]

The Stasi gave him the go-ahead to apply for admission to the West Berlin bar, and Vogel filed his application on July 28, 1955.[44] On September 27, the Stasi officially re-registered Vogel as a Secret Collaborator, or "SC." "Georg" continued to send in reports over the months, most of them concerning Vogel's meetings with Commichau.

In early January, the West Berlin lawyer told Vogel that he thought his chances of quick admission to the bar there would improve if he resigned from the East Berlin lawyers' collective. "Some old farts" on the Committee of Free Jurists, Commichau explained, were holding up his application on these grounds. But Vogel and his wife were also finding his double life a strain. "Sometimes it is hard for me to keep up the charade," Vogel pleaded with his Stasi control officer. The ostentatious wealth displayed by some of his West German contacts seemed to prove Marx's theories about the surplus value of labor. "And then when you hear enthusiastic talk at dinner parties about how it was 'with the Führer in the Reich Chancellery,' you can get sick to your stomach!" Vogel wrote. Once again he asked, "How should I proceed?"[45]

Because the West Germans were concerned about his membership in the lawyers' collective, it took until November 1957 for his admission to the West Berlin bar to come through. The letter bringing the news also informed him that though he was authorized to represent clients in any kind of criminal or civil case, he could not claim the right to housing in West Berlin, which was then strained to the limits by an acute shortage caused by the influx of tens of thousands of East German refugees.[46]

Vogel was now in a position to become something like a double agent. He was clearly working for the East Germans, but he could be useful to the West Germans as well, depending on how cleverly he could play the game of allowing both sides to think he was working only for them. Commichau had already shown an interest in having Vogel represent captured West German spies in East Germany. The Stasi would naturally have an interest in his doing the same for them, in West Berlin. No East German lawyer could possibly undertake such assignments without Stasi connections and Stasi approval, this much would be clear to the West Germans. But to be truly effective, the connection could not be too obvious.

Vogel took his responsibilities to his clients seriously. He chafed under the Stasi's constant presence, and the occasional hindrances placed in his way by small-minded functionaries who sometimes embarrassingly denied him permission to travel to West Berlin to see clients.[47] Without telling his Stasi controllers what he was about to do, he went to Josef Streit once more to ask for help.

The Stasi presence was too obvious, Vogel argued; his clients who saw the agents coming to his office could become suspicious. Vogel was fascinated by the professional opportunities that were opening up to him in West Berlin, but these could be severely constricted unless he had more leeway. "Can't you do something to get these people to leave me alone?" Vogel pleaded.[48]

Streit saw potential uses for Vogel that went far beyond the Stasi's original plans for him to penetrate the "Committee of Free Jurists" and keep the East German secret police informed on what went on behind the scenes in the West Berlin courts. Vogel had been trained in the same precepts of the law as his West German colleagues, and he had shown that he was able to win their trust. He was young, non-Communist, and nonprovocative, unlike the famous Friedrich Karl Kaul, by far the most famous East German lawyer of the day. Streit hoped that Vogel might eventually replace Kaul; Erich Honecker, the roofer from the Saar who was already rising rapidly in the party ranks, was pressing to do more to defend the members of the Free German Youth Organization who were in legal trouble in West Berlin, and the West Germans had told Vogel he would have free reign to represent them.

A few days later, Streit asked Vogel to come back and see him again.

When Vogel walked into the office, Streit introduced him to a well-dressed, brown-haired man about his own age, a tall person whose open manner radiated self-confidence. "Herr Krügler is a serious man you can talk to about these things," Streit told him.

When Vogel explained his situation, "Krügler" nodded and said he would look into it.

Streit called them together again, a few weeks later, and "Krügler" decided that he could trust Vogel enough to tell him who he really was: Heinz Volpert, captain in the State Security Ministry.[49] Vogel soon learned that Volpert operated on quite a different level from the Stasi lieutenants and captains, all Volpert's subordinates, to whom Vogel had been submitting his reports. Volpert was responsible for monitoring relations between the West and East German churches, which had contacts and financial dealings across the border that the East Germans tolerated because they were a source of hard currency. This, too, was in Volpert's area of responsibility.

But what counted for Vogel most of all was that Volpert could understand what he needed to develop his work to its full potential. "Don't worry about it anymore," he told Vogel, and the Stasi visitors abruptly stopped bothering him in his office.

On March 14, 1957, three final entries appeared in Vogel's Stasi file.

The first was a printed form used for decisions to break off relationships with unofficial collaborators. This one, Number PE/H1264157, was for "Georg," whom it identified as Wolfgang Vogel. The grounds were given as follows: "For some time, it has been determined that the SC has been dishonest. Will be handled operationally in the future." It was signed by two persons, including the section head of Section V/5/I, "Volpert."

Volpert also signed the accompanying handwritten "Final report," dated the same day.

> In the course of his activities he developed contacts with enemy offices and persons and was for this reason re-registered on Sept. 27, 1955 as an SC.
>
> In working together, it was determined that in the beginning the SC was ready to cooperate with us honestly and dependably.
>
> For some time however, it could be observed that he was keeping certain things from us. He delivers messages and carries through things on the other side without having an assignment from us.
>
> The checks that have been carried out show that the SC is dishonest.

For this reason the contact with the SC is being broken off and the files are being sent to the archives. The SC will continue to be handled operationally. . . .[50]

Finally, there was a "Notice of Restriction," signed by Volpert alone.

The personnel and working files of SC 'Georg', reg. no. 4148/53, may be seen only by permission of the chief of Section HA V/5, Comrade Capt. Volpert.

From now on, only Volpert and Vogel would know what Vogel's true relationship with the Stasi was. Vogel had met his Mephistopheles, who would soon take him on a journey to realms of international intrigue, espionage, and high politics that this Faust from Lower Silesia had never imagined in his wildest dreams.[51]

CHAPTER TWO

THE ABEL-POWERS EXCHANGE ON THE GLIENICKE BRIDGE

"Mrs. Hellen Abel has retained me to protect her interest."

Having launched Vogel on his career, Volpert and Streit would soon call on his talents in a case of crucial importance to the Soviet Union, and to all of Vogel's later work. Vogel's mission would be to use his Western contacts to negotiate the release of a notorious Soviet spy, Colonel Rudolf Ivanovich Abel, from a federal prison in the United States. But it would take much help from the Soviets to put Vogel in a position to be able to be of assistance.

Abel had been represented at his sensational 1957 trial by a court-appointed American lawyer, James B. Donovan of Watters & Donovan, 161 William Street, New York, New York. Donovan fit every Communist cliche about the connections between the CIA and the American establishment. A theatrically handsome figure with a penchant for self-dramatization, Donovan had served with William "Wild Bill" Donovan (who was no relation to him) in the wartime precursor of the intelligence agency, the Office of Strategic Services, and later had been a member of the United States prosecution team at the Nuremberg trials. Comfortably ensconced in a lucrative practice that handled mostly insurance cases, Donovan had nevertheless answered the call when the New York City bar had asked him to serve as counsel to Colonel Abel. His background and his healthy ego ensured that he could weather any insinuations of pro-Communist bias that might arise. Moreover, the publicity would serve his political ambitions and would relieve the tedium of insurance law.

Neither the American legal establishment nor the Federal Bureau of Investigation (FBI) had any interest in a sham trial that, like Stalin's show tribunals, would have made Abel appear to be a victim of state persecution. Donovan's job was to provide legitimacy by putting up the best possible legal defense, even for a Soviet spy. It was the American way. But in the paranoid and often hysterical McCarthyist atmosphere of the 1950s, few could have doubted from the time of Abel's arrest that he would be convicted, no matter what Donovan told the jury.

In a studio on Fulton Street in Brooklyn, just across the Brooklyn Bridge, Abel, masquerading as a photographer and painter and using a variety of phony names, had run agents and received secret messages from Moscow. He was an ascetic, thin, and dour-looking man who always wore spectacles and usually covered his bald head with a hat: The prosecution portrayed him as an evil Communist intruder who had run a network of secret and sophisticated Soviet intelligence networks conspiring to gather and transmit to Moscow some of the most sensitive defense and nuclear secrets the United States had. The FBI had arrested him in a fleabag hotel in lower Manhattan after a tipoff from a defector, Reino Hayhanen, an inept, bumbling, and alcoholic ethnic Finn whom the KGB had sent to be Abel's principal assistant and courier. After his arrest, Abel had acknowledged his Soviet nationality, though nothing else. He had never admitted to being the clandestine KGB *rezident* in New York City. But he had once made the fatal mistake of taking Hayhanen to the studio, and after Hayhanen had defected, he led the FBI straight to Abel's door.

The trial was held under federal Judge Mortimer W. Byers in a courtroom only a stone's throw away from Abel's lair. The case received reams of coverage in New York's intensely competitive and then still numerous daily newspapers. A hollowed-out nickel, found years earlier on the street by the FBI, had been introduced as evidence to prove Hayhanen's authenticity, for the coin had contained an enciphered message addressed to the courier: "We wish success. Greetings from the comrades," it had said. It was similar to many other exhibits that had been seized from Abel's studio. This evidence included the one-way radio he had used to receive his own coded messages from Moscow; "microdots," or reduced-size messages that could be concealed under the staples of *Better Homes and Gardens* magazines and mailed to drops in Paris; and other paraphernalia of the spy trade.

In the end, Abel was found guilty on all three counts of the indictment: conspiring to transmit defense and atomic secrets; conspiring to obtain such secrets; and failing to register with the United States government as a foreign agent. Donovan convinced Judge Byers to spare Abel's life with an argument intended to be heard in Moscow. "It is possible," Donovan pleaded, "that in the future an American of equivalent rank will be captured by Soviet Russia or an ally; at such time an exchange of prisoners through diplomatic channels could be considered to be in the best interest of the United States."[1]

It had taken the Soviets two years to pick up the hint. In the spring of 1959, they were looking for a counterpart to Donovan, one as loosely and indirectly connected to the KGB as Donovan had been to the CIA, and one who would be content to remain behind the scenes and follow their instructions rather than to posture in public. For the Soviets, Berlin was the ideal place to look for such a lawyer. The Stasi, with its Soviet "advisers" and tight chain of command, could be counted on to find a reliable candidate to fill the bill. The Soviet liaison office, therefore, asked Volpert to designate a candidate; Volpert suggested Vogel. Moscow sent Ivan Aleksandrovich Shishkin from KGB headquarters in Moscow, with cover as the second secretary in the Soviet Embassy on Unter den Linden, to mastermind the strategy that would lead to Abel's freedom.[2]

For this strategy to work, it was essential that Vogel appear to have considerable leeway and not be seen as a pawn of the Stasi or KGB. He would take orders from Josef Streit, through proper East German legal channels, with as little direct Soviet involvement as possible. In the spring of 1959, Streit had rather tentatively summoned him to the party's Central Committee headquarters, a few blocks away from the Soviet Embassy, and asked: "Would you be prepared to take on a case in America? It's a case of espionage, a very serious case."[3]

Vogel, then thirty-four years old, knew only what he had read about the case in East German newspapers, which had portrayed Abel as the victim of an anti-Communist frameup. Vogel had no relationship with any Soviet official, spoke neither Russian nor English, and had never been to the Soviet Union or to the United States. "How is this supposed to work?" he wanted to know.

"You'll be told," Streit said.

Four years of Stasi scrutiny had turned up no evidence of disloyalty against Vogel, though he had occasionally been faulted for lack of ideological conviction or activity. Streit thought he was ready for bigger things. And, a few days later, Volpert turned up in Vogel's office to explain to Vogel his brief.

The Soviets had never before overtly acknowledged having foreign espionage agents and they would not formally do so in this case, Volpert told him. Vogel would represent "relatives" of Abel who had turned up in Leipzig. These "relatives" would write him a letter shortly and had already been in contact with Donovan in the United States. The object was to see if somehow Abel could be released in exchange for another spy.

All contacts with the Soviets, Volpert assured Vogel, would go through him. Vogel would not be compromised or given instructions by the Soviets: the KGB would communicate its wishes through its liaison with the Stasi.[4]

In early July, the woman who would be known as "Frau Abel" duly wrote to Vogel, from Eisenacherstrasse 24 in Leipzig, an address that was almost certainly a KGB mail drop, saying she was staying with relatives there and asking him to represent her interests.[5]

In due course, "Frau Abel" came to visit Vogel at his office in 113 Alt Friedrichsfelde; conveniently, it was not far from the KGB's Berlin operating base in Karlshorst.

"Frau Abel" reminded Vogel of Nina Khrushcheva—a plump, plain woman who looked like a Russian grandmother. In all her meetings with Vogel, she never spoke a word. She was always accompanied by a younger, more attractive woman who spoke German as well as some English and identified herself as Abel's daughter Lydia. An "interpreter" was also usually present, a man who said he was a cousin named Drews and spoke fluent German with what Vogel thought was a Russian accent. Why Mrs. Abel's German-speaking daughter needed an interpreter was a question that only briefly flashed across Vogel's mind; his role was not to question the approach the Soviets wanted to use. "Frau Abel" had retained his services, and now she was a client. By implication, so was the intelligence service she represented. But Vogel had already adopted the view that he was to do his best to deliver whatever a client wanted, and he proceeded to do so in this case.[6]

At their first meeting, Lydia had confirmed that she had already corresponded with Donovan, who still represented Abel in New York City, and gave Vogel his address. "Frau Abel" had first written directly to Donovan, asking him to tell her whether her husband, in prison, needed any help only a few months before her first meeting with Vogel. Donovan wrote back saying the only thing that needed to be taken care of was the ten-thousand-dollar legal fee he was owed for her husband's defense, money he intended to donate to charity. She foresaw "considerable difficulties" in providing the money.

Here was Vogel's cue to make an approach. On July 27, he wrote to Donovan, in the best English the Stasi could supply:

"Mrs. Hellen Abel from the Democratic Republic of Germany has retained me to protect her interest. I am mainly to conduct the correspondence between Mrs. Abel and yourself. Kindly correspond with me exclusively in the future."[7]

Vogel could sympathize, as only another lawyer could, with Donovan's impatience about his fees, and gave him the good news that a first installment of thirty-five hundred dollars was being transferred to Donovan's account at First National City Bank in New York City. Volpert had provided the money from the Stasi's foreign currency accounts, and Donovan soon confirmed that the payment had indeed arrived. By September, the balance had cleared Donovan's account.

Donovan, who had seen some of the letters from the real Mrs. Abel that had been seized when his client had been arrested, was under no illusions that anyone but the KGB had authorized the sending of the money, though he could not have known the technical details. The Soviets, in any case, would pay dearly in irony. Donovan donated the money to three universities—$5,000 to Fordham, his alma mater, and $2,500 each to the law schools at Columbia and Harvard, where his assistants had studied. "It is my belief," he told the court, "that in a land of plenty, such as the

United States, the most effective means of combating totalitarianism lies in the furtherance of sound moral training and a true understanding of justice under law."[8]

The money was but the preliminary step. The only way for the Soviets to secure Abel's release was to obtain another Abel—a hostage of equivalent status. They would not find one until May 1, 1960.

On that day, a little more than a month after the U.S. Supreme Court had rejected the appeal Donovan had made on Abel's behalf, the American spy the Soviets had been looking for literally fell into their open arms out of a clear blue sky. The CIA had thought its new U-2 spy planes, which could fly at seventy thousand feet and higher, were invulnerable to Soviet ground-to-air missiles. But Francis Gary Powers had proved otherwise deep in Soviet territory over Sverdlovsk and had been caught "quite alive and kicking," as Khrushchev disclosed six days later, after he had trapped the United States government in a tangled web of lies about the U-2's true mission. The plane had been conducting reconnaissance of Soviet military and missile sites from which surprise nuclear attack could be launched.

The U-2 flights had been going on for four years, and Khrushchev had known about them from Soviet military intelligence. But, embarrassed by the impotence of his own forces to stop them, the Soviet leader had no more interest than President Dwight D. Eisenhower in revealing the spy flights' existence until he had incontrovertible evidence that he could use to portray the Americans as cynical and hypocritical aggressors. Powers had provided this evidence. Bailing out of his tumbling aircraft, he had failed to pull the destruct switch, and in his wallet in the wreckage of the cockpit, the Soviets had found his identity card, which described him as a civilian employee of the Department of the Air Force.

Grateful, perhaps, for the propaganda value of the windfall he represented, his captors had taken him to Moscow, driven him around the city to point out the tourist sites, and then brought him to the Lubyanka, the hulking KGB fortress near Red Square. There Roman A. Rudenko, the Soviet procurator-general, had asked Powers if his flight had been a deliberate attempt to sabotage the East-West summit the United States, Britain, France, and the Soviet Union planned for later that month in Paris.

Powers had been a spy, not an agent provocateur. But Khrushchev used the incident to embarrass the Eisenhower administration and the president, who had at first presumed that Powers had died in the crash and had tried to pretend his plane had strayed off course on a weather reconnaissance mission. The Soviet leader came to Paris, but refused to attend any meetings unless Eisenhower apologized for sending in the U-2. The summit collapsed.[9]

For the young Wolfgang Vogel, as for all other Berliners, 1960 was a time when the strength of Communism and the Soviet presence in Germany had never seemed more formidable or permanent. To be sure, capitalist West Berlin was an unresolved contradiction in the midst of the "socialist" world; thousands of East Germans were still using the open border between the two halves of the city to get out. The East German leadership under Ulbricht seemed unable to prevent the exodus, but in other respects it apparently had the upper hand. Communism and the separate East German state were here to stay.

Vogel had no particular reason to feel gratitude to the Soviets after what had happened to his family and his homeland. But he appears to have had no doubt that with his new work he was moving with history, elevated to the world stage in a drama of crucial importance. He was intrigued, excited, and swollen with self-importance just as he had been as his father's messenger in Glatz twenty-five years earlier.

The idea of swapping Abel for Powers had been proposed shortly before Vogel had been brought into the case. Oliver Powers, the pilot's father, had written to Abel in prison in early June with the suggestion. But the problem for Vogel was that as yet, the Soviets had never directly confirmed that Abel was even a Soviet citizen, let alone an agent. Also, the cases had to be symmetrical before Powers could be used as a bargaining chip; Abel was already convicted and Powers had yet to stand trial.

In August, Powers went before a three-judge military tribunal in the Hall of Trade Unions in Moscow, in the same crystal-chandeliered ballroom where Stalin's purge trials had taken place in the 1930s. Vogel wanted to attend the trial himself, along with the two thousand spectators. But the Soviets did not want him to go. The whole point of bringing him into the Abel case had been to allow the Soviet state to appear to keep its distance. If Vogel were spotted at the trial, he would compromise that objective. Just wait and be patient, Streit told him.[10]

The U-2 incident had top priority in Moscow. The Politburo and even Khrushchev himself would almost certainly have had to approve the guilty verdict and the ten-year sentence meted out against Powers, a term that struck Vogel as surprisingly light. Though the stage was now set for a high-level exchange, Abel would have to wait a while longer for his freedom. The Soviets thought they would have more to hope for if John F. Kennedy were elected in the 1960 elections, and did not want to give Richard M. Nixon a boost by letting the Republicans take the credit for getting Powers back.[11]

Vogel, meanwhile, saw to the legal technicalities. He received his instructions through Streit; at this early stage, he had not yet even met Shishkin, the KGB official who was his real client.[12] Where "Frau Abel" got her instructions and who wrote her letters were not Vogel's business, nor was where Volpert got the money to pay her husband's lawyer—and Vogel never asked. In September, Volpert provided Vogel with $3,000 from the Stasi's coffers for Donovan to pay the fine that Judge Byers had imposed; the Stasi and the KGB were doing their best to play by the American rules.[13]

The first direct Soviet proposal for an exchange came in a letter sent directly to Donovan by "Frau Abel" herself in May 1961, nearly five months after Kennedy's inauguration. "I remembered of [sic] the letter sent to my husband last year by the father of the pilot Powers," she wrote, in what seems to be Russian rather than German syntax. "I have not read it but if I am not mistaken, he suggested to my husband that some mutual action be taken to help his son and my husband be released. Rudolf wrote to me then that Powers's case had nothing to do with him and I did not consider myself that any benefit could come of it for us or the Powerses. . . . Not knowing how to act, I have decided to ask your advice. . . . what should be done to accelerate our case?"[14]

Donovan, true to his part, immediately contacted the CIA. "I think it is perfectly evident that for the first time we have an offer to exchange Powers for Abel," he wrote to the agency the same day. Now things began to move into high gear, and Vogel withdrew temporarily into the background. Donovan told "Frau Abel" that the United States had recently let an accused Soviet spy go home without trial, and asked her to get her government to make a further demonstration of good faith and interest in arranging an exchange. In June, she reported that she had gone to her embassy in East Berlin and been assured "that if my husband is pardoned, Mr. Powers will be amnestied too. . . ."[15] On August 17, Donovan received two letters: one for her husband, and one for him which contained the breakthrough he had been waiting for, proposing the outline of the deal that would eventually be made: "simultaneous release of both F. Powers and my husband which can be arranged."[16]

"Frau Abel's" correspondence was just as phony as Donovan thought she herself was. It would have seemed more businesslike coming from Vogel instead, but the Soviets were new at this game. What mattered were the results, and the Americans were interested.

These maneuvers were taking place during a politically precarious time. A mounting crisis over the open border with West Berlin was coming to a head that August, even as "Frau Abel" was preparing for her talks with the American lawyer. On Sunday the 13th, the Communists began to seal themselves off from the West with the Berlin Wall.

Just two weeks after the Wall went up, a new dimension to the case arose that allowed the Communists to try to strengthen their negotiating position in the bargaining for Abel. The East Germans had captured another American "spy." Vogel moved back into a central negotiating role.

The new American hostage was a young Ph.D. candidate from Yale University named Frederic L. Pryor. Pryor had come to the Free University of Berlin, in the Western sector, to work on his thesis, which analyzed East Germany's role in the Communist foreign trade system. By late summer, he had finished his dissertation and secured a job with the U.S. international aid agency in Pakistan. Pryor had had help from several East German academics in writing the thesis, and before leaving, he wanted to give them copies of the manuscript, along with his personal thanks. Besides, he thought as he got into his Karmann-Ghia to drive to Checkpoint Charlie on August 25, he could visit Fräulein Bergman, a young woman whom he had taken to dinner a couple of times.

After dropping off the dissertations, he drove to her home. She was not there, and her landlady seemed nervous and closemouthed, refusing even to let Pryor into the apartment to leave a message. When he went back to the street to get into his car, he was suddenly surrounded by Stasi plainclothesmen who told him he was under arrest.

They took him to the Stasi detention center in the Magdalenenstrasse for questioning. Frightened and alone, Pryor surmised they were trying to get him to lead them to Fräulein Bergman, and refused to say what he had been doing in her building. Pryor did not know that only a few days earlier she had escaped across the Wall, and that Stasi agents had staked out her apartment waiting to seize anyone who came to retrieve her personal effects. Pryor's silence only raised their suspicions.

Stasi agents interrogated him nearly every day for six months, mainly about his thesis, which the Stasi had rendered into beautiful German. They had also questioned him about the slips of paper in his wallet—telephone numbers, notes to himself, and old library cards. Though his relationship to Fräulein Bergman had been entirely innocent, Pryor finally gave in to the Stasi's demands and "confessed" that he had been trying to seduce her.

Pryor was never told what the charges against him were, nor when his trial was to take place. But the East German prosecutors had constructed a case of espionage against him centering on his Ph.D. thesis. Under Article 14 of the country's criminal code, it was a crime even to attempt to obtain and publish material that was "in the political or economic interest, or for the protection, of the GDR, to be kept secret." This rubber clause easily covered Pryor's work. At the time of his arrest, just after the construction of the Wall, the East German authorities saw enemies everywhere. "Watchfulness," Stalin's motto, was a license for the Stasi to suspect anyone. Guilt or innocence was sometimes incidental.

Millard H. Pryor, the student's father in Ann Arbor, Michigan, tried to rescue his son by getting in touch with the U.S. Mission in West Berlin. One of his neighbors, William Haber, a professor of economics at the University of Michigan, had worked closely with retired U.S. Army General Lucius D. Clay, a prestigious figure held in awe in Berlin, where he was President Kennedy's personal representative. Clay quickly took a personal interest in the Pryor case and ordered his staff to try their best to get the young man out quickly.

One can only imagine the state of mind of Frederic Pryor's parents when they arrived in Berlin to try to retrieve their son from jail. Crisis after crisis had enveloped the city after the building of the Wall. Images of cruelty and desperation filled television screens every day with pictures of East German families jumping out of second- and third-story windows that overhung the Wall, trying to get to freedom before the Communists could demolish the buildings and seal off the remaining avenues of escape. The United States did not recognize East Germany and could offer none of the normal consular protections to Pryor while he was in Stasi hands. American soldiers and diplomats saw the East Germans as puppets: Khrushchev himself might as well have been holding the keys to Pryor's cell. But the U.S. mission did give the Pryors a list of lawyers in the East whom the Americans occasionally employed to help citizens in trouble. The first one they chose had undertaken the case, but his awkward public statements seemed to do more harm than good. The next lawyer on the list was Wolfgang Vogel.

The Pryors had been warned that any lawyer in a Communist country regarded the state as his principal client and that they should expect very little of whomever they hired. But Vogel charmed them. The way this gentle, smiling, ingratiating man talked and acted impressed them. Vogel seemed interested in their son and in them as individual human beings, not merely as clients. He did not seem to share his government's view that they were class enemies. Vogel seemed eager to try to get their son free; he did not assume that he was guilty as the Stasi charged. After a few meetings, he even opened up with personal details from his own life, telling Mary Pryor—who was Jewish and had told him so—about his Catholicism. Vogel always responded to any expression of religious commitment with a profession of his own belief; his work as a lawyer in an officially atheist society was difficult and often troubling, he told the Pryors, but he took it so seriously that he suffered from stomach ulcers. Mary Pryor's impression was of an honest man who walked a difficult line between his ethical and moral beliefs and his obligations within the East German system of class justice. A measure of trust soon developed between the Pryors and their East German lawyer, so much so that Millard Pryor handwrote a note for Vogel to give to his son when he first went to see him. "You can trust this man," it read. When Pryor's interrogator first told him that his father had hired "Lawyer Vogel," the young man had thought it a bad joke—*vögeln* in German was a vulgar word for fornication.[17]

The Pryors stayed in Berlin for weeks, while Vogel immersed himself in the case. When he saw the Pryor file, he thought the state's case was a weak one. If this was espionage, Vogel thought, then all spies deserve to get out of their jail cells, the sooner the better. If the Stasi had been looking for a counterpart to Abel and Powers, it could have found a better and more plausible alleged spy than a graduate student whose only crime was openly to have sought access to economic data that he did not know was classified.

But in an era when people were being charged and imprisoned just for reading Western newspapers, this was a heinous enough crime, and the young American stood little chance of acquittal. The real secret of the Stasi's interest, Vogel knew from Streit, was that the secret police had somehow persuaded themselves that Millard Pryor was a wartime buddy of Kennedy's secretary of defense, Robert S. McNamara, who as president of the Ford Motor Company had also lived in Ann Arbor.[18]

Toward the end of 1961, an American diplomat, Frank Meehan, assigned to the Eastern Affairs Division of the U.S. Mission in West Berlin, came into the picture. Meehan, who was almost exactly Vogel's age, had been briefed on General Clay's interest in Pryor and met Vogel through Millard and Mary Pryor. Vogel was instantly taken with the American diplomat, impressed by his fluent German and by what seemed a different perspective on Germany than most Americans had. It was the beginning of a lifelong friendship that remained unshaken through decades of superpower tension and made possible many small and large acts of diplomacy and mercy that tempered the inhumanity of the long Cold War.

Meehan knew Germany and the world of Communism better than most American diplomats. Born in East Orange, New Jersey, in 1924, he had been raised and educated in Scotland, and spoke with a Scotch-Irish lilt and intonation. A mischievous pair of eyes twinkled behind Meehan's glasses; he was always alert to a good joke and ready to appreciate the hidden ironies and absurdities of any situation. Meehan thought before he spoke and chose his words carefully, just as Vogel did. And unlike most Americans, Meehan knew his way around the East. He spoke fluent Russian and had arrived in Berlin after a two-year posting in Moscow.

Meehan and Vogel soon found that they could trust each other. As they gradually opened up, they found that they also shared a lively commitment to the Roman Catholic faith, and with it an understanding of human fallibility. American citizens could get into trouble in East Berlin in all kinds of ways; their motives were usually a mixture of the idealistic and the cynical. Meehan understood, Vogel thought, that opposition to Communism was not always the moral cause it seemed. True, some Americans asked nothing in return for risking their own lives to help Germans dig tunnels to smuggle their relatives out to freedom. But others coldly demanded cash to help bring people out in the trunks of cars. Still others, like Pryor, were simply undone by their own naïveté.

Vogel had never met an American quite like Meehan, someone who actually understood how things worked in Vogel's part of the world. Meehan could see beyond the cold war clichés and recognize that decent human beings lived on both sides of the Wall.

No such understanding was struck between Vogel and Donovan, who saw Vogel as a KGB puppet, pure and simple. Following the receipt of Frau Abel's crucial letter, Donovan had received the go-ahead from Washington in early January 1962 to travel to Berlin and try to strike a deal that would free Powers, Pryor, and a third American—a student from the University of Pennsylvania named Marvin Makinen who had been imprisoned in Kiev for taking photographs of Soviet military installations—in exchange for Abel. Vogel, he was told, had sent a message to the U.S. Mission saying that "Mrs. Abel" was confident that all of them could go free in exchange for her husband, but the CIA was not sure how far it could trust these assurances.[19]

Vogel was nowhere in evidence when Donovan made his first trip to East Berlin on Saturday, February 3. It was snowing when William Graver, the CIA station chief, drove Donovan to the elevated station at Bahnhof Zoo. There he boarded one of the East German–operated trains to Friedrichstrasse, the point of entry in East Berlin, to make an appointment with Shishkin at the Soviet Embassy. Donovan reached the embassy after trudging through snow-covered streets that seemed, he wrote later, strangely deserted and filled with oppressive fear.[20] In the consular section next door to the main entrance of the huge neoclassic monstrosity on the Unter den Linden boulevard, Donovan was escorted inside to make the acquaintance of "Frau Abel," her "daughter," and the "interpreter" Herr Drews.

Though he had probably written the message that Vogel had sent to the mission about the proposed three-for-one deal, Shishkin now told Donovan he knew nothing about it. Donovan was aware these were standard Soviet negotiating tactics, but who was Vogel? He thought there might have been another dimension as well, a Soviet determination to keep the East Germans in their place and out of this deal. This would have been fine with Donovan. Donovan had concluded that there was no love lost between East Berlin and Moscow from Shishkin's answer to a question about why the Soviets allowed their embassy to be surrounded by ruined buildings and shrapnel-spattered walls nearly twenty years after the war. "We have not deemed it advisable to eliminate from Berlin all the ravages of war," Shishkin had replied.[21]

The rules began to shift when Donovan met Vogel on Monday, February 5. The meeting was a consequence of a new tactical maneuver by Shishkin, who now said that Pryor's case concerned the East Germans, not the Soviets. Abel's "daughter" and Drews were in the embassy waiting room to accompany Donovan to Vogel's office. The American lawyer's apprehensions grew during the long cab ride to 113 Alt-Friedrichsfelde. The squat, square structure looked more like a back-alley KGB torture chamber than a law office. The entrance was poorly lighted. A flight of rickety wooden stairs led up to a narrow hallway, with bare walls on either side. With Drew following him up the stairs, Donovan had visions of being knocked unconscious and becoming a hostage himself. But he comforted himself by thinking that since there was no place to run, there was no point in worrying.

Vogel was not at all what Donovan had imagined. "In a few minutes, Herr Vogel appeared and ushered us into his own small but well-furnished office," he later wrote. "He was about thirty-seven years old, dark-haired and good-looking with an ever-quick flashing smile. He wore a hand-tailored gray flannel suit, a white-on-white shirt, a figured silk tie with matching breast kerchief and elaborate cufflinks. He looked like many successful sales executives in the United States."[22]

Donovan wanted to know whether the East Germans would produce Pryor at the Glienicke Bridge for a simultaneous exchange with Powers for Abel. "Definitely yes," Vogel replied, showing him a statement signed by one of Streit's section heads authorizing Pryor's release "if the conditions known to you are met by the Americans."[23]

Vogel had been told not to tell Pryor about the plan, apparently because the Stasi hoped the prisoner would keep talking and eventually confess to being a spy. But when Vogel reported to Streit on his discussions with Donovan that afternoon, there was a hitch. The Soviets now wanted to see if they could exchange Abel for Pryor alone, and leave Powers out of the deal. Privately, Vogel was appalled, but he played the game as asked.[24]

Donovan was furious when he returned to Vogel's office later the next day. His anger mounted when he learned that Streit, who had become East German prosecutor-general only two weeks earlier, wanted Pryor exchanged alone for Abel and would try Pryor for espionage if Donovan refused the deal. There appeared to be a contest of wills, Vogel observed nervously, between the Soviet Union and the East German prosecutor-general over the privilege of rescuing Abel. "Nonsense," Donovan snapped. "If Shishkin told the Attorney General of East Germany to walk across this floor on his hands he'd get down and try."[25]

Vogel promised to try to change Streit's mind, and Donovan agreed to delay his departure until after lunch. Donovan obviously regarded Vogel as a puppet's puppet, so he was amazed by what Vogel did next. Looking over his shoulder to make sure Drews could not see him, Vogel gave Donovan a thumbs-up gesture and said *"Nicht zurückgehen,"* "No retreat."[26]

Vogel seemed to be trying to carry water on both shoulders, Donovan thought, and in a way he was. An East German lawyer could scarcely do otherwise when his clients were charged with state crimes. Besides, Vogel was as irritated by the Soviets as Donovan had been. Vogel had still not met Shishkin. He knew he was being used. He had agreed to that when Streit had asked him to come into the Abel case, with Volpert carrying instructions back and forth from the Stasi. But the Soviet "salami tactics" were making him look like a fool.

While Donovan and Drews fenced over lunch in East Germany's premier diplomatic restaurant, the Johannishof, Vogel went off to do battle in Streit's office, where he found Volpert waiting as well. "You can forget about getting Abel for Pryor alone," he told them, expressing heatedly his frustration with being trapped in the maneuvering between the Soviet and East German positions. Streit accepted Vogel's reading of the situation. He asked Volpert to see that Vogel accompanied the American lawyer to the Soviet Embassy that afternoon, to make clear to Shishkin that the Soviets would have to go back to the three-man swap Donovan thought they had already agreed to.

When Vogel introduced himself to Shishkin in his first and only meeting on the case, Donovan believed they were both merely performing a charade for his benefit. Vogel explained to Shishkin, in German, that all the remaining difficulties from the East German side had been removed. That did not seem to matter much to Shishkin, who left Vogel and Drews out in the anteroom and beckoned Donovan into his private office. There he tried one last negotiating ploy that Donovan found outrageous. Donovan had implied at the first meeting with Shishkin that Powers was something less than a national hero in the United States. Now Shishkin claimed that Powers's diminished stature lessened his value as a bargaining chip. So the Soviets would offer only Makinen, the student in Kiev, in exchange for Abel.

Donovan, too exasperated for words, sighed that there was no point in even talking about such an absurd proposal. He would return to West Berlin and would go home to Washington unless he got what he had come to arrange: a swap of Powers and Pryor for Abel.[27]

Vogel reported back to Streit and Volpert that he could not tell how things would finally be resolved. He had done all he could, and the East Germans would have to wait and see how the Americans and the Soviets resolved their remaining differences.

A meeting the following day broke the impasse; the Soviets had exhausted their soundings for weakness in the American position and were now again ready to release Abel, Powers, and Pryor—simultaneously, but separately. Abel and Powers would be exchanged early in the morning at the Glienicke Bridge, safely tucked away from the curious and the news media. But Pryor would be freed separately at Checkpoint Charlie, to preserve the appearance at least of East German sovereignty over his case. Makinen could expect clemency in the near future. Shishkin and Donovan shook hands, and at last the exchange was on, for 8:30 A.M. on Saturday, February 10.[28]

Though Vogel would not be at the bridge on the big day, it was only a few days before then that he finally met Frederic Pryor. Vogel walked into the visiting room at the Magdalenenstrasse jail with the note in Millard Pryor's handwriting telling his son he could trust this man, gave it to him, and pointed to the ceiling. With his lips, Vogel mouthed the word "microphone," a warning that the Stasi would overhear everything they said. Vogel was elliptical, implying that he was not much concerned about preparing a defense. Probably there would be no trial at all, Vogel seemed to be saying, and Pryor could expect to go free very soon, but when and how Vogel did not say. Nor did he mention Abel and Powers. By this time, Pryor expected little from East German justice. Confused and dazed, he was resigned to spending five or ten years in prison, and did not let his hopes rise.

Pryor's Stasi interrogator knew that he was going to be released soon. The orders were direct: Vogel is handling it, it has been cleared, do as you're told.[29] The interrogator spent Friday night in Pryor's cell, telling him his jailers were afraid the dejected prisoner would try to commit suicide.[30]

Saturday, February 10, dawned crisp, clear, and bitter cold. Vogel arrived at the Magdalenenstrasse just as it was beginning to get light and announced to Pryor, who was disoriented and had trouble absorbing the information, that he was free to pack his few things and leave. There was still no mention of Abel or Powers, but Pryor would not have understood anyway. "During that day and the next, I felt quite giddy and irresponsible—as if I had been drugged," Pryor later recalled. He had been cut off from the outside world since his arrest in August. In Vogel's Mercedes he tried to catch up on the news even though a prison guard had also joined them for the short ride to Checkpoint Charlie. At the clearing before the entrance, the guard got out of the car and stood outside. There would be a delay, Vogel said calmly, still not explaining what was happening.

But again Vogel surprised Pryor by quietly asking him to point out all of the Stasi officers he recognized. Once you sup with the devil, Pryor thought, you have to have a long spoon, and you also have to know at all times who is sitting at the table with you.[31] For Vogel, perhaps the scene evoked his own four-year period of open observation by the Stasi. This had ended after Volpert had appeared, but Vogel was never sure that the surveillance had stopped. And so they whiled away the time, waiting for Frank Meehan to arrive as scheduled to take delivery of his countryman.

Before dawn, Donovan had found Abel looking old and careworn in a holding cell on the U.S. mission grounds. He asked his client whether he was worried about what would happen when he went back home to Moscow. "Of course not," Abel replied. "I've done nothing dishonorable."[32]

They went separately to the Glienicke Bridge, Donovan riding with Graver, the CIA station chief, and Abel in a car filled with guards, one of whom, Donovan noted, was one of the largest men he had ever seen, perhaps six feet seven inches tall and three hundred pounds. At 8:20 Donovan walked to the center of the bridge, flanked by the chief of the American mission and Joseph Murphy, another U-2 pilot. At precisely the same moment Shishkin walked toward the center of the bridge from Potsdam, accompanied by two civilians, one of whom was Nikolai A. Korznikov, Abel's direct superior in the KGB.[33] Spies from East and West solemnly shook hands and each then beckoned to his side of the bridge for the final pas de deux.

Abel, flanked by the deputy director of U.S. prisons and the giant guard, walked forward from West Berlin. Powers, wearing a fur hat and accompanied by two men who Donovan thought looked like retired wrestlers, approached from the East German side. Murphy, who was there to verify Powers's identity, asked him the name of his high school coach. Powers could not remember, but did better with the names of his wife, mother, and dog. "You're Francis Gary Powers," Murphy established. In precise and clipped fashion, Shishkin announced that Pryor had been released at Friedrichstrasse, and that Abel could now be exchanged for Powers. "I told him I must confirm this and called for confirmation from our end of the bridge," Donovan recalled. "Someone finally yelled back to me, 'No word on Pryor yet.' "[34]

It was Meehan, nearly fifteen miles away at Checkpoint Charlie, who would have to give that word, and at this exact moment he found himself caught in a similar bind. He had walked over to the East German side, and found Vogel waiting in the car where he had said he would be, with Pryor in the back seat. Okay, Meehan had said, let's go to West Berlin. Vogel motioned for him to climb in, but made no move to start the car. Gesturing at the security types standing around in their imitation leather coats, he told Meehan, "We will be waiting here until we get the word from them."[35]

Back at the Glienicke Bridge, Shishkin expressed anxiety that the diplomatic traffic would soon begin to build up, and pressed to go ahead. "We wait right here until my people confirm that Pryor had been released," Donovan insisted. Shishkin protested that the student had probably been freed already. "Perhaps Vogel is arguing with Pryor about his legal fees," Donovan cracked. "This could take months."[36]

As the time dragged on, Meehan, sitting in Vogel's car, began to worry. "Oh, Jesus, what to do?" he thought to himself. But after an interminable delay, one of the East German security guards came up to the car. Vogel rolled down the window and talked to him for a moment. Then he turned to Meehan and said, "We can go now." After shaking hands with Vogel, Pryor then walked with Meehan the remaining few yards across to the American sector, where Millard Pryor was waiting to take his son back home.

At the same instant, at the Glienicke Bridge, Powers and Abel moved forward and passed each other without making eye contact, each carrying an overstuffed bag. Abel asked Wilkinson for the paper giving him his official pardon, and then shook hands with Donovan for the last time.

Within minutes, Powers and the other Americans were on board an Air Force Super Constellation winging their way through the Berlin corridor to the West. The Air Force crew, Donovan noticed, were treating Powers like anything but a hero. More, he thought, like a pariah.[37]

While they were in the air, the news of the exchange broke in Washington, where it was nearly 3 A.M. The White House press secretary, Pierre Salinger, had known that an exchange of some sort was to take place in Berlin in the early morning hours, and had tipped off a few correspondents to come back to the White House before they went to bed. The news was a sensation that remade front pages around the world, but Salinger had needed the help of a West German correspondent in the briefing room to locate the Glienicke Bridge on the map.[38]

Even with the limitations on his role, Vogel had managed to please all his clients.

Pryor wrote him from Ann Arbor three months after his release. His Karmann-Ghia had been shipped back as promised, even though the clock had stopped and there were a few new dents. Pryor thanked his lawyer for all he had done and said he hoped that he would have the opportunity to help others as much as Vogel had helped him.[39]

Vogel's ability to keep simultaneously the confidences of clients with opposing interests had never been in doubt. Now he had shown that he could serve those interests simultaneously, if he was allowed, like a priest in the confessional, to preserve the integrity of the lawyer-client privilege. It had seemed odd to Pryor that a lawyer who clearly served the Stasi would warn him about surveillance bugs in the prison visiting room, just as it had surprised Donovan when Vogel urged him to stand firm in taking a position that opposed Vogel's own brief. In a less complicated man, this might have been the hypocrisy that Donovan suspected it was. But for Vogel, cases were not abstractions—they concerned the lives of individual human beings, each with an individual tragedy. Vogel's very commitment to his clients also allowed him to preserve his own integrity with the Stasi. Streit respected this and tolerated his demonstrations of independence. After all, East Germany had come out of this exchange looking good.

The Soviets were also satisfied, and soon showed their appreciation by giving Vogel a mandate in similar cases in England and France. They had learned, from the Abel case, that they need not have become so directly involved themselves. Shishkin need not have broken cover to come into contact with the American side as he had done. The CIA had kept its distance, and perhaps its secrets, far more effectively by using Donovan. In the future the KGB would use Vogel in this same manner. He had shown that he had the loyalty, the good judgment, the discretion, and the suave manner with Westerners to handle such negotiations entirely by himself. The Soviets had no lawyers of such sophistication in Moscow, but through the Stasi, they could avail themselves of Vogel's services in Berlin whenever they liked.[40]

Vogel had picked up some important information from his Stasi and Soviet contacts. From "Drews," the Russian- and German-speaking "cousin" who had accompanied "Frau Abel" and her "daughter," Vogel had received the first hint of how deeply concerned the Kremlin was about the continuing flow of refugees from East Germany to the West. For most of early 1961, the numbers had been relatively constant, between thirteen and twenty thousand people a month. But in July more than thirty thousand had fled, and in August their numbers were still rising. Half of the refugees were younger than twenty-five. The country's future was running away, and that something would have to be done was an open secret. What, and when, nobody knew. Vogel got the impression that it would be something drastic, and that it would happen before the middle of August.

Vogel took these developments very personally. One of his closest friends, a doctor named Hans-Christoph Crosta, wanted to leave East Germany. He and Vogel had met at the only East German ski resort, at Oberhof in the Thuringian mountains, in the mid-1950s. They shared a love of the sport and vacationed regularly together. Like Vogel, Dr. Crosta was a privileged man with a secret. He had a prestigious job as a physician to the East German Olympic team, but was deeply unhappy and wanted to get out to the West. Whatever Vogel's special relationship with the Stasi by 1961, he did not betray his friend's confidence. On Thursday, August 10, after "Drews" dropped a heavy hint that something was about to happen at the border, Vogel got in his car and drove to Crosta's home in Merseburg, arriving shortly before midnight. If Crosta wanted to get out, Vogel told him, he had better go soon. Vogel was not sure whether the hints he was getting meant that a wall or some other form of border control was coming, but he left Crosta with the impression that some action was coming, perhaps as soon as that Saturday night.

Vogel had offered only hints and a hunch, but Crosta took him literally, and left, taking his mother with him, on Saturday morning. Vogel even helped, bringing Mrs. Crosta's furs and the family silver to his own apartment in East Berlin.[41] Later that day, he and Eva took it across to West Berlin later that day to the apartment where Crosta was staying on the Keithstrasse, near the zoo. The Vogels stayed until long after midnight.

Toward three o'clock in the morning, Crosta had been listening to RIAS, the American-run German-language station in West Berlin, and suddenly came running out of the kitchen to tell Vogel the news: "The border's been closed. The tanks are at the Brandenburg Gate." East German soldiers with pneumatic drills were digging a ditch at the Brandenburg Gate and everywhere else East German troops and workers were building a wall. Soviet tanks and troops stood behind them, ready to repel any attempt by the Americans to stop the construction.

At first, the Vogels thought Crosta was kidding. Their children Manfred and Lilo were on the other side, in the apartment on the Ostseestrasse, near the center, where the family had recently moved. They had to go back, and drove across the border, even as the jackhammers thundered and the tanks rumbled through the streets. West Berlin border guards and American soldiers who saw the East German plates on the car stared in disbelief. Vogel found himself almost disappointed that the Americans had been unable to do anything to prevent the division of the city. But despite his feelings, the Wall would shape Vogel's life and his career. It would propel him into even greater prominence and in the years to come make his role indispensable.[42]

PART TWO

THE WALL

CHAPTER THREE

THE TRADE IN EAST GERMAN POLITICAL PRISONERS

"There is news that can kill, while pretending to inform."

Phe dramatic and brutal decision to seal off West Berlin with the Wall ended the hopes of easy escape for millions of East Germans suffering under Communism. An "economic miracle" had flourished in the Western zones following the introduction of a stable West German currency, the deutsche mark, and the Marshall Plan. This prosperity had no counterpart in the Soviet-occupied German Democratic Republic. While Germans in the West enjoyed abundance, their compatriots in the East had not been able to obtain even the basic necessities of life. The shortcomings of Communist central planning and the reparations exacted by the Soviets during the early postwar years only made matters worse. Shortages of coal, steel, building materials, fertilizer, and food created a cycle of deprivation and oppression. As in the early 1950s, again tens of thousands of East Germans were seeking to escape by moving West.

As long as Soviet policy held out the prospect of a united, neutral Germany, the border remained relatively open, and East Germans took advantage of the freedom. About 197,000 of them had crossed to the West in 1960, and the floodwaters had been steadily rising, with 153,000 leaving just in the first six months of 1961. All this had ended at midnight on August 13, when East German and Soviet guards began stringing barbed wire along the border.

The Wall opened a new dimension in Vogel's career, one that began in secrecy but would eventually make him a household name in both parts of Germany. For while the Wall could physically stop the movement of Germans from East to West, it could not stop them from wanting to leave. West Germany decried as an outrage the denial of freedom to millions of Germans on the other side of the Wall, and encouraged them to defy the illegal barrier between the two parts of the country. Yet West Germany was powerless to remove the Wall. The Communists soon found they could use this frustration—a frustration felt in homes, in churches, in political parties, and in the government in Bonn—to force the West Germans to recognize the legitimacy of the East German state.

The Abel-Powers exchange had shown the East German Communists that the West was willing to barter for individual freedom, and on the Communists' terms. The East Germans had no doubt that the political pressures on the West Germans to improve the lot of their aunts, uncles, grandmothers, grandfathers, and cousins in the East would force Bonn to bargain with them. And with the Wall likely to stand for a hundred years, the Communists would hold the upper hand.

The Communists also had hostages. The Stasi was steadily tightening its grip inside the country, thwarting attempts by West German intelligence and political organizations to undermine Communist control. The BND, West Germany's foreign intelligence service, the huge CIA station in West Berlin, and the West German Social Democratic Party (whose secret "Eastern Bureau" encouraged clandestine resistance to the forced absorption of the Social Democrats into the Communist party in East Germany[1]) were all maintaining thousands of East German agents. The French, the British, and the other West German parties had more. The Stasi's definition of subversion cast a wide net, and by 1961 more than ten thousand political prisoners or convicted West German spies were sitting in East German prisons.

To try to help these prisoners, Bonn set up a legal office in West Berlin, an agency funded by the Ministry for All-German Questions in Bonn but without a formal connection to it. Vogel had come into contact with the lawyers in this office in the late 1950s, not only with the blessing of Josef Streit and the Stasi, but also with the full approval of the West German lawyers and intelligence officers who had been so anxious to have Vogel join the West Berlin bar. After the Wall had gone up, they had an additional need for Vogel's services: Most of the lawyers who worked in the legal office were West Berliners, who on the 13th of August had been barred from traveling into the East at all.[2] The legal office needed Vogel to represent clients for them on the other side, at least in formal legal proceedings such as bail hearings and filing procedures. Vogel thus had no trouble becoming precisely the kind of legal passe-partout that Volpert had intended him to be when he sent Vogel off to work his way into "Western justice" in 1957.

Vogel's special relationship with Volpert and his connection to Streit put him in a perfect position to play the role of fixer. Vogel was reassuringly German middle class, right down to his collection of ticking antique watches and his habit of drinking mocha coffee in the afternoons from an elegant demitasse cup. He put his Western colleagues at ease just by the formal, dignified way he carried himself, and by the neat, stylish cut of his tailor-made suits—made, not in the West, but patriotically in East Berlin, from Bodo Jahn's tailor shop in Biesdorf. Jahn had not been able to commute to his job in West Berlin after 1961, so he opened the shop in the East. Vogel became one of Jahn's best customers, buying five or six suits a year at five to six hundred East German marks apiece, far cheaper than it would have cost him in West Berlin or in London, but made from bolts of cloth Vogel himself picked out on his negotiating trips across the Wall.

In an age when the image of "Communist" lawyers had been fixed in the Western mind by Stalinist show trials, dominated by such fulminating ideologues as Andrei Vishinsky in the Soviet Union and Friedrich Karl Kaul in East Berlin, Vogel seemed a far less unsettling figure. Vogel could cite Lenin with the best of them, but he was never stridently ideological. Frank Meehan had been struck by his willingness to engage in real conversation, and by Vogel's warmth, in sharp contrast to the frozen faces and expressions of most East Germans he had come across. In conversation with Westerners, Vogel talked like a West German, and he had a ready supply of anecdotes that seemed to attest to a tolerant view of humanity.

Vogel showed no hesitation about criticizing Communist actions he found unacceptable. Meehan discovered this one night a few years after the Wall had gone up when he and Vogel dined with an American friend of Meehan's, John Mapother, a lanky Kentuckian with the CIA station. The conversation turned to a horrific incident at the Wall. An East German man had gotten drunk and decided to try to drive across the border. The East German police barriers had stopped him, but instead of obeying orders to get out of his car and surrender, he had eluded the police and raced on to try again at another crossing point, Spandau. There finally he had been shot to death by the East German guards. Vogel said he knew all about the case. The victim had been totally drunk; the autopsy had shown a blood alcohol level that would have been close to fatal. Mapother was outraged. "I think that makes the fact that the guards killed him even more brutal than if he had been sober," he said. Vogel's reaction surprised him. "Exactly," Vogel responded. "I agree completely. What they did was terrible."[3]

By the law of the state Vogel worked for, to attempt to cross the border without formal official permission was a crime for which people could legitimately be shot and killed. The act of merely encouraging someone to leave the country was punishable by a prison term; just reading a Western newspaper or watching a Western television station was taken as evidence of disloyalty. East German families with television sets had to take care not to point their antennas too obviously toward the West. For an East German lawyer in the good graces of the regime to acknowledge that his state and its security organs could be anything less than infallible seemed extraordinary. Vogel's apparent freedom to criticize thus added to the esteem his Western colleagues held for him.

Arnold Heidemann, a West Berlin lawyer, was amazed by the way Vogel handled the case of an eight-year-old girl whose mother had moved to the East after the Wall had gone up, while the father stayed in West Berlin. The mother wanted to reclaim the child, and her father, whom Heidemann represented, resisted. The East German authorities made the little girl's case into a political cause célèbre. German law usually favored the mother's rights in domestic disputes of this kind, but a West Berlin judge had refused to award custody to the mother because it would have meant cruelly delivering the child into the hands of the Communists.

Vogel, representing the girl's mother and, by extension, his own government, had come up with a novel, even cunning way for the

East German government to save face and allow the child to stay with her father in West Berlin at the same time. Custody of the child could go to her mother in East Berlin, but the child could later declare that she did not want to remain there. "Of course," Heidemann had agreed, "but how do you know she will?" Vogel had smiled. "Because her mother will say she doesn't want to stay," he replied. "She will say this because the state can make her do so. It's one of the few advantages of a dictatorship."[4]

Jürgen Stange, one of the lawyers in the government-supported legal aid office in West Berlin, soon came to know and like Vogel. Stange, a jovial, round-faced man, was ambitious and enjoyed the sense of power and influence that came from operating close to government and intelligence operations. As a West German citizen, not a West Berliner, his passport allowed him to cross the Wall, and he had worked on cases for the Roman Catholic and Lutheran churches, rescuing lost sheep caught in the barbed wire on the other side. Vogel had often been a big help to him.

Stange had his own informal but well-developed connections with the BND. His relationship with Vogel brought a new dimension to the conspiratorial aspect of his work. Vogel's razor-sharp intellect was clearly superior to his own, but they complimented each other. If Vogel was sometimes cool and distant, Stange was hearty and avuncular, the kind of lawyer who would clap his hand reassuringly on a client's back. Stange was better working out a deal behind the scenes than he was in the courtroom, and like Vogel he preferred harmony to confrontation, often achieving it over many glasses of beer and schnapps—often too many glasses, in Stange's case. Both men appreciated the finer things in life. Gradually, Stange and Vogel began to see themselves as a sort of partnership across the Wall. Few who observed them in action together doubted that the stronger partner lived on the Eastern side.

The Stasi was eager to exploit the possibilities of East-West exchanges opened up with Soviet blessing by the Abel-Powers swap, and Heinz Volpert wanted Vogel to play an important role. Vogel's contacts with Stange, and through Stange with the churches, provided the key.

Both the Catholic and Lutheran churches held uniquely ambiguous positions in East Germany. Official Communist policy made life as hard as possible for them. But just as Stalin had needed the moral authority and continuity of the church, so did Walter Ulbricht and the other East German Communists. Although the regime resisted all efforts by the denominations to preserve the vestiges of German unity, both Lutheran and Roman Catholic diocesan lines crossed the border. The East Germans succeeded in forcing the Lutherans, who of the two had by far more adherents in East Germany, to redraw these lines. But over the years, the Communists also sought to exploit the political and financial ties that continued to link the churches East and West, and Vogel soon found ways to use them.

A week before the Abel-Powers exchange, a twenty-eight-year-old West German student from Cologne named Engelbert Nelle, president of the Catholic German Student Union, had been arrested at the elevated station and charged with conspiring to smuggle two East German students to the West. The charge was the result of a misunderstanding. Nelle had gone to East Berlin to the office of Prelate Johannes Zinke, who headed the church's charitable operations in both halves of the city. There Nelle was to meet the two students—as part of his work keeping up contacts with Catholics on both sides of the border, he thought. So Nelle was appalled to learn that the students worked for French intelligence and thought that he had come to help them make their escape through the Wall. The Stasi was waiting for him when he had tried to go back to West Berlin.

Nelle's arrest had unleashed angry protests throughout West Germany. Church groups had engaged Vogel and another East German lawyer from Halle to defend him at his trial, in the beginning of June. Vogel argued strenuously that Nelle was not guilty, but lost the case. Afterward, he quietly approached Prelate Zinke with another solution suggested by the Stasi. Vogel first told the churchman how he had managed to get Frederic Pryor freed back in February by including him in the Soviet-American spy exchange. Then he described an East German physicist whom the West Germans had imprisoned in Düsseldorf as a spy. Perhaps, Vogel suggested, the church could use its connections with the Adenauer government in Bonn to see whether this innocent young man and the physicist could both go home to their families.

It took only a month to strike a deal. At 3 P.M. on July 10, Volpert and Vogel took Nelle to a back entrance of the Friedrichstrasse station to await the arrival of the scientist. After a long and tense wait, the West Germans delivered the Communist agent as agreed. Nelle was then whisked up to the station platform to ride back across to West Berlin, and Volpert had his answer: The West Germans would deal with the East Germans on spies, and church channels had proved to be one reliable and confidential way of getting such deals done.[5]

Johannes Zinke was not the only churchman Vogel found useful in weaving secret connections across the Wall. Kurt Scharf, the Protestant bishop of Berlin, was even more active. Scharf, whom the Nazis had arrested seven times, had been a constant thorn in the side of the Communists in East Berlin until Ulbricht had expelled him when the Wall had gone up. Bishop Scharf's experience with both Nazi and Communist totalitarian regimes had helped him develop shrewd negotiating skills. The spiritual welfare of political prisoners had been one of his main concerns before the war, and it remained so. Despite his expulsion, Bishop Scharf was determined to continue his work on the prisoners' behalf and thought Vogel might be in a position to help.

As much as the Communists objected to the work of the churches, the regime needed commodities and materials that could only be purchased using Western convertible currency. Both the Protestant and the Roman Catholic church organizations in West Germany had this kind of cash in abundance, because the West German government levied a tithe on the income tax of all baptized citizens, unless they expressly renounced church membership, and paid it to the church.

Helping their brethren in the East was an important part of the West German churches' mission. In East Germany, both the Protestant and Catholic denominations operated hospitals, old-age homes, and other institutions that needed medicine, equipment, and maintenance. But the churches were having an increasingly difficult time persuading the Communist authorities to let them send money and materials to their institutions in East Germany. Sending West German marks across was illegal, except at a punitive rate of exchange that amounted to East German government confiscation of most of the money. Church officials had tried to smuggle money across, and had been caught. Threatened in a crucial case in 1957 with prosecution for sabotage, they had agreed to a compromise that gave the East German authorities the control they had sought over this source of hard Western currency. The church could not transfer Western currency from West to East, but if it would undertake to deliver commodities and foodstuffs the East German authorities needed badly, the state would make East German currency available to the church—for the Lutherans, as much as forty million marks a year.[6]

Bishop Hermann Kunst, another worldly and wily Protestant prelate who represented his church's interests in Bonn, had convinced the West German political authorities to agree to this arrangement, for it satisfied one objective of Bonn's German policy— that of preserving human ties across the border. This was how the West German Protestant charity organization, the Diaconate Works, had come to export West German coal from the Ruhr to coal-starved East Germany. Soon it had added steel, other metals, peanuts, cocoa, and grain to its list, getting West German firms that delivered the goods to inflate the bills so that the East German churches would receive even more money than the value of the materials that had actually been shipped. The 1961 erection of the Wall did not affect this "transfer" business in the least; it rose to DM34.7 million that year, and in 1962 continued at nearly the same level, reaching DM33.9 million, the equivalent at the time of more than $8 million.[7]

Kurt Scharf had earned a reputation for courage by his willingness to lead a struggle for freedom for the victims of Nazi repression. After the war, as a leading cleric in East Berlin, Scharf had tried to exert moral pressure on the Stasi to free church members who had been caught up in the ideological confrontation. One method he used was to have names of Christian prisoners in the East read out in West German churches every Sunday, just as the Protestant resistance under the Nazis had read out the names of its victims. Scharf had not been averse to marching straight into the lion's den and negotiating with the Stasi himself on more than one occasion. But the Communists had refused to recognize his election as presiding bishop in both parts of the country in the spring of 1961. From his home in West Berlin after the Wall went up, he continued to use material leverage on the Communists to try to help those on the other side.

In Vogel's recollection, it was the church that first intimated that money, whether paid directly or indirectly, might be a promising way of securing the large-scale release of political prisoners. The emissary who made the suggestion was Reymar von Wedel, a lawyer and influential Protestant layman who served as Bishop Scharf's personal assistant. He knew that Scharf would use money, if that would get the Communists to show mercy to political prisoners. On June 21, 1962, Scharf dispatched von Wedel to ask Vogel what might be done. This mission was to have fateful consequences, and von Wedel's written memoir of it supports Vogel's version of the origins of the human trade.

Von Wedel, a short man whose boyish mien and informal, friendly manner belied his aristocratic origins, was one of the few Germans in West Berlin who could even cross the Wall at this point; he had a West German passport instead of a West Berlin identity card.

Von Wedel was as unsure of who Vogel really might be as James Donovan had been five months earlier. Playing it safe, he told the border guards at the Friedrichstrasse station his intended destination, and an hour later he was climbing the stairs to Vogel's office.

Vogel was out on an errand when von Wedel arrived in the late afternoon; the office manager offered him one of the leather chairs in the waiting room. When Vogel returned, he graciously escorted his visitor into his more elegant private office. Von Wedel, still feeling his way with Vogel, said that he had come on a mission from Stuttgart, where a group of industrialists wanted to try to do something for political prisoners in the East Germany. He had brought a few names with him, and wondered if Vogel could help.

"The Justice Ministry has already told me you were coming. Your arrival was registered at Friedrichstrasse," Vogel told him. Taken aback by such directness, von Wedel felt rather foolish about having tried to hide his real mission behind a phony cover story. Looking into Vogel's open, rather bemused gaze, he decided to drop the pretense.

"All right, I'm not from Stuttgart at all, but from West Berlin," he told Vogel. "And I have nothing to do with industry; Bishop Scharf sent me." Vogel smiled, and admitted that he had found the cover story a bit bizarre; he told von Wedel that they would stand a better chance of making progress by being open with each other. In any case, he said, he would much rather deal with the church than with a bunch of unknown industrialists. Vogel would see what he could do on his side, and would report back through Stange in West Berlin. Von Wedel should stay in touch with Stange.

"I think we've found the golden goose," von Wedel reported the next day to the bishop, who brought him up short, in von Wedel's recollection, by pointing out that more likely it would be the other way around.[8]

In an interview with the author von Wedel said, "I didn't start off with the suggestion of money. I said I wanted to find a way of helping prisoners, and Vogel may have just assumed I meant money." Indeed, Vogel clearly recalled coming away from the meeting with the impression that payment had been proposed, and he took the idea to Streit that very evening. According to Vogel, Streit was skeptical. "Money for prisoners?" Streit said, raising his eyebrows. "I don't know whether we can agree to that." It seemed, at first glance, to contradict every Marxist tenet about the difference between capitalist exploitation of labor and Communist morality.[9]

As a judge and Communist party apparatchik before becoming East Germany's prosecutor-general, Streit had earned a reputation in the West as a ruthless functionary who bent justice to suit the purposes of the Communists and showed no mercy to "enemies of the state." True, Streit talked in rigid ideological classifications and wore a party button in the lapel of his properly shapeless East German suit. But Vogel saw a deeper human dimension in the man, and eventually came to revere him as a father. Streit, in turn, saw and respected professional competence in Vogel and knew how to use it for the party's purposes.

Streit passed the idea of trading prisoners for Western commodities or currency along to Hermann Matern, who headed the Communist party's powerful central control commission and was a veteran of the Communist underground during the war. The proposal must have been music to Matern's ears. Whatever the ideological problems, East Germany needed the money. The country's economy was in desperate shape. So Matern had no scruples at all about accepting the proposal, and told Streit to authorize Vogel to pursue the idea immediately.[10]

On the West German side, Bishop Scharf and Bishop Kunst conferred in Hanover a week after von Wedel's visit to Vogel. There they decided that if it took money to release a group of seventeen church prisoners known to be in the terrible Communist prison in Bautzen, the church would do it. "People are more important than money," Kunst observed, and agreed to clear the idea with the government in Bonn.[11]

It was not long before Vogel let von Wedel know that the East German side was willing to negotiate a short list of names. In return, East Germany would ask for three freight cars full of potash. Could von Wedel provide these? Von Wedel thought he could, but first the church would need to get export permission from the government.[12]

This was easily arranged. The churches had long had clearance to effect such transactions to finance their activities on the other side, and if the church wanted to use money to free people it cared about, the government in Bonn had no objection. Bishop Scharf sent von Wedel to Stuttgart to see Ludwig Geissel, the church's charity director, a wheeler-dealer who negotiated and ran the transfer business.

Geissel, in his published recollection of their meeting, claims to have been initially skeptical. "But, Herr von Wedel—money for human beings, isn't that inhuman?"[13]

Not at all, von Wedel assured him. The church was already supplying steel, coal, oil, and so on to make life better for people on the other side. Helping to get a few of them out was just taking the process one step further.

Geissel easily received export permission for the three cars of potash from the Bonn authorities. Within a few weeks, the first few church prisoners of conscience did indeed go free, and the three loads of potash found their way to East Germany. After this initial swap of human and industrial commodities, two further prisoner lists were negotiated, and an agreement was reached to free twenty children separated from their parents the night the Wall had gone up. There was one prisoner for whom the East Germans wanted a higher price—the pastor of the Marienkirche, one of the biggest churches in East Berlin, whom the Stasi had arrested for helping arrange escapes across the Wall. For this prisoner, the East Germans were demanding about one hundred thousand West German marks, a fortune at the time, to offset the damage they said he had done to the interests of the state. Bishop Kunst, in Bonn, finally came up with the money. Perhaps there really had been some "Stuttgart industrialists" after all, von Wedel surmised.[14]

A peculiarly German kind of sentimentality had suffused all of these talks. Vogel himself felt it. He thought of the desperation he had seen in the eyes of prisoners who had been sitting for years in East German prisons. Children touched a particularly sensitive spot in his heart, he told von Wedel and others. He felt that he could not rest until he had tried to help, and surely they could not do less. Tenderheartedness about children did not stop at the border and, like the good courtroom lawyer he had become, Vogel had no trouble playing on these feelings when negotiating with the church representatives.

Soon West German politicians realized that what the churches could do on a small scale, government could do on a much larger one. The Abel-Powers exchange put the idea of prisoner swaps in the air anyway. Moreover, the trades would flow logically from the sense of national impotence that the Wall and the division of Germany symbolized. Both East and West Germany chafed under it. The West Germans had discovered that the Americans could neither prevent the Communists from building the Wall nor force them to tear it down; the East Germans had discovered that the Soviets could not force the Americans out of Berlin. The East Germans had taken matters into their own hands, albeit with Soviet approval. Now the West Germans, though only indirectly and on a small scale, were willing to deal with them.

Willy Brandt, the Social Democratic governing mayor of West Berlin, sent his aide Dietrich Spangenberg to meet with Jürgen Stange and Vogel to see if the city could do something similar to what the church had done. West Berlin authorities were interested in hardship prison cases, some of whom had been behind bars since 1953. This time Vogel took the initiative. The East German economy was not in good shape, he told Spangenberg; perhaps money was the key. Spangenberg and Brandt were interested, but they could not convince the ruling Christian Democrats in Bonn to appropriate money from the federal treasury to back the idea. But Spangenberg continued to see Vogel; to evade any attempts at surveillance the pair took long walks in the people's park of Wilmersdorf. After several meetings, they arranged for the release of six prisoners, in exchange for a mere twenty-five thousand West German marks.[15]

This was about all the West Berlin government could afford at the time. To get thousands of prisoners out of jail, Bonn simply would have to come into the picture. But Brandt's Social Democrats had little national influence as long as the Christian Democrats were in charge, and some leading Christian Democratic politicians held strong ideological objections to becoming involved in human trade.[16]

But in December 1962, a new man took over as Minister for All-German Questions: Rainer Barzel, an ambitious Christian Democratic politician who had his eye on the chancellor's office in Bonn and was willing to experiment with policies that others would have rejected out of hand. If Barzel got behind the idea of exploring a trade for political prisoners, Stange felt, the business could really get off the ground.

What he and Vogel needed, Stange knew, was to gain Barzel's ear, through someone with impeccable anti-Communist credentials who also recognized that practical policies and moral posturing were often incompatible. Stange thought that Axel Springer, the stridently anti-Communist media magnate, would be the perfect contact. And Stange knew someone in Hamburg who could provide access to Springer—Dora Fritzen, a rich Hamburg shipowner and philanthropist who ran a charity that benefited refugees from Communism and also supported those in need in the East.

So, early in 1963, Stange managed to convince Fritzen to receive Vogel at her estate in Hamburg, to hear a proposal for a way to enable Bonn to help many thousands of people suffering in Communist prisons. When Vogel showed up at her door, Fritzen immediately took to him, feeling that here was a man with a good heart. After explaining how the East Germans had helped arrange freedom for Francis Gary Powers in exchange for Colonel Abel, Vogel said some words that had made an indelible impression: "Frau Fritzen," he had said, "we Germans can do for ourselves what we did for the Americans."[17]

Fritzen agreed that the best way to gain the attention of the politicians in Bonn was to get Axel Springer behind the proposal. Springer's standing in Bonn was impeccable. He had deliberately set out to be a thorn in the side of the Communists in East Berlin, defiantly erecting his West Berlin office right next to the Wall so that its neon sign shone into the offices of the Communist functionaries on the other side. Springer detested the German Democratic Republic so thoroughly that as long as he lived, none of the newspapers he owned ever printed its official name except between quotation marks.

Fritzen herself explained to him the proposal to buy prisoners out of Communist jails. She found Springer skeptical at first. "But that is the purest kind of human trade!" the publisher objected. Fritzen emphasized the good the trades could do. "If your son were in jail over there and you could get him freed by paying money. . . ." she had begun. Springer quickly interrupted: "Say no more." He then got Rainer Barzel on the telephone.[18]

A few weeks later, on the 13th floor of his headquarters in Hamburg, Springer had an aide explain the proposal for prisoner releases to Barzel, who was immediately intrigued. Not long afterward, Barzel met in Munich with a young subordinate of the ministry's Berlin office, a lawyer named Ludwig Rehlinger, and with Stange.

Rehlinger, tall and patrician, had joined the ministry's Berlin office in 1957, partly out of anti-Communist conviction, partly because he was a native Berliner. He had political ambitions and a smooth polish that, with his fastidious dress, combined to give him an almost English manner, inspired perhaps by the time he had spent as an eighteen-year-old prisoner in a British prisoner-of-war camp at the end of the war.

Rehlinger supervised the ministry's legal support for political prisoners in the Soviet zone, many of whom had worked for the West Germans, and Barzel wanted him to explore the East German proposal through Stange and Vogel. A few weeks later, Stange brought the first East German proposal from Vogel: East Berlin was ready to bargain on a thousand prisoners, once an acceptable price was agreed on with Bonn.[19]

The Western legal-aid office knew of twelve thousand political prisoners in whom the churches, political parties, and other official institutions in Bonn had an interest—thousands of former prisoners-of-war convicted of war crimes in mass trials; thousands of civilians serving sentences for such political crimes as "anti-Soviet agitation," "subversion," or espionage. Picking out only one thousand was agonizing for Rehlinger. The responsibility lay heavy on him as he sifted the files, weighing the length of the sentences, grounds for conviction, state of health, and family situation of thousands of prisoners to winnow out those for whom Bonn was willing to bargain. Those whom he did not select, he felt he was condemning to remain behind bars even longer.

Then Stange appeared again with news that made him feel even worse. According to Vogel, East Berlin wanted to cut down the list to five hundred. At a time when people were trying to jump over the Wall, burrow under it, or ram through the checkpoints with trucks full of bricks, perhaps the East Germans did not trust Bonn or were developing cold feet. At the end of the process, Bonn had to settle for only eight names out of the thousand that Vogel had originally offered.[20]

As for the price, Vogel proved to be a hard bargainer. Throughout the negotiations, he was kept on a tight leash by the Stasi. Heinz Volpert, Vogel's Stasi liaison, not only controlled the list of prisoners; he would also handle the money that Bonn was to pay for them.[21]

Volpert instructed Vogel to work out a separate price for each individual, according to a rationale that had its own Communist logic—a new spin on the old maxim, "from each according to ability, to each according to need." Each prisoner who would be sent to the West represented a financial loss to the Communist state. "The training of a doctor costs the state 150,000 marks," Vogel once explained. "Put yourself in the position of the state: every crime has brought damages of some kind."[22] Ordinary workers, even in "the first workers' and peasants' state on German soil," might be worth less. The length of the sentences was also a factor—a person serving a long prison term cost more to get free than one serving only a few years. The exact price for each prisoner has since been lost in time, but in the end, Vogel and Rehlinger settled on 340,000 West German marks for the first eight prisoners, a sum equivalent to something less than 100,000 dollars in 1963.[23]

On September 23, Rehlinger flew to Bonn to secure agreement for the package. The eight he and Vogel had finally selected reflected the West German politics of the day. Rehlinger knew that to gain political backing for a secret project as sensitive as this one, every major political party and interest group would have to have a stake in the results. So, for the Christian Democrats, there were two prisoners on the list, including a cabinetmaker who in 1945 had been sentenced to life imprisonment by a Soviet military tribunal for espionage. Three other prisoners with various sentences had ties to the Social Democrats, the labor unions, and the Free Democratic Party; two youths imprisoned for church activities represented the interests of organized religion, and a solitary anti-Communist activist not affiliated with any party gave the whole package a hint of wholesome nonpartisanship in the greater national and humanitarian interest.[24]

The releases took place a few days later. None of the participants would ever forget the moment. One at a time, the prisoners were taken out of their cells at the Magdalenenstrasse by the Stasi prison guards, brought to the warden, and presented to Vogel and Volpert, who was identified to the prisoners as a "prosecutor." The lawyer and the Stasi man then took each prisoner separately in Vogel's Mercedes to the Friedrichstrasse elevated railway station, the heavily guarded border checkpoint where trains departed for West Berlin.

On the platform, Jürgen Stange was waiting. Vogel handed over the prisoner to Stange, who rode with him across the Wall to the Zoo station in West Berlin, and then to Rehlinger's office nearby. Each prisoner was then given a cup of coffee, welcomed to freedom, and urged not to talk about what had just happened so as not to endanger the next prisoner's release. The first three prisoners came free as agreed by early October, including the cabinetmaker, who sat silently in the West Berlin legal office as he took in the fact that he had, from one day to the next, gone from a life sentence in solitary confinement to freedom in the West. He broke into sobs. "That anyone would think of me!" were the only words the lawyers could understand.[25]

The release of the third prisoner marked the time for the West Germans to pay the first installment of their side of the bargain— 170,000 marks, in cash; there was no way, politically or any other way, that the West German government could write a check to an East German government bank account.

The cash payment posed its own problems for the dignified, orderly civil servant Rehlinger. He had drawn the money from the government treasury, in one-hundred-mark notes, and put it into a large gray envelope. But for a Bonn government employee to take West German taxpayers' money across the Wall and hand it to the Communists was diplomatically unthinkable. What if a West Berlin customs agent stopped him at the border—how would he explain the envelope? What would he say if an East German customs inspector stopped him on the other side? The East Germans had caught a Lutheran Church official doing just this, with the proceeds from West German collection baskets, a few years earlier, and had put him in jail for a few weeks. If Rehlinger took such a risk, the whole arrangement could blow up in his government's face.

So Stange took the money across. Rehlinger drove him to the Lehrter Stadtbahnof elevated station in West Berlin, one stop away from the Wall and a couple away from the West Berlin customs agents, police, and undercover Stasi officers who infested Zoo station, the main depot near the Kurfürstendamm. After mounting the steps to the platform, the two men found themselves nearly alone. When the next eastbound train pulled in and opened the doors, Stange stepped quickly inside, and Rehlinger remained on the quay, waiting for the platform guard to signal the motorman to leave. As the guard gave the standard "stand back" warning,

Rehlinger handed the envelope to Stange, the doors closed, and the train pulled out for East Berlin.[26]

"Who received it there or into what channels it flowed was no longer our concern," Rehlinger later wrote.[27] At that time, the West Germans did not know, and perhaps they never really wanted to. But the truth was that the money went, almost directly, right into the hands of the Stasi. When the train reached Friedrichstrasse station, Stange handed the money to Vogel, who immediately passed it over to Volpert. A few minutes later, Vogel rode with Volpert to the Foreign Trade Ministry, where he watched him give the money to a man named Horst Roigk, himself an undercover Stasi officer. Vogel had held the money in his own hands for only a few seconds.[28]

Volpert wielded all manner of influence, influence that grew as the services he performed for the state brought in more money. So Volpert was eager to make these releases regular occurrences and bring in a regular flow of money to the East German state. But it took two more years for the Communists and the West Germans to be ready for that. The breakthrough, again, came from the West German side, after Adenauer's resignation in the autumn of 1963 and the formation, on October 17, of a new coalition government under Chancellor Ludwig Erhard, author of the West German "economic miracle." Erhard put Erich Mende, the chairman of the junior coalition party, the Free Democrats, in charge of the all-German portfolio and made him deputy chancellor. Mende had Rehlinger explain how his predecessor had used government money to buy freedom for East German political prisoners and approved enthusiastically.[29] But not until April of 1964 did Vogel report to Stange that the East Germans were ready to proceed, this time on a larger scale than before. In subsequent negotiations, including a private meeting between Mende and Vogel in Berlin on May 12, Bonn and East Berlin agreed on a basic rate of forty thousand deutsche marks—then roughly the equivalent of ten thousand dollars—for each prisoner who was to be "sold free" to the Western side. Depending on the length of the prison terms, this basic rate could be doubled, tripled, or even quadrupled for the release of prisoners serving life sentences.[30] Vogel would negotiate the lists and the prices for the East German side; what he did not tell the West Germans was that he would get his negotiating position from Volpert and the Stasi.

But the cabinet in Bonn decided it could not go on sending cash packets across the Wall; it needed to find methods that were both more discreet and more palatable. Politically, the West German government could not turn over the taxpayers' money to the Communists to spend as they liked. But it could give them—preferably indirectly—consumer goods or commodities such as coal and heating oil that would fill empty stomachs and warm freezing schools and homes in East Germany.

On July 8, Mende called a meeting in his office in Bonn to discuss which "political prisoners" Bonn wanted from East Germany and how it should pay for them.[31] This meeting laid the groundwork for a better way of continuing the secret financing.

Bishop Kunst and the Protestant Church were the key. Whereas the Federal Republic of Germany could not have direct financial dealings with the East Germans, the church could and did. So Mende and Bishop Kunst agreed that Bonn could make the prisoner payments through the Protestant charity organization. The church would then make available to the East German Foreign Trade Ministry credits, which it could use to order commodities and consumer goods through West German firms that the charity itself would select.[32]

Bonn was as eager as East Berlin to keep the arrangements quiet. Unauthorized bookkeepers and prying eyes in the Bundestag could be kept guessing by short-circuiting normal accounting channels. Geissel would submit the prisoner payment accounts to the Federal Accounting Office in Frankfurt through Bishop Kunst. The bishop's authority would attest that the church had used the money for humanitarian aid to prisoners in East Germany. If these arrangements were properly carried through, the explanation would be true, and no more than ten people in the government would ever know exactly how it was being done.[33]

The West Germans did not know, but probably suspected in 1964 that all hard-currency dealings of the East German Foreign Trade Ministry were under the direct control of the Stasi. So even the indirect trade voucher payments made by Bonn went to accounts that the Stasi controlled.

The vouchers were simply sheets of white paper without letterhead, listing only the goods to be ordered and the quantity, with two signatures: the director of the church charity organization and that of the deputy director of the Foreign Trade Ministry. It was up to the churchmen and their East German negotiating partners to agree on delivery contracts with the West German firms on the approved lists, and up to the West German economics minister to give Bonn's final blessing, which was always forthcoming.[34] But neither church nor state in West Germany had any way of controlling the ultimate disposition of the funds or the goods, or of ensuring that the East Germans did not simply turn around and sell the goods on the world markets for precious hard currency that Mielke and the party leaders could put to other uses besides pampering the population. This, as it turned out, was precisely what they did.[35]

It was hardly Vogel's job to point out the pitfalls. His job was to carry out the Stasi's instructions and to negotiate the prisoner lists with Bonn. When Vogel and Rehlinger met to discuss the procedure, they liked each other instantly. Both men respected the discipline of the law, and both took the same view that their deeds were not a political, but humanitarian and noble—nothing as crass as trading in souls. Here, Rehlinger thought, was an East German he could do business with.[36]

Vogel would earn no fee or percentage on the trades, but money was no longer a big worry in his life. Unlike almost anyone else in the Communist world, he thought of his own time as money and used it wisely. Vogel kept his father's pocket watch by the telephone on his desk and timed his appointments and discussions carefully. Thanks to the Wall, he had the federal government in Bonn as a client, and its legal-affairs office paid both him and Stange statutory legal fees for the thousands of cases of divided families, property settlements, divorce and alimony payments, and the like that spanned the political division of the Wall. Depending on the number of court appearances, prison visits, and legal papers Vogel had to make, his fees from Bonn could amount to one or two thousand West German marks per case, though usually they were smaller. But soon he would have thousands of cases, and an income in West German marks worth ten times more to him in an economy of scarcity than it would have been if he had lived, like Stange, on the other side of the Wall.

Seen from the perspective of the regime that had created him, Vogel was a useful part of a perfect closed system. The Stasi and Streit would round up and prosecute political prisoners. Obedient East German courts, following Marxist principles of class justice, would jail them no matter what lawyers like Vogel did in their defense. And finally Vogel could bargain for their sale to the West German government for hard currency.

But blinded by its material need, the regime had failed to see that it was also buying itself a long-term political problem. Word of the exchanges for money was bound to get around, eventually. When it did, it would undermine the credibility of the regime that sold the prisoners, not only with dissidents and other ordinary East Germans who had little respect for the government anyway, but also with the loyal Communists who served it. Stasi investigators and prison guards who had worked hard to put political prisoners behind bars and keep them there had little sympathy when a lawyer dressed like one of the class enemy—no matter what his connections—suddenly appeared on the scene and announced that he was taking the prisoners to the West. Vogel often saw such functionaries, in later years, shaking their heads at him in the Stasi prisons in Bautzen or Karl-Marx-Stadt, and wondered to himself what they were thinking.

In the meantime, their bosses in the Stasi and the prosecutor-general's office were thinking that Vogel had better bargain hard and well on the prisoner lists with the West Germans. Bonn wanted most to secure the release of the hardest cases, to free the political prisoners serving longest sentences; these were of course the ones East Berlin least wanted to let go, for theirs had been the most serious crimes.

Negotiations on the names for the first big releases in 1964 took place indirectly and lasted most of the summer. Rehlinger was the chief negotiator for Bonn, Vogel for East Berlin. Stange was the messenger, shuttling back and forth across the Wall with the lists of names.

"On the list was the family name, first name, date of birth, nothing more," Rehlinger recalled. "Stange would come back after a while and say, the GDR is ready to release number 1, 2, 3, and so on, but not number so-and-so—without explanation. And I'd look to see if I could figure out why they were refusing. Then I'd go back and say, 'You have to give us this one and that one, you can't just turn them down.' That's the way it went."[37]

Vogel himself did not decide which prisoners were to be released. The Stasi did that, relaying the names through Volpert, who also passed the West German wish lists to the Stasi's Main Administration for Investigation. This department, which had access to the prisoners' files, then decided whether the Stasi had already gotten all it was going to get from the prisoners, or whether they could now be released. Difficult cases were referred to the minister for state security, Erich Mielke himself. When the lists were in the final stages, Volpert explained fully to Vogel why certain names had been left off, so that Vogel could offer convincing reasons to the West Germans. At the end, of course, officials of the Interior Ministry and from the prosecutor-general's office had to be brought in to do the formal paperwork needed for the prisoners' release.[38]

Stange also had to carry out his consultations through the West German security services. The negotiations went on until early August. Finally, a list of four hundred prisoners was worked out, and it was time to consider how to release the first seventy, in three installments beginning with a busload of twelve on August 14.

Stange could hardly be expected to go over to East Berlin and pick up each one individually, as he had done with the first eight the year before. So Vogel, Stange, and Rehlinger agreed on a procedure, one that was followed for the next twenty-five years, to make the "deliveries" as inconspicuous as possible. The prisoners would be taken from their jails in East Germany, in East German buses bearing GDR license plates, and delivered to an autobahn rest area closer to the West German border. From there they would be transferred into a West German bus that would bring them across at the Herleshausen border crossing point to the refugee reception center at Giessen. Vogel and Stange would personally escort them the whole way, to make sure the agreements were fully upheld.[39]

This first major exchange beginning on August 15 would work well. But there had been one problem Vogel and his Western partners had not thought of, one that Stange discovered only on the 13th, when he went to Vogel's office in East Berlin to prepare for the trip to the border the next day. Only Rehlinger, who was in Bonn, could resolve the problem; Vogel told Stange to call him right then and there.

"We need a second bus," Stange said with some urgency when Rehlinger came on the line. Were more prisoners than expected going to be released? Rehlinger asked. No, Stange told him; he was calling from Vogel's office and he could not answer any more questions, but there would be no problems from the East Germans about clearing a second bus in time for the exchange the next morning, if Rehlinger could arrange it.[40]

Why the extra bus was needed remained a mystery until after

Vogel and Stange completed the release. The prisoners were brought by the East German authorities, as agreed, to the central holding prison of the Stasi in the Magdalenenstrasse in East Berlin, loaded into one bus, and taken on a five-hour journey to the southwest corner of the country. Darkness fell as the Hungarian-made bus came to a halt at the rest area off the autobahn near the exits for Jena and Lobeda, where Stange and Vogel oversaw the transfer to the two West German buses standing nearby. An hour later, the convoy neared the last East German border checkpoint, wound through the concrete barriers, and was waved through into West German territory. Just beyond the border, the route took a detour through rural hills and well-kept, prosperous villages, and the prisoners began to believe that they were *really* going free. They began to smoke and chat, and the tension started to ebb.[41]

Not until the following day did Stange return to West Berlin and tell Rehlinger why he had needed to charter a second bus. It was, Rehlinger wrote later, a story that could only have taken place in Germany, where the regulations must always be followed to the letter whatever the circumstances. The prisoners in this first release had been those with the longest sentences. Many of them had spent long years in East German jails, and, as the regulations provided, they had had to work for minimal wages. But these small sums had piled up over the years as credits on the prisoners' ledgers. The regulations now required that they be paid in East German marks. But these prisoners were being released directly to West Germany, and other regulations made it illegal to take East German marks out of the country.

With German punctiliousness, the East German state security had assembled the prisoners in Berlin, informed them of the sum due to each, and put together for them a small shop full of consumer goods: suitcases, clothing, food, soap, and the like, telling them all to use their allotted quotas. The second bus was needed for their baggage.[42]

Two more buses, on the 18th and the 21st of August, brought the rest of the first seventy prisoners to freedom. The inevitable leak to the West German press was not long in coming. ZONE OFFICIALS RELEASE NUMEROUS POLITICAL PRISONERS, ran the headlines on August 27, although the first stories did not explain why they had been freed. Axel Springer's *Berliner Morgenpost,* however, opined in an editorial titled TOO MANY WORDS that going after the story was not only irresponsible but could cost lives: "We know as well as others that for some time political prisoners—under certain conditions, of course—have been released from the Soviet zone. But we also know that nothing will harm the prospect of release of further prisoners more than too many, too loud words. . . . For there is news that can kill, while pretending to inform."[43]

Mende held a press conference in Bonn the next day acknowledging that there had been releases, and that these had been preceded by contacts between lawyers on both sides. But he was vague about discussing the payments. A front-page editorial October 7 in *Der Tagesspiegel,* West Berlin's best daily newspaper, threatened greater trouble. Joachim Bölke, the independent-minded editor, had found out the whole truth, and saw no reason why his readers should not also be told. Bonn, he wrote, had paid "a high price per head" for every prisoner the East Germans had released. Two days later, responding to the government's attempts to keep the lid on despite his reports, Bölke denounced the arrangement as a "dreadful slave trade."[44] The weekly news magazine *Der Spiegel*'s October 14 issue also revealed that prisoners had been freed and that the government in Bonn had paid for them with shipments of oranges, bananas, coffee beans, and butter for East German consumers.

It was the truth, but the West German government had agreed not to embarrass the East German Communists by making it public. So the West Germans briefed the leading West German newspaper editors, explaining the background and warning that the East Germans could call the whole program off and condemn thousands of prisoners to more years in prison if there were more publicity; the editors were asked to instruct their news staffs to lay off the story, and most complied.

The East Germans had, in fact, used much of the proceeds from this first exchange for scarce consumer goods, which were released to the people in time for the traditional open-air Christmas markets the Communists allowed for their morale-building effect. By that time, 884 prisoners had gone free, and the prisoner trade (disguised in the Protestant Church's accounts as the "*B-Geschäft,*" "B-business," *B* for *Bund,* the German word for "federal," and *Geschäft* for "business") had brought 37,918,901 deutsche marks, nearly 10,000,000 dollars, into the Communist coffers.[45]

On the East German side, there was understandable satisfaction. Streit was well pleased in his protégé. As to Volpert's role, Vogel kept this to himself. Stange knew who Volpert was, but he also knew Vogel did not want him to broadcast his knowledge, and he respected his partner's wishes. Frank Meehan, in the U.S. Mission in West Berlin, assumed that Vogel could have achieved his miracles only through some kind of connection with the East German secret police, but he knew nothing about the details of how Vogel's connections worked and had no reason to question his good faith.

Neither Stange nor Meehan was surprised, in the spring of that year, when Vogel invited both of them to the confirmation ceremony of Lilo, his daughter and younger child, at St. Joseph's Church, a large Catholic neogothic building in the Weissensee section of East Berlin. Meehan was honored when Vogel asked him to serve as Lilo's confirmation sponsor. To have an American diplomat instead of a relative do this, at a time when the act of confirmation itself was frowned upon by the Communist authorities, made the influential Dr. Vogel seem even more self-confident and independent. Anyone else seeking official favor would have put pressure on his children to stay out of the clutches of the church and go to an alternative Communist youth initiation rite instead. The Stasi monitored regular churchgoers and would be sure to have observers among the congregation at this event. But Meehan was proud to do as Vogel asked, walking up to the altar with Lilo Vogel. When he handed Archbishop Alfred Bengsch his calling card, the prelate's eyebrows shot up.

Jürgen Stange listened with growing interest as Bengsch, who later became a cardinal, gave a ringing sermon about the conflict of belief and unbelief, congratulating the young people and their families on having the courage of their convictions and warning them that greater trials might lie ahead. "Wolfgang's had it now," Meehan whispered to him, half-jokingly.[46] It was the kind of thing, Meehan thought, that an East German would do only if he were very sure of himself and of his connections. Vogel had reason to feel secure. But, always pushing the envelope, he had himself been taken aback when Bengsch had boomed out Meehan's name, and he had half expected a visit from the Stasi after the ceremony. But he had nothing to worry about. In the lucrative new trade that Vogel had opened up, the Stasi needed him too much to give him trouble over little infractions such as this.

Besides Vogel, only a few people in East Berlin knew about the trades, starting with Erich Honecker, the Communist party official in charge of security. To the list was added in 1967 the name of

Alexander Schalck-Golodkowski, who took over the East German side of the financial arrangements.

Schalck, as this mysterious and energetic figure was known to all who dealt with him in both East and West, loved conspiratorial dealings with Western negotiating partners, none of whom knew until many years later that he secretly held the rank of lieutenant colonel in the Stasi. He was a wheeler-dealer who knew what he was doing in the world of high finance, a sort of Communist mogul who impressed Western negotiating partners with his expertise in the ways of Western financial and currency markets. His mastery of the patter of exchange-rates, commercial instruments, and legal double-talk was total. With his portly figure and his Western dress, he could have passed for a fast-talking West German businessman. "His style was dynamic, his judgment was excellent," wrote the Lutheran charity director, Ludwig Geissel, of his first meeting with Schalck. "He had a good sense of what was doable, his instinct for pragmatic solutions was highly developed. And what was most important, he obviously had excellent contacts with the top leadership of the G.D.R."[47]

Schalck's job was to milk the West Germans for every mark he could, on behalf of his real boss—Stasi chief Erich Mielke. In 1967, he was put in charge of a new, covert organization called the "Commercial Coordination Area," CoCo for short, with the assignment of running up East German hard-currency reserves by hook or by crook. Schalck had spelled this out himself two years earlier in a letter to Hermann Matern, saying the Stasi's support was essential "because a series of operations like illegal shipments, insurance fraud and other measures that should be closely held are to be carried out by an extremely small number of operatives—not more than two or three—who should be the only ones who know about them."[48] CoCo, though at first part of the Foreign Trade Ministry, was subject only to the controls the secret police and the party chose to exercise over it, and from now on it would handle the financial dealings with the churches, including the "B-business" with the prisoners. Schalck's Stasi control officer, the man responsible for coordinating his undercover activities with the organization at an official level, was none other than Vogel's main contact, Heinz Volpert.[49]

Vogel maintained that his dealings with Schalck were confined mainly to notes or memos written to him or his deputy, another

Stasi officer named Manfred Seidel, after the successful conclusion of one of the prisoner-release deals, to inform CoCo how much to expect in trade credit vouchers. But Schalck's mandate was to build up foreign currency reserves for the benefit of the Communist party, not to pamper the East German population. To handle these foreign currency transactions, including those from the prisoner-exchange business, CoCo set up special secret foreign currency accounts in the official German Trade Bank, accounts that were subject to no auditing controls. Schalck and Seidel were the only authorized signatories, and activity reports went directly only to Mielke, and later Erich Honecker.[50]

How Schalck administered these millions, or whether the Communist leadership in East Berlin followed proper accounting procedures, were questions that would not even have begun to occur to West German political leaders, let alone to a negotiator such as Wolfgang Vogel, in 1967. Church leaders, West German politicians, and Vogel all had no choice about who their negotiating partners were. They had to deal with things as they were.

But whatever they told themselves, the West German government and the churches had become involved with the machinery of East German political repression. The East German state now had a material incentive to put even more people in jail, people it could then offer to sell for more potash and steel and industrial diamonds. By agreeing to the purchases, the church and the West German state had corrupted their moral position and laid themselves open to blackmail. For the East German Stasi, like any monopoly, could jack up the price of its wares, or withhold them, until it got the price it wanted.

But the East Germans, and Vogel, had laid themselves open to something that was even more corrosive. Money and material goods were a temptation to corruption. The amount of money involved in the prisoner exchanges was enormous—67.7 million deutsche marks in 1965, and 56.2 million between 1966 and 1967.[51] As the business grew, CoCo broadened its net to sweep more money into the secret coffers. Manfred Seidel used some of it to supply the Communist elite with television sets, whiskey, luxury automobiles, and Western building materials this same elite was denying the masses in the name of Communist ideology.[52] Schalck and Coco were not only running up hard currency reserves, they were running up a political deficit that would come due when the Wall fell.

The Wall, however, was not about to fall in the mid-1960s, and at that point the Communist leaders had no more second thoughts than Wolfgang Vogel did about what they were doing. By then Vogel had persuaded himself that he was an angel of mercy to his clients, and he enjoyed the many articles in the West German press that portrayed him that way. He told himself whenever he lost a political case to the prosecutors—almost always, under Communist rules—that later he could try to shorten the human suffering of the defendants by getting the West German state to buy them into freedom. He knew how "class justice" worked, but, powerless to change it, he worked within it to mitigate its unfairness. Most East Germans did not question the basic nature of the system that World War II and the Soviet Union had imposed on them, for fear of bringing the wrath of the Stasi upon their heads. Instead, like their parents' generation under the Nazis, they followed orders and did as they were told.

One case among these thousands of political prisoners weighed heavily on Vogel's conscience. In the summer of 1965, he asked Rehlinger personally to put Rudolf Reinartz's name on the list.

Vogel's old protector in the Justice Ministry had now been in prison for ten years, on conviction of espionage. "He was my boss once, and it would be a wonderful thing to get him out," Vogel told Rehlinger. How Rehlinger would react to the suggestion, Vogel had decided, would be a clue to how deeply involved in spying Reinartz might actually have been.

Bonn did agree to include Reinartz, a sign, Vogel decided with no other evidence for the hunch, that the West German authorities might have checked with the Americans and verified Reinartz's services as an American agent.[53]

But Vogel's East German partners had been somewhat more difficult. Hilde Benjamin, who had prosecuted Reinartz, was still in charge of such cases, and she had the right to pass on the prisoner-release lists. When she came to Reinartz's name on the one for September of 1965, she marked it with a Z—for "zurück," meaning "back." Streit, Vogel told friends later, had made a show of crossing out the Z, in his presence. "He stays on the list—I am the state prosecutor-general," Streit said.[54] If he had not already done so, Streit then replaced Reinartz as the father-figure Vogel always sought and revered.

It was just turning dusk on the evening of September 17 when

Vogel drove to the Stasi prison on the Magdalenenstrasse to pick up the man with whom he had mused, in Leipzig, about the quality of mercy for a defendant who had stolen a goat to feed his children. Vogel had to help Reinartz into the car in the prison courtyard—a dozen years in the high-security prison at Bautzen had made it difficult for his old mentor to use his crutches to get around. He was old now, and bitter, focusing his bitterness on Hilde Benjamin whom he blamed for his fate. Vogel decided, driving to his office in Friedrichsfelde, not to ask about the past.

At this early stage, Vogel had to ask for special permission every time he crossed the Wall to visit Stange or von Wedel in West Berlin. This time he had asked von Wedel to come to his office in the East, in order to drive Reinartz to the other side. What reception would await Reinartz there, Vogel could not be sure. His wife had signed her divorce papers years ago—a mere formality, the prisoner had thought.

Darkness had long since fallen as von Wedel drove Reinartz up to his wife's house. The lawyer helped Reinartz carry his suitcase to the front door, and watched as he rang the bell. But no one came to answer. The lights began going out upstairs, one after another. Reinartz rang again, but by now the house was dark. After a few moments, Reinartz sighed and returned to the car. "She doesn't want me anymore," he whispered.

Von Wedel knew of a nearby Swedish Lutheran rest home in the Grunewald section operated by a former opera singer named Carl Gustaf Svingel, who was a man of absolute discretion. For years, Svingel had been a silent partner with the German Protestant church and with Brandt's municipal government in the secretive world of prisoner exchanges and "humanitarian" actions. Drawn to Berlin by the love of a German woman and by a fascination with the political stage, Svingel had given up his musical career to watch the Germans try to build their new democracy and to take on a humanitarian mission between two worlds. His German, in a lilting Swedish accent, was as good as his political connections on both sides of the Wall.

So Svingel had taken Reinartz in. But, finding the man in tears, unable to speak, hobbling with his crutches, he worried about his health. A doctor arrived the very evening of his arrival at the rest home, declaring after examining Reinartz that the patient was suffering from a protein deficiency so grave that he could die unless he was confined to bed and put on a strict regiment of supplements and vitamins. Gradually the program restored his strength, but Reinartz seemed deeply depressed; even visits from his daughter did little to brighten his mood. One evening, Svingel noticed a nylon rope in Reinartz's bag. After a long conversation over a Scotch whiskey, Svingel finally asked, "What's the rope for?" Reinartz only sank into a deep and melancholy silence.[55]

Vogel occasionally dropped in and made inquiries, though he was uneasy about showing too much interest in Reinartz's fate. The Stasi originally had locked its sights on Vogel because of Reinartz's defection, and he was not sure that the Stasi was not still watching his own every move to West Berlin. Once or twice, he called on Svingel at the rest home and inquired after his old mentor. "The Americans" had come to look after Reinartz, Svingel reported— two men in civilian clothes whose names he remembered as Calabrese and Stronk.

Vogel, assured now that Reinartz would not be abandoned, thereafter stayed away. What if the Americans should come by while he was visiting Reinartz? he asked himself. He could not afford to jeopardize his own career again.[56]

Reinartz also had another visitor, the chief of West Berlin counterintelligence, who got him a job in the West Berlin city government but was disturbed by signs of Reinartz's mental instability. The Americans were after him, Reinartz complained, as were West German agents.[57]

In 1966, Reinartz left Svingel's rest home and moved into a small apartment. Svingel, concerned about his mental well-being and his physical disability, stayed in touch with him there. At first, Reinartz seemed to be recovering, and enjoying his work. But the persecution complex was getting worse. Eventually, he was committed to the city neurological clinic in Spandau.

There, Svingel later learned, Reinartz's hostility gradually became fixated on one of his nurses. Reinartz, he heard, would wander up and down the corridors looking for her, and then menace her, screaming her name. Why this nurse in particular was a mystery, the doctors told Svingel. Discussing the case one day with the doctor in charge, Svingel told the professor that Reinartz believed he had spent a decade in prison because of Hilde Benjamin. "That's it," the doctor exclaimed aloud. "The nurse's name is Hilde."[58]

Accompanied by a male nurse from the clinic, Reinartz came to visit Svingel only once more, in November 1972, asking that he come to see him in the clinic at Christmas. When Svingel called the clinic to arrange the visit, he was told that Reinartz had committed suicide.

Wolfgang Vogel also did not learn that Reinartz had died until several days later. By then, the funeral had already taken place.

CHAPTER FOUR

VOGEL'S GROWING REPUTATION

"Most lawyers earn their living from the misfortunes of others."

The Wall created a new strand in the shroud of subversion, surveillance, and espionage that both East and West had spun around Berlin, and a new line in Vogel's practice. "Flight from the Republic," as the Communists defined the act of trying to leave the country without official permission, not only challenged the ingenuity of would-be refugees, but created a whole new field for spies, agents, and mercenaries. Vogel's personal integrity and his determination to do the best for his clients, within the limits that Communist legal practice allowed, made him indispensable, both to the clients and to the Stasi.

Streit seemed to be building up Vogel systematically as the next Friedrich Karl Kaul, the star lawyer who had dominated East German courtrooms for the previous decade. But where Kaul was flamboyant and confrontational, Vogel was substantive and conciliatory, a born seeker of compromise who was effective and reassuring to West German partners who dealt with him behind the scenes.

Vogel's legal briefs and the testimony of some of the young

Westerners—Germans and Americans—whom he represented in the early 1960s show glimpses of his complex personality. His conduct won him the trust of his clients without shaking the Stasi's confidence, and also impressed foreign lawyers with connections to Western intelligence services. This was the heyday of the "escape helpers" who flourished after the building of the Wall, and Vogel used the cases to increase his own leverage on the East German government that sought to control him, even as he satisfied its demands. If this occasionally meant that he could do little to get his escape helper clients off the hook, they had never expected otherwise; and with the prisoner exchanges, he had a secret channel to the West German government to help them after they went to jail. How much leeway Vogel really had depended on the case. The greatest danger was that of self-delusion, that Vogel would overestimate his own importance and come to think that his powers derived not from Streit and Communist power but from the force of his own personality and intellect.

Vogel's was always a risky game, one that was particularly dangerous in the tense atmosphere of late 1961 and 1962, when public outrage against the Wall was high in West Berlin, and Soviet and American tanks often faced each other at the Friedrichstrasse. Escape helpers became targets of special Stasi vigilance. Those who were apprehended were viewed and prosecuted as state criminals. But in West Berlin, particularly just after the Wall went up, the Wall itself was the crime, and helping people to escape across or underneath it was viewed as a noble cause. As long as the helpers stayed within the law, the West Berlin authorities did nothing to try to stop them. Defiance of Communist repression was an act of heroism celebrated in all of West Germany on every June 17, the anniversary of the uprisings in 1953.

The East German state placed high symbolic and propaganda value on trying and convicting people who were caught in such activities. The helpers could not engage West German lawyers to defend them in East German courts, but they could hire someone like Vogel, who would then find himself at the center of conflicting forces pulling on his clients from two sides. The stakes were high, and sometimes the interests of the superpowers were directly involved.

After the Wall, escape helpers discovered tunneling with a vengeance. Those who organized such activities for money had a wide variety of motivations—altruism, selfishness, idealism, greed, cynicism, and naïveté in various mixtures. As the Stasi became more efficient at discovering and arresting them, Vogel was asked by the West German legal-aid office in Berlin to assist in the helpers' defense. There was already much irony in this. The legal-aid office operated under the aegis of Bonn's Ministry for All-German Questions, the same ministry that was constantly and shrilly being accused by East German propaganda of encouraging and financing many of the escape organizations. When he served as their defense attorney, Vogel was pitted against prosecutors who worked for his protector, Josef Streit. Sometimes he and Streit found themselves in the same courtroom, arguing opposing sides of the same case. When Vogel lost, as he did in 99 percent of the cases, he could negotiate secretly, again with the Ministry for All-German Questions, to get these same defendants released for money, though usually not until after they had served half their sentences.[1] With Communism dead and discredited, this looks like a closed circle of legal and moral corruption. But while Communism held more than sixteen million people cruelly in its sway, it seemed, to the West Germans, like an efficacious way of helping people who would otherwise be trapped for years.

In the early summer of 1962, Vogel represented an alleged member of an escape-helpers' group known as the "Girrmann" organization, which had built a tunnel underneath the Jerusalemstrasse a few months after the Wall. The discovery of this tunnel had cost an East German policeman his life. The defense Vogel offered in the trial before the East German high court shows a good lawyer trying to walk a tricky legal tightrope.

Vogel's client was a former East German from Bautzen named Gottfried Steglich who had been arrested at the border two months earlier. Steglich was charged with helping 210 people, including his brother, get out of the country with falsified Western identity papers. The indictment charged that Steglich's group had been paid and maintained by the All-German Ministry, and had been intimately connected to the West Berlin city government, police, and "various secret services" as well.[2]

Vogel had only limited room for maneuver in the defense. The law did not allow him to contest the facts, but at best permitted him to plead for mercy for clients who would get it only if they had made full confessions. As an East German lawyer, Vogel could not question the legitimacy of the measures the state had taken to seal itself off, or of its right to prosecute for "crimes" against these measures.

Steglich had fled the country after 1953 to study at the Technical University in West Berlin. Vogel described his client's involvement in the crime to the court the way an East German lawyer would be expected to do: "He said . . . he had gradually come under the influence of the press and radio. In this way he had come to his negative view of the German Democratic Republic. He hated the security measures at the border." But how had this hatred been instilled in him? "To see the complete answer to this question, we have to go back to the year 1953. With the promise of a free university education he was lured to West Berlin. In the following nine years he was in the flower of development. He had not gone consciously through the war; he was twelve years old when it ended. His father was gone. In the course of time and with continually new forms of cold war, he was then—perhaps not even consciously— prepared for a hot war. The warriors saw their chance coming last year. But their plans were foiled by the protection measures of the 13th of August"—the standard East German euphemism for the Wall.

With Streit listening in the courtroom, Vogel then went on to argue why his client deserved clemency: "Great weight should be accorded to the distinction between someone who has been led to engage in an organized human trade[3] through political demagogy, under the increasingly misleading influence of constant propaganda, and someone who knowingly participates out of sworn hatred."[4] His client had not taken part in the tunnel-digging activities of the group to which he had belonged; he had adopted no conspiratorial alias, had come into "democratic Berlin" under his own name, Vogel said. Steglich had simply processed applications from those who wanted to try to get out, and in only one case, that of his own brother, had he personally influenced an East German citizen to leave.

West German propaganda had said that the outrages of the Wall justified almost any resistance, that the Ten Commandments did not apply to the murderers at the border, Vogel told the court. The prosecution had asked for a fifteen-year sentence for his client, but Vogel pleaded for a lighter one, saying that the West German political authorities bore some of the responsibility for his acts because they had encouraged them.

Steglich received the full fifteen years, despite Vogel's plea, and went back to jail. Vogel had spoken for his client and shown his patriotic loyalty to the state. The young man was, in Vogel's eyes, a victim of larger political forces. He had even said so, though necessarily concentrating only on those in West Germany. If the West German state then later paid money to ransom Steglich free, to Vogel's mind, that would be part of a larger justice. And soon, Steglich would be on one of those buses leaving the Bautzen jail, one of many prisoners who owed their freedom to Vogel's secret negotiations with the "warriors" in Bonn, while the state he served received compensation for the damages their subversive activities had done to it.[5]

Sometimes Vogel saw to it that the state got back more than money, as in the case of Volker G. Heinz.

Heinz, a good-looking blond youth who spoke excellent English, had become fascinated by the activities of the escape helpers while a student at university in West Berlin. In particular, he was intrigued by Wolfgang Fuchs, who had become famous as "The Tunnel Fox."

Fuchs had escaped to West Berlin and hauled his wife and three children over the Wall soon after it was built. He was determined to help as many other people as possible to get out any way they could. Fuchs, whose name means "fox" in German, saw that it would be easy to dig tunnels underneath the Wall and construct exits in the basements of the houses the Communists had vacated on the Eastern side preparatory to demolition. Fuchs dug seven of these tunnels, but to do the digging, he had needed volunteers, whom he recruited from idealists and adventurers at the Free University in West Berlin and elsewhere. He also needed money, which he often got from German magazines eager to have exclusive reports of his successes. Many students, including Heinz, cheered him on in what seemed like exhilarating sport that could mean, literally, life or death for the players. Some risked their own lives to help him get scores of East Germans out.

By the fall of 1964, though, the relentless Stasi campaign against the tunnels had made the technique ineffective. The secret police had evacuated nearly all the buildings within tunneling distance of the Wall and sealed them up; they blocked the sewers, underground electrical conduits, and subway lines with immovable grates or just sealed them off entirely. Fuchs's last tunnel, under the Bernauer Strasse that October, got fifty-seven people out before an East

German guard in uniform surprised them by appearing on the scene. The tunnelers were armed as well, and the East German soldier was killed in an exchange of fire. The ensuing uproar forced Fuchs to abandon tunneling and dream up other ways of helping escapees.

His new methods were scarcely less spectacular, including a well-publicized feat in which he had pulled refugees across the Wall with a hinged ladder mounted onto a truck, in the macabre but somehow appropriate surroundings of a deserted cemetery at night.[6]

One day in the late summer of 1965 Volker Heinz read this story in *Stern* magazine in the rooms of a medical student friend at Berlin University. Looking closer, he was astounded to find his friend's face in the picture: "That's you!" he exclaimed.

After his friend began telling tales of his other adventures, Heinz, then twenty-two years old, became fascinated. The feeling grew when he was finally brought to meet Fuchs in West Berlin. Fuchs saw that Heinz could be trusted, and told him he might be useful in a new scheme he had come up with. He had recruited the Syrian consul in West Berlin, who was willing, for a reward, to smuggle out East Germans in the trunk of his white Mercedes 220 automobile.

This was a smuggler's dream, since the consul's diplomatic plates guaranteed that the East German border guards would not inspect the car at the crossing points. But Fuchs still took precautions, strengthening the car's rear suspension so that it would not sink under the weight of the refugees hiding in the rear and thus draw the attention of the border guards. As a West German citizen, Heinz could travel to East Berlin, and his job would be to meet his clients there, make sure they were unobserved, and get them safely into the car. He would return on his own by subway or the elevated rapid transit line while the Syrian delivered his passengers to West Berlin.

Though he was nervous about the plan, Heinz was fascinated. It would be dangerous; the East German authorities were still handing out fifteen-year sentences for escape helpers. And in the West, the glamour and romanticism that had surrounded their activities when the Wall had first gone up were fading. Many West Germans were beginning to have doubts about rapacious mercenaries who commanded fees of tens of thousands of marks for their services and kept the money in Swiss bank accounts. Heinz did not know or care whether Fuchs was demanding such fees; he himself would do the work for the sheer adventure of it, and his conscience was clear. Fuchs told Heinz he would be given a contact address and a time. He would not know names or have other means of identifying—or inadvertently betraying—the refugees, and it would be entirely Heinz's decision when the Mercedes drove up whether to proceed with each escape or to abort. If he did not signal with his hand to the Syrian consul to stop and let him bundle the refugees aboard, the Mercedes would drive on.

This was something straight out of the movies—authority, secrecy, and the romanticism of struggling to advance a good cause. It was all too much for a young law student to resist. In the autumn of 1965 Heinz, by then enrolled at the University of Bonn, boarded an evening British Airways flight from Cologne to West Berlin and traveled across the border in the dark for his first mission, making a rendezvous with his first pair of escapees—the operations would almost always involve two adults. He saw them safely into the diplomat's sedan, watched its red taillights disappear into the night, and then made his way back across the Wall. He could return early the next morning to Cologne, in time to make his first class in Bonn, and not even his girlfriend would know where he had been or what he had done the night before.

Heinz repeated the operation once, then again, and again and again, despite incredible tension and fear that sometimes made his mouth go dry. On one night, Heinz had signaled to the Mercedes to pull into a remote vacant lot on the outskirts of East Berlin, seen the headlights flash, and quickly forced the two people who had turned up on the site into the trunk of the car. On the way back to the outlying rapid transit station on another occasion, a sixth sense warned him that two men were following him. Heinz ducked into a train waiting at the platform, and as the doors closed before his followers could board, he thought he had successfully evaded pursuit. The border guards at Friedrichstrasse processed his exit papers routinely, and he had been relieved when he finally stepped out of the train on the Western side at Bahnhof Zoo. Fuchs, who listened carefully to his account of the close call, thought Heinz must have thrown off the tail, since he had not been detained at Friedrichstrasse, and agreed that it would be safe for him to go back after a few weeks.

When he did, in 1966, all was apparently normal for a while. On August 13, the fifth anniversary of the Wall, Tunnel Fuchs and his boys even carried off a "spectacular," smuggling out five people in one night. The Syrian consul made two trips instead of one, pocketing the extra pay—Heinz never knew how much he got—with pleasure.

By September 9, Fuch's Syrian-student operation, with Heinz and another man Heinz called his "deputy," had brought across sixty-three people. Shortly before 10 P.M. that evening, Heinz was congratulating himself on the sixty-fourth and sixty-fifth, a man and a woman, when he entered the East Berlin side of the Heinrich-Heine-Strasse pedestrian crossing point near Checkpoint Charlie. Suddenly he felt his wrists being seized from behind. In an instant, he was in shackles and roughly shoved into a car, much the way he had bundled his charges into the Mercedes. But this car brought him to the Stasi detention center on the Magdalenenstrasse for a long and relentless interrogation. "We know who you are and what you've been doing," the investigators told him calmly, but Heinz held out all night long, claiming to be just an ordinary student tourist come to see the night sights in the Communist capital. At five in the morning, the door to the interrogation room burst open. There in the corridor outside was the Syrian consul, and in a cell next door to him was the couple Heinz had put into the Mercedes the night before.[7]

Heinz's interrogators took between three and four months to build the case against him, going over every single detail of all thirty of his successful operations. He was shown hundreds of pictures, including one of his "deputy," and asked to identify anybody he knew. But Heinz had not come this far to betray his friends. He shook his head and insisted that he recognized no one in any of the photographs.

Now Vogel entered the case. Heinz's father had well-connected political friends in Bonn, who referred the senior Heinz to Stange in West Berlin and through him, to Vogel. And Vogel could see that Heinz might be worth more to the Stasi if he were used as a bargaining chip in an exchange rather than being given a long prison sentence, as a deterrent example to other "escape helpers."

Vogel's first contact with Heinz came in the Stasi prison in Hohenschönhausen about a month before his trial, which was to be held at the end of June 1967.

But Vogel made the meeting with Heinz purely a formality. Vogel had come into the visiting room with his index finger held vertically before his mouth and his eyes rolling up towards the ceiling, a sign Heinz took to mean that the Stasi had the place thoroughly bugged and that anything said would be overheard. Though Heinz was burning to ask all kinds of questions, he understood that Vogel just wanted him to keep quiet. Vogel seemed to regard the state's case as ironclad, or at least so Heinz concluded from the way he left the further details of preparing the defense to an elderly lawyer Vogel had hired as a legal assistant. His meetings with this elderly clerk left Heinz feeling discouraged and pessimistic about his chances at trial, an impression strengthened by the older lawyer's desultory questions. Heinz began to realize that he might have to serve a prison sentence of ten years.

A week before the trial began, Vogel made another brief visit and delivered a cryptic message hinting that, though the verdict would undoubtedly go against Heinz, he nonetheless could expect to be released very soon afterward. Heinz did not understand why, but he began to feel hope for the first time. At the trial itself, which began at the Berlin City Court on June 29, there were two surprises. The first was Heinz's "deputy," who was introduced into the courtroom and asked, by the trial judge, "Do you know Mr. Heinz?" "Of course," came the answer. "What do you say to that, Mr. Heinz?" asked the judge. "Do you still maintain you don't know him?" "I see no reason to deny it any longer," Heinz said, resigned to the inevitable. The second surprise was the sentence: not ten years, but twelve. Stunned, back in the cell in Hohenschönhausen, Heinz began to wonder if Vogel was a man of his word after all.

Only a week later, two Stasi officers came to his cell and said he would be released, if he would cooperate with them and undertake assignments as an agent for the East Germans in the West. Heinz was noncommittal, and after another day and a half, the Stasi officers gave him a bundle of codes and rendezvous addresses, swore him to secrecy, and left him to his own devices.

Early in the morning of July 11, Heinz was given back his clothes, 7.50 marks, and put into a big light-blue West German-made BMW with East German number plates and a Stasi driver. The man took him wordlessly on a four-hour trip south and west of the city, toward the West German border. It was a splendid, blue-sky summer day, and Heinz's spirits rose—even more so when the car stopped at a parking lot off the autobahn and he saw Vogel waiting, with another man he learned was Stange. Vogel's car, an Opel Kapitän, brought him to the border at Herleshausen and to freedom, in exchange, Vogel told him, for two captured East German spies whose names and backgrounds Heinz would never know.[8]

Vogel said nothing about the approach the Stasi had made to his client, and Heinz did not mention it to him. Days later, he did report it to Stange, who urged him to go directly to the West German authorities and tell them everything. Heinz took this advice and gave a full account to counterintelligence in West Berlin.

Vogel could put himself in Heinz's shoes, which fit him uncannily closely. Who better than Vogel could understand how a young law student could find himself over his head in subversive intrigue? He had been there himself a decade earlier, escaping punishment only because of his own willingness to cooperate with the Stasi and his political connections with Streit.

Heinz's political connections in Bonn had made him a hostage of special interest to the East Germans. His father's friend was Hanns-Martin Schleyer, a powerful West German industrialist who had interceded with a former school classmate in the West German chancellor's office. At the request of the chancellery, the Ministry of All-German Affairs had then put his name on the prisoner exchange lists Vogel negotiated, as a "special" case.[9]

Vogel's bill came a few weeks later, a sum on the order of fifteen hundred marks. It was reasonable given the circumstances, Heinz thought, though he was surprised to find it was payable in West German marks to a bank in West Berlin. Vogel had better connections, and was doing better, than he had realized. But Heinz, who later became a lawyer himself, could understand that, as well. "Most lawyers earn their living from the misfortunes of others," he shrugged.[10]

How well, Heinz could not have known. Slowly and erratically, the prisoner-release business with Bonn was growing. There were 884 prisoners in 1964, 1,555 in 1965, 961 over the courses of 1966 and 1967, by which time the government in Bonn had paid more than 160 million deutsche marks to get them free. The East Germans did not pay Vogel for his work or his expenses in negotiating the exchanges, but he was making plenty of money in hard Western currency, from the West German government and from clients such as Heinz. The East Germans taxed it at only a minimal rate and let him keep it in West Germany.[11]

Streit and Volpert were carefully and systematically helping their protégé to build his reputation in other ways as well. In 1966, Streit assigned him to defend two accused German war criminals in widely publicized trials the Communists wanted to reflect well on their carefully cultivated antifascist international image. For propaganda purposes, the more important case was that of Dr. Horst Fischer, a doctor at Auschwitz who had successfully hidden in East Germany after the war until mid-1965 and who had largely confessed his crimes. Streit himself led the prosecution that March, demanding the death penalty; his protégé pleaded for mercy for his client.

"Every accused, even this one, is legally guaranteed the right to defend himself through a lawyer," Vogel reminded the court. But he refused to insult the memory of the Nazis' victims by pretending the crimes to which the defendant had confessed did not require punishment: "The leeway for the defense lies only in the area of sentencing," Vogel had said, "and here it can only be between life imprisonment and the death penalty."

But the purpose of the death penalty, Vogel had pleaded, was "not atonement or even revenge. It is not necessary to impose a death sentence against this defendant in order to deter others inside the country, for Fascism has been absolutely liquidated in the G.D.R." Against fascist influences from outside, Vogel told the judges, East Germany was more than adequately protected by "the government measures of August 13, 1961" that had built the Wall.

The court condemned Fischer to death, but Streit was pleased by the way Vogel had performed his role.[12]

In the shadows away from such show trials, Volpert was encouraging Vogel to develop the lines to the Americans that he had first picked up during the Abel-Powers negotiations. Here, too, the Wall provided Vogel with many opportunities and clients, for it was not only young German students such as Heinz who became involved in escape operations—sometimes Americans were caught up in them as well.

One of these was Benjamin Franklin Whitehill III, a twenty-one-year-old Stanford University student who, along with a nineteen-year-old British boy, had been arrested in August 1965, only hours after arriving in East Berlin. Whitehill was the son of a wealthy oil company operator in Tulsa, Oklahoma, and he was on a classic European tour, paid for by his father. Berlin was a long way from Tulsa, and nothing he had heard about the "awl bidness" had prepared the boy or his British companion for a classic passport scam.

The boys had gone over to East Berlin on a day trip. But when they had arrived at Friedrichstrasse to return to West Berlin, the

East German guards told them their passports and currency-exchange documents had already been used by two people who had passed through earlier.

The pattern was a common one. Since both Britain and the United States had occupation rights for all of Berlin, most British and American passport holders were automatically entitled to twenty-four-hour day passes, which were numbered and registered and had to be kept with their passports and handed back on return to West Berlin. When the Wall first went up, escape helpers often persuaded foreign tourists to lend their documents to East Germans who could use them to cross; the rightful owners need only claim that their passports had been lost or stolen. Many young people, hard up for money, were willing to undergo the risk and the unpleasantness of a delay in return for payment. But the Stasi had not bought Whitehill's story. Now he was in jail in a country where American consular officials could offer no protection at all.

The Whitehill family immediately became highly alarmed, fearing that their son might be a hostage in an East German plot to shake down wealthy Americans for big money. So they asked their lawyer in Washington, a soft-spoken Georgian and former official of the U.S. Immigration Service with the unusual name of Ricey S. New, to fly to Berlin to see what he could do to help.

The U.S. Mission in West Berlin had given New the standard reference to Stange and his East German contact, Vogel, and in due course New had gone over to see Vogel in his office in East Berlin. The two men liked each other from the start. New was a tall, courtly man with a laconic southern drawl, an open face, and a handsome head of wavy hair. Despite the language barrier, the two men found they had much in common; to the East German lawyer, New seemed a bit like himself: nonconfrontational and concerned primarily about his client's interests. And because New's former government connections promised good contacts with the Johnson administration in Washington, the Stasi placed no obstacles in Vogel's way to developing a relationship with New. Vogel was eager to do so. Young Whitehill might very well have "lent" his passport, Vogel thought, but if he had done so, he had been a victim of sharp operators. A speedy and humane resolution of this case would pay greater dividends, for Vogel and for the East German government, than a show trial of the naïve young American who had clearly gotten in over his head.

Vogel negotiated Whitehill's release on August 28, having Stange announce that the East Germans had let him and the British student go because of their "ignorance of conditions in East Berlin."[13] In New York, Whitehill told reporters he might have been asleep when he "lost" his passport for some hours in East Berlin.

Vogel earned no fee on this case, but he had collected an IOU from Ricey New worth far more than money, to him and to the Stasi. New was fascinated by the atmosphere of East Berlin and flattered by Vogel's attentions. Now, only two weeks later, he received a letter from Vogel in Washington, saying that there were several other Americans in East German prisons whom they could try together to get released.

Among these was a Wisconsin dairy farmer's son, a student at the Free University named John Van Altena, Jr., who spoke fluent German and had been preparing for law studies at the Free University. Since school did not start until November, during the summer of 1964 Van Altena worked for Lufthansa Airlines in Hamburg, where he became acquainted with Werner Kloss, a swashbuckling blond giant whose cousins in East Berlin had tried unsuccessfully to leave the German Democratic Republic and were now prepared to try desperate measures to get out. Van Altena agreed to help by smuggling out Jürgen and Bärbel Rabe and their four-year-old daughter, Sabrina, in the specially modified trunk compartment of his 1959 Ford.

The arrangements were painstaking. Using a hammer, chisel, a hacksaw, and metal shears, Van Altena and Kloss cut down the fuel tank and chopped out part of the car body over the differential, creating a space between the rear seat and the enclosed trunk compartment just big enough for an adult and a small child to squeeze into. The men were proud of their handiwork; they thought the East German guards would find no exterior signs of the rebuilding job even if they slid a mirror beneath the car to inspect the underbody. And, with the special customs-free plates Van Altena had arranged for the car, the inspection should be only cursory and their chances of making an escape excellent.

The plan was for Van Altena to drive the mother and child out on October 9, on the East German national holiday weekend, the 15th anniversary of the German Democratic Republic, and then return on the 10th to smuggle the father across. To ensure success, the little girl would have to remain quiet with her mother once they squeezed into the secret space, which was so tight that it required a foam-rubber form over the differential. So when Van Altena arrived at 8 P.M. on the 9th to pick them up, he was relieved to find the girl sound asleep from a dose of tranquilizing drugs.

Carrying a concealed automatic pistol, Van Altena drove into Checkpoint Charlie at about 8:30 P.M. He whispered to Bärbel in the seat behind him to be sure that she and the child remained quiet until they had reached West Berlin. But the East Germans were waiting for them. After a long and thorough search of the car failed to reveal the hidden cargo, some guards took Van Altena inside a narrow hallway behind the commander's office while others systematically dismantled the car. Spread-eagled against a poster on the wall, Van Altena slipped, and in the ensuing body search his guards discovered the automatic weapon.

The interrogation later that night had its own horrors, including a fright when guards burst in and said that the child had been found dead in the car, from a drug overdose. This, fortunately, was only a bluff. The horror at the trial the following January was real, however; Friedrich Karl Kaul offered what Van Altena thought a half-hearted defense, and the American was given one year for possession of a concealed weapon and seven years at hard labor for "smuggling of East German citizens."

Freedom became a possibility for Van Altena a year later, in mid-September 1965, after a notice arrived in the prison mail that Wolfgang Vogel was to take on his case and would try to arrange a visit with him after Van Altena signed the necessary power of attorney. Vogel's name meant nothing to the young American, but when a fellow prisoner told him that Vogel was the man who had arranged the Abel-Powers exchange, his spirits brightened considerably. The first meeting with the lawyer occurred shortly after the New Year, in the Magdalenenstrasse jail. Vogel made it clear that the case would be difficult, but explained that he had asked New to help. By the first of April, Vogel said, the lawyers should be able to tell how much longer Van Altena would have to stay in jail.

Vogel called New in Washington and asked him to get to Berlin before February 4, when he would arrange for permission to visit Van Altena in the Magdalenenstrasse. New did not stand to make a dollar from the case, but Vogel intrigued him as much as he intrigued Vogel. His curiosity shot even higher when Meehan told him after he flew in that the very fact that Vogel had been able to arrange the visit to an East German jail was a good sign. "The case must mean a lot to him," Meehan said.[14]

New was wearing a spy's trench coat with the collar turned up when Van Altena first met him in prison on the appointed day. Making introductions, Vogel cupped his hands to his ears and motioned toward the ceiling, to indicate Stasi bugs. New said that he had spoken with the boy's parents in Wisconsin and found that they had been worried about the condition of his foot, since he had complained of a torn ligament that had immobilized him for months. Clearly, Van Altena thought, New and Vogel did not want to talk about negotiations for his release because the room was bugged. But New did tell him, "With any luck, you can expect to be released by the Ides of March."

New was off by only a day. On March 16, 1966, the Stasi supervisors at Hohenschönhausen presented Van Altena with a document signed by President Walter Ulbricht, reducing his sentence from eight to two-and-a-half years and making him eligible for immediate parole because he had already served half of the new term.

Van Altena was then taken, one last time, to the Magdalenenstrasse holding facility, where Vogel picked him up at 3:25 P.M. and drove him out of the prison yard once and for all. The destination was not West Berlin but Vogel's office in Friedrichsfelde. Vogel said there was someone who wanted to meet him—Maxwell Rabb, president of the United States Committee for Refugees, who told Van Altena that he had helped arrange his release.

By now it was time to get across the Wall. Vogel took both men outside, where his new light blue Mercedes was waiting.

"This is how you should smuggle people out," Vogel grinned to Van Altena, as he started the car. The young American looked to Rabb to see if he knew what he meant. "Watch this, John," Rabb told him. "This will show you who Vogel really is."

Van Altena's last border crossing through the Invalidenstrasse checkpoint was, as he later described it in his book about his imprisonment, a memorable one. Normally, the few East Germans authorized to make border crossings at all approached them with caution. They looked to the *Volkspolizei* and the Stasi guards before making a move and obeyed the traffic signals with meticulous care. Vogel showed complete disregard for the speed limit signs and cared not a fig for the guards who had stopped and torn apart Van Altena's car a year and a half before. Instead of slowing down for the concrete cement blocks and steel barriers at the Invalidenstrasse, or stopping and showing his passport and those of his passengers, Vogel took the course at speed, tires squealing as the

Mercedes slalomed through the barriers. And instead of drawing their pistols or blowing their whistles, or slamming the gates shut, the guards saluted as Vogel roared through.[15]

By now, Vogel had completely captivated New, who thought the East German lawyer was the most fascinating person he had ever met.[16] Vogel encouraged New in this belief. His visit to Van Altena in a prison in East Berlin was the first time any American lawyer had ever been allowed to do such a thing, Vogel told him. On the other side of the Wall, Meehan, too, was impressed. But Vogel had developed his relationship with New for a purpose, a purpose that served the Stasi's interests and had Volpert's full approval.

Vogel had contacts in America and with American officials that a secret Stasi agent could only dream of. Any sophisticated American lawyer or diplomat knew perfectly well that Vogel must have had a relationship of some kind with the Stasi. That much was perfectly obvious, and practically out in the open. And the Stasi connection was precisely what made him so fascinating and, indeed, invaluable: He could get people out of trouble whom no one else could help.

The Stasi deliberately steered "intelligence" cases his way, perhaps to increase Vogel's allure. In September 1967, he was entrusted with the pro forma defense of a man the East Germans alleged was an American CIA agent, a twenty-seven-year-old truck driver from Rhode Island named Peter T. Feinauer. He had been charged with a variety of crimes, including smuggling East Germans across the Wall, between 1961 and his arrest in October 1966. The list of subversive activities ascribed to Feinauer by Streit's office went on for pages and pages. He had worked for the Ministry for All-German Questions; he had worked for the CIA station in Dahlem as a paid agent; he had been assigned to prepare anti-Communist propaganda and recruit other agents for "West German and American imperialism." Feinauer had confessed, after spending seven months in investigatory arrest. A dangerous man indeed, in the Stasi's eyes, and Streit was demanding a fifteen-year sentence.[17]

Vogel pled before the sentencing commission of the Greater Berlin City court for a shorter term, on the grounds that Feinauer—much like Colonel Abel a decade earlier—might have wanted to spy, had been fully equipped to spy, but had not actually managed to do much spying at all.

"It is certainly essential to draw a distinction between whether a secret service receives information that might also be in the newspapers, and whether confidential material from an important institution disappears, or military intelligence is passed on," Vogel told the court. "In determining a sentence, this is and should remain of importance. . . . Not everything that is held to be important and is withheld from the public is a state secret, the High Court once said in a published opinion."[18]

Vogel always tried to put himself in the shoes of the people he defended. He had no trouble doing so in the case of this one. "When the accused was recruited in October 1961, he was still quite young. He was twenty-two years old, not yet very long in West Germany or West Berlin, but long enough to have been set up and incited by those who recruited him. Why this happened has to do with the context of his personal development, but also with the context of the situation in which he found himself then as a twenty-two-year-old young man. He was in financial difficulties, and was about to be drafted. He was lured by the offer of a deferment. At home, he had no one he could ask for advice; his relationship to his mother was and is not of the best. He was all on his own, and he could not cope with the conflict. I would even like to say that precisely because he was vulnerable, they concentrated on him, for it is a well-known practice of the American secret service to target people who find themselves in difficulties, or are artifically brought into difficulties."[19]

Vogel continued: "Some come over here, others stay on the other side of the Brandenburg Gate, or appear at the most in the mask of a so-called diplomat. . . . Those who are recruited, assigned and sent off the way the accused was, are merely the tools of these others. Whatever he may have done, in comparison with the others he remains only a tool. The best years of his life, his youth, have gone down the drain. For him, that is really the worst punishment."[20]

Vogel was putting into words acceptable to an East German court some of his own feelings about the way the Stasi had exploited his own vulnerability fifteen years earlier. He would return many times in the years that followed to the theme of how all intelligence services cynically exploited human weakness and often abandoned their victims to their fates after they were caught. But in an East German court, the words were bound to fall on deaf ears. The state had already made up its mind about what justice in this case was to be. Vogel's plea for a reduced sentence was rejected, and Feinauer got the full fifteen years that Streit had requested.

But Feinauer, as an accused agent, could be a freed in an exchange of spies.[21] He thus fit into the larger political purpose both Vogel and Volpert had had in mind, each viewing it from his own perspective, Vogel's at the time being to cement personal trust with Ricey New.

Volpert had asked Vogel when he had last met with New whether the American could be trusted enough to pass on a message. By February 1966 Vogel did trust New, and the confidence was mutual. Vogel did not tell New where the message had come from; New was no fool and could have figured it out. What Vogel did tell New was this:

There is a prisoner in the federal penitentiary in Lewisburg, Pennsylvania, an American named Robert Glenn Thompson, who is serving a thirty-year sentence as a Soviet spy. Could New visit Thompson in Lewisburg and deliver a message—a message that was simple and straightforward, and would not compromise New at all? "Tell him this," Vogel said. "We haven't forgotten you."[22]

CHAPTER FIVE

EXPEDIENCY AND INDISPENSABILITY

"If I didn't know you so well, I'd say that was blackmail."

On both sides of the Wall, the players in the new game of human trades were feeling the rush of excitement and the intoxication of operating at the margins of superpower politics, a game that could be addictive. For the East German Communists, driven by their hard-currency habit, Bonn's payments for the prisoner releases had become a badly needed fix, one that they could use to deliver opiate to the masses at times such as Christmas when a sudden influx of oranges and tangerines from the prisoner trades made the rigors of Communism seem more bearable.

For Wolfgang Vogel, there was the exhilaration that came with being treated as a privileged insider, entrusted by his government with sensitive negotiations only a handful of people knew about, and the rare perquisites of a handsome income in Western currency, a luxury Western automobile, and a diplomatic passport that, together with a word from Volpert to the Stasi border guards, allowed him to breeze through the strict frontier controls and deliver to freedom human charges who would forever think of him as a kind of savior. Vogel was becoming not only a trader of political prisoners, but a broker in spies, and business had never been better.

His relationship with Volpert had long since transcended the conventional idea of Stasi control officer and secret agent. Though Volpert apparently continued to refer to Vogel as "Georg" in internal Stasi documents, Vogel had become much more valuable to the Stasi than any "informal collaborator" or undercover officer could be, and the relationship between the two men reflected his status. Vogel found Volpert approachable and flexible, willing to give him all the leeway he needed. Vogel was the lawyer, Volpert would tell him, and when he was negotiating with his Western colleagues he was free to use his own judgment about tactics, within the broad guidelines Volpert provided. Volpert had at first always come to Streit's office to give Vogel the lists of prisoners to be released, and the price to be demanded, but as he and Vogel had grown more comfortable with each other, they began working directly together. Volpert would come to Vogel's office in the Reilerstrasse, or in Streit's office, or Vogel would go to Volpert's; they had no need to meet in secret Stasi safe houses or undercover apartments.[1] Volpert was always present when Vogel made his trips to Bautzen to take the prisoners on the buses to Herleshausen, and gradually a bond of friendship developed between the men; they began to socialize together, and the Vogels would occasionally dine at the Volperts' home.

But Volpert had not risen to Erich Mielke's side and acquired his broad-ranging power because of his likeability. The prisoner releases were, from the Stasi's point of view, a shrewd and ruthless business, and Volpert did not hesitate to press Vogel to serve the Stasi's ends. Bonn wanted freedom for political prisoners and for family reunifications as badly as East Berlin needed the money they brought in. By creating a business that now, year for year, involved more than a thousand prisoners and their families, the East Germans had created political leverage they could use to extract concessions—or simply more money—from the West. Bonn had laid itself open to blackmail, and Vogel would be asked, in his diplomatic way, to extract it.

It had been made clear almost at the beginning of the prisoner exchanges that the Communists did not shy away from blackmail. The case was that of Count Benedikt von und zu Hoensbroech, the scion of one of West Germany's oldest and wealthiest noble families. As a young West German student, idealism led him to help people get out of East Germany. He had some success, smuggling out refugees in the sealed-off compartments of furniture moving vans, until the Stasi had arrested him in September 1963.

His arrest, which took several days to become publicly known, caused a political sensation in West Germany. His prominent family had a name, money, extensive landholdings in the Rhineland, and influential connections in the Bonn government—Heinrich von Brentano, the West German foreign minister, was a cousin. The East Germans tried to get Hoensbroech to write von Brentano suggesting that a letter from the foreign minister to the East Germans would lead to clemency, a crude way of tricking the West German government into recognizing the sovereignty of the German Democratic Republic.

Telling himself that it took the devil to fight Beelzebub, the young count then hired the notorious Kaul. Kaul did not personally see to the defense when the case of Hoensbroech and two codefendants came to trial in Chamber 1B of the Berlin City Court in July 1964, in an atmosphere of cold war hysteria. Phrases such as "hyenas of humanity" and "human commerce" rang through the indictment and the inevitable judgment. The court found Hoensbroech's operation to have been approved and secretly supported by the "criminal" West German government, blinded to ordinary human decency by its class hatred of the first workers' and peasants' state on German soil, and Hoensbroech was sentenced to ten years in prison.[2]

The official prisoner-release program with Bonn that Vogel had begun was only in its infancy, and with the approval of the Stasi, Kaul began private negotiations with the Hoensbroech family. He suggested that a ransom payment of two million deutsche marks would adequately compensate the East German working class for the damage this nobleman inflicted on its interests and might secure his safe return.

The Hoensbroechs had kept the government in Bonn informed, but the West Germans felt that a precedent of this kind would upset the 40,000 marks per capita release payment system, and Erich Mende, the Minister for All-German Affairs, insisted that Hoensbroech's name be included on one of the regular lists at the regular price. He telephoned Stange in Berlin, Mende wrote later, and sarcastically told him, "Please ask your colleague Vogel in East Berlin whether a count is worth fifty times more than a worker in the workers' and peasants' state of the G.D.R."³

Vogel conveyed the message to Volpert, and, according to Mende, the East Germans were shamed into dropping Kaul's ransom demand. Kaul himself also withdrew from the case, and in the fall of 1964, after a year in prison, young Hoensbroech was taken in civilian clothes to the visitors' room and introduced to Vogel, who identified himself and then nodded to one of the three uniformed police officers present to read a letter from Walter Ulbricht granting a pardon. But he had never requested one, the count objected; Vogel calmed him and urged him to let matters take their course. His good behavior in prison, the letter went on, had entitled him to a reduction of his sentence by half; the time remaining was now being commuted to a suspended sentence.

Vogel then invited Hoensbroech to follow him into his car, an Opel, and personally drove him through the Heinrich-Heine-Strasse border crossing. Vogel offered him a Western cigarette and merely nodded to the border guards, who did not even ask to see the East German's identity card before letting him through.

But Mende had not been as successful as he had pretended in fighting the attempt at blackmail. The East Germans had not capitulated—they had only dropped their price, to 450,000 marks. The Bonn government paid only 40,000, but the Count's father had to come up with the remaining 410,000 out of his own pocket, transferring the money to a Swiss bank account as Kaul had originally suggested.⁴

The East German attempts at blackmail were not confined to its pure form—money—as the case of Harry Seidel showed; Seidel, a famous East German racing cyclist, had fled to West Berlin on the first anniversary of the building of the Wall. He, too, had worked with the tunnelers in those early days, but on November 14, 1962, he had been caught by armed Stasi agents while pushing a group of escapees through a tunnel at a remote section of the Wall. Seidel had been armed and started to shoot to try to cover the last escapee. In the exchange of fire, he was shot in the leg and two East German guards were wounded. Seidel was tried and sentenced to life imprisonment on December 29, 1962, for "acts of violence endangering the state" and "peace-threatening aggression."⁵

Seidel had been one of the earliest prisoners on Rehlinger's lists in 1964 and 1965 and was one of the first to be rejected. But the West Germans had kept insisting, and finally Rehlinger, in tough negotiations with Vogel, had managed to get Seidel included in a release scheduled for September 13, 1966. A few days before, to Rehlinger's surprise, Vogel informed him that because of the public interest that would be expected in this case, his side now found itself unable to agree to let Seidel go. Rehlinger heard alarm bells ringing: The East Germans had already agreed in writing to release the prisoner, and if they were now allowed to go back on their word, they would try it again, and again.

"If Seidel doesn't appear as agreed, I'm going to hold up a boat," he told Vogel, who knew that the agreement in this case included a shipping contract for a load of animal feed that would soon be on its way to Rostock harbor.[6] Vogel went back to Streit with the message that the whole arrangement would come apart if his credibility were undermined. Seidel was on the bus as promised on the 13th of September.

The East Germans knew, however, that they were onto a good thing and kept trying to increase the price Bonn had to pay. The stakes went up when the West German Social Democrats joined the government in an all-party coalition in December 1966 and a new minister for All-German Questions, Herbert Wehner, succeeded Erich Mende. Wehner, an ex-Communist and one of the most powerful people in the Social Democratic leadership, found upon taking office that Vogel had brought an East German demand for an increase in the price for prisoners—one that would raise it to sixty-six thousand marks per head.[7]

Rehlinger, as Wehner's chief civil servant in charge of the prisoner negotiations, was incensed and said so; but he also recognized that the demand could not simply be rejected out of hand. The fact that Bonn had agreed to a basic rate of forty thousand marks meant, he realized, that the West was already in the game. But the East Germans had to realize there were limits or they would keep raising the stakes. So he urged Wehner to slap down the new demand.

To Rehlinger's surprise, the gruff Wehner, who would later help make Willy Brandt the first Social Democratic chancellor of the country, was furious at him, accusing Rehlinger of endangering the entire program of prisoner releases and family reunifications. Perhaps, Wehner hinted, Rehlinger, a Christian Democrat, was sabotaging him deliberately for political reasons.

Wehner's passion about the humanitarian issue and his desire to help fellow German ideological victims across the border were understandable. Wehner, a shoemaker's son from Dresden, had been a Communist in his youth and had spent the Nazi years in exile in Moscow and later in prison in Sweden, where he had undergone an ideological conversion to the cause of social democracy. Wehner spoke no English, would never travel to America, and after his wartime experience had little use for Soviets: he was a patriot, through and through, of the German people and saw his mission as working in whatever ways he could to lessen the miseries they had brought down on themselves by the Nazi defeat and occupation by the superpowers.

Wolfgang Vogel came to know this man well and to revere him right alongside Streit, for without Wehner's blessing much of what Vogel did behind the scenes over the next twenty years would not have been possible. Ludwig Rehlinger, too, for all the differences between his own views and Wehner's, could understand and respect the latter's motivation on the issue of the prisoners. Wehner's choleric outburst over the principle of price soon passed after he brought out his pipe and he calmed himself. In the end, Wehner decided to let the East Germans save face. The nominal per capita price per prisoner stayed the same, 40,000 marks, but Bonn would see to it that the overall amount paid to the East Germans rose, ostensibly to include the costs of allowing the prisoners' families to join them. The prisoner release payments did rise—from 24.8 million deutsche marks in 1966 to 31.5 million marks in 1967, with every prospect of rising steadily higher every year thereafter.[8]

In East Berlin, Erich Mielke, since 1957 the minister of State Security, saw that Bonn could be manipulated. Mielke, too, had spent the Nazi years in Moscow, but Mielke was of a different order than either Vogel or Wehner. Mielke had been born into a working-class family in Berlin at the end of 1907 and had grown up in its hardscrabble milieu. He joined the Communist party and, after becoming unemployed in 1930, had plenty of time for demonstrations. In 1931 he had been allegedly involved in the cold-blooded murder of a Berlin policeman by a Communist self-defense group and had fled to Moscow. He returned to fight on the Communist side in the Spanish civil war and work for the Comintern in Belgium and France, where he was interned into a labor battalion during the Nazi occupation. Mielke was brutal, ruthless, and clever, a shrewd political animal who had worked his way to the top of the

Stasi through methods that had included blackmail of anyone who stood in his way.

Fiercely loyal to Moscow and a personal supporter of Comrade Stalin, Mielke took the KGB seriously when the Soviets began pressing him to get the West Germans to release an agent who had served them spectacularly well until his arrest in 1961. This was Heinz Felfe, perhaps the single most successful Soviet spy of the entire cold war. Mielke was determined to use Vogel's new leverage with the West Germans, through the trade in spies and political prisoners, to get Felfe out. He instructed Volpert to introduce Felfe's name into his discussions with the West German authorities.

The West Germans categorically refused even to discuss Felfe's release, not least because General Reinhard Gehlen, the legendary chief of the West German intelligence organization, had never forgiven Felfe for the enormity of his betrayal. The explanation of the Soviets' insistence lay in the nature of what Felfe had done and the reasons why he had done it.

Felfe, tall, agile, athletic, and nearly bald, wore the thick plastic spectacles of a German professor and had an extraordinarily sharp mind, honed to the rigors of the law in studies at the Bonn University after the war. But it was for his skills as a former Nazi intelligence officer and former police detective that both the Americans and the Soviets had become interested in him. And it was for the love of Dresden, his native city, the Florence of the Elbe, that Felfe had given his loyalty to the Soviets.

What had caused him to do it was the savage British bombing raid on Dresden in mid-February 1945, carried out with the help of the U.S. Air Force. A terrible firestorm killed tens of thousands of German civilians already demoralized by the coming inevitable loss of the war, and killed any sympathy Felfe might have had for the Western victors when it ended. "I loved Dresden as a man can only love his homeland," Felfe said later. "When I took the train from Berlin, I always stood in the corridor when we pulled in, to admire the wonderful silhouette of the city. I had all my friends and boyhood friends there. But in the raids, the house of my parents had been hit and burned out, and when they went out the next morning they were strafed, old people, my father was already in his seventies, carrying their last suitcase, with all their papers, taken under fire from the air. And with that fell the last inhibition I had to going over to the Soviets."[9]

Felfe had been captured by Canadian troops at the end of the war and taken to a prisoner-of-war camp in Holland, because of his SS foreign intelligence work, before being released in 1946. He collaborated briefly with British intelligence and then worked as an interrogator at a refugee camp, checking the political backgrounds of new arrivals, until 1951, when two Dresden friends who had also served with the SS, Hans Clemens and Erwin Tiebel, recruited him for the Soviets. A trip to the KGB's Karlhorst operating base followed in August 1951, when Felfe first met his Soviet controller, a man whom even years later he would identify only as "Alfred," out of affection and respect for Alfred's knowledge and love of German culture, and for his personal loyalty to Felfe.

Fearful of the coming rearmament of West Germany, the Soviets recruited Felfe to penetrate the new intelligence organization that Gehlen was setting up and to report to them everything he could find out about its activities.

Gehlen quickly recognized Felfe's talents and brought him to the West German intelligence organization's headquarters in Pullach, near Munich, putting him in charge of the Soviet division of its counterespionage department. At first, the CIA had held the organization directly under its operational control, building it from the remnants of Wehrmacht intelligence operations that had been aimed at the Soviet Union during the war, and funding it from Washington; later it became the BND, the Federal Intelligence Service, under the direct control of the German chancellor's office. Felfe was one of its most brilliant officers, a master of counterespionage who ran double agents with admirable skill and efficiency and seemed to know every detail of what was going on inside the KGB's Berlin operating base at Karlshorst, keeping an elaborate scale model of it on display in the organization's headquarters in Pullach, complete with such information as which senior Soviet officer used which private bathroom.

Felfe knew these things because he was often there himself, making secret forays before the days of the Wall to Karlshorst to confer not only with "Alfred," but with the chief KGB officer in Germany, General Aleksandr M. Korotkov, for debriefings. On one of these rendezvous, in 1958, Korotkov had suggested that perhaps Felfe could be even more useful in some other job.

"Couldn't you try to get yourself into the Foreign Ministry?" he asked. The Soviets were looking for someone to tell them what Bonn was up to politically. Felfe remained a soldier in the front lines of Allied counterintelligence instead, juggling the complicated double lies of pretending to discover Soviet spies while actually protecting them, since he was one himself all the while.[10]

Modesty was not one of Felfe's virtues, and by the early 1960s his arrogance had attracted the attention of a CIA counterintelligence specialist named Clare Petty.[11] The American had been tipped off to the existence of a traitor in the Gehlen Organization's ranks by a walk-in from Polish intelligence, an agent code-named Sniper, who said that it had been penetrated at a high level. The CIA's suspicions had also been aroused by the high life Felfe was leading in Munich, with a ten-room chalet in the mountains and a son in a private school much too expensive for his 1,700-mark monthly salary.[12]

In 1961, he had carried his arrogance a step too far. It was his wartime friend Clemens who got him into trouble, calling with an appeal for help. "Alfred" had sent a letter Clemens either could not or would not decipher. Felfe told him to send it to him by registered mail, but the BND was waiting for the package when it arrived and found within it a page of coded instructions from Felfe's KGB case officer. The CIA copied the message, resealed it, sent it on, and waited to spring the trap.[13]

The end had come on Monday, November 6, at Pullach. Felfe's interrogation lasted for several unpleasant weeks. At his trial with Clemens and Tiebel in July 1963, Felfe described his performance over the preceding decade as having been like "dancing at two weddings, with the Soviets and with Gehlen." He had, by his own testimony, sent fifteen thousand photographs and virtually every intelligence document he could lay his hands on during all that time, betraying dozens of agents in East Germany and abroad, code names and cover addresses of informants, communications codes, verbatim counterespionage reports, minutes of committee meetings, lists of suspects and Eastern agents under investigation in West Germany, profiles of his colleagues, and much, much more.[14]

For his systematic betrayals, large and small, that singlehandedly reduced most of the BND's work up to 1961 to meaninglessness, Felfe received fourteen years' imprisonment, one less than the maximum term. But he also knew he had the unspoken commitment of his old Soviet friends to stand by him and get him out of jail.

For that, Wolfgang Vogel offered the most promising channel. General Korotkov asked Mielke to get "the lawyer," as Vogel was openly referred to within the Stasi instead of by his old code name, to start trying to negotiate Felfe's release early in the 1960s. Also at KGB request, Vogel tried to bargain for the release of Alfred Frenzel, a member of the West German Bundestag who had been arrested in 1960 for working for Czechoslovakian intelligence. But Vogel had gotten nowhere on either case. The first hope of change, the Soviets thought, came in 1966, when a young West German woman had fallen into a KGB trap in Kazakhstan and given them a hostage. Vogel spent much of the autumn of 1966, at Volpert's strong urging, trying to negotiate a package deal including both Frenzel and Felfe, in exchange for the release of the young woman whose case had become a West German national sensation.

The victim was a thirty-one-year-old reporter for the *Frankfurter Rundschau,* a Frankfurt newspaper friendly to the Social Democrats. Martina Kischke had developed a fatal romantic attraction to Eastern Europe, the Soviet Union, the Russian language, and an engineer named Boris R. Petrenko who lived in Alma-Ata, the capital of Kazakhstan. In August 1966, she was ready to marry him, flying in with a white bridal gown and every intention of giving up her life in the West and becoming a Soviet citizen to be at his side. But Petrenko had been deceiving her all along. Instead of marrying her, he delivered her into the hands of the KGB, planting in her purse a package of cigarettes containing microfilm photographs of classified military documents, which the KGB found when it arrested her on August 8 in Petrenko's chauffeur-driven office car. Not until two weeks later did the Soviets let the West German Embassy in Moscow know that she was being held in Alma-Ata, charged at first with "seditious activity" and later, with espionage for West German security services.[15]

The Soviets could not have set off a stronger wave of hostile German propaganda against them if they had deliberately tried. Martina Kischke looked just like what she was—a vulnerable, tender-hearted young German idealist full of romantic ideas about peace and understanding who edited the women's page of her newspaper and wrote travel articles urging her fellow Germans to drop the anti-Soviet prejudices so much in vogue at the time. Now, after transferring her to the KGB headquarters in the Lubyanka in Moscow a month after her arrest, her interrogators had insinuated that she was General Gehlen's lover.[16]

The outcry in West Germany was enormous. Karl Gerold, the editor of the *Rundschau,* vowed that not a single Soviet representative or journalist would cross the newspaper's threshhold as long as she remained in jail. "We are ready to do our best, together with the Soviet Union, to work for the peace of this world," he wrote. "But we are not ready to let ourselves be treated like dogs." Left-wing and right-wing newspapers, radio, television—the entire red-to-black constellation of the West German press—rallied enthusiastically to Kischke's defense.

Kischke's newspaper had immediately contacted Vogel to try to arrange her release, and Vogel had agreed. But even Kischke's case had not been enough to get the West German government to back down on its refusal to release Heinz Felfe. Bonn was prepared, though, to release Frenzel, a native of Czechoslovakia and a former Communist who at Vogel's suggestion had given up his German citizenship and taken Czech papers, in exchange for Kischke and three minor Western agents.

Vogel conducted his negotiations with the KGB through Volpert, who informed him in late December that the deal was on. Now, finally, two days before Christmas, Vogel would get his first trip to Moscow, and his one brief taste of the Lubyanka. Vogel went to Moscow in style. Early in the morning of December 23, Vogel was brought out to Schönefeld Airport and given a Stasi escort to what he was told was the personal plane of Walter Ulbricht himself, for the three-hour flight to the Soviet capital.[17]

The ride was comfortable, with white-uniformed stewards serving an ample German breakfast. Immediately after landing, a procession of KGB cars met the plane, and Vogel was escorted straight to Dzerzhinski Square, entering the massive Lubyanka building through the same metal side gate so many victims of Stalin's purges had passed through. Vogel wondered, briefly, whether he would get out again himself.

The cars stopped in an underground garage, and Vogel rode an elevator up to the second floor, climbed a flight of stairs one floor higher, and was escorted into a comfortably furnished office. There he was greeted by a man who identified himself, in broken German, as an officer. The man was well dressed, dark in complexion, with dark eyes, reserved and correct in his behavior—a ladies' man, Vogel decided, sizing him up. Kischke had never known him, either, except as "Lieutenant Colonel Fokin." Today Fokin was all business. "You are, for us, a lawyer for international cases," he told Vogel, thanking him for his help in the Abel exchange and expressing confidence that they would continue to do business together.

Then he pressed a button on his desk, the door opened, and in came Martina Kischke.[18]

Kischke had never seen or heard of Vogel before Fokin introduced him to her as "Lawyer Vogel from East Berlin." Kischke thought the KGB had brought him in to represent her perfunctorily at a show trial. But this man was surprisingly well dressed and good looking, she thought, for an East German. And she could scarcely believe her ears as Fokin explained that Vogel would escort her in a special plane back to East Berlin and take her to the border at Wartha-Herleshausen, where she would go free that very evening.

"I congratulate you," Vogel told her, smiling and offering his hand, the first time anyone had done this in more than four months, causing tears of joy and gratitude to flood into her eyes. She barely had time to pack her things before the trip to the airport; the bridal gown was kept behind as state's evidence. "We're flying direct to Berlin," Vogel whispered to her, in the black KGB car that took them to the plane. "I went up the gangway," Kischke remembered later. "Vogel, two people with him, my interpreter and two KGB officers followed. In the cabin there were tables covered with white cloths and chairs. A steward was serving Armenian cognac. The Russians raised their glasses. 'As a guest you are welcome in our country at any time,' one of the officers told me." She hardly knew whether to laugh or cry.[19]

On the three-hour flight back to East Berlin, Vogel found Kischke reserved at first, but the cognac, and his reassuring manner, soon warmed her up. He told her that the Soviets had tried to get Felfe for her, but that in the end she was traded for Frenzel instead. "But I have no money to pay you," she protested. "That's all taken care of," Vogel assured her, telling her that her newspaper had engaged him.[20]

After the flight to Schönefeld, there was another four-hour journey, in Vogel's Mercedes, to the West German border at Herleshausen. Just before the car went through the final East German checkpoint, the three lesser agents had gotten in and wordlessly ridden across with Kischke and Vogel to the West German side; she thought they were Stasi officers.

Frenzel got a hero's welcome in Czechoslovakia, but he was a dying man, of little use to Czech intelligence or to the Soviets.[21]

Not so with Heinz Felfe. After Vogel's failure to get his release in 1966, the Soviets became even more insistent, and at Volpert's insistence, Vogel kept Felfe's name at the top of the lists for agent exchanges. But nothing had come of it. By the end of 1968, Felfe had been in jail for seven years. Now Vogel was instructed to try again.

He went directly to Wehner with a new proposal, one that Mielke would have viewed as a giveaway that Bonn could scarcely refuse: Felfe in exchange for eighteen captured West German agents, fifteen men and three women held by East Germany. One man for eighteen was, on its face, an attractive offer, and Wehner had tried to get approval for the deal. But given Felfe's almost mythical symbolic importance, Chancellor Kurt-George Kiesinger, a Christian Democrat, and former Nazi like Felfe, had vetoed it.

Vogel now came back to Wehner with an ultimatum that raised the political stakes to a new level and made clear that the Soviets were prepared to force the East Germans to use their leverage on Bonn to their own ends. Wehner knew that Vogel had negotiated permission for the release of several hundred political prisoners and their relatives who had already been told that they would be allowed to go West in 1969. Vogel now reminded him that these people were "sitting on their suitcases," a phrase Wehner himself often used to describe their plight. But if Bonn insisted on refusing the offer of eighteen spies for Felfe, the East Germans would tell all of them to unpack and stay where they were.

"In case of refusal," Vogel explained, "I am obliged by my side to warn that there will be negative consequences for the humanitarian efforts."

This was, for Wehner, unthinkable. Puffing on his pipe, he peered up at Vogel and narrowed his eyes. "If I didn't know you so well, I'd say that was blackmail," he said.

"If you can't do your part, we can't do our part either," Vogel countered. "Call it what you will, I see it nearly the same way, but I have no choice."[22]

By mid-1968, Felfe had served more than half his sentence, and under German law was technically eligible for parole. Wehner did not like blackmail, but he did not like standing on principle on the backs of political prisoners and pensioners, either.

"These are people, not tomatoes," Vogel pointed out, holding up the list of family reunification cases held up by the deadlock over Felfe. "So what are we going to do?"

After a long pause, Wehner answered. "We'll keep negotiating."[23]

Vogel visited Felfe in his Bavarian prison in Straubing just before Christmas, to keep him in the picture. Vogel was reserved and discreet, knowing the prison rooms were bugged on the Western side of the Wall just as they were on his own; but he had let Felfe know that he could probably count on going free within a few weeks. The West Germans had already kept him behind bars for seven years, longer than any other captured East German spy.[24]

Vogel's negotiating ploy had worked. The West Germans were resigned to surrendering to blackmail on the political prisoner issue, but they were determined to make sure they got their money's worth in agents. Rehlinger's office began with a list demanding twenty-six in return for Felfe, instead of the eighteen that Vogel had originally offered.

In the end, only three more names were added to those eighteen; the Soviets agreed to throw in three German students who had been convicted of espionage and anti-Soviet activities in Moscow. By early February, Vogel had negotiated the package, and now he would make his second—and last—flight to Moscow, to pick up the three students. Again, the East Germans put a government airplane at his disposal.

This time, he did not have to experience the *frisson* of passing through the forbidding metal doors of the Lubyanka. The KGB took its international lawyer to the Sovietskaya Hotel, normally reserved for high-ranking party guests, where the Soviet Foreign Ministry threw him a dinner. The next morning, he was taken back to the airport to take custody of the three students, who at this time were brought directly to the plane.

The release of two of the students was apparently intended as a gesture to the CIA, which had been as reluctant as the Germans to let Felfe go. Their cases attested as eloquently to the dilettantism and clumsiness of some American methods as Felfe's attested to the professionalism of the KGB's. Peter Sonntag and Walter Näumann had been fourth-year students at Heidelberg University in the summer of 1961, when an American "friend" had offered them a unique chance to make the first trip of their young lives (Sonntag was then twenty-two and Naumann was twenty-seven) to the Soviet Union. The two had been arrested on September 17, 1961, at the end of a month-long automobile tour during which they had followed instructions, they testified at their trial that November, to look for and photograph Soviet rocket bases. They took fifteen thousand pictures on three hundred rolls of film, but the photos showed only radar installations, power stations, high-tension power lines, radio towers, and "license plates of military vehicles," according to the Tass account of the trial. The men pleaded guilty to espionage and were sentenced to twelve-year prison terms. Now, more than seven years later, Vogel was bringing them out to freedom, along with a third student from Heidelberg, Volker W. Schaffhausen, twenty-six years old, who had pleaded guilty in Leningrad in April 1967 to charges of smuggling anti-Soviet literature into the Soviet Union for an émigré organization in Frankfurt.[25]

Freedom came for all of them, and for Heinz Felfe, on Friday, February 14, 1969, in the dark at the remote snow-covered border crossing point of Herleshausen. Two West German police officers drove him from Straubing.

"You know," one of them said to Felfe, "between the two German states, at the moment, nothing is going right. The only thing that works is your lawyer Vogel—when he says this or that will happen, it's the only thing that does. He's the only link between our two countries that anyone can depend on anymore."[26]

They arrived an hour before the 7 P.M. deadline set for the exchange, and played a round of cards and sipped coffee together until it was time to go to the final rendezvous, a former fishermen's shack near the crossing that belonged to the German border police.

Felfe could see little outside, where by now it was pitch dark, but within a few moments, the door opened and in stepped Rehlinger. It had been hard for the West German official to get the Gehlen Organization to agree to the release. To intelligence agents, trapping an agent such as Felfe was like a small victory in a war, and releasing him was a betrayal. Rehlinger felt the West German intelligence people looked at him with a certain hostility and wondered for a moment if Vogel had similar problems on his side.

So Rehlinger was curt and formal to Felfe. "Good evening," he opened. "Herr Felfe, the federal president has pardoned you, and as a lawyer, you will be aware that this means that you are being released conditionally, and if you commit any other crime in the next five years, you will have to serve the rest of your sentence. You're a free man. As far as we are concerned, you are a citizen of the Federal Republic, you can stay here if you want, or you can go over there. The decision is entirely up to you."[27]

As Rehlinger left the little shack, Vogel walked in, with Jürgen Stange by his side. "So, here we are at last," he smiled at Felfe. Moments before, Vogel had been on the bus with the three West

German students and the eighteen East German prisoners, some with life sentences, crossing the border toward Herleshausen. Now it was time to take delivery of the main figure in the exchange.

Vogel and Stange asked Felfe to step outside into Vogel's car. Though the release was supposed to be taking place in secret, flashbulbs popped. Vogel drove into the no-man's land and then stopped next to another car, asking Felfe to step into it for the final journey, a kilometer or so into East German territory. At the border crossing point, the headlights illuminated a man standing at attention holding a bouquet of red carnations with two red ribbons. "I greet you in the name of the German Democratic Republic," said this greeter, a high official of the Stasi, "and I congratulate you. There is someone who wants to see you over there."

A few feet away was "Alfred," who came over to welcome Felfe back to the fold, Russian-style, with a bear hug and kisses on both cheeks. "It's past time you came," the Soviet told him. "I've been in Berlin for the past two years, just to be here when you came out, but it all took a lot longer than we thought it would."

"Alfred" had his own car ready—two cars, even, he joked to Felfe, in case one broke down. They drove to the barrier at the border point and were saluted by an East German major of border guards. "Is the operation over?" he asked. "Can I open the border again now?"

As the barrier rose to let them pass, Felfe saw a vast traffic jam, at least twenty-one buses full of travelers who had all been waiting for hours while the border was closed for the exchange. The first of the more than one thousand people sitting on their suitcases whose fate had led Herbert Wehner to prevail on Bonn to let the traitor go, were finally free to leave.[28]

By the fall of 1969, Wolfgang Vogel had become a man to be reckoned with. For an indigent boy from the provincial backwaters of Silesia, he had done very well for himself indeed. He was pleased with himself, and more important, his protector Josef Streit was pleased, rewarding him with a title much prized by Germans on both sides of the Wall: "Dr. Vogel." The honorary doctorate was conferred on October 17 by the German Academy for State and Law Studies in Potsdam at Streit's insistence, over the objections of Hilde Benjamin, Vogel's old nemesis at the Ministry of Justice. While she was in office, two years earlier, she had blocked Vogel's candidacy, having a notation made in Vogel's personnel file that she considered the honor unjustified. But by now she was in retirement and could no longer place obstacles in his way.[29]

By now Vogel had outgrown the dingy walkup in the Lawyers' Collaborative branch office on the Alt-Friedrichsfelde and had been allowed in 1968 to establish his own private law practice, a rare privilege. He moved to a new office, a three-story stuccoed house with a steep tile roof at No. 4 Reilerstrasse, which he bought for sixty-eight thousand East German marks. This sum was beyond the reach of ordinary East Germans, but Vogel was hardly ordinary.

The office was in the Friedrichsfelde section, close to the rapid transit station, so easy both for his ordinary bread-and-butter East German clients to find and only a short drive away from Volpert's office in the Stasi headquarters on the Normannenstrasse. It was a discreet meeting place, in a quiet neighborhood of fruit trees and garden plots where East Berliners grew strawberries, planted flowers, and relaxed on warm summer Sundays. Here Western clients could come and be assured of privacy; here, too, Jürgen Stange could visit unobserved to go over the monthly prisoner lists.

Vogel's business depended on secrecy. He frequently warned his West German negotiating partners, as he warned the prisoners on the buses before they crossed into West Germany, that loose lips could bring the whole enterprise to a halt. Vogel himself did not fear the effects of publicity—far from it. One of the standing instructions his secretaries had—one they took as seriously as the joking "The boss is always right" rule that he had hung up on the wall outside his private office—was to keep clippings of all the newspaper articles they could find that mentioned the "chief." James Donovan's book about the Abel-Powers case and the German-language serialization of it in *Der Spiegel* had been lovingly entered into the Vogel archive. The archive contained magazine articles and clippings entered into chronological loose-leaf binders that filled whole shelves, along with hundreds of letters from grateful clients, and the occasional testimonial from Western officials and lawyers who found dealing with him a pleasure.

Vogel thought of himself as the reliable, discreet messenger-intermediary, and it was important to his self-image that Streit and Mielke and, for all he knew, Walter Ulbricht thought him as dependable as any Western official did. He prided himself on his indispensability. The little boy who had delivered letters of mediation and conciliation in Wilhelmsthal for his schoolteacher father, and been rewarded with a silver coin, was now carrying out missions of state importance for governments East and West. He was being rewarded handsomely not only in coin but, more important to him, in esteem. Indeed, Vogel cloaked himself in respectability, too much so for some of the strait-laced Communist officials he dealt with. His weakness was vanity. Increasingly, it showed in his clothes.

Not for Wolfgang Vogel the drab, brown, synthetic-fiber, shapeless Soviet-style suits and cheap plastic shoes the East German Communists donned to show loyalty to Moscow. Vogel had the provincial's innate need to display urbanity, and no little artistic talent. With all the money he was making from the West Germans, he could easily have afforded to buy all his stylish Western suits on the Kurfürstendamm, but he stuck loyally with Bodo Jahn in East Berlin. In his colored shirts, bright ties, and suits cut to the mod Western style of the late 1960s, with rakish pocket angles and wide lapels, Vogel cut a dashing figure on the colorless streets of East Berlin. Or he would have, if he had needed to walk on them; but by the late 1960s Vogel had his own Mercedes—"needing" it, he told Streit and others who raised their eyebrows, because only a Mercedes was powerful enough and had heavy enough suspension to make bearable the almost weekly four-hour trips down the bumpy, Hitler-era autobahn to Herleshausen.

But the Mercedes, the clothes, and the money were all things he could have had in the West as well, working for any one of the large West German firms that would have been more than happy to hire a lawyer of his talents. It was the feeling that he was indispensable that kept him in East Berlin, the feeling that his country's top leaders had picked him out and entrusted him with secret missions so sensitive that he felt like one of them.

The truth was that Wolfgang Vogel had a dream job that fascinated him, and he was having the time of his life. He had long since justified the faith in him that had led Josef Streit and Heinz Volpert to take him out of normal Stasi channels and put him in a special category of his own. Whatever occasional repugnance Vogel felt for the Stasi methods he often came across in the course of defending clients was more than overcome by the material rewards. And, Vogel told himself, he was helping hundreds and even thousands of people who would otherwise be condemned to spend years in jail—political prisoners and spies alike. Innocent or guilty of the crimes the Stasi charged them with, they were all worthy of pity in Vogel's eyes, and there was profit in pity as well.

It took a bit of the ambulance-chaser to do this kind of work well. Vogel kept his own files, tracking newspaper accounts of the arrests of Communist spies in the West and Western agents in the East, and tucking the names away to bring out again when the time came to bargain for a swap. Vogel did not always wait for his Western negotiating partners to give him names: he would sometimes make suggestions of his own, quickly relaying any signs of acute interest so that his own side would not miss any good opportunities. He enjoyed the trips to Bautzen and Herleshausen to pick up the prisoners and enjoyed the drinking sessions with Stange and Reymar von Wedel that sometimes followed. And he enjoyed the feeling of success that came with every prisoner released—a feeling of satisfaction that, Vogel imagined, could only be compared to what a doctor or a surgeon felt after saving a patient's life. He always gave his best, and this was recognized by his clients even on the rare occasions when he failed.

If his clients appreciated his single-minded devotion to his work, his family did not. Manfred, his son, like many others in their late teens or early twenties, chafed at the contradictions between the drab and regimented daily life of East Berlin, the affluent society they all could see by tuning into West Berlin television, and the claims of Communism's superiority made daily by East German propaganda. How, Manfred wanted to know, in the typical simplistic way of youth, could his father work closely with a regime based on lies? That his father could see them too, and try to mitigate the evil, was not something the son could accept. He began saying, loud enough for the Stasi to hear, that Franz Josef Strauss, the ultraconservative Bavarian, was his hero. Strauss was not then, not yet, one of the Stasi's favorites; his behind-the-scenes collaboration with Schalck-Golodkowski, the financial wizard who controlled the proceeds of Vogel's prisoner release program, would come only much later.

Vogel's marriage had also come apart under the strain of his demanding career. He worked from early morning far into the night and was constantly traveling to West Berlin or West Germany for the prisoner exchanges, so he had little time for his family. He began telling Western friends that Eva, Lilo, and Manfred would be happier on their side of the Wall than on his, but that his job was so important he felt he had to stay on and keep working. Finally, he confided these thoughts privately to Streit, who was supportive and arranged in 1966 for Vogel's family to leave, quietly, for West Berlin. Divorce had followed in 1967. Manfred followed in his father's footsteps and registered at the University of Innsbruck in Austria to study law; eventually, he too settled in West Berlin to practice there, a few miles as the crow flew, but a world away from his father's practice.

Moving into a small bachelor apartment in the Moldaustrasse, not far from his new office, Vogel could now devote full time to his work. He had begun to drink more frequently—too heavily for his own good, thought some of his friends and his enemies. Every East German apartment building had a secret Stasi snoop who spied on the occupants and reported on their ideological loyalty and personal habits. Publicly, a sort of petty-bourgeois morality was proclaimed. Neither Ulbricht nor Honecker, who had divorced to marry Margot Feist (a future hard-line Communist education minister), was in a position to cast the first stone where private morals were concerned; Honecker's affairs with one of his secretaries later became notorious. Vogel uncomfortably found himself summoned to Streit's presence on one occasion to explain a Stasi report that on the previous night, Vogel had been seen inviting a minor into his apartment and later kissing her goodbye.

"Yes," he fumed, outraged. "My daughter visited me and spent the night."

Streit dismissed the complaint, but looked into his protégé's eyes. "Wolfgang," he sighed. "Why don't you find yourself a good woman, fall in love, and settle down again?"

In 1969, Vogel was finally able to go to him with good news. "Josef," he told him, "I've become attached."

"Well, thank God," the prosecutor-general exclaimed.

"There's just one hitch," Vogel continued. Streit groaned when he heard what it was: "She's from West Germany."

Streit could imagine what the petty Stasi bureaucrats who submitted the denunciations would say about this: It's not enough for Vogel that he has a Mercedes; now he has to have a Western floozy to go with it.[30]

A client had brought Wolfgang Vogel and Helga Fritsch together. Werner Ufer was a West German swimming coach and a close friend of Helga's in Essen, the Ruhr industrial town a long way indeed from the bustle and sophistication of Berlin. Helga had long wanted to see the German metropolis, on both sides of the Wall, and finally she had talked Ufer into making the trip with her. The swimming coach had his own interest in going to East Berlin; the East German sports machine, which routinely cleaned up most of the swimming medals in the Olympic Games every four years, was something he wanted to find out more about. So when they made the trip, in 1968, he brought a couple of letters to one of the country's top swimmers.

When the East German customs officials at the Heinrich-Heine-Strasse crossing point discovered the letters, they suspected Ufer of having something more than mere correspondence in mind and put him under arrest. Helga was allowed to go free, and the West German authorities she asked for help put her in touch with Vogel. The easy part of the case, for Vogel, was convincing his authorities that the case against Herr Ufer had been just a misunderstanding. The hard part, for Wolfgang as well as for Helga, was deciding what to do about something else: their mutual attraction.

Vogel, at forty-three years old, was at the height of his powers as a lawyer. His old-fashioned polished manners, his courtliness, his ability to use words to charm and flirt swept the twenty-eight-year-old girl from the Ruhr right off her feet, despite the differences in their ages. It was clear to both of them as soon as Vogel had managed to get Ufer out of jail that they wanted to spend the rest of their lives together. If they did, though, they would have to make a fundamental choice: Either Vogel had to start a new life with Helga in West Germany or she had to come and join him in East Berlin.

Vogel did not want to leave. He enjoyed what he was doing, and word was spreading around the German Democratic Republic, in the prisons at Bautzen and Hohenschönhausen and the Magdalenenstrasse, that when there seemed no other way out of a difficult situation, Lawyer Vogel could work magic. By this time thousands of cases had proved it. The prisoner exchanges with Bonn alone had allowed 7,379 condemned individuals and their families to leave for West Germany, and the business was growing, with an annual turnover in payments from the government in Bonn of nearly fifty million marks. People in their misery had come to depend on Vogel, he thought, concentrating all their hopes on him as their last and only hope. He felt—and needed to feel—desperately needed.

If he simply packed up and left for the West, he told Helga, he would be betraying all these people, betraying a humanitarian cause. East Germany would punish the very people whom he thought it his mission to help for Vogel's defection. He could see from the scowls on the faces of Stasi guards when he went with the buses to pick up the prisoners in Bautzen that some of them would be only too glad to be rid of his unwanted, meddlesome nuisance. And no one, Vogel thought, could fill his shoes: build up trust on both sides of the Wall, not only with a high Stasi officer such as Volpert but also with the lowliest prisoner accused by the same Stasi of a political crime. Vogel told himself that a good criminal lawyer had a calling like a priest's.

Although he had ceased to practice his Catholicism after his marriage fell apart, Vogel was still a believer in the secrets of the confessional and in the integrity of the lawyer-client privilege. A promise to a client had to be made good, and he could not leave hundreds, indeed thousands, of clients to rot in East German jails. He could imagine the pleasure a Stasi interrogator would take in telling one of these prisoners that his lawyer had just made himself scarce. And Vogel knew that his own self-esteem would not survive the thought—which East German propaganda would surely make—that he had been interested only in the money all along and had finally found an excuse to cash in his pot of gold.[31]

Vogel even went to Essen to plead his case with Helga's parents, who listened and told her that only she could decide what to do with her life. In 1969, she made her decision, coming to East Berlin to work in the Reilerstrasse as a secretary.

Streit had tolerated Vogel's infatuation, and given permission for the move, but there had been resistance in powerful quarters. Kaul, Vogel heard indirectly, had referred dismissively to his new companion as "a love dame from Frankfurt." Enraged, Vogel told Helga she should go immediately to Kaul's office and tell him that she came from Essen, not Frankfurt, and then watch his face turn red. The Stasi surveillance reappeared, and this time even Volpert said he was unable to get it stopped. As Volpert's two primary responsibilities, the activities of Vogel and Schalck-Golodkowski, had become more complex, Volpert had been detached from his duties in the section responsible for church affairs and earned special status as a general all-around assistant to Mielke, with a salary and perquisites that generated considerable jealousy among his

Stasi colleagues. They went right ahead investigating Helga, who had to be cleared of any suspicion of working for the West German BND. The West German intelligence service obviously also had Vogel in its sights, so for the next few years, Helga was not permitted to travel to the West at all. She was constantly shadowed, even when she went to buy groceries.[32]

Helga, who became Vogel's second wife, stabilized his life and provided enormous moral and physical support, both at work and at home. For further stability and release, the Vogels decided to get out of the city, escape at least on weekends from the pressures of clients and negotiations. A routine case had acquainted Vogel with the Schwerinsee, a small lake an hour's drive southeast from his office. Vogel had been taken with the peace, quiet, and beauty of the little lake. He had asked a local man to find him a waterfront property for sale; and the man had turned up a plot on an island connected to the main road, and the autobahn to Berlin, by a little causeway. It was owned by a woman who lived in West Berlin—in those days people could continue to own property after they moved West, as pensioners had been permitted to do for some years—and Vogel paid her twenty thousand deutsche marks, about five thousand dollars, in addition to the four-thousand-mark price in East German money for the plot of land. He and Helga paid local workers thousands more to build a large, two-story wooden vacation home, had it insulated and winterized, planted a large garden running down to the lake, and bought a sailboat.

The house became quite comfortable by East German standards, though it would have looked quite out of place in the Hamptons or in St. Moritz. It was more like a comfortable Russian dacha. A long driveway led to a covered garage, where the Mercedes could be tucked away; the entrance to the house led past a guest bathroom and directly into a kitchen outfitted with the latest West German technology. Behind the kitchen, the Vogels built a glassed-in terrace looking out on the lake, with a view through a rose garden where a kitschy miniature windmill turned with the breezes.

In the living room were a large dark-wood eighteenth-century wooden German cupboard, overstuffed chairs, a sofa, a table, and a glass vitrine with shelves of birds—porcelain birds, of all shapes and sizes, most of them from the famous East German works in Meissen—for Vogel means "bird" in German. In a corner niche near the window were two large baroque wooden statues and some nineteenth-century Russian icons. Upstairs, Vogel built himself a study and placed a handsome antique desk at the picture window, from which he could look out at the water.

Whatever the Stasi's vigilance over his new wife, Vogel obviously enjoyed the good graces of the high and mighty. The Stasi's counterintelligence spies might be mistrustful of Vogel's new companion, but Streit's confidence in him was unshaken. He had big plans for his protégé, and on the first of August, with a written power of attorney, he made Vogel, in all but formal rank and name, the equivalent of a high-ranking official of the East German government:

> The government of the German Democratic Republic appoints you with immediate effect, until written cancellation, as permanent legal adviser and in special cases as legal representative.
> This appointment extends in particular to the representation of the interests of the German Democratic Republic vis-à-vis the Federal Republic of Germany, the special political entity of West Berlin and other states.
>
> Berlin, 1 August 1969
> Dr. Streit[33]

Vogel framed it on his office wall in the Reilerstrasse, next to an autographed portrait of Streit, and within sight of his desk near the east window. "Sometimes," he liked to say, with an air of mystery, "behind a lawyer, there is a government, or an agency—who knows?" From 1969 onward, when Vogel spoke, his partners on both sides of the Iron Curtain knew that he spoke not only for himself but for the German Democratic Republic and all its "competent organs," including the Stasi. In negotiations for the release of Stasi prisoners and captured agents, Vogel had become, in effect, the Stasi's officially appointed counsel.

But Jürgen Stange, his counterpart in West Berlin, saw a danger in all this. It seemed elementary to him that Vogel was not negotiating freedom for political prisoners held by the Stasi over its objections; after all, the Stasi finally approved the lists of names of prisoners to be released. Yet Vogel insisted that he had often had to overcome tremendous resistance to keep certain names on the lists. For all his connections with Streit, and for all Volpert's efficiency and hard work, Vogel was basically a glorified messenger, an executive organ doing what the party and its sword and shield, as the Stasi (like the KGB) thought of itself, allowed him to do. Vogel's ego did not permit him to see himself in such unexalted terms.

Vogel's main objective was freedom for as many prisoners as possible. But his reputation was also important to him, a reputation for being able to deliver. Some of his clients' very lives depended on this ability. Vogel wanted to help, but the only way he could was through close cooperation with the Stasi. "Two souls dwell, alas! in my breast," Goethe's Faust had lamented, a plaint Vogel could make as well. As long as the Wall stood, the contradiction remained, undiscovered and ultimately malignant.

PART THREE

TRADER OF SOULS

CHAPTER SIX

VOGEL BECOMES A POLITICAL CONFIDANT

"Why don't you go to Berlin?"

hen Chancellor Willy Brandt's Liberal-Social Democratic coalition came to power in October 1969, the character of the relationship between Germans and Soviets and between Germans and Eastern Europeans changed for the first time since the end of World War II. Vogel's career took on a more deeply political direction, drawing him ever more into the very center of power in East Berlin and making him almost an ambassador, in the eyes of the new authorities in Bonn. In contrast to the hesitant, more skeptical attitude of his predecessors, Brandt believed passionately that the East-West confrontation was a mortal peril to Germans and all other Europeans, and those around him were eager to carry further the unofficial channels of communication Vogel had opened for them to East Berlin. A momentous change of leadership in the East also soon put Vogel into a key position of influence and elevated his reputation, in East and West, to new heights.

Brandt, as governing mayor of West Berlin when Honecker had built the Berlin Wall, knew from firsthand experience what confrontation could lead to, and more important, what it could not achieve. Unyielding refusal to recognize reality would not make life any better for Berliners either side of the Wall, he believed. And reality, at the end of the 1960s, was a strong and assertive Communist empire that began at the East-West German border and showed no sign of collapse. Brandt and his advisers had a vision of "small steps" that would first reduce and then eliminate the most irksome practical irritants that hindered contact between people on either side, and gradually lead from confrontation to cooperation, and eventually to convergence of the Communist and capitalist societies of Europe.

The goal was change as a result of rapprochement, "*Wandel durch Annäherung,*" as Brandt's foreign policy genius, Egon Bahr, a former East German journalist who had worked at his side since the 1950s, called it.[1] Brandt had already begun to lay the foundations for change as foreign minister in the West German grand coalition government from 1966 to 1969. Bahr had chosen to join the Social Democrats when he had come to West Germany because he had concluded that he could not agree with the basic choice that Konrad Adenauer's Christian Democrats had made in the early 1950s—that the integration of the western half of the country in the European Community and the Atlantic Alliance was more important than the eventual reunification of both sides.

This integration had been the most important reason why Adenauer had insisted on strict isolation of East Germany. Now Chancellor Brandt and his foreign minister, Walter Scheel, wanted to move, in their "small steps," to end that isolation—with the goal, the same as Adenauer's of eventually undermining it and making unification possible. Clearly, any improvement in relations had to start with the Soviet Union and with the new leadership in Moscow that was consolidating under Leonid I. Brezhnev.

The Soviets were initially suspicious, correctly sensing the dangers to East German independence. But the Brezhnev leadership also saw a chance to gain new leverage with West Germany and its association with the Western Alliance, which Moscow was eager to exploit for its own purposes. But Ulbricht, the dogmatic, crusty, and inflexible East German Communist leader who had served Khrushchev so well, stood in Brezhnev's way. Even more, he stood in the way of the ambitions of Erich Honecker, his longtime protégé and, since November of 1956, secretary of the Security Commission of the German Socialist Unity Party's Central Committee, and thus in effective control of the Stasi apparatus. Thus it was by no accident that when Bonn's policies changed, Moscow saw the need for someone more malleable to replace Ulbricht, someone who would be able to exploit the opportunities Brandt and his new policies made available to the Soviet Union and the German Democratic Republic, without allowing Bonn to drive a wedge between them.

In the early 1970s the Soviet leaders clearly saw Honecker as the only candidate. But Brezhnev reminded him: "We have troops on your territory," he told Honecker in a talk in the Crimea on July 18, 1970. "Without us there wouldn't be a G.D.R." Ulbricht had acted as though he knew better than the Soviets did how to build socialism on German soil. "This superiority on the part of the G.D.R. has to go," Brezhnev had told Honecker. "It's hurting us all."[2]

By the spring of 1971, Honecker was ready to oblige him.

Honecker, born in the Saarland in 1912 and a roofer by trade, had been a member of the Communist party underground under the Nazis. He had been working as a courier between party cells in Czechoslovakia and the Reich when the Gestapo arrested him on December 5, 1935, in Berlin, carrying a suitcase with incriminating subversive materials hidden in the base. Honecker confessed, compromising the Czechoslovakian Jewish courier with whom he had met and the leader of the secret Communist youth organization in Berlin. Later, in a smuggled note from his cell seized by the Gestapo, he betrayed the name of still another Communist resistance functionary. Apparently because of his talkativeness, Honecker was sentenced to ten years in prison, while the youth leader he had betrayed, Bruno Baum, got thirteen.[3]

His official autobiography, and all the hagiography of the state he later headed, mentioned none of this and nothing about the party reprimand he received for it after liberation in 1945; the betrayals came to light only long afterward. Honecker fell to work after the war building the Free German Youth (FDJ in German) as a mass organ of agitation and propaganda among young people. In the beginning, as the Communists felt their way along, the FDJ was nonpartisan and all-inclusive, but by January 1948 it had taken on so many of the traits of Stalin's Komsomol that three prominent founding members of its central commission withdrew in protest.

All this had suited Walter Ulbricht at the time, and he had promoted his crown prince steadily to ever more powerful positions in the party and state security apparatus. In the meantime, Honecker was quietly building support inside the Politburo, step by step. One of the first and most important steps had come in 1957, when Honecker had helped Mielke engineer the takeover of the Stasi. Mielke had tapped the telephones of the security minister he ousted, Ernst Wollweber, and used the transcripts to prove to Ulbricht that Wollweber had been disloyal.

Ulbricht, who had taken on the functions of East German chief of state as well as party leader, was increasingly autocratic, dictatorial, and out of touch. He had never lost the vision of a united, Communist Germany, and thought it could be brought about by pushing East German economic development so hard that the country, with a quarter of the population of the Federal Republic, would out-produce the West German economy. Günter Mittag, the party's economics chief, warned that such a course would soon lead to massive distortions and popular unrest, but Ulbricht pushed for annual increases in labor productivity of 10 percent. The country was being driven to the brink of economic catastrophe, Honecker warned the Central Committee at the end of 1970. Ulbricht was taking on ruinous foreign debts, to the Soviet Union and to capitalist countries, and permitting little real discussion of his policies in the Politburo.

Strengthened by a decision of the Central Committee not to publish Ulbricht's rebuttal of these arguments, Honecker and thirteen other members of the Poliburo wrote a secret letter to Brezhnev in Moscow on January 21, 1971, posing the key question: "More and more, Comrade Walter Ulbricht is led by feelings of infallibility," they reported, asking that Brezhnev suggest to Ulbricht that he give up the position of first secretary of the party and content himself with his ceremonial functions as chief of state. On April 12, Brezhnev told "Dear Comrade Ulbricht" that his time was up. Brezhnev called Honecker in Berlin to tell him, "Erich, I've thought it over, and we'll do what . . . you've suggested."[4] Ulbricht announced his resignation as first secretary to the East German Central Committee on May 3, "suggesting" that the members elect Honecker to replace him.[5] The crown prince was now the reigning monarch, doomed to follow his protector's fatal trajectory.

"Brandt is under pressure from two sides," Brezhnev had told Honecker in the Crimea less than a year before. "He has to reach agreements with us. He hopes that way to achieve his goals with respect to the G.D.R. Social-democratization of the G.D.R. . . . . We

will not permit a development that weakens our positions in the
G.D.R., will not permit the *Anschluss* of the G.D.R. to [West
Germany]. On the contrary—the delimitation, the trenches between
the G.D.R. and the F.R.G. will get deeper."[6]

Delimitation was the key word of Honecker's policy in the early
1970s.[7] It was rooted in inferiority complexes, his own and his
country's. Honecker, a small man with a nervous smile and a high-
pitched voice that sounded strangled when he tried to impose High
German on his native Saarland patois, looked, in the company of
Brezhnev and the other Warsaw Pact leaders, like an insecure
schoolboy trying hard to be the teacher's pet, his jacket bravely
buttoned tight and cut in the shapeless style favored by Big Brother
in Moscow. Whether he had the stature to hold his own and preserve the Communist position in Germany against the pressures
from the West was apparently not at all clear to Brezhnev in 1971.
Some of Bonn's allies were also deeply concerned that the basic goal
of Brandt and Bahr was the unification of the country, and that
they were willing to palaver with the Soviets to achieve it. Henry
Kissinger, Richard Nixon's national security adviser and secretary
of state, was particularly suspicious.

The United States, preoccupied with extricating itself from its
ill-fated involvement in Vietnam, watched uneasily as Brandt normalized relations with Romania, the Soviet Union, Poland, Czechoslovakia, and the other Eastern European states between the late
1960s and 1972 and in 1972 negotiated the keystone of the new
edifice of *Ostpolitik,* the Basic Treaty between the two German
states. The United States, Britain, and France had managed to
salvage guarantees that they would preserve their interests in Berlin, signing the Four-Power Treaty defining West Berlin's status as
a separate political entity closely linked to West Germany, but
some American diplomats felt it had been a close-run thing because
the Germans were for the first time following an agenda of their
own.

The Basic Treaty changed fundamentally the terms of the long-
running debate on German unification. As before, the West German state held to the hope of unity inscribed in the constitution and
continued to offer citizenship to all East Germans who could find
their way across the Wall to claim it. But for the first time, Bonn
recognized the legitimate existence of the German Democratic Republic. West Germany would set up a "permanent mission" in East

Berlin and allow the East Germans to build one of their own in Bad Godesberg. And since West Germany had stopped refusing to recognize any country that maintained diplomatic relations with the East Germany, the United States, Britain, and France were now free to set up their own embassies in East Berlin and offer effective consular and legal protection to their citizens there for the first time since 1945. Transit agreements enabled many more West Berliners and West Germans to travel back and forth over East German highways to the beleaguered city, and to do so with greater assurance of personal security than at any time since 1961. More East Germans, at first only small numbers of elderly pensioners, but gradually more members of younger families, were allowed to visit relatives in the West, and for small currency exchange fees, West Germans and West Berliners could again visit friends and families in the East.

Honecker's accession marked a fundamental change for Wolfgang Vogel and his work. For Honecker made clear, almost from the very beginning of his tenure, that he would take personal control of the whole area of Vogel's activity, the so-called "humanitarian efforts" that until the early 1970s had constituted almost the entire spectrum of political and diplomatic contacts between the two German states. Honecker named Vogel his personal emissary for such matters in May 1973 and began meeting with him personally—always in Honecker's office, never at his home in the elite leadership residential compound in Wandlitz.[8] Despite the formality—it was always "Herr Vogel" and "Herr Honecker"—there was little doubt that Vogel had truly arrived.

In the autumn of 1972, as the negotiations on the Basic Treaty were drawing to a successful conclusion, Honecker had granted a spectacular general amnesty that freed an estimated twenty-five thousand prisoners serving sentences for the commission of all kinds of crimes, political and nonpolitical. He allowed 2,087 to go West without any West German government payment at all. But he also used his personal authority to take control of those payments. Internal party documents later revealed that only Honecker and Schalck-Golodkowski controlled the bank accounts through which Bonn's regular payments for the political prisoner releases passed, and in the early 1970s these were nearing the one hundred million-mark level every year.

·   ·   ·

An important complication arose from the establishment of official relations for Vogel to overcome. Some middle-level West German officials had begun to wonder if the time had not come to cut out the cut-out man. About to become the first West German "ambassador" to East Berlin (the terms of the treaty had carefully called the two emissaries "permanent representatives"), Günter Gaus, a haughty north German intellectual and journalist, asked if there were really any need to continue relying on Dr. Wolfgang Vogel or to keep paying millions of deutsche marks a year through Protestant Church channels to keep the busloads of political prisoners rolling.

And they were rolling, every two weeks, from places such as Bautzen, Rummelsburg, and Hohenschönhausen, the most notorious of the Stasi's jails, to the remote border crossing at Herleshausen. Twice a month Vogel and Stange would drive to the East German side of the border at Wartha to greet the prisoners, explain why and how they had been chosen for release, and then escort them on the short winding detour through the hills into West Germany—the Hitler-era autobahn being impassable at the border because of a bombed-out bridge that had never been rebuilt after the war.

The new German cooperation opened by the Basic Treaty would permit, among other things, the West Germans to build new autobahns through East Germany. The authorities in Bonn felt that the trade in political prisoners should be made official as well. East Germans who wanted to apply to settle in the West should not be made to feel that the only way to get there was to be arrested for a political crime; they should now be able to go to the West German mission on the Hannoverschestrasse in East Berlin and apply for visas, simple as that.

It was a naïve assumption on two counts: First, the Stasi had the mission, in a modern office building just off the Friedrichstrasse, under constant surveillance, and for years afterward it relentlessly pursued all unauthorized East German citizens who dared pass the armed Stasi guard outside the building to talk with the West Germans inside. And second, the East Germans still wanted the money they got for releasing their political prisoners.

Between the signature of the treaty in December 1972 and its ratification by the Bundestag the following spring, a bitter and closely fought political debate raged in Bonn. The authorities in

East Berlin were doing their best to influence the result. Vogel told one of his clients, Gerhard Kreysa, who had been jailed for trying to escape to West Germany and was now hoping to be allowed to join his wife there, that the government had imposed a freeze on family reunifications until the treaty was ratified.

Nothing was more central to Germans' definition of themselves than their attitudes toward the division of the country. The concept underlying Brandt's policy—that there could be two separate German states in one German nation—was bitterly disputed by the Christian Democratic opposition parties. Even after the Bundestag voted to approve the treaty, the conservatives threatened to keep it from going into effect by challenging it in the West German constitutional court.

Honecker was determined to show Bonn that despite the establishment of official relations between the two states, East Germany would still make the rules on who was allowed to leave the country, and Bonn would still have to pay for the prisoner releases. In May 1973, without a word of public explanation, Honecker cut off the releases altogether.

Herbert Wehner, whom Brandt had asked to take over the Social Democratic parliamentary leadership in the Bundestag after their triumph in the 1972 elections, had negotiated with Vogel an agreement to release more than three thousand people. Merely one day later, the East German authorities brusquely informed more than two thousand of them that permission had been withdrawn, although they had all been issued travel documents and were packed and ready to go.

Vogel was designated as the emissary to explain to the West Germans what was needed. And he knew who would listen: Wehner, who often had made it clear to Vogel that he believed the interests of ordinary Germans were frequently more important than the interests of the state.

Vogel flew to the Cologne/Bonn airport and had himself taken straight up to Wehner's apartment in a modern condominium-cooperative complex high over Bad Godesberg, where Wehner lived with his stepdaughter, Greta, who later became his wife. Vogel had brought a trump card, a willingness to take political risks that was not only based on his growing intimacy with Erich Honecker but had also been encouraged by Wehner himself.

.   .   .

Wehner was a unique figure in postwar West Germany, a former Communist who had known Ulbricht and Honecker and the others before the war and had lived in Moscow, for a time, in the Lux Hotel, together with the rest of the exiled German Communist leadership. But he began to be disillusioned with Communism when the KGB had questioned his loyalty and put him through bitter and painful interrogations in the Lubyanka. Sent to work in the Communist underground in Germany and Sweden after the German invasion of the Soviet Union, Wehner had been arrested in Stockholm in 1942 and sentenced to imprisonment at hard labor for "endangering Swedish freedom and neutrality." After a wave of arrests, Wehner's enemies in the Communist party charged him with betrayal, and they had declared him a "renegade" and a traitor to the movement.

His imprisonment also led Wehner to an inner ideological conversion. After some leading Swedish politicians secured his release from prison, where he had spent twenty-nine months, in late 1944, he emerged as a socialist—a "convert," he would say later, "one who has been burned." Returning to West Germany after the war, he became a disciple of the Social Democratic party's (SPD) leader, Kurt Schumacher. Ulbricht and other German Communist comrades never forgave him for what they saw as both personal and class betrayal.

After the war, Wehner had been the architect of the SPD's move to the middle ground. But he, like Vogel, was a quintessentially German figure. With his ever-present pipe, his white, swept-back hair, his contorted facial expressions, and his colorful interventions in Bundestag debates, "Uncle Herbert" as long as he lived was instantly recognizable on any West German street. Television watchers treasured his eruptions—he once dismissed a Christian Democratic opponent as a "garden dwarf."

But Wehner's Communist background, his fiery temperament, and his paranoia barred him from ever being recognized as the party's titular leader, a fact that he resented deeply and held against those who did rise to the top, including Brandt. Brandt, like Wehner, had fought the Nazis, going to Norway in 1933 and, after its occupation in 1940, to Sweden, where he had met Wehner and helped organize the German Social Democratic Party in exile. Brandt would never have been chancellor but for Wehner's having forced the party to abandon the Marxist principles of class struggle and workers' ownership of the means of production, in the so-called Godesberg Program of 1959. Brandt's Eastern policies had had Wehner's full backing. In 1972, the cornerstone of East-West relations was coming into place, but technicalities endangered the whole edifice. The Soviet Union was threatening to cause trouble because Bonn was insisting on placing a federal environmental office in West Berlin, a step Moscow interpreted as undermining the recognition of Berlin's separateness in the Four-Power Treaty of 1971 and in the Basic Treaty with East Germany. And now Bonn's insistence on bureaucratic formalism threatened the whole secret prisoner-exchange program. Brandt was not being strong enough. The treaties would remain dead letters unless they were filled with life, and if Brandt could not or would not do it, Wehner would. For he had had his own secret channels to the Germans on the other side of the Wall, and one of the most important of them ran through Wolfgang Vogel.

Wehner's years in Sweden had left him with some lifelong friends. One of them was Sven Backlund, son of a prominent Swedish Social Democrat Wehner had known in Stockholm. Backlund had been Swedish general consul in West Berlin in the early 1960s, was also a close friend of Willy Brandt's, and in 1973 became his country's ambassador to Bonn. When Wehner became minister for All-German Affairs and required discreet channels of communications to the other side, Backlund had introduced him to Carl Gustaf Svingel, the Swedish operatic tenor who had given up his singing career to run the rest home where Vogel's first protector, Rudolf Reinartz, had spent most of his last days.

Backlund and Svingel, both fluent German speakers, were shrewd political operators and idealists who, like Wehner, saw their life's work as helping to overcome the ideological and physical barriers of the cold war. More important, perhaps, both were men who were thrilled by the idea of being entrusted with secrets. Svingel's church connections had also made him aware of the secret arrangements that Kurt Scharf, the Lutheran bishop of Berlin-Brandenburg, had made through Vogel to secure the release of church prisoners. Svingel and Backlund found these channels useful when it came to getting Swedish construction workers in East Berlin out of trouble after a few succumbed to the temptations of the black market, or of love, and were caught trying to smuggle East Germans across the Wall. Svingel's rest home was a useful place for meetings that no one wanted to become public, and his discretion was absolute.

Svingel, a good-looking Nordic type with a predilection for wearing bow ties, could do wonderful impressions of the gruff, cantankerous Wehner, and loved to retell the exotic stories Vogel told about his own past—the tragedy of Reinartz and his encounters with Streit and Honecker. Wehner and Vogel had come to know each other well from the prisoner-release negotiations. They often met at Svingel's retreat, where they could talk informally, without the knowledge or interference of West German government officials. Soon they were seeing each other almost once a month, talking not only about the ongoing negotiations on prisoners but also about broader political questions. Wehner, who liked working in the shadows, concluded that Vogel might be able to facilitate contacts on a higher level with some of his former Communist comrades. So in 1968 he left with Vogel a letter asking him formally if he was prepared to go beyond the confines of his mandate on humanitarian matters and arrange contacts with East German political figures to work for broader understandings, with the intention, he said, of getting "over and around the Cold War." Vogel quietly passed the letter to Streit, who circulated it to higher instances. But in 1968 Walter Ulbricht had been in charge in East Germany, and Ulbricht regarded Wehner's efforts as dangerous attempts at ideological subversion, warning his party colleagues against any contacts. So the message had gone unanswered.[9]

But in mid-1973, Ulbricht was out of power and close to death. Vogel knew that Honecker and Wehner had worked together in the Communist youth organization in the Saar in 1934, trying to head off Hitler's annexation of the territory, which had been awarded to France in the settlement of World War I. After annexation, when the party had been forced to go underground, the two men had parted ways, Honecker to Paris and Wehner to Moscow. But, unlike Ulbricht, Honecker had retained a place in his heart for his former comrade. "Herbert Wehner had had it up to here with conditions in Moscow," Honecker remembered later, speaking about the atmosphere of terror and recrimination in Stalin's wartime rule. Many loyal German Communists had been arrested in exile and perished in the gulag. Perhaps, if the KGB had arrested and interrogated Honecker as it had done Wehner, he acknowledged, he too might have chosen a different path after the war.[10]

The fascination between Honecker and Wehner was mutual, and they began using Vogel as an indirect channel of communications. Five times in 1970, Vogel flew to Hamburg to talk to Wehner at home in his working-class constituency on weekends.[11] These weekend visits became routine, and by 1972, the two men had become so well known to each other that Vogel put a picture of Wehner on his office wall, next to Streit's.

Now, at the end of May 1973, in Wehner's book-lined study in Bad Godesberg, Vogel explained that the West German government's insistence on cutting off the humanitarian payments was keeping two thousand innocent people sitting on their suitcases. "What can we do?" Wehner asked. "Make a suggestion."

"I think you should talk with the Number One about it," Vogel replied. "Maybe he isn't aware of what's going on. You know him from the old days, and maybe that will give you something to work with. Why don't you go to Berlin? I think he'll receive you."

It took Wehner only a few moments to decide. "I've got to ask Willy Brandt," he said, but he could not get the chancellor on the telephone. "Greta," he bellowed to his stepdaughter, "we're going East in the morning."

Wehner drove across the border the night of May 30, to the astonishment of West German border guards who said that usually government officials of his rank gave prior notification of their trips. "I'll have to clear this with higher authority," the officer in charge said, "the only exceptions are for retired people." "I'm a pensioner," Wehner snapped back, and drove off with Greta into the dark toward Berlin and Honecker's summer residence, the Hubertusstock on the Werbellinsee, on the city's northern outskirts.[12]

Wehner had not gone without covering his back. Knowing that Wolfgang Mischnick, his counterpart in the Free Democratic Party's parliamentary leadership in Bonn, was in Dresden on a visit, he arranged for Mischnick, too, to drop in for afternoon coffee and cakes with Honecker. So it was, with Wehner smoking his pipe and Honecker pouring coffee, that the people of East and West Germany found them on the front pages of their newspapers on June 1.[13] The official communiqué made the visit seem nothing out of the ordinary, but it caused a sensation in Bonn as well as East Berlin. Most of the German government had been taken completely unawares by Wehner's *"Nacht und Nebel"* trip. Charges flew through the air, most of them not hard to imagine: Wehner was conspiring with his old Communist comrades, selling out, and so on.

In fact, Wehner and Honecker did resolve the impasse over the "humanitarian efforts." The Communist blackmail worked, as it nearly always did. Wehner agreed with Honecker to leave the arrangements as they had been, and Honecker told him that, from then on, Wehner could consider Vogel as the Communist leader's personal agent. Given these assurances, Honecker told Wehner, "I'll take care of it." As soon as Wehner had left, "Number One" ordered East German officials to resume the transport of political prisoners across the border without further delay.[14]

By taking the "humanitarian area" directly under his personal control, Honecker had greatly increased Vogel's power and leverage with the Stasi, which considered Wehner a prime objective. Now Vogel had made him into something close to an East German agent of influence in Bonn. Vogel continued to see Wehner regularly over the years, filing detailed reports on his talks when he returned to East Berlin. And as the two men became friends, Wehner became increasingly frank, treating Vogel to long and excoriating criticisms of Brandt, finance minister and rival Helmut Schmidt, and their policies. Volpert saw to it that all these reports ended up on Erich Mielke's desk in Stasi headquarters, where they were analyzed extensively for their numerous revelations about the real intentions and attitudes of the people who decided government policy in Bonn.[15] Would it have shocked Vogel's West German conversation partners to know that their messages were going not only to Honecker but also to the Stasi chief? It seemed to matter little in those days. Vogel was aware only of a steadily growing respect shown to him by all whom he knew in Bonn, a respect due to his powerful connections to the Stasi among other agencies.

But all those connections, and all Vogel's skills as a mediator, would be put to a severe test over the next eight years in the spy scandal that was about to break and bring Brandt down with it.

CHAPTER SEVEN

THE EAST GERMAN SPY WHO BROUGHT DOWN CHANCELLOR WILLY BRANDT

"I'd figured on seeing you a lot sooner."

When Herbert Wehner returned from his surprise meeting with Erich Honecker at the end of May 1973, Günther Nollau, the president of Bonn's Federal Office for the Protection of the Constitution, the equivalent of the American FBI in domestic counterintelligence, was waiting to see him at his apartment on the hill above Bad Godesberg. Nollau did not come to discuss the details of Wehner's meeting in East Germany, though Willy Brandt later complained that Wehner, increasingly irascible and impetuous in old age, had been irritatingly secretive about the meeting. Rather, he warned Wehner that Bonn's counterspies were hot on the trail of an important East German agent, one whose name was yet unknown but who was believed to be aiming for the leadership of the Social Democratic Party. All that was known for certain, Nollau reported, was that the agent's first and last names began with a *G.*[1]

Günter Guillaume was soon to become the most notorious Communist agent since Rudolf Abel. His unmasking tested the rapprochement between the two Germanies and strained the entire edifice of détente between East and West. The Stasi had put Guillaume where he was, the Stasi had brought down Willy Brandt, and then, from 1974 to 1981, the Stasi pushed Wolfgang Vogel to get Guillaume out of a West German prison. Bargaining for Guillaume's release required all of Vogel's skills in diplomacy, political tact, and negotiation with opposing intelligence services. In unexpected ways, it also made clear the limits of his power and influence as a negotiator, both for the East Germans and for the Soviet Union.

Nollau's domestic intelligence service and the other West German agencies had been slow and ineffectual in following up the the original lead. On May 29, Hans-Dietrich Genscher, then Brandt's minister of the interior, came to the chancellor with a warning like the one Nollau had given Wehner, based on the same information. Had Brandt a colleague with a French-sounding name? Genscher asked. Brandt had indeed: Günter Guillaume, a relatively junior member of his staff in the chancellery who had been working as Brandt's liaison with his party since January 1970. Why did Genscher want to know? Because, Genscher told Brandt, Nollau had asked for permission to put the man under observation. There was no proof that anything was wrong, and Guillaume should go on working as before to avoid arousing his suspicions. The security people simply wanted to check out a tip. The chancellor pointed out that Guillaume was to accompany him on his summer vacation in Norway in July. Guillaume was even going to bring his wife, Christel, and their son. Did Genscher think that Brandt should take a different personal assistant? No, Genscher replied the next day, after checking back with Nollau. Perhaps the suspicions were unfounded, after all, Brandt thought. The security officials would take care of it.[2]

The West German security apparatus failed miserably in the Guillaume case, in the view of the man perhaps best qualified to judge—Markus Wolf, the legendary head of the East German spy machine, the Stasi's Hauptverwaltung Aufklärung (HVA). "He never should have got that far, because his origins were known to West German counterespionage," Wolf gloated in the East Berlin newspaper *Junge Welt* in June 1990.[3] Wolf was correct. In April 1954, the Gehlen Organization had reported that a Günter Guillaume had "infiltrated" West German publishing houses, at a time when he was known to be working for an East Berlin publisher called Volk und Wissen, a front for the Stasi.[4]

Günter and Christel Guillaume were only two of the 279,189 East Germans who registered as refugees in West Germany in 1956, the year of the Hungarian uprising, and Wolf had already calculated that these hurrying masses were excellent cover for "sleeper" agents. The Guillaumes had settled in Frankfurt, joined the Social Democratic Party, and risen through its ranks to the elected city government, and from there to Bonn, helped especially by Georg Leber, who later became defense minister.

The intelligence reports warning against Guillaume had not been lost in the files; they had come right to the surface when he had applied for a job in Brandt's chancellery in 1969, been considered by security officials, and then been disregarded. The officials of Nollau's service had cleared him without reservations for access to papers with the classification of up to top secret in 1970 and cleared him again, in the fall of 1972, when he was proposed as the chancellor's personal assistant for liaison with labor unions. Although Brandt personally found little about Guillaume's personality that was attractive—he was too servile and self-consciously ingratiating, Brandt thought—he had given in to the urgings of Leber and others and let Guillaume take the job.[5]

"The placing of Günter Guillaume in the Chancellor's office, let alone directly under the Chancellor, was not the result of careful planning by our service," Wolf wrote later, but, he added, "Bonn was still a temptation for us."[6] So when Guillaume had risen that far, the Stasi convinced itself that it had gotten lucky. The East Germans had convinced themselves that they needed agents who could tell them things they could not learn from the newspapers and magazines in one of the least security-conscious capitals of the Western world. Among these things, Wolf explained, was early warning about when the West Germans began preparations to move the government apparatus in Bonn to an underground war headquarters in Ahrweiler, a move that could be the first warning that World War III was about to break out. On such fantasies did even highly efficient security services wring their multi-billion-mark budgets out of governments East and West during the cold war.

But the East Germans did not worry much about the possibility that their infiltration could come back and hit them where it hurt if Guillaume were discovered. Wolf tended to leave decisions on whether an agent should be pulled out to the agent himself, in the first instance, since the agent would normally be the first to get a hint of being under suspicion. So in this case the decision on when to call it quits was left with Guillaume.[7]

Had the East Germans reacted properly to the first signs that Guillaume was under surveillance, in the summer of 1973, history might have been different. Christel Guillaume's control officer, another Stasi woman who regularly met with her in Bonn to take delivery of secrets the spies had harvested, had spotted signs of trouble while they were eating in an outdoor restaurant in Bonn. A man sitting at a nearby table, she noticed, was carrying a briefcase from which a camera lens was protruding, and he had just pointed it directly at them. "Watch out, don't turn around," she had told Christel. "We have just been photographed."[8] Back in East Berlin, Wolf admitted later, the significance of the incident had not been properly evaluated; the Stasi assumed that only Christel was being watched, or perhaps the control officer, but not the main agent himself.

Guillaume and his wife were not arrested until April 24, 1974. But when the security agents finally came for him, Guillaume saved them the trouble of proving their case, announcing that he was an officer and citizen of the German Democratic Republic and demanding to be treated accordingly. The news of the arrest provoked a huge political scandal with international ramifications. For when Brandt had gone on vacation to Hamar, in the Norwegian mountains, in July of 1973, the Guillaumes had indeed gone with him, and Günter Guillaume had handled all the chancellor's official correspondence with Bonn—including four confidential and twelve secret telegrams, some of them from Washington.

In his memoirs, Brandt played these down.[9] But a parliamentary investigation of the bungled West German security operation made clear that the investigation of Guillaume had been incredibly incompetent. Nollau had canceled surveillance of his activities in Norway that summer, when Guillaume had been managing the secret message traffic. Four months later, while Brandt was spending a weekend with friends in southern France, Guillaume had begged permission to go with him, and later claimed to have met unobserved with his Stasi controller in a nearby museum. Guillaume had even rented a room in the same hotel where Brandt's security officers were staying, falling asleep after drinking a round with them and drowsily telling one who gently woke him to return a notebook that had fallen out of the spy's pocket, "You pigs, you won't get me."[10]

Appalling as the security lapses were, they were soon overshadowed by what the chancellor felt was character assassination directed against him. Guillaume had spent weeks with Brandt during the 1972 election campaign, crisscrossing the country on the chancellor's special train. Conservative newspapers, never friendly to the Social Democrats, began to report that the spy had been collecting notes on Willy's love life on the campaign trail, notes that the Communists could use to blackmail him into even greater concessions. Brandt was outraged on April 30 when Justice Minister Werner Maihofer reported to him that he had heard the federal prosecutor's office was investigating charges that Guillaume had been procuring women for the chancellor. Brandt kept his temper. The next day, Genscher brought even worse news: a written summary of Brandt's extramarital liaisons with several women that Guillaume might have known about. Even in his memoirs, written fifteen years after the events, Brandt's bitterness fairly radiates from the pages. He had endured subtle allegations of disloyalty for years because of his Norwegian self-exile. Always subject to mood swings, he now became deeply depressed, convinced that even some of his police guardians were now on the side of political enemies who were determined to use the Guillaume affair to get rid of him.

Brandt, sixty-one years old in 1974, was growing weary—weary of constant battles with the Christian Democrats over his Eastern policy, weary of insinuations from the German right wing that he had been a traitor to his country in Scandinavia and was a traitor to it again now, weary of the behind-the-scenes wrangling with Herbert Wehner, weary of fights with the labor unions over excessive wage demands that raised levels of unemployment and inflation to unheard-of levels in postwar Germany. His triumphs—the Nobel Peace Prize, Germany's re-emergence into the ranks of respectable West European nations, even his election victory a year and a half earlier—all seemed long ago and far away. His marriage to Rut Brandt, who had been with him since his exile in Norway, was beginning to collapse. So, late Monday night, May 6, he submitted his letter of resignation to President Gustav W. Heinemann, citing "negligence in connection with the Guillaume espionage affair."[11]

Brandt's letter was not released until midnight, well after every

German morning newspaper had rolled off the presses. German television had gone off the air and would not come on again until early the next afternoon. So for most of that Tuesday, most Germans did not even know that their chancellor had resigned. Before the parliamentary group of his party that day, Brandt said that he had based his decision "on my experience of office, on my understanding of the unwritten rules of democracy and on my desire not to let my personal and political integrity be destroyed."[12]

Nobody professed to be more surprised than Erich Honecker in East Berlin, and he had begun trying to ward off political damage even before Brandt's resignation by sending Vogel to Bonn with a message. On May 3, Vogel flew secretly to Bad Godesberg to tell Wehner that the East German leader had not known that an active East German spy had been sitting in the chancellor's office. Mielke had assured him, Vogel said, that Guillaume had been "switched off" by the Stasi as soon as he had risen to the Chancellor's office. Wehner had given the message to Nollau, who had reacted skeptically.[13]

Brandt, too, was skeptical, and remained so years later even after Honecker personally assured him that if had he known Guillaume had been where he was, he would have ordered him removed. Brandt had been told this before, by Valentin M. Falin, Brezhnev's ambassador to Bonn at the time and, later, Mikhail S. Gorbachev's chief adviser on Germany. Falin, on Brezhnev's orders, had delivered a message to Brandt in early May, telling him that the Soviet Union had had no knowledge that Guillaume had been an East German agent. Brezhnev had been outraged, Falin claimed later, when he had been first told about it in the spring of 1974. For there were suspicions in Moscow that Honecker had deliberately engineered the spy scandal and sacrificed Guillaume as a way of bringing Brandt down.[14]

Much speaks for this Soviet theory, including the casual way in which the East Germans reacted to the surveillance of Guillaume's wife. Honecker had good reasons to feel personally threatened by Brandt's popularity. During a ground-breaking visit by the chancellor to the East German city of Erfurt in 1970, the first time a West German leader had ever been to East Germany, local crowds, in defiance of a massive Stasi security presence, had welcomed the chancellor as a hero. Long into the afternoon, they had chanted, "Willy Brandt! Willy Brandt! Willy Brandt!" outside his hotel in a deliberate snub to East German Prime Minister Willi Stoph, who was also present. Brandt's popularity was a political danger Honecker had sought to contain with his policy of delimitation, but it had remained, and so Honecker must have been secretly delighted by Brandt's unexpected resignation, however much the Soviets might have been dismayed. Vogel had not questioned the truth of the message of regret that Honecker had asked him to deliver to Wehner; he was hardly in a position to do so, and he was not so inclined. But in the Soviet view, the mere fact that Vogel was delivering messages through back channels confirmed that Honecker had been up to something behind their backs.[15]

Helmut Schmidt, Brandt's finance minister, took over smoothly as chancellor on May 14, and Honecker knew that Schmidt, for his own domestic political reasons, would find it in his interest to continue to treat East Germany as a fully equal negotiating partner. Honecker's overtures to Schmidt began, Brandt thought, almost before he had been able to clear his desk in the Palais Schaumburg.[16]

The Guillaumes had not brought down Willy Brandt, the East Germans convinced themselves; they had merely provided the pretext for his resignation, a judgment shared by most West German politicians of the time.[17] Nevertheless, the case had been a colossal embarrassment on the world stage. Brandt, who had earned the respect and affection of millions of people around the world and won a Nobel Peace Prize for laying the building blocks of reconciliation between Germany and its Communist neighbors, had been brought down by Communist perfidy. The Guillaumes paid heavily for what they had done; in December 1975 Günter Guillaume received a thirteen-year sentence, and Christel an eight-year term. Their imprisonment weighed like a stone on East-West German relations, and better than anyone in the Politburo, Wolfgang Vogel knew that it would take a long time to remove the weight. But, pressed by Markus Wolf, Honecker wasted no time in letting Vogel know that from now on getting the Guillaumes free was to be the top priority in his negotiations with the West German leaders.

Schmidt, a former defense minister who spoke fluent English, was better trusted in Washington than Brandt had been, at least by the Ford administration and Secretary of State Henry A. Kissinger. Schmidt was a close friend of the French president, Valéry Giscard d'Estaing, and his whole orientation was more toward the Atlantic than toward the Urals. But his succession as chancellor had not changed the fundamental reasons why West Germany had sought better relations with the East. The guiding principles of Schmidt's foreign policy remained firmly based on Brandt's *Ostpolitik*. The Stasi had brought Brandt down, and Schmidt would never have agreed to talk to Vogel if he thought he had been a commissioned Stasi officer. But Schmidt was as fascinated by Vogel, who came at the very least with the Stasi's blessing, as Wehner was.[18]

The reason was Vogel's closeness to Honecker. Schmidt had never met the East German leader, and given the circumstances of Brandt's downfall, a formal summit any time soon was out of the question. But they would be seated next to each other in July 1975 in Helsinki at the meeting of the thirty-five-nation Conference on Security and Cooperation in Europe. Schmidt was eager to make of this meeting a substantive occasion. And, like Kissinger, he preferred to use private back channels to arrange it.

Vogel suited Schmidt's purposes perfectly. He offered a more useful and flexible way of communicating messages to Honecker than official, but cumbersome, German-German channels, and was more discreet, besides. Vogel was scrupulously accurate as a rapporteur—conveying the views and nuances from Bonn to East Berlin no less precisely than the other way around, Schmidt felt, and in perfect confidentiality. He was a useful "letter carrier," the new chancellor decided, a channel that entailed none of the usual risks of misunderstanding, inflexibility, or preoccupation with loss of face always involved in government-to-government communications. Schmidt, like Wehner, eventually came to trust Vogel "without reservation."[19]

By the time the summer began, Vogel had become a frequent flier on the midday British Airways shuttle from West Berlin to Cologne. He talked with Schmidt and Wehner about the agenda for the Helsinki meeting between the two German leaders. Bonn wanted further East German concessions on humanitarian issues, and a cancellation of the East German decision two years earlier to double the mandatory currency-exchange fee for West Germans visiting the East. In return, Schmidt told Vogel, Bonn would be willing to discuss an investment of millions of marks on rebuilding and new construction of autobahns that all these visitors used on their visits in East Germany. Schmidt even began sharing his assessments of the international situation with Vogel, knowing that Honecker would get them, precisely as delivered, hours later.[20] The East German foreign minister, Oskar Fischer, was a personal friend of Vogel's so there were no ruffled feathers there. Schmidt soon felt comfortable enough with Vogel to invite him to his vacation home on the Brahmsee lake near Kiel, an unpretentious summer bungalow far more modest than Vogel's own.

In Helsinki, Schmidt and Honecker met much more formally than their emissaries, but thanks in part to Vogel's preparatory negotiations, their encounters in the conference rooms of the Finlandia Hall in Helsinki went smoothly. Schmidt assured Honecker that he was as interested in the continuity of relaxation of tensions with the East as his predecessor had been, despite the regrettable and superfluous interruption of the Guillaume affair, and asked Honecker not to jump to false conclusions when domestic political considerations in Bonn troubled the atmosphere. "If anything appears unclear to you, ask me yourself. We've a good opportunity to do that today, and for the future, we have established useful channels."[21]

Honecker was well pleased. On October 30, Vogel's fiftieth birthday, the East German leader pinned onto one of his lawyer's well-tailored lapels the East German Meritorious Service Medal in gold, for "extraordinary service in the founding and development of the socialist social order, and the strengthening of the German Democratic Republic."

But there was one thing Vogel could not bring up with Schmidt without setting him off like a rocket. And that was the subject of Günter Guillaume's release. Schmidt simply would not hear of it, and when Vogel went to ask Wehner to help, the old man just grunted that there was nothing he could do about it. But Honecker and Mielke wanted to get Guillaume out of prison and back home, out of the way of high state policy, as soon as they could. "Wherever I go in the world, they hit me over the head with the case," Fischer, the foreign minister, complained.[22]

Vogel knew he would have to find leverage to use, the same way he had done in the Abel-Powers and Felfe cases. For Guillaume, he needed a counterpart, someone the West Germans or their American allies wanted badly enough to offer Guillaume in return. And Vogel hardly needed to chase after leads anymore; his reputation for having connections all over the Communist world brought leads to him.

In early March 1976 Richard D. Copaken, a lawyer from Covington & Burling in Washington, D.C., contacted Vogel to ask for help in resolving the mystery of a missing Soviet defector named Nicholas G. Shadrin. Shadrin, Vogel thought at first, might eventually become the key to Guillaume's release. For here was a case with as many moral ambiguities and political embarrassments for the Americans as Guillaume had posed for the East Germans. Vogel plunged in with high hopes.

"Shadrin" was, in reality, Nikolai Fyodorovich Artamonov, a Soviet Navy sub-commander who had fallen in love while on a training assignment in Gdynia, Poland, with a woman named Ewa Gora and had fled across the Baltic with her to Sweden in 1959. They went to the United States, where he had taken on his new identity as Shadrin, after the character in Pushkin's short story "The Captain's Daughter," and worked for American intelligence.

Shadrin had abandoned a family in the Soviet Union, and quite a family—his wife was the daughter of Admiral Sergei Gorshkov, the architect of the modern Soviet Navy—and he had been sentenced in absentia to death for treason. In 1966, a man with a Russian accent had called the home telephone number of Richard Helms, then director of the CIA. Eventually, the caller—"Igor," to the Americans—identified himself as an KGB officer and offered to work for the Americans if they would help him string along his superiors in Moscow by letting him find and recruit Nikolai Artamonov, ostensibly as a double agent for the KGB.

The offer of this complex double game attracted at least part of the American intelligence community, and Shadrin, who had become bored with his routine naval intelligence work, was prevailed upon to take on this more exciting and risky assignment. Apparently he was never told how it had come about; perhaps James Jesus Angleton, the CIA's legendary chief of counterintelligence, had doubts about Shadrin's genuineness as a defector and wanted to test him. Whatever the truth, the assignment had ended badly and messily when the CIA let Shadrin agree to meet a Soviet contact in Vienna, for the second time, in December 1975.

On Thursday, December 18, Ewa and Nicholas Shadrin checked into the Bristol Hotel. The first contact with the KGB took place, as scheduled, at 6 P.M. that day, and Shadrin was told to come alone to the steps of the Votivkirche, a huge neo-Gothic church that happened to be directly opposite the U.S. Consulate, for a second meeting Saturday night. He left the room that evening, telling his wife that he would be back by the time she returned from the opera. She never saw him alive again.[23]

Shadrin's CIA "protectors" had no idea what had happened to him, which led his wife to suspect that he had either been left inexcusably to meet alone with the Soviets, without American backup surveillance or protection, or else sacrificed deliberately for reasons she could not understand. After concluding that the CIA was stonewalling her, she hired Copaken to get to the bottom of the mystery. He asked for the assistance of the State Department, which referred him to the U.S. Embassy in Vienna and in particular to its deputy chief of mission, Vogel's old friend Frank Meehan.

Meehan knew when an intelligence operation had gone badly wrong. Shadrin's disappearance, in a city that was as much of a center of intelligence intrigue as Berlin was, certainly looked like a foul-up, if not something far worse. Privately, Meehan was as baffled by the CIA's performance as Copaken was. But the Soviets were also stonewalling every official American request for information on what had happened to Shadrin. The State Department had made Meehan its main point of official contact with Vogel, since the two men had known each other since the Abel-Powers negotiations. And when Copaken came to Vienna in March 1976, Meehan, with approval from Washington, arranged an appointment with Vogel in Berlin.[24]

Copaken, a brilliant and persistent Harvard lawyer, soon demonstrated that he was not to be underestimated either inside or outside a courtroom. Meehan told him he could trust Vogel. "Frank said he had never had occasion to doubt his credibility," Copaken recalled, and he flew off to Berlin on March 7 for a rendezvous the next day with Vogel in Carl Gustaf Svingel's rest home in the Western sector.

Arriving in his room at the Berlin Hilton, Copaken found the telephone ringing. Svingel was on the line. Vogel was ill, he reported. Copaken offered to meet with him at his bedside in East Berlin.

"You don't understand," Svingel told him. "Our friend will be well precisely at 10 A.M. Monday." Svingel's days on the operatic stage were long past, but he never made simple arrangements when he thought a complicated plot would do.

The delay left Copaken with a weekend to kill, not an easy task in a German city where shopping hours ended not long after noon Saturdays and where there was nothing to do Sundays but visit museums and look into the windows of the tightly closed stores. His wife had asked him to check out the Rosenthal china for her if he got a chance, and so he wandered around West Berlin peering at crockery for much of the weekend.

On Monday morning, at about 9:30, he took a taxi to Svingel's address. When he saw the house, he thought to himself that Charles Addams couldn't have designed a more appropriate venue for a meeting with a secret Communist agent. Svingel was friendly and cheerful. Finally Vogel swept in in his Mercedes, greeting Copaken warmly and then handing him a wrapped present. Undoing the paper layers, Copaken discovered that the gift was a little brown china dachshund, exquisitely done. "Meissen," Vogel pointed out, in case the provenance had escaped his new American contact.

Copaken did not speak German. Mice? he wondered, and looked down at the floor with alarm. Vogel reached over and turned over the porcelain dachshund so that the crossed swords of the Meissen royal porcelain factory showed—the most precious gift he could offer from the German Democratic Republic. Perhaps it was merely chance, but Copaken strongly suspected that Vogel, or someone acting for him, must have been following him the entire weekend, during all those visits to the china shops.

Vogel heard out Copaken's explanation of the Shadrin case non-committally, as Svingel interpreted. "What proof or circumstantial evidence do you have that Shadrin was abducted by the Soviets?" he asked. Copaken told him that there was none, only that the Americans thought it extremely unlikely that a man who had defected more than fifteen years earlier would have suddenly changed his mind and voluntarily gone home. "Shadrin is probably in a box," Vogel warned, skeptically; "I have no mandate to act in this case." But, he went on, if he was to get one, his dealings with Copaken would have to remain absolutely confidential. The "cardinal rule," he warned, was that Copaken must not permit the United States government to echo through official diplomatic channels any matters Vogel took up with him in their private channel. If this did happen, Vogel warned, it could have dire consequences for Copaken's client.

Vogel spoke the truth—he had no mandate. He was on a fishing expedition, with Streit's approval. But he also made it clear to

Copaken that if the Soviets did have Shadrin and were willing to swap him, the price for his release would be Günter and Christel Guillaume.[25]

Copaken returned to Washington, and on March 17th, Vogel sent an encouraging message. In the fractured English that Helga, whose sister was married to an American and lived in San Antonio, was sometimes able to conjure up for Vogel, it read: "The case has been researched. One has informed me that the staying of this man is unknown." Shadrin's whereabouts were unknown—which meant, as Copaken saw it, that since he was not in some unmarked grave in a cemetery reserved for Soviet traitors, Shadrin might be alive, and there was everything to play for.[26]

Copaken duly reported to the CIA that Vogel had made clear that he wanted the Guillaumes, but needed to know whom the Americans could offer in a possible trade for them. Within a few days, Copaken had been given a list of captured spies to take back to Berlin. The Americans, of course, could not offer Guillaume; that was up to the West Germans. But the negotiations could go on in the meantime.

Vogel began trying to reel in the line.

At his next meeting with Copaken, again in Svingel's residence on March 22 with the Swede acting as interpreter, Vogel leafed through the CIA's list.

"This guy's dead," Vogel said, flipping the page.

"This one's been dead two years."

Vogel peered over his wire-rimmed reading glasses with a look Copaken judged to be sympathetic. This East German barrister seemed to have better and more up-to-date inventories of captured spies than the CIA. But Vogel did not exaggerate his powers. He was encountering "resistance" on this case, he said, without elaborating, from his own side. "I'm sorry that at the moment things are so negative," Vogel apologized. "The problem for the Russians is that Shadrin is a traitor." A letter from President Gerald Ford to Brezhnev would make clear the high-level American interest in the case, Vogel said, and he would see to it that Erich Honecker personally got the letter to Moscow. "Honecker would not come back empty-handed," he assured Copaken.[27]

Despite what he was telling Copaken, Vogel still had no mandate from Brezhnev to negotiate for Shadrin. He did not even have an idea if the man were still alive. What he did have was his East

ogel and his family in Wilhelmsthal in the early 1930s. From left, Wolfgang Vogel, Charlotte
ogel (sister), Elfriede Vogel (mother), Gisela Vogel (sister), Walther Vogel (father), and Hans
ogel (brother). COURTESY OF WOLFGANG VOGEL

Wolfgang Vogel in Luftwaffe flight training in late 1944.
COURTESY OF WOLFGANG VOGEL

ogel's first law office at 113 Alt
iedrichsfelde in East Berlin. The stairway in
e shadows on the right is where American
wyer James Donovan feared he might be
tacked while negotiating the
bel-Powers spy swap in 1962.

sef Streit, Vogel's mentor and the
osecutor general of East Germany

WATTERS & DONOVAN

SHOREHAM BUILDING
WASHINGTON 5, D. C.

161 WILLIAM STREET

NEW YORK 38, N. Y.

TELEPHONE
WORTH 4-3553

March 19, 1962

Herr Wolfgang Vogel
Berlin-Friedrichsfelde
Alt-Friedrichsfelde 113
Berlin, Germany

Re: Marvin William Makinen

Dear Herr Vogel:

By letter dated March 2, 1962 Oliver S. Allen, Esquire,
of the Massachusetts Bar, submitted to Leonid I. Brezhnev,
Chairman of the Supreme Soviet Presidium of the Union of
Soviet Socialist Republics, a petition for clemency upon
behalf of Marvin William Makinen by his father and step-
mother.

A copy of this petition has been forwarded to me by
Mr. Allen and, at his request and the request of the
Makinen family, I ask that you undertake to ascertain
from Mr. Shishkin at the Soviet Embassy whether favorable
consideration cannot now be given to this petition since,
due to the manner in which my Government publicly
explained the release of Francis Gary Powers, the effect
has been to assist in the creation of a better climate
in the matter of relations between the United States and
the U.S.S.R.

Sincerely yours,

James B. Donovan

JBD/MM

Key correspondence in the Abel-
Powers exchange: Abel's note,
handwritten after his release, asks
Vogel to cash a check Abel received
from his lawyer, James Donovan.
Donovan's letter asks Vogel to follow-
up on the promised release of another
prisoner in light of the "better climate"
in East-West relations created by
the exchange.

Fn. E. Förster, z. Hd.
R. I. ABEL
LEIPZIG N 22
EISENACHER STR 24

Oct. 15, 1962

Dear Mr Vogel, would it be
possible for you to cash
the enclosed check which I
received from Mr Donovan
and send the proceeds to me
at the above address ?
I shall be very grateful
to you for this service.
Sincerely Yours,
Rudolf I. Abel

ɔlfgang Vogel in his office at the height of his career in the mid-1970s. COURTESY OF WOLFGANG VOGEL

Another successful exchange: A happy Vogel (third from left) with (from left) Jeffrey H. Smith, Robert Glenn Thompson, and Shabtai Kalmanovich in front of Vogel's Mercedes.
COURTESY OF JEFFREY H. SMITH

The start of the Shcharansky deal: Vogel (center) in New York city wi Rabbi Ronnie Greenwald (left) and New York Congressman Benjamin Gilman in 1978.

One of the biggest spy exchanges Vogel engineered, June 11, 1985, a the Glienicke Bridge. Heinz Volpe Vogel's long-time Stasi contact, ca be seen (second from right) walkin away from the bus.

February 1986: a happy ending to a long ordeal. Anatoly Shcharansky celebrates his release with Vogel (left) and Frank Meehan, U.S. ambassador to East Germany.
COURTESY OF WOLFGANG VOGEL

ogel and German hancellor Helmut Kohl 1990.
GE KUNDEL-SARO

The Glienicke Bridge, site of Vogel's most famous exchanges in the era of the divided Germany, in 1991.
CRAIG R. WHITNEY

The twilight of a long career: Vogel
outside his office and in his home.
CRAIG R. WHITNEY

German bosses pushing him hard to do anything he could to secure Guillaume's release, and evidently giving him plenty of leeway to use his judgment. He could see that, like himself, Copaken was engaged, and well connected, and willing to go to bat in Washington to do whatever it took to get to the bottom of whatever had happened to his client.[28]

On April 16, Copaken went to the west wing of the White House to meet with William Hyland, then on Kissinger's staff. Hyland told Copaken that the administration had decided on a compromise. There would be no letter from Ford to Brezhnev. But Brent Scowcroft, Kissinger's top deputy, had signed one addressed to Mrs. Shadrin. Hyland gave the letter to Copaken and said that Vogel could deliver an authenticated copy to Brezhnev through his own channels. The first paragraph made clear that President Ford was personally concerned about Shadrin's whereabouts, and that a resolution of the case would lead to an improvement in U.S.-Soviet relations. The second explained that the United States was aware of the unofficial channel being used to convey the letter, and had confidence that it could bring positive results.

Though still puzzled by the White House's standoffishness, Copaken pronounced himself reasonably satisfied. He would leave that very evening for West Berlin and deliver the letter to Vogel, he told Hyland. But Kissinger's aide was deeply skeptical that Vogel had any special inside relationship to the Kremlin. "The Vogel connection," he said, "I always believed and still believe was totally phony."[29] All Vogel was trying to do, Hyland suspected, was to make Honecker happy by somehow conning the Americans into pressing for Guillaume's release, with sleight-of-hand about the Shadrin case.

Packing that afternoon for his trip, Copaken was surprised at home by an alarming call from Hyland. On instructions from above, Hyland said, he had called Counsellor Yuli Vorontsov of the Soviet Embassy into the White House and told him about the letter Copaken was bringing to Vogel. Hyland knew that this directly violated Vogel's "cardinal rule," and seemed sheepish. Copaken feared the worst. As he understood it, Vogel had specifically warned that such an action would be taken in Moscow as a signal that the United States did not want Shadrin back at all, dead or alive.

In his talk with Hyland, Vorontsov had taken umbrage at the suggestion that the Soviets had been responsible for Shadrin's disappearance. "We don't know where this man is," he had huffed to

Hyland. "If we did, we would tell you." And as a professional Soviet diplomat, he was irritated at the unofficial and non-Soviet channel. Kissinger had had a perfectly good one that had worked for years, with Ambassador Anatoly F. Dobrynin, who could come and go at the State Department almost as easily as its regular employees. "Why do you need an East German messenger? Vogel does not speak for us," he warned Hyland. "Perhaps Vogel knows where 'Shadrin' is—perhaps he is in West Berlin," he suggested sarcastically, adding that in Soviet eyes, Shadrin was still a Soviet citizen answerable for a capital crime.

Vogel was scarcely less distressed when Copaken told him what had happened. One channel at a time was the way he understood his own cardinal rule, and if the Americans were opening a second, official channel on Shadrin, he would probably have to bow out.

Indeed, after Vorontsov's conversation with Hyland, the Soviets slapped Vogel on the wrist. When he next saw Copaken in Svingel's house at 4 P.M. on April 18, he read from a written statement: "The Soviet side wishes no further discussion, and warns of possible attempts at political blackmail. What Secretary Kissinger was told still remains valid, including the statement that the Soviet side reserves the right to return to the question of Artamonov's [Shadrin's] return to the Soviet Union."[30]

Again, Vogel emphasized discretion. His mandate to negotiate on the case, he warned, would only be valid if he had ironclad assurances from Copaken that there would be no repetition of the breach of confidentiality with Vorontsov. He repeated the point in a letter that Copaken received in Washington on May 3.

But on May 13, Kissinger himself entered the fray, briefing Dobrynin about the whole case, apparently also emphasizing that whatever else the United States might be willing to do for Shadrin, it was not willing to pressure Chancellor Helmut Schmidt to free the Guillaumes—not in mid-1976, less than six months after they had been sentenced. When Copaken returned to Berlin one last time to see Svingel, he was told that Vogel could no longer meet with him on the case, because the Soviets had taken umbrage. On June 6, back in Washington, Copaken received a letter from Vogel telling him, with regret, that his "mandate" had been withdrawn.

Perhaps the truth was that Vogel's fishing expedition had taken him a little too far. Josef Streit warned him off the case. The Soviets were not interested in having Vogel involved in this one, Streit told him, without further elaboration. According to Vogel, this was the first indication he had been given that the Soviets were displeased. Copaken remained skeptical, and blamed Kissinger for scuttling Vogel's efforts, apparently deliberately. "Vogel may or may not have been on a fishing expedition, or if he had begun on one, he may have been finally handed the pole only to have it yanked back out of his hands when Kissinger moved against Shadrin," he wrote.[31]

Vogel could no longer use Shadrin as a lever to pry the Guillaumes out of jail. He would have to persist, and to come up with other names.[32]

The next one that Vogel tried to use to exchange for Guillaume was Adolf-Henning Frucht, a physicist whom a secret East German military tribunal had tried for espionage in early 1968. Vogel had defended Frucht, scion of a distinguished family of German scientists, apparently at the Stasi's orders. Frucht had originally asked for another lawyer, but his Stasi interrogator had told rejected his choice: "You can't have him. Take Herr Vogel, he's good too."[33] Vogel's name was new to Frucht, who had not known that his wife had already approached Vogel for help.

Frucht had been director of a scientific institute in Leipzig, and had passed to American intelligence information on secret East German programs to develop chemical weapons. He had confessed to much, but not all, of his espionage activities during interrogation. Vogel, who had come to see him for only a few minutes before the trial had begun, had read the indictment and asked, "Is this true?" Frucht acknowledged that it was. "What kind of sentence do you think you'll get?" Vogel asked. "Ten or fifteen years," Frucht guessed.

"You'll probably get life," Vogel corrected him. "Did you really have to tell all this to the investigators?" he asked, looking at the ten-page indictment. Then he had uttered the crucial words: "The best thing is for you not to testify. Our best chance will come after the trial."

Frucht's three judges had unpromising names—Hammer, Nagel, and Sarge, "Hammer, Nail, and Coffin" in German—and the prosecutor's name was Richter, for "Judge." The prisoner would be lucky, Vogel thought, not to get a death sentence. But the verdict had been life imprisonment, for "serious crimes committed on behalf of imperialist secret services." Later, in Bautzen prison, visiting

Frucht on one of his trips to pick up the political prisoners that Bonn had bought free, Vogel asked him, alluding to the BND, "Did you ever have any contacts with the people in Munich?" Frucht had not; his only contacts, always through an intermediary, had been with the Americans. "Too bad," Vogel had told him. "If you had, maybe you wouldn't have had to sit here behind bars for so long." Frucht remained suspicious; but his wife, a frequent visitor to Vogel's office in the Reilerstrasse, was persuaded that he was doing everything in his power to help.[34]

Vogel went to see Herbert Wehner in his Hamburg constituency three times during 1976, and how to get Guillaume out of prison always figured in the discussions. When Vogel mentioned Frucht's case to him, Wehner was incensed to learn that the Americans had not lifted a finger to do anything to get him out of jail for eight years. "Orphans" such as Frucht always irritated Wehner, who felt that whatever loyal agents had done, on either side, they were owed loyalty back by those for whom they had worked. The Stasi was certainly showing its loyalty to Guillaume; Wehner could dismiss Vogel's attempts to obtain his freedom, but he could not despise them. But leaving somebody like Frucht in the lurch was something he could despise, for deeply German reasons. The Americans treated their German agents with contempt, Wehner feared, precisely because they were Germans.[35]

Schmidt simply would not hear about exchanging Frucht for Guillaume. Vogel got Frucht out of prison in June 1977, in an exchange with Jorge Montes, a high-ranking Chilean Communist jailed by Augusto Pinochet in the coup against Salvador Allende.[36]

Guillaume would not become a commodity of exchange until Schmidt finally decided that he needed to clear the air for another summit meeting with Honecker. This did not happen until 1981, and by that time the world was a changed place.

Moscow's deployment of medium-range SS-20 missiles in the European theater, and President Jimmy Carter's insistence on making the Soviets live up to their human rights promises, had led to a rapid deterioration in East-West détente. But the hopes that détente had aroused in both German states were hard for their leaders to ignore. Honecker and Schmidt had been trying to meet since 1977, but the growing tensions on both sides made a German-German summit politically impossible.

By the early 1980s, the Solidarity movement in Poland seemed to be testing the limits of Soviet patience; Schmidt, a friend of the former Polish Communist leader Edward Gierek, thought Solidarity's activities were a dangerous temptation to the Soviets to roll in with tanks and crush the challenge to Communist power. The Polish border was only sixty miles from West Berlin, and Schmidt feared that armed Soviet intervention would also have unforeseeable consequences for the Germans.

The mounting tensions were undermining Schmidt's own political base in the Social Democratic Party. The chancellor viewed himself as a friend of America and had always considered the Atlantic Alliance the bedrock of West German independence. It had been Schmidt who had first called attention to the dangers posed to Western Europe by the deployment of Soviet medium-range SS-20 rockets in the mid-1970s, Schmidt who had pledged Germany to the NATO response that matched the SS-20s with American missiles, but offered the possibility of negotiations that would reduce or eliminate all such weapons on both sides in the future.

The Soviet invasion of Afghanistan in 1979 and the election of the Reagan administration a year later brought the contradictions in West German politics to a head. Schmidt wanted some sign of hope to give his people, a sign that relations between the two Germanies, at least, would not go into the deep freeze. He had twice put off Honecker's invitation to make a state visit to East Germany, most recently in August 1980, because of the threatening crisis in Poland.

As soon as he took office in 1981, President Ronald Reagan began a tremendous American military buildup, and instead of cultivating better relations with the Soviet Union, the new administration dismissed it as an "evil empire." The talk and the tensions profoundly unsettled millions of West Germans who had never known war and had believed passionately in détente. Now many people inside Schmidt's Social Democratic Party began charging that his pro-American policies were exposing them to the danger of nuclear annihilation, and he needed something to pacify them. He needed, as well, something to pacify his increasingly restive coalition partner, Hans-Dietrich Genscher, now the foreign minister, whose tiny Free Democratic Party was suffering in the public opinion polls so badly that it feared for its continued existence in the next elections.

In this tense and complex atmosphere many Germans, not for the first time and not for the last, wanted compromise with the "evil empire," not confrontation with it. Schmidt, who shared some of their fears about the recklessness of the Reagan administration, sought to show by example that, even in crisis, East and West could continue dialogue and avoid confrontation.

As the prospect of outright Soviet intervention in Poland seemed to recede, Schmidt invited Brezhnev to come to Bonn in November. Honecker was pressing him to accept his invitation to come to East Berlin the following month, and Schmidt wanted to accept.[37]

Vogel was pressed into service as a diplomatic sherpa once more, shuttling back and forth between Bonn, Hamburg, and Berlin to prepare for the summit. But first, Günter Guillaume had to be gotten out of the way.

By the middle of the summer of 1981, Guillaume had been behind bars for seven years, more than half the sentence he had received a year and a half after his arrest. The scars caused by his contribution to Willy Brandt's demise had healed. If the West German secret services were prepared to release him, by now, at last, Schmidt would have no objection to letting him go.

It had not been Schmidt but Edgar D. Hirt, Vogel's regular negotiating partner in what was by now called the Ministry for Intra-German Relations—less offensive, to East Germans, than the Christian Democrats' earlier name for it, the Ministry of All-German Affairs—who had brought the word to Vogel at the end of August. Vogel had come to know Hirt well, better than his predecessor Rehlinger. Edgar Hirt was no stuffy Christian Democrat but a man of simple German origins like Vogel himself, twelve years his junior. He, Vogel, and Stange had taken to addressing each other informally, as "*Du,*" as if they were members of a secret fraternity together—indeed, in a way they were. Hirt had known Guillaume well and had been on similarly intimate terms with him, as well, before his arrest. And afterward, from time to time, Hirt, as the chancellor's designated official handling humanitarian affairs, had visited Guillaume in Rheinbach prison. He was worried about Guillaume's high blood pressure and kidney ailment.

"If you want to get any of your agents out in exchange for Guillaume," Hirt had told the West German security chiefs, "you'd better act fast. We won't get much back for a cadaver."[38]

Vogel had stepped up the pressure, too, in 1980, warning with concern that the authorities in East Berlin might throttle down the prisoner exchanges and the family reunifications, inflicting pain and hardship needlessly on the innocent ordinary people both sides meant to help, unless Bonn relented.

It did, and things began to move the following year. In late March, still insisting that Guillaume was not up for negotiation, the West Germans secretly released his wife at Herleshausen, in an exchange for six imprisoned German agents. One of these was a well-known West German journalist, Peter Felten, who had been sentenced to twelve years in 1979 on charges of espionage. Christel Guillaume had served seven years of her eight-year sentence.

By the first of October, Vogel and Hirt had finally hammered out an agreement. The East Germans agreed to pay a heavy price for the spy in the chancellor's office, releasing eight captured agents of West German, American, and British intelligence services, including three who were serving life sentences.[39] The entire exchange was to be carried out in secret; the names of the prisoners were never to be made public, and Hirt himself made arrangements to ensure that the West German press got no wind of the actual deed. Guillaume's physical ailments had forced the West Germans to transfer him to the Bonn University clinic on the Venusberg, an isolated spot on a forested hilltop to the west of the town, and reporters and photographers lay in wait outside the gates.

The BND hired a repair-service delivery van to smuggle Guillaume unobserved out of the hospital and into a waiting helicopter for the one-hour flight to Herleshausen. But the proprieties also had to be observed. Hirt himself, who was about Guillaume's height and stocky build, drew an advance from the federal treasury to go into Bonn to the C & A Department store to buy the prisoner a presentable new blue-serge suit, a dress shirt, and a red tie. The West Germans wanted him looking well cared for when he went back home.[40]

Vogel was waiting, in his Mercedes, in the house trailer the West Germans had brought up to the border crossing point, away from the prying eyes of the press, for the exchange. It was dark when Hirt and the two security men accompanying the prisoner arrived.

"I'd figured on seeing you a lot sooner," Guillaume grinned wearily when he shook hands with Vogel.

Erich Mielke had wanted even the devil's advocate to be kept in the dark for part of this fall evening. Vogel was not to take Guillaume across the border, for Mielke had not wanted him to see who was in the reception committee. So it was Hirt who brought him, under the floodlights, to the striped metal barrier pole, and saw him home to the country that had sent him West secretly twenty-five years before. He had done more damage single-handedly to East German interests than all the West Germans agents combined.

Vogel had not minced words when Streit and Mielke had questioned why he had been unable to secure Guillaume's release much earlier. "This case brought down a government and changed history," Vogel had told them. "It will take time for the grass to grow over it."[41]

But by the late 1970s and early 1980s, the West Germans and the East Germans needed each other too much to refuse to have anything to do with each other merely on account of a spy who had brought down a chancellor. The existence of the Vogel channel enabled Schmidt to proceed toward a normalization of relations at a time when his main ally, in Washington, did not want him to.

Honecker entrusted much of the work of preparing Schmidt's visit to East Germany to his unofficial negotiator, and the visit finally went ahead in December 1981, after Brezhnev had given the green light. Through Vogel, Schmidt had told Honecker that he wanted to talk in full confidence, *"fortiter in re, suaviter in modo, cordialiter in modo,"* hoping, inventing the Latin as he went along, that Honecker would get the idea that Schmidt wanted relations to be as positive as they could be given the uncertainties on the broader international scene.

Through Vogel, Honecker had made it clear that the lines of international policy were not their concern, and the two German leaders could try to keep taking small steps to reduce the tensions between them. Schmidt had hoped to persuade Honecker to rescind a raise in the daily minimum amount of hard currency West Germany had to exchange on visits to the East, a sudden increase the East Germans had imposed in 1980 from 6.50 marks a person to 25 a day, a sum that was beyond the reach of many elderly pensioners. The result was that the number of Western visitors had fallen by half.

Vogel had encouraged the West Germans to expect some progress. He also encouraged Klaus Bölling, the West German ambassador in East Berlin, in the belief that the chancellor would be able to meet some of the local people during an excursion to the countryside not far from the meeting place, an official guest house on the Werbellinsee, just north of Berlin.[42] But in truth, Honecker's room for maneuver was more limited than Vogel had led the West Germans to believe. East Germany needed the money too badly to reverse the decision on the minimum exchange. And a sudden dramatic turn of events in Poland cast a shadow on the plans Bölling and Vogel had negotiated for a visit by the chancellor to the old cathedral town of Güstrow in Mecklenburg, in north Germany near Rostock.

The morning of December 13 had brought the news of the imposition of martial law by General Wojciech Jaruzelski. Schmidt got the impression that Honecker had had no better idea than he had of when the Communists would be forced to crack down. Schmidt thought Honecker seemed almost relieved that Soviet troops and tanks had not gone in, for if they had, the East German leader would have been forced to express his approval. This would have been politically awkward, but no more awkward, perhaps, than Schmidt's presence on Communist territory not a hundred miles from Polish soil. "Herr Honecker was just as upset as I that this was necessary," Schmidt told a press conference, hoping it was true, and trying to quiet the uproar already beginning at home about what some thought amounted to West German complicity in the invasion.[43]

The Stasi turned Schmidt's visit to Mecklenburg into farce. The snow-swept streets were lined with people, all of them men, and almost all of them Stasi officers. "We won't hide him away if he goes to the provinces," Vogel had promised. But in its insecurity, the Stasi had hidden the local population away from possible political or ideological contamination by the chancellor, showing not only the West Germans but Vogel the limits of his powers. It was not the first time, and it would not be the last.[44]

CHAPTER EIGHT

CORRUPTION

*"If I had had a mocha cup in my hand,
I would have dropped it."*

The source of Vogel's power and influence was his connection with the Stasi and the Communist party leadership, a connection that greatly magnified his talents as a lawyer, made him indispensable to his Western contacts, but also drew him into the dark, corrupt side of the regime. Vogel had worked to help thousands of people reach freedom, but he also made money because his government had held them in bondage. Vogel worked hard for his money, but he owed every penny he made to his connections with a system that was becoming more arbitrary and corrupt with every passing year. By the mid-1970s, he had become, in all but the formal sense, a member of the ruling elite. How much Vogel knew about the regime's lawlessness, and the extent of his complicity with it, were questions that would arise only much later. For the time being, the Communist way of doing things was shrouded in secrecy, a situation that suited many of the shadowy characters involved in the business that East and West Germans did with each other in the murkier recesses of the cold war.

Vogel's work from the mid-1970s through the mid-1980s brought him into daily contact with the moral corruption that underlay the system he served. It was almost built into the prisoner-release program, which the Communists were by now treating like just one more of the shady businesses that Alexander Schalck-Golodkowski ran with smoke and mirrors, with no objections from the West Germans. At the working level where the dirty business of peaceful coexistence got done, expediency, not moral integrity, was the guiding principle. And Vogel was no more immune to damage than some of his Western negotiating partners were—and no more interested in publicity about the extent of the corruption.

This decade was a time when the East German regime was becoming increasingly arbitrary and autocratic, and Vogel was often appalled. But self-preservation usually made him keep his disdain to himself. The Stasi was capable of terrible things, things Vogel was not always able to do anything about, as an unfortunate couple named Otto and Bärbel Grübel discovered.

They had unsuccessfully attempted to cross through the swampy woods from Czechoslovakia to West Germany with their two small children, Ota and Jeannette, in the summer of 1973. Because they had sedated the children to keep them quiet, they had irresponsibly placed their lives in danger, an East German court ruled after they were picked up by border guards and imprisoned; the children were taken away and placed with foster parents. The Grübels were convicted and sentenced to two years and ten months in prison.

Otto Grübel heard of Dr. Vogel's reputation for being able to work miracles in cases like this from fellow inmates in the Rummelsburg prison, and wrote to him in hopes of getting himself and his wife on the West German government's prisoner list and then using family reunification procedures to get the children out.

Vogel replied encouragingly in the early spring of 1975, saying that he had applied for permission for the entire family to leave the German Democratic Republic. And in March both Grübels were moved from Berlin to the Stasi prison in Karl-Marx-Stadt, a sign, according to their fellow prisoners, that release was not far off. There, later that spring, they were taken separately to meet Vogel and Jürgen Stange in one of the prison's visiting rooms. The Stasi had the room bugged, so to get his message across, Vogel seated Stange behind him while he talked with each Grübel separately. To each Vogel explained that they had to make a choice: They could remain in the East Germany, and possibly recover their children, or they could go to West Germany and risk never seeing their children again. Stange, by his facial expressions and gestures, left Bärbel Grübel with the clear impression that Vogel was signaling that they should go West, and he would take care of things later.[1]

So they risked it, boarding one of the buses to freedom on May 21, 1975. On the bus, Stange's friendly manner made the prisoners feel like breaking out a bottle and celebrating, something the West German lawyer usually did at the end of each of these missions, and sometimes earlier than that. Stange, too, had profited handsomely from the trade in political prisoners and enjoyed both the reputation that had come with it, and the gratitude of those who owed their freedom to him. Yet he also showed signs of being troubled by some part of the trade. Stange often drank heavily. Of course, few prisoners on a bus journey that was taking them away from Communist jail held a little too much good cheer against him.

Gratitude also went to Vogel, grave, gray, and dignified; he was touched by the occasional letters he got from former inmates after they arrived in the West. But more than a few also thought of him as, at least partly, a representative of the system that had kept them in jail.

The Grübels had become free West German citizens, but they knew nothing of the whereabouts of their children. Stange assured them that they would soon be free as well, and Vogel, after the New Year, as good as promised it, enlisting their support for a plan to get the children placed in custody of Bärbel's mother and then get permission for her to emigrate to West Germany. The Grübels agreed, but something went wrong and in July, the grandmother came West alone.

By this time, the Grübels had asked Reymar von Wedel, the Lutheran Church's lawyer in West Berlin, to use his connections with the Church and with Vogel to try to help them. But at the end of August, von Wedel gave Grübel ominous news: "Herr Vogel is meeting internal resistance," he told him. Two weeks later, Vogel himself met with the Grübels, confessing: "There are people in the G.D.R. who don't want your children to leave. If we don't succeed by October 20, I don't see any more hope."[2]

In the end, Vogel could do nothing to get the children out. In this case, Vogel claimed, even Heinz Volpert could not tell him who had blocked their release. Vogel asked Josef Streit whether Margot Honecker, minister of the People's Ministry of Education and the party leader's second wife, had interfered; it was her ministry that enforced the laws enabling the state to take children away from parents who had placed them in danger or had simply failed in their "socialist duty" to raise the children as loyal citizens of the East Germany. Margot Honecker, a hardline ideologue whom Vogel found far less sympathetic than her husband, could have prevailed on Honecker not to let the children go. But Streit assured Vogel that she had had nothing to do with the case.

Circumstantial evidence points to Erich Honecker himself. The case had been the subject of a series of critical articles in the aggressive weekly news magazine *Der Spiegel* at the end of 1975, so critical that East Germany expelled the magazine's East Berlin correspondent, Jörg Mettke. Such a decision would have had to have Honecker's approval. Moreover, the case had become a political controversy in Bonn. Honecker's honor and pride had become engaged too directly to let Vogel negotiate a compromise that would have looked like a concession that the East Germans had been in the wrong.[3]

But according to Streit, other instances had been responsible. Vogel never found out who was responsible, but suspected interference by middle-ranking Stasi functionaries jealous of his status and determined, in this case and others, to show him they knew how to keep him in his place.[4]

The conservative West German Christian Democratic opposition unleashed a barrage of questions in the Bundestag at Egon Franke, the gruff and secretive Social Democrat who had replaced Wehner as Intra-German minister. The Christian Democrats had tried and failed in 1972 to bring down Brandt on the question of establishing relations with East Germany and the Eastern European countries. How, they asked now, could Bonn go on negotiating with an inhuman regime that, almost like the Nazis, took children away from their parents? And how long, under these circumstances, could Bonn go on buying prisoners from such a regime? The public airing of these issues became increasingly acrimonious and contentious, and Vogel himself came under fire for carrying on a questionable trade in human souls.

Vogel also knew that not all was kosher in the secret hard-currency financial empire Schalck-Golodkowski had built to try to keep the German Democratic Republic, or at least the Communist party, solvent. His "Commercial Coordination" empire, CoCo, became independent from the Foreign Trade Ministry in 1976, making Schalck answerable only to his superiors in the Stasi and to Günter Mittag, Honecker's economic czar in the Politburo. CoCo controlled the money that Bonn paid for the release of political prisoners, paying it into the secret hard-currency bank accounts controlled directly by Erich Mielke and Honecker himself, from where it went into the pot used to buy embargoed Western technology, weapons, raw materials, and anything else the Communists wanted.[5]

Schalck and Heinz Volpert also had other ways of using political prisoners to bring in West German money, ways in which Vogel was implicated.

In the early years, people who had left East Germany could continue to own property there and to sell it after leaving, though under restrictive rules that set a price ceiling at prewar—1936!—property values. Communist ideology forbade "speculation," so there was no real property market anyway. Vogel had often dealt with West German lawyers on such sales, on behalf of clients who had rented properties in East Germany from such absentee owners and now wanted to buy them; on occasion, he had even quietly been able to arrange sales for West German marks, though technically this was illegal.

With the move toward normalizing relations between the two German states at the beginning of the 1970s, East Germans were allowed to receive marks from their relatives, and Schalck set up hard-currency stores in East Berlin and other cities so that the state could soak up as much of this hard currency as possible. Furthermore, the rules were tightened for the few people who were legally permitted to give up their East German citizenship and leave for the West. In 1977, the Ministry of the Interior and the Ministry of Finance issued secret regulations instructing that people who wanted to leave the country had to sell their property and valuables at prices the state dictated.[6] This was, in fact, blackmail, and the state made lawyers who helped the emigrants into its accomplices. But this was accepted at the time, in both East and West, as simply the way the Communists did things.

Vogel knew about some of the underhanded practices of Schalck-Golodkowski's operations. In April 1975, for example, Schalck had brought him into a case involving an antique dealer named Siegfried Kath. Kath had managed to make himself rich, by East German standards, by combing the castles and country houses in the East German countryside for valuable artifacts and then selling them to Western buyers for deutsche marks, through an affiliate of CoCo, a front company called Art and Antiques, Inc. He had done so well that Schalck's deputy, Manfred Seidel, had set up a branch of the affiliate for Kath in an abandoned water mill near Pirna, making him a copartner in the business along with Horst Schuster, one of the two principals in Art and Antiques, Inc. Kath had earned himself healthy commissions, with such benefits as a West German Audi 100 car, and filled the house with nearly a thousand antiques of his own.

Seidel soon concluded that Kath was looking out for himself more than for the Stasi's business. On April 18, a troop of Stasi agents and a prosecuting attorney had knocked on the door of the water mill and arrested Kath on charges of embezzling nineteen thousand East German marks.[7] The investigation dragged on into early 1975. Kath had not yet been formally indicted when, in early April, a prosecutor from East Berlin had come to visit him in the Stasi jail in Dresden to suggest that he engage a new lawyer: Wolfgang Vogel.

Kath wrote on April 23, and a few days later, Vogel came to see him in Dresden. He had good news: the prosecution had agreed not to indict, if Kath would give up all his property and belongings to the state as compensation for the estimated 150,000 marks in "damages" that his activities had caused. And if Kath and his wife wanted to leave for West Germany, Vogel could arrange that as well.

It was dawning on Kath by then, he later told the news magazine *Der Spiegel,* that Seidel and company were a band of thieves, an impression strengthened by their suggestion, on the eve of his resettlement, that if he kept his mouth shut about the state's business methods in the antique trade, they would help him get started again in the West. Nevertheless, he took Vogel's advice and left behind his antique collection, with a value later assessed at more than 600,000 marks, giving power of attorney over his possessions to Horst Schuster, the partner with whom Seidel had set up Kath in business.[8] And on June 6, 1975, with no more criminal investigation against him pending, Kath went free across the Wartha-Herleshausen border.

An extensive report on the Kath story in *Der Spiegel* at the end of 1978 insinuated that Vogel, who had a fine appreciation of antiques himself, might have been involved in the profiteering. Vogel vigorously disputed the suggestion; he had bought all his antiques privately and honestly, he insisted. But he had warned Reymar von Wedel about CoCo: "Don't have anything to do with those people. They're involved in one rotten thing after another."[9] If nothing else, the Kath case showed how true this was, and showed that Vogel knew it. But if he had any vigorous objections to what Schalck and Seidel had done, he kept them to himself, and he collected a fee and expenses totaling 3,605 marks from Kath for managing to get him out.[10]

Whether Vogel knew about the systematic deception that Schalck was practicing on the West German government is less clear. Bonn was making its annual payments for political prisoners on the assumption that the trade vouchers it sent to East Germany were being used to buy food and consumer goods for the oppressed population. But by the mid-1970s, CoCo had the system firmly under its control. The Communists were indeed converting the trade vouchers into hard Western currency by selling commodities on the world markets, sometimes even before they reached East Germany, through phony front companies the Stasi set up in Liechtenstein. Some of the West Germans involved might have known about the process, but deliberately kept their eyes closed—always, of course, so as not to jeopardize the prisoner releases. By 1974, more than a hundred million marks a year from this source were flowing into the secret account controlled directly by Erich Honecker. It was entirely up to the Communist leader to decide whether to use the money for shoes, apples, and bananas for the people or for Western computers, bugging devices, and weapons for the Stasi—or simply to keep the money in the East German reserves.[11]

The state's need for hard currency continued to grow, and, through Volpert, Schalck instructed Vogel in 1977 to negotiate a hefty increase in the per capita price for political prisoners. For several years, the number of political prisoners the West Germans were buying free had been increasing, reaching a level of well above one thousand a year, and two or three times as many family reunifications. The head price of forty thousand marks a prisoner had really been only a base price, in any case. When Bonn gave Vogel lists of names, Vogel turned them over to Volpert, who returned them with a notation beside each one. A prisoner serving a short sentence, three or four years, could go for forty thousand marks. But for the release of a prisoner on a life sentence, Volpert would write "3X" after his name, a demand for triple the regular price. The West Germans would then respond, through Vogel, until final agreement was reached.[12]

Volpert instructed Vogel to negotiate a uniform price that would reflect the actual average of what the West Germans had actually been paying per prisoner over the years. After some discussion, the West Germans had agreed, setting the price at 95,847 marks, Vogel later related, so that no outsider would easily be able to figure out what it was—a uniform price per head.[13] Vogel himself was also earning more money from the West German government. His annual fees for taking care of the legal details that needed to be settled before the prisoners Bonn bought free could leave East Germany had risen to about 300,000 marks a year, paid by the West German government.[14] But with thousands of such cases every year, and considerable work involved, Vogel thought he had earned the money. Every prisoner released had to be legally pardoned by the courts and the East German Justice Ministry, and every case involved a raft of paperwork and visits to talk with individual prisoners in the Stasi jails in Bautzen and Karl-Marx-Stadt and Berlin.

The Stasi also authorized Vogel to "sell" prisoners privately, to friends or relatives who offered large sums of money. Usually, the offers came by themselves. Dr. Eberhard Hoene, for example, a lawyer from West Berlin, had come to Vogel in 1980 with a request from the family of a pair of brothers in Dessau who had applied for permission to emigrate, but had been denied it on the grounds that one of them had been employed in secret government work and could not leave for five years. The regular government-to-government channel was thus unavailable. But Hoene had solved cases like this with Vogel several times before—with private money, and so in this case he pressed Vogel to find out if a large sum would persuade the Stasi to change its mind. Vogel made inquiries through Volpert, and came back with a positive answer: 250,000 marks would do the trick. A well-off relative of the brothers in the Rhineland provided the cash, which Hoene delivered to Vogel in the spring of 1981, and the families were immediately allowed to leave. When Hoene reported this transaction, like the earlier ones, to the West German government authorities in Berlin who were in charge of the prisoner-release program, they raised no objections. Vogel kept none of the money for himself—it went directly to Volpert, who passed it on to CoCo—but he collected a fee of 5,000 marks, which was also paid in cash.[15]

Vogel later acknowledged that he had arranged about twenty such private "sales" over the years, mainly for people who had either political connections in West Germany or with the church.[16] More often, he claimed, he had urged clients to leave things to the regularly established government channels and save their money.[17] In truth, there seemed to be little moral distinction between the private sales and the public ones. The West German government discouraged private offers because it did not want the impression to arise that it favored East German prisoners with access to private wealth. If anybody was to pay organized bribes to the Stasi, it should be Bonn.

The prisoner-release operation had become so well known by the late 1970s that questions began to be raised about whether the East Germans were putting some people behind bars just to be able to raise hard currency by selling them off. Vogel did not believe this was the case, but he could see from talking to clients that people who were desperate to leave the country had sometimes deliberately committed "political" crimes in hopes of being bought out later by Bonn. He was reminded of a Jean Gabin film about a Parisian *clochard* who went to his lawyer every fall asking for legal advice on how to get jailed just long enough to get through the winter. Breaking a store window usually did the trick, until the clochard inadvertently smashed a jeweler's display case and got himself sentenced for attempted grand larceny, and jailed right through the summer. Clients were now coming to Vogel and asking detailed questions about which paragraphs of the law they could break that would ensure them of being condemned to short terms as political prisoners, and then included on the West German lists. You cannot be assured of any certainty that you will get on the list, or that some official somewhere won't scratch you off, Vogel told such people. It was dangerous for ordinary people to try to play such games with the Stasi, Vogel knew. He could do it, but it was irresponsible to let clients try.[18]

Vogel's own relationship with the Stasi had always been fraught with contradiction. He had resented being blackmailed into cooperating with it in the early 1950s, yet he had become a close friend of Heinz Volpert, who had helped make Vogel what he was. Volpert was also Schalck's control officer, but he was much more than that. CoCo had been as much Volpert's idea as Schalck's, and its success had earned Volpert a quasi-independent status that irritated many people within the Stasi. Volpert reported directly to Mielke, outside the regular chain of command, though he rose only to the rank of colonel. Vogel benefited from Volpert's connections, and indeed owed his own special status to them. Their questionable financial dealings were none of his concern.

Occasionally, Vogel revealed hints of his conflicted feelings. One client who did not fully appreciate it at the time was a traveling West German salesman from Osnabrück, Gerhard Strunk, who had been arrested on the East German autobahn in August 1977 on the way to a meeting in East Berlin. Strunk's Stasi interrogations had lasted for most of a year, as the secret police built a case of espionage and economic sabotage against him. Constantly, the interrogators told him that he would be let off with a comparatively light sentence if he confessed, but that if he refused to cooperate, he would get a life sentence. Strunk was no spy, but he knew that an East German court was hardly likely to acquit him, and the Stasi had twelve witnesses prepared to testify that he had tried to recruit them as agents for the West German BND.

Strunk's relatives in Osnabrück had engaged Vogel to defend him. Meeting with him in the Stasi jail, Strunk had been suspicious. "I did not have the courage to trust Dr. Vogel, because for me he was a 'G.D.R. lawyer,' " Strunk wrote later. Nor did he trust Vogel's advice not to confess, as the Stasi interrogators were pressing him to do. He went ahead and gave them what they were asking for.

About two weeks before his trial, in June 1978, Vogel asked Strunk what rank he had held in the BND. "Since I hadn't been in the Bundeswehr or any other military organization, I wasn't familiar with the ranking system," Strunk wrote. "Since my Stasi interrogator [a senior lieutenant] was about my age, I told Dr. Vogel that I had been a senior lieutenant in the BND. He then responded that I wasn't a senior lieutenant, but a captain. 'You are not a captain in the BND, but the Captain of Köpenick,' " Vogel mocked him, alluding to the Carl Zuckmayer comedy about an ex-convict who pretends to be a military officer.

At Strunk's trial in the Superior Military Court in Berlin, Vogel had openly alluded to his dissatisfaction with the Stasi's conduct by saying that he could not square the case with his conscience as a lawyer. Strunk was convicted and sentenced to fifteen years' imprisonment. Vogel was outraged, and immediately lodged an appeal. Finally, he succeeded in obtaining freedom for Strunk by getting him included in an amnesty on September 24, 1979. Cases such as these left a bitter taste in Vogel's mouth, for they tainted not only East German "justice" but all who, like himself, thought it should live up to its name.[19]

But even the amnesty, announced by Honecker in connection with the German Democratic Republic's thirtieth anniversary, was corrupted by the leadership's need for hard currency. More than two thousand former prisoners had been released across the border to West Germany in the last big amnesty seven years earlier, but this time, of the 21,928 people freed, only four East German political prisoners, including two well-known dissidents, Rudolf Bahro and Nico Hübner, had been permitted to go West. The result in the Federal Republic was a public uproar. Once again it had been made clear that Honecker would do nothing for free that he could make Bonn pay hard currency for; once again, there were questions about whether the Federal Republic was being played for a sucker. And once again, the East Germans reacted by threatening to stop the releases altogether. The last bus transport from Karl-Marx-Stadt had left on October 9. When there would be another one was highly uncertain.

Vogel skillfully pinned the blame for the breakdown on the West Germans, granting one of his rare interviews to a West Berlin newspaper, *Der Abend,* and hinting that the opponents of detente were more interested in propaganda than in the welfare of individual clients like those he represented. "I see dark, black clouds on the horizon in this respect," he said, "now that it has become fashionable to make honest help grist for the scandal and gossip market. Let the people who are doing the damage take over my office consultations from now on."[20] Contemplating the possible consequences of their own outrage, the West Germans, as always, backed down, the press got the word to go easy, and the prisoner transports resumed in March 1980. For the East Germans did, in fact, need the money.

The Christian Democrats would clean up the political prisoner business, but they did not stop it after they took power again in October 1982. According to documents later found in Schalck's files, Chancellor Helmut Kohl's Bavarian coalition partner and rival, the legendarily anti-Communist Franz Josef Strauss, brought the news in late 1983 that the chancellor wanted a change. Behind the scenes, Strauss had found Schalck the kind of Communist he could do business with, and he told him that Kohl was debating whether the prisoner-release and spy-exchange business ought to be done differently in the future. "The Chancellor is of the view that in the future, important cases should be dealt with directly between the Federal Chancellor's office and the Permanent Mission of the G.D.R. in Bonn, bypassing the lawyer Dr. Vogel," Strauss told Schalck, who responded that this would be out of the question. "I got the strong impression," he reported later to Mielke, "that Strauss has a view no different from our own of the position and person of Attorney Vogel."[21]

So the prisoner releases continued. "One day, one of us is going to have to stop this," Vogel had told Rehlinger in one of the sessions over the list. But it would never be Bonn that called off the program. As Rehlinger later wrote, "As long as the G.D.R. would grant freedom to innocent persons only in exchange for economic concessions, the Federal Republic of Germany was not in a position of being able to say no, on the grounds of the moral rules of democracy and probably also on legal grounds."[22]

But by the mid-1980s, the prisoners in the exchanges were of a totally different category from those of twenty years earlier. Then, political prisoners had been, by and large, people who had struggled against the establishment of the Communist regime—Social Democrats, for example, who had resisted the forced merger of their party with the Communists, or people accused of sabotage of state-owned industry, or labor unionists who had taken their calling too seriously in a state where unions were instruments of production just like state-owned factories. Now political prisoners were, in the vast majority, people accused of trying to flee the country, or of crimes associated with trying to flee. The game of getting arrested, and then getting freed by Dr. Vogel, seemed merely to add to the general atmosphere of moral corruption.

Vogel also discovered that his "humanitarian efforts" had the effect of subtly undermining the system of repression, in small ways, diminishing respect for the police who arrested the prisoners, for the prosecutors and judges who sent them to prison for wanting to leave, and for the Stasi guards who watched over them in prison and then saw them board the bus to freedom solely because their government was willing to sell them to the West Germans for money. Even the prisoners could see these things. Karl-Ulrich Winkler, a twenty-year-old rebel who was released on November 25, 1981, noticed when he and other lucky inmates were told to get ready to be transported to Karl-Marx-Stadt, the first station on the way West. "We could often tell by the mood of the pigs whether or not a transport was coming. Before the transports, they were especially moody and bothered us more than usual. They knew that we'd soon be free in the West, and they'd still have to be guarding the jail," Winkler wrote. Riding in the bus behind Vogel's car—now a blue Mercedes—from Wartha into the no-man's zone before the crossing to Herleshausen, Winkler wondered whether the other passengers had the same thought that was going through his mind: They had wanted to leave, had tried to flee and had been arrested. Now they were getting what they had wanted, and it must have irked their jailers. At the border, when the two Stasi guards accompanying the "transport" had gotten out, the West German bus driver had announced over the intercom, "We're rid of them." The bus had echoed with the cheers of the prisoners.[23]

But the regime needed fear to maintain itself in power, and people were losing their fear. Instead of a safety valve, the prisoner releases had become a political time bomb, for the regime and for everybody associated with it, including Vogel. "People began risking more themselves, because in the back of their minds they were figuring, 'If it goes wrong, I can always be bought free,' " Vogel said. "Somebody would hang out a banner saying 'Long Live Gorbachev,' or go to the Friedrichstrasse Station and show an identity card without a visa and say 'Let me go to the West,' hoping to be arrested and later bought free."[24] Step by step, doors and cracks were being opened in the Wall. Every time an aunt was allowed to visit an uncle across the border, every time a prisoner took the bus from Wartha to Herleshausen, every time an East German politician went to Bonn to negotiate or a West German politician came to Berlin, or Erfurt, or Rostock, the cracks grew wider, steadily weakening the structure of oppression.

The weaker they got, the more paranoid the old leaders like Mielke became, extending the Stasi's snooping far and wide throughout the society and authorizing it to do terrible things to coerce its citizens into behaving as it wished.

Even when he tried to alleviate the worst of these abuses, Vogel sometimes ran the risk of complicity by association. What, for example, were people in West Germany to make of a letter like this, written by Vogel to Rüdiger and Beate Hobusch, a couple held in the Stasi prison in Karl-Marx-Stadt in July 1984?

You know that a decision on the custody of your daughter Patricia has not yet been made. As I have been informed by the court in Halle, it is to be expected that neither you, Mrs. Hobusch, nor you, Mr. Hobusch, will be awarded custody. The consequence would be remand to an orphanage.

"This could be prevented, if Mrs. Daniel from Wismar got custody. She told me in May of this year that she would be agreeable. If you concur, please transmit to me an appropriate written statement for the court in Halle. Only in this case do I see the possibility of success for your application for release from citizenship.

Respectfully,
Dr. Vogel
Attorney-at-law

"In my eyes, that's extortion," Hobusch, later released from the prison, told a hearing of the German Section of the International Society for Human Rights in Bonn–Bad Godesberg. When asked who "Mrs. Daniel" was, he acknowledged that she was his mother-in-law.

The case was an outrage nevertheless, as the society was right to imply in its documentation pamphlet published later. But it was wrong to pin the blame for it on Vogel. The letter had been presented to the Hobusches not in a personal meeting with Vogel himself but by a Stasi officer in the prison in Karl-Marx-Stadt. The true outrage was what the state had already done to people like the Hobusches, and might yet have done if Vogel had not been able to intercede.

Systematically, Stasi agents had driven the parents apart. Beate Hobusch had been a twenty-four-year-old hairdresser, and her husband a thirty-one-year-old industrial assembly-line worker when they had applied to leave Halle for West Germany in 1979. The Stasi not only disapproved their applications, it set about to ruin their lives with a campaign of personal disinformation. The pattern was a familiar one, documented many times over in the similar cases that would come to light after the Stasi files began to leak out to the public after unification. Stasi agents told Beate that her husband had been lying when he said he was working overtime, and that he had actually been visiting his girlfriends instead; they even told her that he had become a Stasi informer. Rüdiger was told that his wife had been playing around with other men in the pubs in Halle, and even, once, that she had not come to work at all for two days. The campaign had worked; the Hobusches began to argue, they separated, and in May 1982 they were even divorced. A complaint to the human rights society against denial of permission to emigrate had landed both of them in trouble on a charge of "treasonous transmittal of information," and after their arrests in November of that year the child, and Hobusch's son from an earlier marriage, had been taken in state custody. Both parents were sentenced to more than six years' imprisonment.[25]

Vogel's intervention saved Patricia for the family, leaving her in Mrs. Daniel's care. He also managed to get permission for the Hobusches to leave for West Germany in September and enabled the child to be reunited with them later.[26]

It was not Vogel's fault that the East German state enforced draconian laws or used immoral methods, he thought. When he succeeded in mitigating such evils, he thought he deserved credit and praise, not accusations that he had become an accomplice. Vogel, unable to understand why people he had helped sometimes turned against him in this way, was deeply hurt, and took consolation from the scores of letters from more properly grateful former clients. Vogel thought of these as bouquets, the flowers German patients traditionally give a surgeon after a successful operation, and the reproaches hurt like stabs into the quick.

But a few, a very few, of the hundreds of thousands of people whose settlement in West Germany he arranged, through family reunifications and prisoner releases, even held the fees he later charged them in marks against him. Dr. Wulf Rothenbächer, a human rights group officer whom the Stasi had imprisoned on political charges in East Germany, had taken Dr. Vogel as his lawyer and then complained bitterly about the bill for 623.97 marks in West German currency that he had had to pay after Vogel had gotten the Bonn government to buy him freedom. "Human trade on behalf of the Stasi," Dr. Rothenbächer charged, as if Vogel's West Berlin bank account had been proof enough of the accusation.[27] That it would have been impossible, under East German law, for Vogel to send a bill in East German marks to a client in West

Germany seemed, to such critics, beside the point. The amount was the equivalent of only a few hundred dollars in the early 1980s.

But, multiplied by thousands over the years, such amounts piled up. The West German government paid the fees for thousands of such cases—as much as 1.5 million marks a year—and much of this money went to Vogel. Besides this, after 1984, he received from Bonn a blanket annual retainer of 360,000 marks to cover the expenses and routine work of handling a minimum of 6,000 cases a year. By then Vogel was generously paying underlings to do much of the ordinary legal work for him in courts around the country, but these payments were in East German marks, not West German currency. He was doing very well indeed by doing good. In a country where the state imposed poverty on most of its citizens and called it socialism, Dr. Vogel could see nothing wrong with his high lifestyle. There was nothing in Marx that stipulated that Communists had to be poor, he insisted.

The "Datscha" he had bought on the Schwerinsee had grown, over the years, into something that looked even to the East German craftsmen and carpenters who worked on it more like an estate than a cabin. The front gate and a wall on the quiet street opened up on a richly planted garden, acres and acres of manicured grass, roses, and shrubs, watered in the summer by irrigation pipes and hoses. The Mercedes sheltered safely in a garage built onto the side of the house, with a lean-to roof to keep the snow off in winter. The back lawn led down to a gazebo on a pier, with another garage for a sailboat. And inside, a kitchen with all the latest West German appliances, a Miele dishwasher, a washing machine, and a dryer; in the living room, a dark wood antique cupboard from Potsdam, and a glass vitrine displaying Meissen and Dresden-China birds, Russian icons, statues, Oriental carpets. It was not luxury, by West German standards; it was comfort, with overstuffed sofas and chairs and kitsch, the kind of life millions of people could live in the *Bundesrepublik.* But in East Germany, outside of the walled-in Stasi compound in Wandlitz where Honecker, Mielke, and the rest of the Politburo lived, there was nothing like it at all.

Vogel's neighbors did not hold his lifestyle against him; he was always willing to put his connections to work to help them. He was besieged by requests to help people get the permission the Communist bureaucracy required for the smallest things—to buy a van, to build an additional room in their homes, to buy glass to replace a window—but he was always happy to be of service. Helping people, he liked to think, was the central purpose of his life. But it also fed his sense of righteous self-importance. Vogel would even take moral short cuts to help people because, he told himself, the end justified the means. At the time, few people in East Germany worried much about whether powerful people paid much attention to the proprieties.

Vogel had been glad to help when Peter Pragal, then a correspondent from the West German *Süddeutsche Zeitung,* asked him to help an East German friend, Waldemar Zapff, who had run afoul of the authorities and was trying to emigrate in 1980. When Vogel heard the details of what the Stasi had done to Waldemar and Vera Zapff, he was appalled. Pragal's mother-in-law and Waldemar Zapff's mother had gone to school together before the war, and as he had been about to begin his assignment to East Germany in 1974, he had written to the Zapff family in hopes of establishing personal contact. His letter had been intercepted by Stasi agents who had tried to pressure the Zapffs into collaborating by spying on Pragal. Waldemar Zapff had refused. The Stasi then charged him with economic crimes and imprisoned him until 1980. After his release, Zapff wanted to leave, and Pragal had asked Vogel to help.

The Zapffs owned two properties, a house in Köpenick and a cottage on a small plot of land on the Baltic Sea resort island of Rügen. Vogel told Waldemar Zapff—rather unpleasantly, Zapff told his friend later—that he could get him permission to leave, but that he would be obligated by the Interior Ministry's regulations to dispose of the properties first. Vogel could also expedite this, but he told Zapff that according to the rules of legal practice, he could not also represent Zapff in the sale.

Zapff sold the house to a man on a list of state-approved buyers that Vogel provided who later turned out to be a Stasi colonel, though Vogel professed to know nothing of the connection. But weeks later, Zapff came to Vogel and said he had been unable to find a buyer for the property in Rügen. Waving the paper fixing the assessed value of the property, 14,100 East German marks, he pleaded with him to buy it himself, threw the key down on Helga Vogel's desk, and said, "At least go take a look at it."[28]

When he finally went to see the property, Vogel was disappointed. It was barely one thousand square meters, or less than one hundred feet on a side, and the cottage was just a shack. But he thought it might be handy as a place to keep a sailboat, and since the Zapffs wanted to get out quickly, he agreed to buy it in Helga's name. She signed the contract on August 11.

The Vogels tore down the cottage and, with their own considerable resources in deutsche marks, built a rather more luxurious vacation home, one envied by all the neighbors. It was a marvel to them that Dr. Vogel had seemed able to import every brick from the West, but in reality all the work had been done by the Stasi, at Volpert's direction. Vogel secretly paid 803,709.10 East German marks for the work.[29]

So now the Zapffs were free at last. Vogel had taken the bungalow off their hands and facilitated the sale of the house in Berlin. Getting out was all they had wanted; the Zapffs never thought they would be back. Vogel did not think he had taken advantage of them; he had done them a favor. And as for the sale of their home, he thought it was not his business who the purchaser was. The Ministry of the Interior–approved lists helped clients who were anxious to leave, by shortening the time it took to get official approval for the sale of their property. That was what was important, as Vogel saw it—not who the purchaser was.

Vogel's services could be used by the Stasi, as other lawyers and notaries were also used. His emigration cases were piling up and speed was of the essence. In mid-1982, Vogel had not asked who Walter Henning really was when he appeared in his office to complete the formalities on the sale of a house in Wandlitz for Ulrich Pietzsch, an artist whose wife had lost her job as a solo ballet dancer with the Deutsche Staatsoper for political reasons. As soon as the Pietzsches applied for permission to leave, the Stasi's Department XXII, which was responsible for counterterrorism operations, moved to acquire the house, which was close to the leadership compound and could be used as a secret observation post. Henning was commissioned to buy it for the Stasi, with twenty thousand East German marks and authority to pay off two mortgages on the property. This he did, on June 14; the Pietzsches had been only too happy to be rid of it and to leave.[30]

Vogel was willing to bargain with the devil to get his clients what they needed. One day his double standard would be his undoing, as in the West it was already becoming the undoing of his main negotiating partner in the Social Democratic government in Bonn.

For on the West German side, too, lower-ranking churchmen and officials over the years had often not worried very hard about the moral dimensions of their secret dealings with the Communists.

Edgar Hirt, Vogel's main negotiating partner with the government in Bonn on spy exchanges and prisoner releases during the 1970s, had one standing order from Egon Franke, the minister for Inner-German Relations: Keep it quiet. On the most delicate cases, Franke would often tell him, if there were only two people who knew what had been done to solve them, that was already one too many. "Don't talk so much about it. Just get it done."[31]

Two more different men than Vogel and Hirt would be hard to imagine. Hirt was no lawyer; he was a political functionary, a scholarship student of humble social origins twelve years Vogel's junior. He had found his home in the Social Democratic Party, where he worked with Franke as one of the back-room boys who got things done while Brandt and his highfalutin intellectual friends such as Egon Bahr had been dreaming up their *Ostpolitik* and winning the Nobel Peace Prize for the chancellor. Franke was widely regarded as politically unassailable. He had impeccable credentials, having been imprisoned by the Nazis and sentenced to hard labor; he was also a man of few words, and Hirt fell under his spell.

Men such as these had had a bit of a complex when they had finally taken over the government from the Christian Democrats; they felt a mixture of inferiority and resentment. Konrad Adenauer's party claimed to have built West Germany out of the ashes, but it had built it with good German workers who belonged to the Social Democrats' constituency, not the Christian Democrats'. The "Sozis" had also resented Adenauer's attempts to dismiss them as "Reds," attempts that were successful long after Herbert Wehner had transformed the party platform. So many years of Christian Democratic government had led, not surprisingly, to a clubbiness between the government and many of the firms that did business with it, particularly, Hirt found, in the secret program of collaboration with church charities and commodity and shipping companies that arranged the payments for East German political prisoners.

By their very nature, these arrangements were an invitation to corruption. Everything was on a wink and a nod, with financial procedures that no private corporation's accountants would ever have approved. Hirt was no man of the world, no smooth operator, but a simple man with a well-developed sense of political loyalty to such rough-and-tumble operators as Franke who had brought him to where he was. He had struck up an easy friendship with Stange, finding his informality quite congenial. Vogel's frequent visits to Bonn were also welcome diversions from the usual Bonn routines, and Hirt found the East German lawyer to be a man of his word. Gradually, Hirt, Stange and Vogel began to think of themselves as a team, a band of brothers secretly doing battle in a noble cause.

Of the three, Vogel was clearly the superior intellect and the dominant personality. And in one respect, his side clearly held the negotiating advantage: East Germany possessed the political prisoners, the hostages to German division. West Germany could only try to get them out, on conditions the East Germans could dictate. To Hirt, the fact that his government and his chancellor had sanctioned what amounted to a secret business to get some of them out, and that both Protestant and Catholic church leaders were a part of it, meant that whatever it took to get them free was all right. Franke encouraged him in this belief. The minister did not want Hirt to haggle; he wanted him to get the job done and not to trouble him with the details. "The instruction of my minister, and of the cabinet at the time, was not to leave anything in writing about all these activities," Hirt insisted.[32]

Hirt was only too willing to comply, and East Germany was not the only Communist country demanding money in exchange for political concessions. Romania, for example, was demanding money to release the hundreds of thousands of ethnic Germans who lived there. Hirt began looking around for a discreet source of secret funds, and soon he put his finger on one: Heinz Thiel, director of the Catholic Church's Caritas charity in West Berlin, who worked closely with the Intra-German Ministry. Thiel was no ascetic churchman but a wheeler-dealer who could have come from the same mold as Egon Franke. He, too, shunned the limelight, was interested mainly in results, and was not too fussy about bookkeeping when it came to trying to help people living in a Communist dictatorship.

So when Edgar Hirt came to him with a proposition, Thiel was all ears. "There are some sensitive cases that can't be solved in any other way but cash," Hirt told him in confidence. He explained that Franke had authorized him to ask whether some of the money the church received every year from the ministry could be given back to him, in cash, for Hirt to use in making payments—payments for spy swaps, individual humanitarian cases, and the like.[33] The ministry would reimburse Caritas with surplus funds from its general budget that were always left over at the end of the fiscal year.

Thiel went along with the suggestion, agreeing to provide cash for "special cases," which for all he knew could be not only in East Germany, but in Romania, Poland, Hungary, or anywhere else the government needed money for special humanitarian operations. All he knew was that Jürgen Stange would have authorization from Hirt to call for the money; Thiel was to give him whatever amount he asked for, no questions asked. "It was not a formal legal agreement," Hirt said; "it was an arrangement."[34]

So now there was a new secret channel, even more hush-hush than the prisoner exchanges. According to Hirt, the Romanians had proved quite cash-thirsty indeed. Entire families of ethnic Germans seeking to emigrate and claim German citizenship had sometimes been arrested by the Securitate, the secret police arm of the most ruthless dictatorship the Communist world had known since Stalin's death. The official protests Hirt said he had made at the Romanian Embassy had had little effect. Bonn was willing to pay money to get East German political prisoners free, the Romanians had told him. What made Hirt think that the same means would not be effective with his country?

Hirt began inviting the ambassador or his deputy chief of mission into the ministry, for a chat and a cup of coffee, sometimes, he claimed, wordlessly slipping an envelope with 50,000 or 60,000 marks in it across the table. Freed with money thus drawn from the Caritas, the arrested ethnic Germans began to turn up at Frankfurt airport.[35] He paid the Bonn station chief of the Polish secret service 400,000 marks, Hirt claimed, so that a professor and his family could emigrate from Warsaw.[36] And in his last year in office, Hirt said, he had authorized the payment of 468,000 marks to the South African secret service in exchange for the return for the release of Aleksei M. Kozlov, a KGB spy for whom the East Germans were prepared to release eight West German agents.[37]

Possibly none of this would have come to light if Hans-Dietrich Genscher and his Free Democrats had not decided, in October 1982, to abandon their coalition partners and put the Christian Democrats back into the chancellor's office for the first time since 1969, with Helmut Kohl at the helm. Egon Franke, who had led the Intra-German Ministry for thirteen years, was now replaced by Rainer Barzel, who asked his old friend Ludwig Rehlinger to come back into the ministry as junior minister. Among Rehlinger's responsibilities was the work with which he was more familiar than almost anyone else, the "special efforts of the Federal Government in the humanitarian area." But in the transition, Rehlinger discovered that Franke had not allowed his predecessor to supervise Hirt's work.

The real shock came when Rehlinger learned that Hirt had been taking back some of the government's money in cash from Thiel. Oh yes, Thiel had told him, Franke had personally approved the arrangement, and Stange had often come by to pick up thousands of marks at a time. Thiel had receipts for all of them—a total of 5.56 million, the equivalent of about three million dollars, between 1978 and 1982. Stange himself had no idea what most of the money had been used for.[38]

Hirt insisted that all of the money had been needed for "humanitarian purposes," delicate matters that were in no one's interest to disclose. There were no records because, following Franke's instructions to keep the arrangements secret, Hirt had shredded all the papers.

When Rehlinger reported on the results of his investigations, Barzel had turned pale. A national election was coming the following March, and the last thing any of the national parties wanted was to turn the decades-old program of secret humanitarian payments to the East Germans into a political football.

So, in effect, they tried to bury it. The first thing they did was to dismiss Stange from his sinecure as Vogel's Western counterpart in Berlin. The second thing they did, in effect, was what Hirt and Franke had done—they "lost" the missing money. The all-party committee that monitored the secret traffic with the East Germans, purposely limited to three persons in the interests of keeping it secret, met several times and examined both Franke and Hirt, but it never got to the bottom of the affair. What had happened to the missing money, obtained by "gross violation of procedure" and illegally withdrawn from parliamentary accountability, the committee could not determine, it concluded on February 11, 1983. It recommended a criminal investigation to try to solve the mystery.

The same day, Franke made a statement assuming full responsibility and assuring the public that when it came to helping people in trouble, in East Germany or elsewhere in Eastern Europe, everything the federal government in Bonn had done had been on the up and up. "Any doubt that the funds under discussion were used for anything except humanitarian questions is resolutely rejected by me," he said. "The application of budget rules appropriate in other areas was completely impossible in this one, in view of the difficulties to be overcome and the need for absolute secrecy."[39]

Vogel claimed to have been unaware of Stange's role in the cash arrangement that Hirt had made with Caritas.[40] When he had first heard of the problem, Vogel had been appalled, worried that the scandal could jeopardize the entire framework of the prisoner releases worked out so carefully over the years, and even sounded out Schalck about finding some way for CoCo to provide Hirt with the missing money, to save them all considerable embarrassment. "But what if they discover it somewhere?" Schalck objected.[41]

Ludwig Rehlinger, back in the Inner-German ministry again after Chancellor Helmut Kohl took over the government, was also worried about the consequences. The new Christian Democratic government in Bonn wanted to keep the flow of political prisoners coming, and worried that the East Germans would stop it if they thought they were suspected of involvement in West German corruption. So Rehlinger had quietly informed Vogel of his findings. As far as Bonn could tell, he told him, none of the money had gone to the East German side. The government would be glad to state this publicly if the East Germans liked.

The Bonn prosecutor's office considered charges against Stange, dropped them, and eventually indicted both Franke and Hirt in the spring of 1984 on charges of negligence and suppression of evidence. But the investigators stumbled around in a fog of unspoken deals, contradictory assertions, and evasions by the various intelligence services. When the case finally came to trial in the summer of 1986, most of the testimony over the course of the six months it lasted was given in secret. When his turn came to testify, on July 21, Wolfgang Vogel told the judge in open session, "If I had had a mocha cup in my hand when State Secretary Rehlinger told me the news, I would have dropped it." "Do you have mocha over there?" the judge had asked. "Rest assured, we have mocha too," Vogel had replied. None of the missing money had gone to East Germany, directly or indirectly. Franke was a man of few words who had apparently given Hirt free reign to negotiate as the minister's alter ego, as Vogel saw it; Hirt had seemed to him as dedicated, concerned, and upright as any of his predecessors or successors. But Thiel and Stange had told him that what had become of the money was their problem, not his. "I hesitate to think what may have happened with it," Vogel said. "They were both such decent people."[42]

Stange's three days of testimony were among the many that were closed to the public, and for Hirt they were, in his words, a "catastrophe." Unable to recall any concrete details, unable to reconcile his testimony with Franke's, incoherent and, as far as anybody could tell, completely drunk, Stange was ordered by the judge to undergo a blood-alcohol test, which proved, however, to be negative. He was in shock, and among the reasons was that his close friend and colleague Wolfgang Vogel seemed to assume that he was guilty of having taken some of the money for himself. He distanced himself from his friend, and in his testimony, he was very reserved, Stange complained. He sank deeper into alcoholism, with long absences from his office his assistants explained as "illnesses," and became increasingly bitter about Vogel. "When my birthday came around, he came to visit me, but his opening words were only 'I don't have much time,' " Stange said later.[43] Hirt, too, felt that Vogel let him down, but his own testimony about having to make cash payments to secret services, East and West, was hard for the court to accept. "Herr Hirt," the judge kept telling him, "if you could produce evidence to support your testimony, you would do yourself a favor." Hirt vainly protested that Franke had ordered that everything be kept secret, and that this was why all traces of the irregular dealings had disappeared. Hirt had shredded them. "Whom do you think you're kidding?" the judge had asked.[44]

Franke, Hirt's minister, testified only that he had left all the details to Hirt and had assumed that he was acting at all times in accordance with sound legal and budgetary procedure. "Suddenly he could barely remember that I had ever worked for him at all," Hirt said bitterly.[45] Officials of the South African Embassy denied that they had received even a pfennig for releasing Kozlov or anybody else.

In the fog of the Cold War, the truth disappeared into the mist. Franke was found innocent, but Hirt was sentenced to three and a half years in jail. The presumption was that he had lined his own pockets, though none of the missing money was ever found in Hirt's possession.[46]

In 1986, Wolfgang Vogel's reputation was at its peak. Jürgen Stange and Edgar Hirt, his Western counterparts, were broken men, but Vogel was secure. The details, sordid or otherwise, of how he earned his living in East Berlin were secrets that seemed destined to remain forever safe behind the Wall. For at the Glienicke Bridge that February, he had achieved one of his greatest triumphs—the release of the Soviet dissident Anatoly Shcharansky in an East-West swap of agents, a goal for which Vogel had worked for nearly nine years with steady and single-minded dedication.

CHAPTER NINE

FISHING EXPEDITIONS

"I can get you Shcharansky."

ogel's reputation as a trader of spies entered its golden age
with the case of a man who was never a spy at all: Anatoly
Borisovich Shcharansky, whose championship of human
rights made him a martyr and a cause célèbre in the West.
From 1977 until the moment of Shcharansky's release in February 1986, Vogel worked steadily to obtain freedom for a
man the Stasi and the KGB insisted had been an American intelligence agent. It was a time of high tension in the East-West relationship, one that tested all Vogel's skills as a mediator. During most
of these nine years, he worked on his own, without a real mandate
from the Soviet side to bargain for Shcharansky's release. But there
was a growing sense among East German Communist leaders during this time—when the Moscow leadership was adrift and senile—
that East Berlin, too, was on its own, and they let Vogel dangle
Shcharansky before his Western contacts in hopes of reaping diplomatic benefits from his success.

That Vogel finally did succeed despite the obstacles was indeed
testimony to his personal skills, but also to the ambiguities and

tensions of this critical period of the cold war. Success came at the end of a series of spy swaps involving the release of scores of agents on three continents, but it was made possible by the intense reactivation of the informal American channel between Vogel and Frank Meehan, the career diplomat who had met him in Berlin during the Abel-Powers negotiations in 1962. Over the course of Shcharansky's imprisonment, Meehan followed the strands of the case as deputy chief of mission in Vienna and Bonn, and finally as United States ambassador to East Germany.

The secret of success, in the end, lay in its diplomatic ambiguity. During the entire period of Vogel's negotiations, the Americans insisted that Shcharansky was not an agent, but bargained for his freedom with captured Communist agents as if acknowledging that he were. Vogel might have been on a fishing expedition during most of the period, but he had the successful angler's most essential attributes: patience, persistence, and as much fascination with the sport itself as with bringing back a prize.

Anatoly Shcharansky had been arrested in Moscow on the afternoon of March 15, 1977, after visiting the Moscow apartment of his friend Vladimir Slepak.[1] Shcharansky, then a twenty-nine-year-old computer specialist, had been trying to describe to two of their American journalist friends what it was like to be followed around constantly by the KGB. Shcharansky had earned the right to be bitter, but his irrepressible sense of humor always allowed him to laugh at the innumerable absurdities of Soviet life, and now he hit upon the perfect idea of showing the two foreigners what he was up against: Just come with me, he told them, and I'll show you. When the KGB men had bundled him off in a Volga, the journalists first thought that Shcharansky had staged an elaborate practical joke.

Son of a lifelong loyal Communist, he had grown impatient of the intellectual paralysis in the Moscow of the early 1970s and, as a Jew, decided to emigrate to Israel in 1973. But because he had done computer work at the Oil and Gas Research Institute in Moscow, the authorities denied him an exit visa on the grounds that he was a bearer of state secrets. In KGB logic, he was then classified as a security risk and dismissed from the institute.

Shcharansky joined forces with other "refuseniks," Soviet Jews who had been denied permission to emigrate but left in political limbo. He became an active member of the Soviet human rights movement that sprang into being to monitor the Soviet Union's compliance with the Helsinki Accords on human rights, signed by thirty-five countries at the Conference on Security and Cooperation in Europe in 1975. The Moscow Helsinki Group was one of the first, bringing in such towering figures as Andrei D. Sakharov and his wife, Yelena Bonner, who called attention to abuses through frequent press conferences with Moscow foreign correspondents, many of whom did not speak Russian. Shcharansky, who spoke English fluently, became a sort of translator and public-relations man for the dissident and refusenik groups and befriended many of the correspondents. Soon menacing-looking KGB shadows in unmarked Volga sedans and black leather coats were following him constantly.

By 1977, the KGB saw the little group as a dangerous threat. The Soviet secret service began plotting its move against Shcharansky after he organized a computer survey of former prison-camp inmates, with the object of publicly revealing the extent and locations of all the far-flung sites of the gulag. Shcharansky had gotten Robert C. Toth, a science reporter for the *Los Angeles Times,* interested in the story, and Toth's newspaper had given it big play. At a time when the Carter administration was making human rights the centerpiece of American Soviet policy, the KGB singled out Toth and his work on the computer survey Shcharansky had organized as an example to the rest of the U.S. press corps in Moscow. Toth was arrested, accused of espionage, persuaded to sign a Russian-language confession he could not read, and expelled from the country. It was only a matter of time before the KGB collected Shcharansky himself. When it finally charged him, in the summer of 1977, it was with a capital crime: Treason, under Article 64 of the Russian Federation's criminal code, for allegedly working as an American agent of the CIA. Washington denounced the charge as an outrageous fabrication, and U.S.-Soviet relations began a long, cold, downhill slide for which Moscow got all the blame.

For Vogel, the first feeler of interest from the West in engaging him to obtain Shcharansky's release had come in the spring of 1977, very soon after Shcharansky's arrest, from a flamboyant politician and dealmaker named Samuel Flatto-Sharon. Vogel's reputation as the mysterious fixer of the Communist world was well established in Israel, and Flatto-Sharon was not afraid to walk in the shadows; he had arrived in Israel from France in 1971, just ahead of fraud and embezzlement charges by the French police. In 1977 he was running for a seat in the Knesset, and the announcement that he had appealed to Vogel to help get Shcharansky free was politically popular. He was also serious. But Flatto-Sharon could not risk arrest by traveling to Germany. His parliamentary secretary was another shadowy character named Shabtai Kalmanovich, who had come to Israel from the Soviet Union six years earlier and yet had mysteriously managed to preserve influence and connections there. Because his patron could not do that, Kalmanovich became the intermediary with Vogel, and soon made his way to the office on the Reilerstrasse.

Vogel informed the East German Foreign Ministry of the approach, and went to see Streit in his lakeside dacha near Rauchfangwerder. "Is there any objection to my trying to do something in the Shcharansky case?" he asked, arguing that success would resound to the credit of the East German regime, and of Erich Honecker as well. "It has to go through the *Sektor*," Streit answered, meaning the Justice Section of the SED's central committee, which would keep the party leadership informed and clear Vogel's moves with the Stasi liaison to the KGB.

Honecker had told Vogel that he was free to make any negotiating move that seemed appropriate for the fulfillment of what both men always referred to as Vogel's "humanitarian" mandate. By now, Vogel knew Honecker's mind well enough to know what was appropriate and what was not. He also knew that Honecker had become increasingly confident of his ability to act on his own, without clearance from Moscow on every conceivable move. Once Streit had reported what Vogel was proposing to do, he could cast his line into the murkier eddies of the cold war and see what rose to the bait.[2]

As far as Vogel knew from Streit and others, Moscow had no objections to what he proposed to do. There was only ambiguous silence, which was hardly surprising. Publicly, the Soviets were insisting that Shcharansky was an American spy, and publicly, the Carter administration was just as vehemently denying it, blasting the Soviets for this and for other human rights violations. The U.S. moral posturing included a letter to Sakharov and meetings in the White House with expelled Soviet dissidents. These actions were personally offensive to Brezhnev, who denounced them as unacceptable interference in Soviet domestic affairs. East-West relations had cooled noticeably since the days of the more "pragmatic" diplomacy of Henry Kissinger's realpolitik during the Nixon and Ford administrations.

Vogel knew that the rules in his game had not changed. It would be difficult to trade Shcharansky as an agent unless and until the Americans "snapped up" a big enough Soviet spy to make a bargain worth their while. To him, in a way, it was irrelevant whether Shcharansky was a spy or not, though he liked to think that he had a nose for the truth in such matters. His nose told him this time that Shcharansky was a hostage to politics.

"I don't think he is a spy," he once told Streit, who had snapped at him: "Which side are you on? Where's your ideological standpoint?"

In part, it rested upon his ego. Vogel had his eye on a Nobel Peace Prize, which he thought might come his way if he could bring off a trade with a man so widely regarded as a hero.[3] And to get one, Vogel, whether through naïveté or willful disregard of what the world thought, was willing to take help from wherever he could get it. Kalmanovich and Flatto-Sharon were promising leads, and Vogel was eager to follow them.

Flatto-Sharon was eager to have Vogel's help in Mozambique, in a case that had figured prominently in most Israeli newspapers for the previous year. He knew that the Stasi's sizeable foreign intelligence mission in Mozambique would give the East Germans considerable leverage.

The details were these: A young Israeli pilot named Miron Marcus, flying a light plane on a business trip from Rhodesia to Capetown for his South African father-in-law, had run short of fuel in stormy weather and landed by mistake in Mozambique on September 4, 1976, at an airbase used by African National Congress guerrillas. Mozambiquan soldiers had opened fire on the plane, killing Marcus's brother-in-law and wounding him slightly before taking him prisoner.

The East German advisers in Mozambique concluded that Marcus was more or less what he appeared to be—a "little fish" in the world of espionage, but one that could be useful to them nonetheless. When the Shcharansky case became important in the West, the Stasi whiffed a possibility of using Shcharansky and Marcus to secure the release of somebody else, a Soviet agent who had been imprisoned in the United States for nearly thirteen years. So the request Heinz Volpert had relayed to Vogel from the Stasi had been clear: Use the American and Israeli interest in Shcharansky to see if you can get Thompson.

Robert Glenn Thompson was the man Vogel had asked his American lawyer friend Ricey New to visit in the federal penitentiary in Lewisburg, Pennsylvania, a decade earlier, to bring him the simple message, "We haven't forgotten you." Vogel personally had every reason to remember this bizarre, lanky American—or perhaps not an American—with a beard. Thompson had written to Vogel from Lewisburg on August 2, 1965, addressing the letter to 78 Normannenstrasse, Berlin, German Democratic Republic—the Stasi headquarters. Three months earlier he had been sentenced to thirty years in jail for "espionage against the United States allegedly for the Union of Soviet Socialist Republics," as he put it in his letter.

"It is my desire that you represent me in a possible exchange. I believe that you will find that I have been a citizen of the Union of Soviet Socialist Republics since the year 1957. It is my desire if an exchange can be worked out to return to the U.S.S.R. or the German Democratic Republic and continue in my peaceful life," Thompson had written. His wife and children, Thompson wrote, also wanted to "leave the hostile environment of the United States as soon as transport is available." If Vogel had any doubts about who he was, the prisoner assured him, Erich Mielke or the Soviet Embassy could surely eliminate them.[4]

For the FBI, Thompson was an American citizen, born in Detroit on January 30, 1935, who had enlisted in the United States Air Force at the end of 1952 after he dropped out of high school. Thompson, the federal authorities charged, had begun spying for the Soviets in 1957 and had continued snooping for the next eight years in West Berlin, Montana, Detroit, and New York City, supplying the Soviets with photographs, military manuals, code books, data on missile sites, and other information. Finally, federal agents had swooped down on him at the heating oil company in Long Island that was his cover. He had pleaded guilty before trial at Federal Court in Brooklyn, he claimed, because he had expected to get a five-year sentence and then be deported. Shocked by the thirty-year-term that he had received instead, Thompson had broken his silence and written to Vogel to get him out.[5]

In early 1978, Vogel was not greatly concerned about who Thompson really was. Streit had told Vogel that Thompson was, in fact, a KGB asset, but instructed him to negotiate for Thompson's release as if he had belonged to the Stasi.[6]

Vogel kept up the momentum by bringing new names into the package, all the while saying that his real goal was the release of Shcharansky. The new name was another young American—"a case like Pryor," Vogel had told Meehan, who was now deputy chief of mission at the U.S. Embassy in Bonn. Alan Stuart Van Norman, then not yet twenty-two years old, was, as Frederic Pryor had been in 1961, an American graduate student in Berlin who had fallen in over his depth. Van Norman, a biology student from Concordia College in Windham, Minnesota, had been arrested by East German border guards on an automobile trip from West Berlin to Munich on August 2, 1977. In the trunk of his car, East German border guards had found the huddled figures of an East German couple and their young son. Van Norman had just been sentenced to two-and-one-half years in prison for attempting to arrange their escape. He had insisted that he had not taken any money for his services, an assertion that Vogel used with the Stasi as an argument for clemency.

Van Norman was a valuable bargaining chip for Vogel. Vogel flew to Cologne airport on February 22 to see Meehan, giving the American diplomat the clear impression that while Thompson was the number-one priority on his list, he was also eager to talk about Shcharansky. To Meehan, the hint of Vogel's interest in discussing the Soviet dissident was encouraging—but it was far from clear that it would lead to anything soon.[7]

For Vogel, the new connection with Flatto-Sharon had already paid an unexpected dividend in the form of a new American contact in New York City, a character outside of all his previous experience of life. Ronald Greenwald, born in Manhattan's Lower East Side in 1934, became Vogel's American rabbi, an orthodox Jew who earned his living not by reading from the Talmud but by wheeling and dealing in the world of American and Israeli politics, and in commodity trading in southern Africa.

Greenwald was bigger and heavier than Vogel, six feet tall and heavyset, as disheveled in his rumpled suits and protruding shirt-tails as Vogel was fastidious. Friendly and outgoing—the kind of streetwise New Yorker who knew his way around everywhere and was never intimidated by anybody—Ronnie Greenwald stuck to his religious beliefs, wearing a yarmulke and always observing kosher rules. Like Vogel, he mixed good deals with good deeds, teaching seminary courses, running a summer camp near his Catskills home in Monsey, N.Y., and doing campaign work for the Republican party among the Jewish communities there and in Brooklyn at a time when most New York Jews considered it practically a sin not to vote for the Democrats.

It was not divinity that earned Greenwald his living—it was commodities, trading in the salt of the earth, aluminum, and other raw materials in a business he ran out of a modest tenth-floor office on lower Fifth Avenue in Manhattan. He, too, had Soviet connections; phosphates, copper cathodes, urea—whatever the Soviets had to sell or trade, Greenwald found buyers for it. He also had many business contacts in the South African black "homeland" of Bophuthatswana, dealing in aluminum ore and ingots so industriously that the U.S. State Department required him to register as its official foreign agent. He was a close friend of his congressman, Representative Benjamin Gilman, who had owed his campaign victory in Rockland County in the 1972 election in part to the entrée into the Orthodox community that Greenwald had provided.

Greenwald's political connections had led Flatto-Sharon to call on him in Israel, during a session of the World Conference of Synagogues in February 1978. Flatto-Sharon asked if Greenwald could help get Shcharansky free. Explaining how he had already taken up the contact with Vogel, Flatto-Sharon outlined the three-cornered deal involving Mozambique, Israel, and the United States and spoke excitedly about how Vogel had hinted that Shcharansky might be included as well. The rabbi was so excited that as soon as he had hung up the phone, he had called Gilman at his home in New York, where it was only about 5 A.M. "Congressman, I am sorry to wake you, but I'm sure you are going to want to help get Shcharansky out," Greenwald began. Gilman was groggy with sleep. "Ronnie, have you been drinking?" he asked.[8]

But by early April, Gilman was as enthusiastic as Greenwald was. Vogel had all but perfected a deal to get Marcus and Van Norman released in exchange for Thompson, and he was still holding out the prospect of release for Shcharansky as well. Both New Yorkers were intrigued by Vogel, though Greenwald had had some initial misgivings. The thought of dealing with a mysterious spy lawyer in the Communist part of Germany who had done God knew what during the war had been a bit much for him. Vogel spoke no English, and Greenwald had no German, but the rabbi's

Yiddish made communication possible. Greenwald found the Vogels' attentive charm flattering and seductive, but genuine. At first, Ronnie Greenwald had been "Rabbi Greenwald" to the formal Dr. Vogel, but gradually they had struck up a real friendship. Vogel would welcome his exotic friend to the garden behind the house on the lake at Teupitz, and ask Helga to pick tomatoes and squash for him. Then Vogel would boil Greenwald an egg in a special tin pot that had never been used to cook anything else, and set the food before him on the table in the terrace behind the kitchen. *"Das ist kosher,"* Vogel would assure him, and the rabbi would eat.

American officials were attracted to the deal Vogel and Flatto-Sharon seemed to be working out, even though Shcharansky was not included. Thompson had by now spent thirteen years in jail, and was clearly losing any value he might have had as a bargaining chip. Here was a chance to get two young men—an Israeli and an American—out of Marxist prisons, and the Carter administration gave its approval to pardon Thompson and set the deal in motion.

The State Department officer who was put in charge of the technical details was Jeffrey H. Smith, a former Army Ranger turned lawyer who specialized in law enforcement and intelligence matters. Earlier, he had helped negotiate the treaty that restored Panamanian sovereignty to the Canal Zone, attracting the favorable attention of Ambassador Ellsworth Bunker and career foreign service officers. Smith, an athletic, open, and friendly man, was imbued with the military's cheerful "can do" spirit. His good working connections in the intelligence and defense communities led his colleagues in the State Department to respect him as a practical man who could talk both with CIA "spooks" and military "jarheads" more easily than the striped-pants set could. Smith could get things done. His first inkling that something was up in the Thompson case came in early April, with an abrupt telephone call from a colleague in the State Department's Office of the Legal Adviser. "If we want to get somebody out of jail in this country, how do we do it?" had been the question.

At about the same moment in East Berlin, Vogel was preparing for a meeting with Kalmanovich on April 10. First he had checked to see if there had been any news from Moscow about the possibility of Shcharansky's being included in the deal. He had found only stony silence. Because he had no mandate from Moscow to deal for his release, Vogel warned Kalmanovich that secrecy was of the essence. There had already been news stories speculating about a release, and if the Soviets thought that Vogel was behind the stories, all prospects would be off, Vogel warned.

Kalmanovich had been undeterred, cabling Greenwald in New York with the news, "The Shalosh for Zar is looking good." Vogel cabled his boss in Israel with some exasperation, as rumors continued to fly: "As I cannot reach Herr Kalmanovich at this time, may I once again with good reason ask for absolute discretion. Any publication would be harmful, for now and also later."[9]

The State Department was no happier than Vogel about the publicity. A lawyer representing Lawrence K. Lunt, a CIA agent who had been held in a Cuban prison since 1965, got wind of the deal and threatened legal maneuvers to prevent the State Department from releasing Thompson unless it got Lunt out at the same time. Vogel had tried to help arrange Lunt's release, but that agreement had come to naught because of revelations that the CIA had plotted with the help of the Mafia to assassinate Fidel Castro in the early 1960s. Thompson might be Lunt's last chance, the American lawyer thought, but time was running out. Volpert was pressing Vogel to go with what he had, saying that the arrangements in Mozambique had been set. So when Vogel received Kalmanovich in his office on April 10, he gave the Israeli a letter to take to Congressman Gilman in Washington, spelling out a deal that excluded Lunt altogether.

DEAR MR. GILMAN:

At the request of Mr. Sharon from Tel Aviv, may I confirm to you that I can guarantee the release of Herr Miron and Herr Norman. This is, however, conditional on Mr. Thompson being freed simultaneously.

If you agree, I would send you a binding letter on when and where Messrs. Miron and Norman are to be expected. In return I would also expect a similarly binding letter on when and where Mr. Thompson is to be expected.

In the very complicated and difficult Shcharansky case, a resolution is not possible at this time. But I will continue my best efforts and believe that agreement in the abovementioned matter could be a good omen for similar arrangements. Vogel[10]

Kalmanovich brought the proposal to Frank Meehan in Bonn the next day. Vogel, he reported, had said he could have Shcharansky out "in the next couple of months."[11]

Volpert's Stasi connections worked wonders for Vogel in Berlin and in Mozambique. In America, where Vogel had never been before, he was counting on Kalmanovich, Greenwald, and his old friend Ricey New to help him. Vogel made plans to fly to the United States to pick up Thompson in Lewisburg, and even drew up a formal contract, typewritten in German on his office stationery:

It is agreed:

1) Mr. Kalmanovich will provide Attorney Dr. Vogel by 17.IV.1978 *an official document* that Mr. Thompson will be freed on 30.IV.1978 and can fly on this day with Attorney Dr. Vogel from New York to Berlin (West).

2) Simultaneously with the exit of Mr. Thompson from Berlin (West) to the GDR Herr Norman will be released to Berlin (West). (Friedrichstrasse elevated railway station)

3) Mr. Miron will arrive in South Africa at 1600 hours Central European Time on 23.IV.1978 and will be picked up by his wife, accompanied by Mr. Kalmanovich, at the border. The exact location will be made known at the proper time.

Handwritten into the letter was the correction of the minor error about Marcus's name: "Mr. Miron is Miron Marcus," the note said, and at the bottom were spaces for the signatures of Vogel and of Kalmanovich, as Flatto-Sharon's agent.[12]

On the 14th, the State Department called Meehan with the news that the United States had decided to release Thompson for Marcus and Van Norman. Meehan was also authorized to pass the information on to Kalmanovich, who would be coming through Bonn on his way back from Washington the next day. The Israeli wheeler-dealer was pleased to get the letter, since he would be seeing Vogel immediately after visiting the U.S. Embassy. Kalmanovich did call on Meehan in Bonn, and on the 18th, Meehan telephoned Vogel to make sure there would be no more complications from the East German side.[13]

Still, Ben Gilman wondered as he flew in a small plane to the airstrip at Siteki, Swaziland, near the Mozambique border, how could a lawyer in East Berlin actually make anything happen way down here in the bush? Gilman, Greenwald, Kalmanovich, and Miron Marcus's young wife had all come halfway around the world on Vogel's word. The American Congressman's doubts grew stronger after the plane landed and the party continued by car. It wound its way farther and farther into the African countryside, over dusty trails to a tiny point on the border called Goba, a border station that seemed to be in the middle of nowhere.

But a deal was a deal. Miron Marcus, blindfolded, soon appeared walking down the trail, with eight armed Mozambiquan guards leading the way. Greenwald crossed the cement platform that marked the border and asked him, in Hebrew, "Do you know what today is?" He had to answer his own question—"Passover, the time of our freedom"—and he had been moved to tears.[14]

The next day, Meehan flew to see Vogel in Jürgen Stange's office in West Berlin, to make the final arrangements for the next phase of the deal. This was to be the exchange of Thompson for Van Norman the following weekend. *Newsweek* magazine had somehow gotten a scoop on the whole thing, and the West German press was full of speculation about Shcharansky's imminent release.

Vogel now made his first trip to the United States. He took Kalmanovich with him when he flew to Washington on the 26th to make the final arrangements for Thompson's release from custody. Vogel was looking forward to seeing his old friend Ricey New in Washington as well. New was waiting for him in Gilman's office when Vogel walked in on the 27th. Gilman, still flush with excitement over his African adventure, congratulated Vogel on the successful release of Miron Marcus and introduced him to Jeff Smith, who had meanwhile succeeded in making the arrangements for Thompson's release.

Gilman had a less welcome "surprise" for which Meehan had prepared Vogel: a meeting with Richard Copaken, the American lawyer who represented Ewa Shadrin, the wife of the Soviet defector who had mysteriously disappeared in Vienna in 1976. All Vogel could tell Copaken and his client was that at the moment, nothing could be done; if the situation ever changed, he would of course try to do his best.[15]

This out of the way, the group fell to working out the scenario for a simultaneous exchange of Thompson and Van Norman in Berlin on May 1. They also worried about how to get Thompson to that point after his planned release from Lewisburg on April 30. The negotiations provided that Vogel and New would be driven to Lewisburg to ascertain that Thompson did, indeed, want to go to East Germany. He would be escorted to John F. Kennedy Airport in New York City, where Smith would join the party and take him to West Berlin. Only there would Thompson be formally released from U.S. custody.

Vogel was flying first class, so Smith got Pan American to upgrade him. Then he learned two appalling facts. The first was that the American prison authorities believed Thompson to be mentally unstable. The second was that since the FBI's jurisdiction did not extend overseas, Smith might be on his own with a maniac 30,000 feet over the Atlantic.

"There is this guy who has been in jail all these years and some stewardess is offering him a drink, and he's mentally not all together. What am I going to do?" Smith thought to himself. But Smith had not been a West Point graduate and Ranger for nothing. In his pocket, he packed a coil of nylon rope. He would tie Thompson to his seat next to Vogel, Smith decided, if worse came to worst.[16]

Emerging from Lewisburg penitentiary on parole on the morning of the 30th, Thompson was all smiles. In Pan Am's Clipper Lounge at the airport later, he waxed eloquent before a crowd of reporters who had somehow materialized despite the pledges of secrecy from all sides. "I did my duty for humanity," he insisted. But once on the airplane, Thompson turned into a pussycat. Smith relaxed and left the rope in his pocket. In West Berlin the next morning, all went as planned.

Helga Vogel was already waiting at the U.S. Mission there, with Alan Van Norman in tow. Thompson had a present for his East German lawyer—two of his abstract paintings, which did not quite fit with the antiques and Meissen porcelain in Vogel's office on the Reilerstrasse. But there, they got pride of place anyway on the wall of the waiting room corridor outside.[17]

Both Moscow and Washington had gained important knowledge from the Thompson case. Prodded by Greenwald and Gilman, the State Department had reactivated the American channel to Vogel, through Frank Meehan, obtaining through it the most important results since the Abel-Powers exchange of 1962. To the Carter administration's State Department, at least, the "Vogel channel" had seemed important enough to keep open, and after Meehan went off to be Ambassador to Czechoslovakia in 1979, this channel had been assigned to the U.S. Embassy in Bonn.[18] Vogel had also arranged a new back channel for himself, in Ronnie Greenwald's connection to Representative Ben Gilman in Washington.

Most important, Vogel had established something else that Moscow took note of. He had demonstrated that the United States government, for all its public denials that Shcharansky had ever worked with the CIA, would not refuse to talk privately about including him in a spy swap, whatever it said in public about his innocence of the Soviet charges that he had been an American spy. Spy or no spy, Shcharansky had become a Soviet intelligence asset—a hostage. He may have been the best one they had had since Francis Gary Powers.

The publicity about the Thompson case had embarrassed Ronnie Greenwald. Who was this East German lawyer he was dealing with, some of his friends wanted to know, and how could he be sure Vogel wasn't a Nazi? Imprudently, Greenwald asked Kalmanovich to see whether Israeli intelligence knew anything about Vogel's past, and instead Kalmanovich snitched to Vogel. "The rabbi isn't sure you're kosher," Kalmanovich had told Vogel. Ben Gilman had checked on him in Washington, but the only information in the files suggested that as far as having a Nazi past went, Vogel was clean.[19]

Greenwald knew how sensitive Vogel was to insult or slight, and was afraid that Kalmanovich's indiscretion would alienate him. Both he and Gilman wanted Vogel to keep trying on Shcharansky. You got me into this, he told Kalmanovich, now help get me out of it. Greenwald came up with the idea of asking Gilman to nominate Vogel for the Nobel Peace Prize if he succeeded in getting Shcharansky his freedom. Kalmanovich thought this such a brilliant idea that he got Flatto-Sharon to do it right away, and on June 5, the Israeli legislator told world news agencies that he had sent a letter to the Norwegian Nobel Committee in Oslo nominating "this great individual and his far-reaching humanitarian concepts" for the prestigious award.[20] Nothing could have been better calculated to flatter Vogel's ego or to ensure that he would continue to work hard for Shcharansky's release.

Vogel needed Greenwald for the same reason Greenwald needed him—to keep the negotiations going. The passage of time, Vogel thought, would make the Soviets more amenable to letting

Shcharansky go, but they would do so only for someone who was in a roughly equivalent situation—charged but not yet convicted of espionage. If there were any chance of securing a deal on these terms, Vogel would have to move quickly.

He knew that the secret world of espionage often played cynical games. Some spies spied simply because they had been trapped into doing so by the other side's counterespionage tricks. Vogel was by now confident enough of his talents and of the power of his international reputation to protect him, and he spoke with contempt of the gumshoes he often had to deal with. In private, he was no less harsh on the KGB and the Stasi than he was on the CIA or the BND.

Vogel owed much of his reputation, and most of his career, to what they did, and to the seriousness with which they did it. Where would Vogel be without the KGB, the Stasi, and the CIA? In effect, he needed all of them, just as they needed each other to justify themselves. That all such organizations were basically cut from the same bolt of cloth and shared the same set of values was something about which Vogel had little doubt. In Shcharansky, the KGB had a valuable hostage. Vogel had little from the other side to bargain with in exchange for his release. There would be little movement, he thought, until the other side "snapped up" a human prize of equal value.

Vogel was undeterred, driven now by his own personal ambition and ego. But he continued to be frustrated, not only by the Soviets, but sometimes by the Americans as well, for reasons of high politics.[21]

Carter had insisted publicly and privately in letters to Brezhnev that Shcharansky was innocent of any connection with the CIA, and he did not want to contradict his own insistence by being forced to swap him for any Soviet spies the Americans might catch. "Your president," Vogel told Greenwald, putting his index figure to his temple and twisting it, "must be crazy." The Soviets, he thought, would feel challenged now, and would stage a show trial of Shcharansky, dashing any hopes of a swap before legal proceedings could go any further.[22]

This was precisely what happened. The old men who ran the Soviet Union were determined to reject Carter's attempts to meddle in their internal affairs by demanding freedom for Shcharansky because he was innocent of the charge against him; that was for them to judge, and they needed Shcharansky behind bars for their own reasons: he was a symbol of resistance to the system of repression and control that kept them in power, resistance that had to be crushed. The verdict was arranged when his trial finally came in July, with scores of his relatives, dissident friends, and Western correspondents barred from attending. The harsh sentence was thirteen years in prison and internal exile, and it began the darkest period in the U.S.-Soviet relationship since the crises over Berlin and Cuba in the early 1960s.[23]

But Vogel was undeterred. He dangled still more names in front of Smith and Greenwald, always with Shcharansky as the possible ultimate prize. East Germany's position at the center of the cold war carousel gave it plenty of leverage of its own; it had plenty of prisoners with connections to the Americans, and perhaps one of them could provide the key. He got Lothar Loewe, a television correspondent who had been expelled from East Berlin for broadcasting one evening that Erich Honecker's guards were shooting would-be escapees at the Wall "like rabbits," to take to Washington a list of about thirty names of convicted CIA prisoners sitting in East German jails and tell his American contacts that the CIA was not doing enough to try to help get them out.[24]

Eventually, the CIA succeeded through Vogel in obtaining the release of one of its most valuable agents in East Germany, a man named Franz Saretzki, who had worked as an American mole in the East German State Planning Commission for more than a decade before his arrest in 1969. Vogel finally delivered him in March 1983, in return for a captured East German agent, collecting only about a four-hundred-mark fee for arranging Saretzki's pardon.[25]

But still there was no movement on Shcharansky.

A deal began to seem less likely than ever with the advent of the Reagan administration, whose hard-line policies sent U.S.-Soviet relations into a deep freeze. The renewed moral condemnation of the "evil empire" and the greatest peacetime rearmament in American history blew a cold wind into Central and Eastern Europe that plunged the Soviet Union and its Warsaw Pact allies into a fragile state of brittleness and put relations between the two Germanies into a new context, one that paradoxically gave new impetus to Vogel's efforts on behalf of Shcharansky.

To the Germans, who knew that if World War III ever broke out they would be right on Ground Zero, the early 1980s were years of extraordinary psychic strain. The West Germans, who had always been America's staunchest European allies, began to march by the hundreds of thousands in anti-American nuclear disarmament rallies. Schmidt's Social Democratic Party, under the pressure of this growing movement, began moving away from the centrist, pro-NATO positions its own chancellor espoused, creating tensions with Genscher's Free Democrats, who finally abandoned them and brought Kohl's Christian Democrats back into power.

In East Germany, Erich Honecker had a growing antiwar movement on his own hands, one the Communists had first tried to direct into anti-NATO channels. But growing ideological rigidity in the aging leadership in Moscow and in East Berlin was creating a widening rift between the better life the people wanted and the old platitudes that were the only thing their leaders could deliver.

For the East German leadership, reducing tensions between the two Germanies would deflect the mood of discontent by preserving the illusion of normality. Honecker wanted very much to accept an invitation that Helmut Schmidt had extended to him at the end of 1981 to be the first East German leader to visit West German territory. Kohl, who had succeeded Schmidt as chancellor in 1982, was no less eager to keep the tensions under control, and Honecker, who was turning seventy that year, wanted one last time to see his home town of Wiebelskirchen in the Saar. But Moscow barred Honecker from making the trip. The KGB also continued its stony silence in answer to Mielke's inquiries about whether Vogel could finally go ahead and arrange a swap for Shcharansky.

The Americans kept pressing, and Smith and Vogel continued to see a lot of each other during the early 1980s, carrying on a lively correspondence about the list of allegedly abandoned American agents in Bautzen that Vogel had slipped to Lothar Loewe. The list made depressing reading: the East Germans always meted out heavy sentences in espionage cases. Some of the people on this list were in for life, others for ten or fifteen years—stretches that made it difficult for the Americans to come up with equivalent cases of their own to bargain with. Smith submitted lists, names on pieces of paper with no letterhead that had been compiled by an American interagency working group in Washington; Shcharansky's name was always at the top, and Vogel had never indicated that getting him out was out of the question. But there would be no real movement on in any case—especially Shcharansky's—Vogel knew, until the Americans had someone of equivalent "value."

. . .

For Vogel, the next chance for a possible breakthrough on Shcharansky came on November 4, 1983, when the FBI arrested an East German physicist, Alfred Zehe, when he arrived in Boston for a conference of the American Vacuum Society. The charge was espionage. Alarm bells rang all over the Stasi headquarters on the Normannenstrasse in East Berlin, for though Zehe was not a full-time spy, East German intelligence had used his expertise in evaluating and targeting sophisticated Western technology it was under heavy pressure to obtain.

Zehe, a professor at Dresden University, regularly spent half the year at the University of Puebla in Mexico. In exchange for giving him permission to travel, the Stasi had obligated him to serve as a consultant when asked, and Zehe had been made well aware of the rules of conspiratorial work. One of them was that under no circumstances was he to travel to the United States.[26]

Why Zehe had disregarded these instructions was not Vogel's concern. All he knew was that Volpert was pressing him to get Zehe out of prison, and fast. Money, Volpert made clear, would be no object, and Vogel was to use his American connections to get legal representation in the United States as fast as possible.

Vogel did indeed put his American connections to work—all of them. He called Richard C. Barkley, political counselor at the U.S. Embassy in Bonn, and asked whether the United States government could help find a German-speaking lawyer in Boston. Barkley relayed the request to the State Department in Washington. There the matter came to Jeff Smith's desk, and Smith began inquiries in Cambridge, looking for a lawyer who would be "sensible" if and when the opportunity for a trade of Zehe for other agents arose.[27]

Vogel, who never put all his eggs in one basket, had not limited his inquiries to the State Department. He also used his back channel, calling Ronnie Greenwald in New York City and asking him the same question: Could he find a good lawyer for an East German professor who had just been arrested by the Americans, a lawyer who might have an interest in advancing Shcharansky's cause? If he could, Vogel would come to the United States right away to discuss the case. Greenwald immediately called somebody he had played basketball with in Brooklyn's Borough Park as a young man—Alan M. Dershowitz, a Harvard Law School professor and Shcharansky's attorney of record in the United States. Dershowitz demurred at taking Zehe's case because of the possible conflict of interest as Shcharansky's lawyer. But he had enthusiastically recommended a friend, a Boston lawyer named Harvey A. Silverglate, who would be certain to give Zehe his best effort.[28]

So it was Silverglate, a skilled lawyer just as combative as Shcharansky, and just as dedicated to resisting government attempts to encroach on individual freedoms, who took on Zehe's defense. Silverglate's view of the FBI's actions in this case was one of undisguised contempt. Streetwise in the same way the rabbi was, Silverglate smelled entrapment when he started looking into the facts: A U.S. Naval Intelligence undercover operative had gone fishing on Embassy Row in Washington, D.C., waving around outdated secret documents on submarine sonar-detection technology and trying to lure a spy from one or another of the Communist embassies to come out and take the bait. This operative had gone into the East German Embassy, asked to see someone who might be willing to pay for secret American defense information, and been told that no one was interested. The FBI had ordered him to go back in, and someone had finally nibbled. The East Germans wanted the documents turned over in Mexico City, they said, because there was no one capable of properly evaluating their significance in Washington.

So, in Mexico City, the East Germans had called in Zehe to look at the documents. The U.S. authorities charged that he had done so on at least three different occasions in 1982 and 1983, and that he had delivered secret documents personally to East Berlin three months before his arrest. Silverglate argued that Zehe had neither gone looking for the information nor received it directly from the Navy undercover agent. He had simply been present when it was turned over in Mexico and had given a professional view of it as requested. Neither had he seen any harm in traveling on to Boston for the scientific conference, but once in American jurisdiction, he had been hit with the full weight of the espionage statutes by the FBI—for acts allegedly committed not in the United States but abroad.[29]

As Silverglate saw the issues, the United States was trying to extend its jurisdiction in an unacceptably broad way. If an American academic physicist had been called into the Pentagon and asked to advise as to the meaning of a classified East German document, would the United States find it acceptable if the East Germans arrested him for espionage when he went to East Berlin for a conference? Hardly, Silverglate thought. And the documents Zehe was charged with seeing had been "obsolete documents about obso-

lete technology," he argued. Selected by Naval Intelligence itself as
bait for Communist spies, the papers could hardly contain vital
national secrets.[30]

Silverglate enthusiastically represented Zehe at his arraignment
in Boston on November 17, a few days before Vogel's arrival. Vogel
had asked Smith for a visa and told him he wanted to come to
Washington. But the State Department lawyer was miffed that
Vogel had gone behind the government's back to retain Silverglate
in the case, and told Vogel his visa would be good only for Boston
unless he could show that some greater purpose would be served by
coming to Washington. Vogel assured him that it would—the Zehe
case was just a piece of the puzzle that would one day lead to
Shcharansky's release.[31]

Wolfgang and Helga Vogel arrived in Boston, on their second
trip to the United States, on Thanksgiving Day. Greenwald flew up
from New York to meet them for dinner at the Parker House, the
venerable hostelry near the Common, but to the rabbi's surprise,
Boston was closed up like a tomb on the holiday. He could not even
offer the Vogels a traditional Thanksgiving dinner, for turkey was
not on the menu of the coffee shop, the only place in the hotel that
seemed to be open.

Silverglate, like Greenwald, spoke enough Yiddish to be able to
communicate after a fashion with Vogel, who told him he was there
in his capacity as the East German government's special legal representative in the case, and assured him that there would be no
problem with paying the American's fees. They had breakfast,
again at the Parker House, on Friday morning. Silverglate looked
to see if there were any U.S. government spies around, and spotted
an assistant U.S. Attorney he knew a few tables away. "I am sure
we are being followed, but it's always hard to tell who is following
you, the KGB or the FBI or the CIA," Vogel joked with him.
"They look alike, they think alike, and they act alike." He was sure,
Vogel said, that the FBI and the KGB bought their agents' trench
coats from the same central manufacturer.[32]

Vogel knew exactly what he was talking about. "When you're
abroad," Streit had told him, "assume that everything you have
said will already be known here by the time you return." It was not
for nothing that he always signaled to his clients in East German
prisons to watch what they said, and he and Helga assumed that his
office and even their home were thoroughly bugged by the Stasi. In

a way, it was a sort of protection—it left them always on their guard, he thought.[33]

Confident that Zehe's case was in the best of hands, Vogel left a retainer on a rapidly mounting legal bill, and then called Smith at home in Virginia from the hotel, promising that if he got permission to come to Washington, he would bring proposals that could lead to movement on Shcharansky. Greenwald, he told him, had already reserved a room for him and Helga at the Capitol Hyatt Hotel, near Union Station. Smith relented on the visa and arranged to meet him at the hotel bar at 6 P.M. that day.[34]

He had picked the bar before ever having been there, but when he walked in and saw its name, Smith laughed aloud. He was to talk with the mysterious East German spyswapper about trading spooks in the "Spy's Eye." Vogel found this equally droll, but was unfazed; with a State Department interpreter, they got down to business.

"So what is it that you have for us?" Smith asked. "I think if you give us Zehe and some others," Vogel told him, "then we can do Shcharansky." Encouraged by the good news, Smith drew out of his pocket the latest American wish list, with Shcharansky's name on the top. It included not only a score of Germans who had worked for U.S. intelligence agencies or the BND in East Germany, but other Soviet political prisoners, and several being held in Poland and Czechoslovakia as well. It was, Smith conceded, an all-encompassing list, but if Vogel was serious about finally resolving the impasse over Shcharansky, it was not an unrealistic basis for negotiations. Vogel accepted it, and said he would be back in touch after he had reported back to East Berlin.[35]

But Smith was taken aback by the letter he received from Vogel a week later, reporting that the reaction to the American proposals had been more negative than he had expected. The Americans had asked for too much, Vogel said. Anxious to keep the momentum going, Smith's ad hoc interagency group lopped a few names off and sent back the revision to Vogel, still with Shcharansky at the top, and were rewarded just before Christmas with a more encouraging reply, and an invitation to continue the talks in East Berlin. "Jeff, would your family mind if you missed Christmas?" Secretary of State George P. Shultz asked his negotiator, who persuaded him to let him delay his departure until December 26.[36]

But once again, Vogel had discouraging news when Smith arrived in East Berlin. Indeed, Smith thought, Vogel seemed very cool, handing over a two-page, double-spaced memorandum in German that was surprisingly blunt, accusing the Americans of making outrageous and unprecedented demands that were not serious, and of trying to bargain for convicted prisoners with people who had not yet even been tried.

Smith's journal entry after the meeting gave the flavor of the bargaining: "I added that when he told us that we could have all of them, he would surely understand why we would have such a high bargaining position. Would he make a counter offer? No. He said what he needed now was a pause. I asked what was the chief objection to our proposal—was it the size, or the overall political situation? He said it was the size, plus the uncertainties [about the] sentences." His side, Vogel pointed out, could hardly be expected to release a prisoner serving a known, twelve-year sentence in exchange for someone who had not yet been before a judge but might be liable to life imprisonment. On both sides, the arrested spies were *Spielmaterial,* human chips in an international poker game.[37]

Smith did not contest the description, but he was baffled. The only possible explanation seemed to be that in his eagerness to get some movement in the case, Vogel had gone too far in his conversation in Washington. Back in East Berlin, the Stasi must have hauled him back by the scruff of his neck with the tough memorandum. But Smith did not want to give up. He pressed Vogel to refine the two lists, to make them into something more manageable for future negotiations, to explore the limits of his mandate. The two men worked away on the two pieces of paper, Smith dropping a few names from his list, Vogel from the East German one. But Vogel was clearly not ready to make a final agreement. "Ask me in writing to make a formal counteroffer," he finally suggested, playing for time, and Smith wrote out a request.

Vogel promised to get back to him within a week, saying that he had to check with East German Foreign Minister Oskar Fischer. In private, Vogel seemed as amiable as ever. Smith and Barkley bought Vogel a turkey from the PX, presenting it to him as an "American chicken" that had flapped in just a bit late for Christmas; the Vogels returned the thought with a carved nutcracker from Thuringia and a wooden Nativity set for the Smiths' family Christmas tree back in Washington.

On his return to the other side of the Wall, Smith found a telex from "Wolfgang and Helga" wishing him peace in the New Year, and proposing the next meeting in early February. He flew back to

Washington on December 30, still unclear about what had gone wrong. And he would not be much enlightened when he returned to Berlin as Vogel had suggested in February 1984. All that was clear, Smith concluded sadly, was that Vogel would not be able to deliver Shcharansky any time soon.[38]

The reason lay more in Moscow than in East Berlin. For in Moscow, early 1984 was not a good time for making difficult decisions. Yuri V. Andropov, the KGB chief who had succeeded Brezhnev as Soviet leader in 1982, had refused to approve Shcharansky's release on security grounds, and Andropov was on his deathbed as the two lawyers were meeting in Berlin.[39] Konstantin U. Chernenko, the tottering old Brezhnev crony who succeeded Andropov after his death on February 9, would last only a little more than a year. Whenever the East Germans relayed queries to the KGB about whether Vogel could negotiate for Shcharansky's release, Volpert and Streit told him, all they got in reply was silence. Vogel had winged it, holding out the prospect of a deal on Alfred Zehe on his own initiative, but he had gone too far. To avoid embarrassment, all he could do was delay.[40]

Smith could hardly hold it against him, even though he had correctly guessed that Vogel had simply been angling. Whatever embarrassment there was was strictly between the two negotiators. Neither U.S., Soviet, nor East German prestige was involved. In any case, Smith was soon leaving for another job, with Senator Sam Nunn's Armed Services Committee. The State Department asked him to keep his diplomatic passport so that he could rejoin the negotiations in case there was a break. The Americans wanted to keep the Vogel "channel" open, and negotiations on a package for Shcharansky continued despite the temporary impasse.

The delay gave the security services more license than they had enjoyed in years to play their games of cat and mouse, and on both sides, they were taking full advantage of it. Vogel now had more than twenty names of agents being held by the Stasi, and Polish intelligence had made available half a dozen more. The Communists had more reserves in the bank, but the United States was also beginning to pile up "assets" rapidly.

There was Marian W. Zacharski, a Polish intelligence operative posing as a businessperson, arrested in California in June 1981 by the FBI and charged with paying a disgruntled employee of Hughes Aircraft $110,000 over four years to supply film of highly classified documents on weaponry and radar. By 1984, Zacharski was serving a life sentence in a federal penitentiary in Tennessee.

There was Penyu B. Kostadinov, a Bulgarian trade official in New York City who had been trapped by an FBI sting operation at the Top of the Park Restaurant off Central Park in September 1983. The federal authorities had supplied a cooperating graduate student with specially selected classified government documents on nuclear weapons security, enticed Kostadinov into taking the bait, and then nabbed him red-handed out on the street. He was under a charge of espionage and conspiracy to commit espionage, but the Bulgarians were insisting that he had diplomatic immunity.

And there was Alice Michelson, a sixty-seven-year-old East German woman arrested as a KGB courier in October 1984 at New York City's Kennedy International Airport just as she had been about to board a plane for Czechoslovakia. The Stasi had asked Vogel to do for her what he had done for Zehe, and with Greenwald's help, he had found a lawyer for her—Leonard Boudin, the well-known New York civil liberties attorney. Vogel also asked Greenwald to visit her in prison, making a point of telling the rabbi that she was Jewish. She too had been caught in a "sting," trapped by a U.S. Army sergeant posing as a spy who had passed her a cigarette pack and a tape recording of classified information to take to Czechoslovakia.

East German spies were by now beginning to make Vogel a regular visitor to the United States. He was back again in November 1984, to bring Silverglate a check for his work on Zehe's behalf and to consult with Boudin on the Michelson case.[41] Vogel then went on to Washington, where his main State Department working contact had become André Serena, Smith's successor as assistant legal adviser for law enforcement and intelligence.

On November 27, the day after Vogel flew back to Berlin, he took on two more Communist clients charged by the Americans with spying—Karel Koecher and his wife Hana, whose case bore some superficial similarities to Robert Thompson's. Koecher had come to the United States from Czechoslovakia as a refugee from Communism and worked for Radio Free Europe before being hired as a translator by the CIA in Washington and New York City in the mid-1970s. On November 27, the Koechers, too, had been waiting to board a plane at John F. Kennedy Airport, on their way to Zurich. The day before, they had sold their cooperative apartment at 50 East 89th Street, a fashionable Upper East Side address where the comedian Mel Brooks and the tennis star Ivan Lendl also lived. Koecher, who had been on the board of the cooperative, had even had the chutzpah to try to bar Lendl as a possible Communist a few years before. The FBI arrested the couple at the airport and charged Koecher with having been an "illegal" planted by the Czech intelligence service who for more than ten years had passed every CIA secret he could get his hands on straight to the StB, the Czechoslovakian secret service, in Prague. Hana was not charged, but detained as a material witness.[42]

Vogel had led the American authorities to believe that their best leverage in any possible barter for Shcharansky was Zehe, but Harvey Silverglate had taken on Zehe's defense with a vengeance, barraging the court in Boston with petitions for dismissal on grounds that included lack of U.S. jurisdiction, since all the allegedly criminal events alleged in the indictment had occurred on foreign territory. Silverglate told Vogel that he expected to win. "All the East Germans did is bite, they didn't go out looking for this stuff; you went shopping on Embassy row," Silverglate told the prosecutors.[43] Vogel, reporting back on the case through Volpert, now had to contend with an additional complication. The Stasi would not want to barter for Zehe if it thought it had a chance of getting him free for nothing, on a legal technicality.

Perhaps "nothing" was not the right word. Vogel was staggered by the fees he was paying to Silverglate, though Volpert had not flinched. The bills mounted, finally, to $360,407.50, with some of the money brought by Ronnie Greenwald, $10,000 or $50,000 at a time, in the interests of speeding Shcharansky's release. Boudin's fees for Michelson were on a similar scale, amounting to well over $100,000, Greenwald later attested, and Volpert also arranged for these amounts to be transferred through Vogel's accounts to the United States.[44]

Silverglate managed to get his client out on bail, and installed him in a small apartment in Boston's Back Bay, close to the court, to which he was required to report almost daily. Silverglate soon became aware that not only the FBI but the East Germans were keeping the professor under close surveillance.

Zehe was skeptical about the scenario the government was offering to his lawyers. Take a guilty plea, the prosecutors were saying, and we'll try to get you leniency when you're sentenced. Zehe could not be sure, any more than his lawyers, that this would ever lead to an exchange and a return home, but a taste of American prisons taught him he did not want to do much time on this side of the Atlantic. The plea-bargaining was hedged with mistrust, on both sides. Silverglate's team got the impression that the FBI knew Zehe was not exactly another Colonel Rudolf Abel, but believed that he was holding back and not telling all he knew about the way East German intelligence operated.[45]

Zehe threw a major monkey-wrench into the bargaining one crisp morning early in January 1985. Stop the plea bargaining, he said; he wanted to defect and stay in the United States. He asked for two FBI agents to be waiting for him in Silverglate's office on Broad Street in downtown Boston after he arrived with his East German escorts. Wary of the city's capricious parking regulations, Zehe's East German minders stayed in their car, and the FBI men had no trouble slipping him out the back door. Hours later, Silverglate finally took pity on the men patiently waiting in the automobile, and called the East German Embassy with the news that Zehe would not be coming back that day.

In East Berlin, the Stasi was furious, and pressed Vogel to get to the bottom of the matter. He called Silverglate in Boston and asked what was going on. Zehe had decided to stay in the United States, Silverglate told him, mindful of who else might be on the line. Vogel was soon on the telephone to Greenwald, as well. "Where is he?" "I can't tell you," the rabbi answered. "Is he alive?" Greenwald assured him that Zehe was fine. "Well, tell him that if he wants to stay, that's his business, but he shouldn't forget that he has a wife and children here," Vogel warned. It seemed to Greenwald, at the time, less like a threat—though it had certainly come from the Stasi as a threat—than a sober statement of the facts of life in any Communist country.[46]

But the Stasi did not need to threaten Zehe to get him to come home. The U.S. government refused to accept him as a bona fide defector, and pushed him back into the Stasi's arms.[47] Now the defense was in an awkward spot. Zehe could plead not guilty, go to trial, and publicly testify that he wanted to defect, but then the East German government could bring charges of treason against him and retaliate against his family. Or he could plead guilty to the charges, hope for a light sentence, and try to arrange things with the East Germans. His FBI debriefers remained adamant about rejecting his claim to defection and pressed him to tell everything he knew.

Vogel sent him a message of reassurance through Greenwald,

assuring Zehe that he was still trying to arrange an exchange, and that if he did return home, Vogel could guarantee that he would not have to fear retaliation by the East German authorities. It was a concession Vogel had demanded from Volpert as a condition of his further cooperation in getting Zehe back, and the Stasi had agreed to it.[48]

On February 21 of 1985, Zehe decided to trust their assurances and throw in the towel. He pleaded guilty to the eight counts of the indictment, and received a sentence of eight years' imprisonment and a fine of five thousand dollars.[49] Silverglate was discouraged and cynical. "He had no choice," Silverglate concluded. "Our government wouldn't accept him."[50] It was Zehe's fate to remain a pawn, in the hands of both the American and the East German governments, in the ongoing game for greater stakes.

In the late winter of 1985, further bargaining for Shcharansky looked hopeless, both for Vogel and for his Western negotiating partners. The package that was supposed to have included him was complete. But without Shcharansky, the United States would hold back the Koechers. Most of the rest of the names in the package were German—though most of the German spies held in East German jails had been accused of working for the United States.

Vogel did not relish the trip to Mielke's vast office in the Normannenstrasse to secure the minister's signature of approval for the deal, but when it came to exchanges of agents, Mielke always insisted on personally clearing the releases. Sitting there in his service uniform with the collar unbuttoned, in front of the vast telephone console he loved to use to summon and intimidate his scores of subordinate commanders, Mielke narrowed his eyes skeptically, jabbing the paper with a finger. Four prisoners from the West—Zehe, Zacharski, Kostadinov, and Michelson—against twenty-five from the socialist side, how could that be a balanced bargain? he asked. He had negotiated long and hard, and he could assure Comrade Mielke that a balance had been struck, Vogel replied. Most of the agents Mielke would release were minor figures compared to Zehe and Michelson, and besides, Vogel argued, "he"—the personal pronoun Mielke always used when referring to Honecker—was eager to use this swap to improve relations with the Americans.[51] Mielke knew this was true, and signed. "The lawyer," he later told his subordinates, had been at the negotiating table, not he himself, and "the lawyer" knew his trade.[52]

Erich Honecker was eager to make the deal. His efforts to build on détente with the West Germans, détente that was essential for him to shore up the country's failing economy, were thwarted by the continuing impasse in U.S.-Soviet relations. At this point Honecker, like Vogel, seemed to be at the peak of his career. He thought of himself as the most dependable and loyal Soviet ally in Eastern Europe, and he was beginning to earn grudging respect as a statesman even in West Germany. He liked to think of himself, as Vogel liked to think of himself, as a man who could mediate between East and West even at a time when they were too stubborn or proud to make gestures on their own. East Germany, so often vilified in the past, would earn respect for a spectacular humanitarian gesture, and Dr. Vogel had prepared the way very effectively.

Honecker made one last attempt to see if Moscow was ready to relent on Shcharansky, Streit reported to Vogel, but got no answer in reply. Then Honecker decided to proceed without the Soviets and go ahead with the rest of the package, if the Americans and the West Germans were willing.

The Americans had started negotiating this list to get Shcharansky out, and had shown their good faith by keeping his name in the forefront during three years of negotiations. With the exception of the Koechers, whom they wanted to keep in reserve for the day when the Soviets were willing to talk about Shcharansky, the Americans and their German allies were ready to go ahead, with the hope that one day they could get him out yet.

Honecker was not the only prideful politician eager to reap political benefit from what was bound to be a spy-swap spectacular. Richard R. Burt, the U.S. Assistant Secretary of State from European Affairs, was about to be named U.S. Ambassador to Bonn, and was eager to take a prominent role. Burt, an arms control specialist who had briefly worked as a diplomatic correspondent for *The New York Times* in Washington, was conservative, brash, brilliant, and politically ambitious. Vogel fascinated and puzzled him at the same time, for Burt, like most of Vogel's Western negotiating partners, had only a vague idea of the sources of Vogel's influence all over the Eastern bloc, and was mystified and intrigued by his ability to deliver. He was also drawn by Vogel's sartorial fastidiousness, for the dark-haired, handsome, and athletic-looking American diplomat shared Vogel's *faible* for fancy dressing. If a spy spectacular was going to take place, Burt wanted to be an equally visible presence on the scene at the exchange on the Glienicke Bridge, in the middle of June.

But first Vogel had to undertake yet another round of prison visits in the United States. On April 14, he and Helga flew to New York City to consult with Silverglate and Boudin. A month later, on May 17, the Vogels returned to obtain final consent from Michelson and Kostadinov at the federal detention facility in Manhattan. The Vogels' next stop was Lake Placid, where Zehe was kept in the federal prison that had been built out of part of the village for the Winter Olympics in 1980.

Vogel's mission to Zehe was a delicate one. Vogel reassured the prisoner that he had nothing to fear by returning home. He had told Streit and the others that it was clear that Zehe had been pressured into saying he wanted to defect, and that there would be no reprisals, though there might be some intensive questioning and considerable explaining to do. "If I stayed here," Zehe had asked, "could I get my wife and children out to join me?" Vogel knew there was little hope of that, and told his client so. In the end, with a heavy heart, Zehe agreed to trust his assurances, and to return home.[53]

The Vogels immediately drove back to New York to catch an airplane for Memphis, where Zacharski was held. The Memphis prison, Vogel thought, bore comparison badly with Bautzen, which was dubbed the "Yellow Horror" by its inmates. America—especially its system of justice—was baffling in many ways. East Germany had done away with the death penalty (though not at the Wall, which remained lethal for would-be escapees), yet capital punishment still survived in the United States. Vogel thought of twenty- or twenty-five-year sentences as being extremely long, but in the United States they seemed routine. The slums of Harlem and the Bronx that the Vogels saw on their motorway journey made the worst of bombed-out Berlin or Leipzig look good by comparison.

Rather than spend the weekend in Memphis until their next appointment with Burt in Washington on the following Monday, the Vogels flew to Miami, simply to get a look at Miami Beach and stroll along the shore. Vogel also could not resist browsing through the posh haberdasheries, and bought himself a handsome dark-blue jacket. He was wearing it on Monday when he walked into the State Department to report to Burt that all the arrangements on his side were now complete. "What's this?" Burt crooned, feeling the lapels and complimenting Vogel on his good taste. "At least now you know there are more interesting things to see and do in America than visit jails."[54]

Back in Berlin, it was time for the choreography of the exchange, always important as a symbol of the interests of security and prestige that had to be carefully balanced, in appearance as well as reality. That the political stakes were high was apparent, among other things, from the level on which the negotiations were held. Burt's deputy, Deputy Assistant Secretary of State Tom Niles, came over from Washington to work out what amounted to a formal diplomatic protocol with Vogel, blocking out the scenes, the steps, the pas de deux, the formal bows to the right of every prisoner to decide to stay rather than return to the other side. By June 10, it was complete. Vogel and Burt would be joint impresarios, and the exchanges would be simultaneous, all twenty-nine crossing the border at the same time in a grand *chassé-croisé,* with their relatives having the right to follow with their household effects by July 20. Finally, there was a general clause: "Both sides recognize that this procedure may be complicated by human error and uncertainty and undertake to implement it in a spirit of compassion and flexibility."[55]

June 11 dawned gloriously, a sunny, summer morning in Berlin, and a wonderful day for a stroll across the Glienicke Bridge for twenty-nine people who had not seen much beyond their prison bars for many months or years. With the agreement of both sides, the West Germans had arranged for discreet news coverage of the exchange. No correspondents or reporters were allowed at the scene, but a television crew was there to videotape the proceedings, which would be broadcast over the national West German television evening news. The Vogels managed to get the raw tapes themselves, and after the Wall fell would watch them at home, with a sigh of nostalgia for the great days gone by.

Taken from the West Berlin side of the bridge, which was closed to the regular licensed military spy traffic of the four powers' military attachés for the several hours it took to set up and carry out the exchange, the tapes make fascinating viewing even today. There is Richard Burt, looking eager and purposeful in an exquisitely cut gray suit, arriving early and pacing nervously. He has secretly slipped away from a meeting in London to fly to Berlin just to be here, and now he is talking to aides and American security men with microphones in their lapels and receivers in the ears and peering across the bridge to the barriers on the Potsdam side. Then Vogel, dapper and businesslike in a brown double-breasted suit whose lines are no less elegant or Western than Burt's, is driven up by Helga in a golden Mercedes with East German license plates, IS-92-67, and rolls down the window to give the all-clear. Birds are singing, the water is blue under the green girders of the bridge, and there are sailboats out on the lake. The Vogels drive the few hundred feet over to the East and Burt remains on the Western side; then the Mercedes returns, and Vogel comes out to tell Burt that the Communist prisoners, too, are ready to go. Vogel gets back in his car, Burt gets into a black State Department limousine, and they both cross to the East German side. There Vogel takes Burt by the arm and points out where the prisoners will be emerging from the barricades. American military photographers now converge closer to the scene, accompanied by two military jeeps with soldiers in flak jackets.

But the exchange itself is not tense or dramatic; it seems relaxed and anticlimactic, with buses and van moving to and fro as if bringing two groups together for a church picnic. The prisoners from the Communist jails come out dressed in T-shirts, stretching and yawning and looking disbelievingly across the Havel to West Berlin. A big red, white, and black Mercedes bus in the German national colors then drives across from West Berlin to receive them. As they board with their satchels, bearing their meager few belongings, they look like a group of middle-class Germans on a sightseeing tour.

Vogel stands next to a blue Chevrolet van from the American Mission that has brought over Zehe, Michelson, Zacharski, and Kostadinov. The lawyer beams as they emerge, welcoming them back with warm words, embracing Zehe, who looks particularly happy to be coming back home and betrays no nervousness about the consequences of his attempt to defect, and accepting a hug from Alice Michelson. Standing a few feet away, at the gap in the barrier, stands another smiling figure who looks like a tour guide, welcoming back all four of them, a tall man in an open sports jacket, unafraid of the cameras on the other side: Heinz Volpert, the fixer's fixer, the senior Stasi officer on the scene, urging the four prisoners onto an East German bus bearing a sign SONDERFAHRT, "special journey." Volpert is everywhere, giving orders to the border guards, directing traffic, always in the background, finally melting away offstage and leaving Vogel and Burt alone in the spotlight as the scene reaches its end. They say goodbye to each other and get into their limousines, roaring off back to the city.

Honecker would bask in the reflected afterglow, but not for long. For soon his "humanitarian gestures" would begin to unravel the structure of repression that he had built with the Wall. And in Moscow, Gorbachev would begin a series of "reforms" that in a few short years would lead to the collapse of Communism and the disintegration of the Soviet Union.

Wolfgang Vogel had, as yet, no inkling that his own work was contributing to this undoing. This day, though fallen short of its original aim of achieving Shcharansky's release, was a triumph, and in the evening Vogel took the American and German teams, Burt included, to dinner at the Palace Hotel, East Berlin's finest, to celebrate. "To Herr Vogel," Burt wrote on this evening, "a talented, extraordinary and very humane man. You have taught me that one must never lose sight of the human element in foreign policy." Tom Niles wrote Vogel three days later, "Some played important roles, but you are the only person whose role was absolutely essential, without whom this entire project would never have happened."[56] Vogel had been touched by the way Burt, far from all the television cameras, had wept, in the bus with the prisoners, when Vogel had told them that they owed their freedom to President Reagan. Vogel also remembered Jeff Smith and all their years of negotiating on the exchange, sending him a little model of the Brandenburg Gate with the date, June 11, as a memento.

But Vogel also remained determined to see through Shcharansky's release. He had not come this far, had not bargained for his freedom with scores of agents, to be satisfied with failure.

CHAPTER TEN

A DISSIDENT'S JUMP TO FREEDOM ACROSS THE GLIENICKE BRIDGE

"The knot has been cut."

By the summer of 1985, Anatoly B. Shcharansky had outlived the aging Soviet leadership that had put him in prison. He had served more than seven years of his thirteen-year sentence and, like Sakharov in his exile in Gorky, had become an international cause célèbre. Vogel had come to think of getting Shcharansky out of prison camp as a goal that would be the crowning glory of his career, and, driven by personal ambition, he had been working hard at it the whole time. Scores of captured spies, East and West, had his hard work to thank for their freedom. But time after time, Vogel had been forced to strike Shcharansky's name from the lists after Streit or Volpert reported that Moscow would not give the go-ahead—or, more accurately, that there had been no word from Moscow at all. First Brezhnev, then Andropov, and finally Chernenko, unwilling to admit that the Communist empire was crumbling or to acknowledge the consequences, had simply been afraid to let Shcharansky go.

Now, as the longest days of the year began and the golden domes and crosses of the Kremlin sparkled under the brilliant Russian summer sun, a new era was dawning. A new and younger Soviet leader had succeeded the last of Stalin's generation, and Mikhail S. Gorbachev was prepared to show his country and the entire world that he was ready for sweeping and fundamental change.

But Gorbachev was a cautious politician, a compromiser who worked by consensus. In June 1985, he had been leader for only three months. So, he began his move on Shcharansky by gathering the leadership around the table in his Kremlin office and telling them that seven years of unrelenting military and political confrontation with the West had brought the Soviet economy to the brink of a perilous crisis. Even the hard-line leaders of the KGB knew this was true. Their old mentor Andropov had seen economic paralysis coming and had tried to exhort the people to work harder. But exhortation had had little effect. Gorbachev and his close ally Eduard A. Shevardnadze, soon to become a full member of the Politburo and foreign minister, knew that the country needed to break out of the stagnation and the self-imposed isolation of the past and engage the nation and the West in a new process of renewal and dialogue, step by step. But they had to begin somewhere.

In the eyes of the entire world, Shcharansky had become a symbol of Soviet repression and inflexibility. His release, Gorbachev and those close to him knew, would be an unmistakable sign of the clear break they wanted to make with the past. But even Gorbachev could not just give Shcharansky an amnesty, commute his sentence, and put him on a plane for the West. The KGB had arrested him as a spy, and the KGB was a powerful force, a fraternity with its own rules and its own loyalties. Gorbachev could not afford to affront it with a gesture that would undermine the legitimacy of the judgments it had made as the party's "sword and shield."

Shcharansky had exhausted whatever usefulness he had had as an example to keep other Jews in the Soviet Union from challenging the authorities. And time after time, the Americans had shown that they were willing to negotiate with Vogel for Shcharansky's release, in exchange for agents neither they nor anybody else would deny were genuine spies. By finally putting the negotiations for Shcharansky in the hands of an East German lawyer who was as much respected by the West as by Moscow's loyal allies in the German Democratic Republic, Moscow would save face. Whatever it said publicly, the West would be implicitly agreeing that Shcharansky was an agent, just as the KGB had been insisting since

1977. This was the argument that, within the Politburo, had carried the day. It took a vote of the decision-making body to authorize his release, but even Viktor M. Chebrikov, the Andropov protégé who had run the KGB since 1982, gave his consent. Returning to the KGB headquarters in Dzherzhinsky Square, he ordered his first chief directorate to send a telegram to the KGB's chief liaison with the East German Stasi, Major General Gennady Titov, telling him the East German leadership could give Vogel the mandate.

Vogel was elated when Streit relayed the message he had been waiting so long to hear. "The knot has been cut," Streit told him.[1]

Arranging the big swap on the Glienicke Bridge on June 11 had been no small accomplishment for Vogel, and Honecker had been grateful and unstinting in praise. The German Democratic Republic was becoming respectable even in Washington. And Honecker was eager to keep the momentum going. Now Vogel could go to work, finally, on the big one, the one he had wanted all along.

Vogel's Western negotiating partners had never been fully aware of either the sources or the limits of his powers. He had deliberately kept his connections with Volpert quiet, in part because the Stasi wanted him to, in part because it flattered Vogel's ego that his Western contacts thought him so powerful he could get the vast Stasi apparatus to bend to his will. Vogel's connection to Honecker was by now well known; what was not so well known was that it was Honecker's political connections with the Soviet leaders that gave Vogel any influence in Moscow—Honecker's connections, and the Stasi's KGB liaison in Karlshorst. Vogel himself had not even been to the Soviet capital since 1969.

At the same time, Honecker, like other East German leaders before him, was finding that his own interests and those of his Soviet protectors did not always coincide. By mid-1985, he had become obsessed with the idea of making his often-postponed visit to West Germany, despite previous Soviet objections. Maintaining decent relations with the West Germans was important to him for a number of reasons, not the least of which was the money that trade and the secret prisoner deals kept flowing into the increasingly starved Communist coffers. For East Germany, too, was entering a serious financial and economic crisis, one that only Honecker and his chief Politburo lieutenant for the economy were fully aware of, and carefully kept secret.

.   .   .

On Vogel's next trip to Bonn, only a few days after the spectacular exchange of June 11, he went to see Ludwig Rehlinger in the Ministry of Intra-German Affairs, on the Godesberger Allee, telling him that "his side" was ready to talk about another exchange of agents, this time including Anatoly Shcharansky.[2]

Bonn let Washington know that the situation had changed for the better. The interagency committee that Jeff Smith had assembled began putting together the list of agents the CIA, the Defense Intelligence Agency (DIA), and other U.S. organizations wanted to get out. In Bonn, Rehlinger convened his own ad hoc group, bringing in Chancellor Kohl's office, the Interior Ministry, the Justice Ministry, and the Foreign Ministry. Rehlinger, Vogel, and Olof Grobel, Ambassador Burt's political counsellor, worked diligently to shape a mutually acceptable catalog of spies. By September, Meehan, as U.S. Ambassador to East Berlin, was again firmly in charge of the Vogel portfolio, doing much of the coordination with Washington. Burt was not exactly pleased by a negotiating chain of command that put him in the second string, but he loyally put up with it, and the negotiations proceeded apace—fast enough, Rehlinger thought, to make a release look possible by September or early October 1985.[3]

That it took longer was partly due to the list-making procedure itself. It spoke volumes about the differences between East and West. In the West, there was give-and-take, the clash and play of bureaucratic interests, with the final decisions made by the politicians. The American ad hoc interagency committee was much like the West German one; Justice, the FBI, the CIA, and the State Department met to discuss the names to convey to Meehan and Grobel to give to Vogel, and to discuss the merits of the names on the lists he provided to them. The White House was kept informed, but did not chair the meetings; the State Department's legal adviser did that. The West German side, as Rehlinger described it, worked much the same way, with the chancellor's office, in immediate charge of the German security services, also having a seat in the negotiations.

Across the Berlin Wall, it was the Stasi that was in control, deciding alone over the lists of spies, just as it made the decisions about which political prisoners the West Germans could buy free. First a committee in the Stasi's investigations department cleared the names; difficult cases—those the East Germans did not want to let go but whom the West insisted on—went to the minister himself, Mielke, for his personal decision. Then Volpert traveled to Vogel's office to get the lists he had received from the West, and Vogel prepared an untitled memorandum for the record with whatever explanations or other information about the cases he had been given by his negotiating partners on the other side. Vogel's own trips to the Stasi headquarters were reserved mainly for discussions with Mielke, usually at the end of a negotiation.[4] "Though Mielke played a decisive role, he did not come to the meetings," Vogel said. "Probably he spoke to Wolf, and then worked out [the list] with him. I would get the result, these lists, and then be told to negotiate from them. I had no authority to add or eliminate names from the lists; I had authorization to make suggestions, but not to decide."[5]

In October, Vogel had been rewarded for his achievements with the honorary title of professor, conferred by the East German Academy of Sciences for State and Law in Babelsberg. In his acceptance speech, Vogel was so confident of his own and his country's growing prestige—and of the accolades that both would receive if the Shcharansky release took place in full view of the news media—that he suggested that in future, exchanges of agents be treated as "normal" events, even in the East German media. The suggestion was noted with interest, and even welcomed, in the West, where many people had come to view such events in the same way. And by the end of October, Vogel knew that this time there would be no more major hitches on Shcharansky.

There was only a slight complication. The United States had asked that Andrei Sakharov be included in the release. The Soviets were willing to release Sakharov, Vogel learned, but only in the same way they would let Shcharansky go—by expelling him from the country and depriving him of his citizenship. Sakharov, in exile in Gorky, had made it clear he had no intention of agreeing. He would rather stay in exile and fight for his rights as a Soviet citizen, free to stay or go West as he chose, rather than submit to treatment as a criminal.

The final package for the exchange began to take shape only after the U.S.-Soviet summit in Geneva in November 1985, when Gorbachev confirmed to President Ronald Reagan that Shcharansky could go free once the negotiations were complete. The pulling and hauling took a full two months. Part of the delay had been caused by the West Germans' reluctance, and finally refusal, to turn over one of Markus Wolf's best agents—Lothar-Erwin Lutze, who had penetrated the Defense Ministry in Bonn and had been arrested with his wife, Renate, a secretary in the defense minister's private office, nearly a decade earlier. The West Germans were not yet ready to forgive Lutze, one of many so-called "Romeo" cases masterminded by Wolf in the 1970s and early 1980s, for seducing his way into access to more than a thousand secret documents and NATO defense plans that he passed on to the East German spy service.[6] And part had been caused by Vogel's inability to obtain the release of a captured spy the Soviets were powerfully interested in getting out of jail, Arne Treholt, a Norwegian diplomat and former junior government minister who had been arrested at Oslo airport in January 1984. He had been on his way to Vienna to deliver a suitcase full of secret documents to Gennady Titov, the KGB's chief liaison to the Stasi. Titov put enormous pressure on Mielke—and Mielke passed it on to Vogel—to try to get Treholt out in a swap. The Norwegians would not hear of it, and gave him a twenty-year prison sentence after his trial ended in June 1985.[7]

The negotiations continued, with telephone calls and meetings with Grobel and Ludwig Rehlinger in Bonn. Vogel jetted back and forth from Berlin, the adrenaline rising as he contemplated the prospect of success. For it was challenge of deals like this, not the fees (indeed, he never collected a cent from the Americans) that attracted him; it was power, the sense of involvement in high affairs of state to which no one else was so privileged.

Driving in behind the fearsomely barricaded doors of the Stasi's Normannenstrasse headquarters, a vast, high-tech complex of new and old buildings as big as the CIA, Vogel would sometimes remind himself that most East Germans were afraid even to walk past on the sidewalks. On the blocks around, the Stasi had painted false fronts, windows with German lace curtains and neatly painted blinds, to give the impression that this was just a quiet residential neighborhood. Going up to the office to deal with Mielke, then seventy-nine years old and as fearsome a despot as there was anywhere in the Communist world, Vogel would summon up his courage.

The older he got, the more despotically Mielke behaved. He liked to terrorize his officers, summoning them in to the big staff auditorium to hold a two-to-three-hour speech and then spotting someone dozing in the back row and figuratively hauling him up by the scruff of his neck: "You, there, this concerns you, too." Sometimes, meeting with Mielke and Honecker in the SED headquarters building, Vogel had been shocked at the level of discourse. Agreements, treaties, lawyers' protocols all meant little to Mielke, who had erected a vast apparatus in the service of the state and saw everything as a simple question of power. After one of these seminars, Vogel would come down to Helga in the car, pale and shaking his head. He had learned from experience not to mention his own doubts about whether Shcharansky was really an American agent; Mielke would narrow his pig-eyes and remind Vogel that he, too, was not above suspicion. Vogel, after all, was only a messenger.[8]

Still, even at such moments, Vogel felt indispensable, an intimate of the mighty and powerful, uniquely trusted as much by the CIA as by the KGB, by West German intelligence and by the Stasi alike. Who else, he asked himself, could perform such a mission; who else was there for the prisoners to turn to? He swelled with pride, becoming once again the little boy carrying messages from his father to the neighbors through the cobblestone streets of Glatz.

The Americans had negotiated for Shcharansky for most of eight years as if he were a spy. But they had always insisted that he was not, and that if it came to an exchange he would have to be kept clearly separate from any agents. Vogel would have his hands full in arranging the *mise-en-scène*. This package, like the previous one, would be big, with agents from many countries. Honecker and Mielke had the special communications lines humming between East Berlin and Moscow, Prague, Warsaw, and Sofia as the package took shape, and it was one for which Honecker could count on the gratitude of all of his most important Communist allies.

Vogel had succeeded in getting the biggest prize for Czechoslovakia: Kael Koecher, the agent who had infiltrated the CIA and had been stoutly maintaining his innocence since his arrest a year earlier. His wife Hana, freed on bail, was having some success with a publicity campaign aimed at obtaining their release, and the Czechoslovakian secret service, the StB, was playing its part in the charade by refusing to acknowledge that the Koechers had worked for it. But the Americans insisted that Koecher had been funneling defense secrets to the StB for years and were offering to pardon the Koechers as part of the exchange only if the couple renounced their American citizenship and accepted voluntary deportation.

The West Germans would also be getting enormous political benefits out of the exchange: Since it was taking place on their territory, they would share much of the credit for obtaining Shcharansky's freedom, and Vogel had gotten from Rehlinger a pledge to release Detlef Scharfenorth, a forty-three-year-old East German economics expert who had been arrested in Cologne in 1985. Scharfenorth had aroused the suspicions of Bonn's counterintelligence experts by asking the Cologne University's student employment office to advertise for market researchers, who were to apply to "Dr. Detlev Gensel" in a Cologne hotel. The jobs turned out to be intelligence assignments; Scharfenorth had been sentenced to four years in jail, sneering at the judge's comment that he had been "a valuable worker" for the Communist side.

For the Poles, Vogel had succeeded in getting the West Germans to agree to release Jerzy Kaczmarek, an intelligence officer who had infiltrated the West German office for emigrants and returnees in Bremen to determine how West German officials handled security checks, information that would come in handy for any one of the East's secret agent networks. Kaczmarek had been arrested in March 1985 but had not yet been tried.

And finally, Vogel had gotten someone the Soviets wanted badly: Yevgeny M. Zemlyakov, thirty-nine, a member of the Soviet trade mission in Cologne, sentenced by a court in Düsseldorf in September to three years' imprisonment for espionage. He had been convicted of trying to obtain precision electronic measuring instruments, directional broadcasting antennas, and high-frequency transistors for wireless data transmission equipment, all on the NATO embargo list of military and intelligence technology that could not be sold to the Soviet Union or Warsaw Pact countries. Moscow had waited only a day after his conviction to let Vogel know that it wanted him brought safely home.[9]

In return, from the Eastern side, Mielke had agreed to release Wolf-Georg Frohn, a forty-year-old East German researcher for the Carl Zeiss optical works in Jena, who had been in Bautzen prison since 1980. A CIA control officer in Hanover, a distant relative, had promised Frohn that he could get him secretly to West Germany in exchange for information on precision optics research under way at the plant. The Stasi had arrested him, and Frohn was sentenced in 1981 to life imprisonment.

There had been particular West German interest in Jaroslav Javorsky, a forty-three-year-old Czech who had been imprisoned for almost as long as Shcharansky. His father, an internationally known tennis player and member of the Czechoslovakian Davis

Cup team, had decided on one of his trips to stay with his wife in West Germany, leaving Jaroslav at home until he had finally been able to get permission to visit them. He, too, had decided to stay and applied for political asylum in West Germany, but he had left his fiancée back in Czechoslovakia and made the fatal mistake of going back to try to sneak her out in October 1977. Condemned on December 13, 1978, to thirteen years' imprisonment for espionage, illegal flight from the country, and violation of currency restrictions, Javorsky had become a favorite cause of Chancellor Helmut Kohl's conservative Bavarian rival, the blustery former defense minister, Franz Josef Strauss. Behind the bluster, Strauss had been secretly arranging deals with the East Germans and urging Kohl to provide huge trade credits to the East Germans, with whom he hoped to be on good terms if his day as chancellor ever came, so Honecker had had every reason to prevail on his Czechoslovakian counterparts to do him a favor by releasing Javorsky.

Finally, the East Germans were prepared to release Dietrich Nistroy, a fifty-year-old West German medical equipment salesman. He had been arrested during a trip to East Germany in 1981 after making one visit too many to an institute for radiation technology, not selling but spying on behalf of the West German BND. A Communist military tribunal had sentenced him to life imprisonment the following year.

But Shcharansky was the centerpiece, politically and symbolically on an entirely different plane. So the most delicate question that remained for Vogel to negotiate was the choreography of appearances. This was something Mielke and even the Soviets were now willing to leave entirely up to the impresario of the Glienicke Bridge, and in January 1986, Vogel came into his element.

Shcharansky or no Shcharansky, Rehlinger and his wife took their annual ski vacation every January in the Austrian resort of Gerlos, often inviting the Vogels to join them. The Rehlingers were in the Austrian Alps now, staying in their favorite hotel, a place called the Gaspingerhof, the kind of comfortable family hotel that serves coffee and apple strudel with whipped cream to guests who included few of the rich and famous. It was favored instead by Dutch families who came for quiet relaxation and sober après-ski afternoons, and it had an annex across the street that was accessible by a tunnel under the road.

With Vogel pressing to get the case settled before the hardliners could change their minds, Rehlinger invited everybody to the resort on January 23, bringing his secretary down from Bonn. In the negotiations on the final arrangements, Grobel represented the U.S. Embassy in Bonn, and Meehan the American mission in East Berlin. The team sat down at the table in the Gaspingerhof's best suite to thrash out the details. One of the most troublesome was what to do about the Western news media, which were already speculating feverishly about when Shcharansky would be released, and in exchange for whom. Vogel surprised the group by announcing that his side was prepared to carry out the exchange in public, again at the Glienicke Bridge. Moscow wanted its gesture to be seen and fully appreciated, and East Germany wanted to claim full credit. Vogel was also attentive to Meehan's concerns about the way the exchange would look. Shcharansky, Vogel said, could be released first, before the others, so that no one would get the impression that he was simply one of the agents.

The protocol of the Gerlos meeting, typed up in German by Rehlinger's secretary, is one of the more fascinating documents of the cold war.

1. Prof. Dr. Vogel declares that he is authorized by the Chairman of the State Council of the G.D.R. to give assurances that

   Shcharansky, Anatoly
   Niestroy, Dietrich
   Javorsky, Jaroslav
   Frohn, Wolf-Georg

will be pardoned or freed from criminal prosecution by the respective responsible state authorities. All named persons, as well as members of their families, can go to a country of their choice.

   Ambassador Meehan declares that the couple
   Koecher, Karel
   Koecher, Hana

will be freed from criminal prosecution, on condition of a guilty plea by the husband, renunciation of American citizenship by the couple and departure from the U.S.A. by both. Attorney Prof. Dr. Vogel will expeditiously arrange the fulfillment of these conditions in the USA.

   State Secretary Rehlinger declares that

Zemlyakov, Yevgeny
Kaczmarek, Jerzy
Scharfenorth, Detlef
will be freed from criminal prosecution or pardoned.

2. Should one of the persons named in (1), with the exception of the Koechers, not wish to leave the state in which the person is now located, a free and unimpeded interview of this person by a person delegated by the other side will be arranged. If this person holds to this position during the interview, the obligation will be considered as having been met. In such a case the guarantee of the right to emigrate to a country of the person's choice will remain.

3. The obligations entered into in (1) and (2) constitute a whole. The obligations will be met simultaneously.

4. The agreement will be carried out on Feb. 11, 1986, at 3 P.M. at the Glienicke Bridge in Berlin.

The date and time were tentative. So were the approvals of Rehlinger and Meehan, for their governments. Of the participants, only Vogel said he was authorized to sign for his government, and he did so with a flourish. In a relaxed mood, the entire company then adjourned to the hotel restaurant for an Austrian supper of venison and roast potatoes.[10]

Vogel told Meehan that he expected no trouble in persuading the Koechers to drop their defense and come back home; he planned to leave Berlin that Sunday and would return two days later, on Tuesday. This surprised the U.S. ambassador. Kael Koecher had pleaded not guilty in December 1984, despite the FBI's contention that he had volunteered an account of his espionage activities for Czechoslovakian intelligence for the fourteen years prior to his arrest. Now his story changed. The confession had been false, he said, and he had made it as part of a plan to build a legend as a double agent for the Americans. Hana Koecherova, who had been jailed for contempt of court for refusing to testify to the federal grand jury investigating her husband's case, won an appeal on the grounds that she could not be forced to give incriminating testimony about her spouse, but, though now free on bail, she was still being held in the United States as a material witness.[11]

The Vogels arrived in New York as scheduled, and as usual, the federal jail on the lower west side of Manhattan was the only place on their itinerary. As Vogel had predicted, the negotiation with the Koechers was no trouble at all. He walked into the jail, told Koecher his name, and showed him his identity card. "O.K.," Koecher said. End of negotiation. Koecher pleaded no contest to the espionage charges, signed a declaration attesting to his willingness to return to Czechoslovakia, and agreed that he and Hana would renounce their American citizenship before being turned over to the Communist authorities at the Glienicke Bridge. Vogel returned to his room in the Essex House, called William M. Woessner, head of the German Desk at the State Department, and said that, with this final obstacle out of the way, all they needed to do was confirm the date—the sooner the better, Vogel thought, because now momentum counted for everything.

They confirmed the 11th of February as the date, moving up the time to early morning, and on Monday night the Vogels boarded a plane for Munich, to make the final arrangements with the West German BND.

In the taxi on the way in to Munich from Riem airport the next morning, Vogel heard on a radio news broadcast that the date had already leaked, and groaned. By now, the Soviets would be fattening up Shcharansky in Moscow, getting him presentable for his flight to East Berlin, but they would want everything to go according to plan. Both sides had agreed to some publicity on the day of the exchange, but Vogel had imagined something more like the controlled access the media had been given to the big swap of June 1985, when the television tapes had been taken under official supervision. Now scores of journalists would be descending on the Glienicke Bridge, threatening to turn a discreet exercise into a media circus.

The 11th of February would be a Tuesday. By the previous weekend, not merely scores but hundreds of journalists from all over the world had flocked to West Berlin for what was clearly being treated as a major world event. For more than a mile along the Königstrasse, their cars, trailers and vans lined the roadway, with cameras, antennas, generators, and portable telephone booths making it look like an outdoor bazaar: a shivering, impatient, excited crowd awaiting the sale of long-sought goods, and meanwhile trading wild rumors. The weather had turned bitter cold, with a light dusting of snow, and Rehlinger, observing the scene, felt sorry for the freezing Fourth Estate. Major General John H. Mitchell, the U.S. military commander in Berlin, issued an order barring the unruly crowd from the last stretch of the road to the bridge from noon Monday until 6 P.M. on Wednesday. At least the assembled journalists knew when the end was coming, but in fifty-six hours you could easily get a bad case of frostbite. But the diplomats decided there was nothing to do but go ahead.[12]

Vogel was worried about something else. Shcharansky was now in a sense his client, but they had never met. Vogel was afraid, he told Meehan, that when Shcharansky arrived the next day, he would think of him merely as another of his oppressors. "I'll vouch for you," Meehan assured him, thinking that a meeting with Shcharansky the day before the release would also give him a chance to satisfy himself about the prisoner's physical and mental state. Vogel said he would have the Stasi bring Shcharansky to his office after his arrival, and Meehan could meet him there. They would be left in privacy, Vogel was sure. Looking for Shcharansky at the Reilerstrasse office would be the last idea that would occur to any of the journalists gathered at the bridge, for it was too simple.[13]

The day before the negotiations in Gerlos, Anatoly Shcharansky had suddenly been plucked out of his labor camp in the southern Urals and put without a word of explanation aboard a special plane to Moscow, where guards had brought him to Lefortovo Prison. For nearly three weeks, the guards told him nothing about why he was there, and he received no explanation for being awakened at dawn Monday, given a set of civilian clothes, a suit and tie, and instructed to put them on. There was no explanation of where they were going when his KGB escorts put him into a car, none while it slowly dawned on him that the destination was the international airport, Shcheremetyevo, and still none after he was taken up the ramp onto an Aeroflot plane. None as the aircraft rolled down the runway, none as it headed steadily west, as Shcharansky could tell from the position of the sun. Two hours into the flight, there came a cryptic pronouncement from the KGB officer in charge: Shcharansky was being deprived of his Soviet citizenship and expelled from the Soviet Union, an occasion he solemnified by suggesting that perhaps the KGB officer would like to defect and come with him. But in all seriousness, he began to hope against hope that perhaps, at last, he was on the way to join his wife, Avital, in Jerusalem.

As the plane came down to the runway, Shcharansky had still not been told where he was going, but could see that most of the aircraft on the ground were painted in the red and white colors of Interflug, the East German state airline whose headquarters was at Schöne-feld Airport on the outskirts of East Berlin. Again without explana-tion, he was bundled off into another car and driven toward the city, to a small KGB safe house in Karlshorst, and turned over to a new set of East German guards.

It was nearly dark on the Reilerstrasse when the unmarked Stasi Wartburg brought Shcharansky up to the stuccoed house, and he was escorted inside to Vogel's ground-floor office. The time was just after 5:15 P.M.

Inside, Meehan was waiting with Vogel, watching the clocks tick away on the wall opposite the visitors' couch. Meehan had just begun to fret about whether there had been a hitch, when the padded door to Vogel's inner office opened and in came one of the shortest men he had ever seen. "He wore a heavy, dark blue topcoat that was too big for him, and a gray suit, also a few sizes on the generous side. The trousers rippled down in folds that hung over his shoes onto the floor. He took his hat off, the familiar Russian winter hat with ear flaps tied up on top. He was quite bald, Lenin-like almost," Meehan thought. "I noticed from the start the sharp cool glance. Nothing beaten down about that." Shcharansky, of course, had no idea who the men were. Meehan, who had brushed up his rusty Russian for the occasion, introduced himself as the American ambassador to the German Democratic Republic, whereupon Shcharansky launched into fluent English, glad of the chance to speak it after so long. It occurred to Meehan that he was the first Western person Shcharansky had seen or talked with in almost a decade. Moved, he told Shcharansky that he had only one more night to wait before he would be a free man, and that the United States had arranged to fly him immediately to Frankfurt, where Avital would be waiting for him to continue on to Israel.[14]

Shcharansky did not lose his composure, and coolly began ques-tioning the ambassador and Vogel on the details of the procedure. Meehan told Shcharansky that he would be part of a package, but that the United States was not lumping him together with the other prisoners, who were intelligence agents. The arrangements had clearly separated him from the others, and he would be released first, on his own, before the agents.

"I know President Reagan helped," Shcharansky told him, though he was not aware that the president and Gorbachev had discussed his case at their summit in Geneva a few months earlier. In the camp near Perm he had had access to a library, where he found an anti-Semitic book that denounced Reagan for taking up his cause, among that of other Soviet Jewish dissidents. He hoped to be able to express his thanks to the president himself later, he said, but in the meantime, would Meehan convey his appreciation through diplomatic channels?

He had no luggage, only the clothes on his back and a tiny prayer book, he said, but he was concerned about some books and letters from his deceased father that he had had to leave behind. He wanted these more than anything else, and the authorities had promised to send them to his mother, Ida Milgrom, in Moscow. Vogel promised to check, but observed that in East Germany letters received by prisoners were the property of the state. Not so in the Soviet Union, Shcharansky assured him.

Vogel then told Shcharansky that he and Meehan were hoping to negotiate the release of Sakharov, and asked him to be discreet in his public comments. Shcharansky seemed noncommittal, Meehan thought. Helga Vogel walked in, greeting Shcharansky warmly and offering a cup of hot tea, which he gratefully accepted. How long had he known he was going to be freed? Vogel asked the prisoner. "Since I got a tie."[15]

Vogel found himself deeply moved. Here, in his office at last, was one of the most celebrated political prisoners of modern times, on the verge of obtaining freedom that Vogel was thrilled to think he would be given credit for. Vogel asked Helga to come in with a flash camera, asked Meehan to sit next to him and Shcharansky on the couch, in front of the large painting of Venice by the nineteenth century Dresden artist L. T. Choulant that dominated the visitors' alcove. Vogel wanted this picture for his children and his grandchildren. Surely, as long as people would talk about the unusual work Vogel had done, this was the moment they would remember best. Vogel put his left arm around Shcharansky, his right hand on the prisoner's knee, and was touched when Shcharansky took it in his own. The look in Vogel's eyes as he smiled into the camera was almost beatific.

But Shcharansky was still on the East German side of the Wall, still a Communist prisoner, and it was Vogel's job now to get him to the other side with as little hitch or fuss as possible. Shcharansky would spend the night in the safe house and would be taken soon after dawn directly to the Glienicke Bridge. When all the other prisoners in the deal had been assembled, he would be released, first, to the custody of the American ambassador to Bonn, Rick Burt. Burt would take him directly to the West Berlin airport, and they would fly to Frankfurt, where Avital would be waiting to continue with him to Israel that same day. Good luck, Meehan and Vogel wished the prisoner, amazed at his poise and self-assurance, and watched him go back out into the night with his guards.

Meehan heaved a sigh of relief. Shcharansky, although thin and pale, seemed in good physical health. He was obviously in sound mental condition, perfectly aware of what was happening to him, and, under the circumstances, in excellent spirits. Vogel, too, was glad the meeting had gone smoothly, relieved that Shcharansky would play his part in the next morning's events with dignity and honor they could all share in. Vogel accepted Meehan's assurances that Shcharansky had never been a CIA agent; it was not for him to judge what political or strategic motives the Soviets had had for keeping him in prison camp for so long. Shcharansky was simply one more of the cold war's victims, one more victim for whom he, Vogel, could take credit and satisfaction for delivering to safety.

It was still dark Tuesday morning when the journalists and camera teams began assembling at the police barricades, one thousand feet away from the Glienicke Bridge, and there was a dusting of new snow on the ground. They stamped and rubbed their hands in the cold, since the temperature stood at 21 degrees Fahrenheit. The sun was up, taking some of the frigid edge out of the air, when shortly before 9 A.M., as arranged, Vogel, Richard Burt, General Mitchell, and a flock of assistants and U.S. marshals assembled at Tempelhof Airport in West Berlin to await the arrival of the U.S. Air Force C-130 aircraft that was bringing in the five people to be released by the Western side. The Koechers had relinquished their U.S. citizenship at the American Consulate in Frankfurt the previous day.

The plane eased up to the apron, silenced its roaring engines, and lowered the tailgate. U.S. military police moved into position around it, sealing off the area around the assembled dignitaries and the VIP lounge of the terminal nearby. West German officials moved up to the plane, went aboard, and the minutes went by. Nothing happened. The problem, Rehlinger soon learned, was a collision between two different worlds, but not quite the one he had expected. American regulations required that the U.S. marshal accompanying the Koechers and the German prisoners handcuff them on the short walk between the plane and the VIP lounge. German regulations, which applied to the other three of the five prisoners on the aircraft, provided for no such thing. U.S. marshals and German police were thus facing each other down, three hours before high noon at Tempelhof, and nobody was blinking.

Rehlinger asked Burt to clear the aircraft of all official personnel and let him try to arrange a solution to the standoff. German law says you don't have to be handcuffed, Rehlinger told the prisoners, but we're in the American Zone and American rules say you do. You know you're going to go free anyway in an hour. It's up to you. The prisoners shrugged, and the U.S. marshal clicked on the handcuffs.[16]

Vogel was appalled at the scene. The Stasi would not bring its hostages to the bridge in manacles. Burt tried to explain that the regulations were the regulations; the marshals had no choice. Vogel got out of his gold Mercedes, following the Gerlos script, and talked briefly with each of the prisoners, getting their assurances that they were ready to go home as previously agreed. Meehan joined the party at about 10 A.M., and shortly before 10:45, the convoy, led by the Mercedes and brought up in the rear with two dark blue U.S. Air Force minibuses, rolled up to the Glienicke Bridge. The television crews bustled into action, cameras clicked, the limousines barreled through the now-open, red-and-white-striped pole barriers and onto the bridge. Vogel and Meehan proceeded across the dividing line to the Potsdam side, passing the Soviet sentries to the left and pulling up sharply to a halt just before the barriers.

Behind them, the American military drivers in the vans executed a screening maneuver, one they had kept secret until now, just in case the Soviets or the East Germans tried at the last minute to make it look as if Shcharansky had been a spy after all. The two vans pulled up to the middle of the bridge and straddled it, blocking the view for the cameras and causing a storm of infuriated outrage to boil up from the assembled press. The limousine carrying Burt and Rehlinger also pulled up and turned as well, pointing back to West Berlin to whisk Shcharansky away without the need for any time-consuming maneuvers after his release, again to get him out of the way before the agent swap.

But thanks to Heinz Volpert, the East Germans did exactly as Vogel had promised. The Stasi officer, wearing a heavy jacket, remained in the background and held back the release of the agents while Shcharansky and Vogel waited alone next to the green East German van that had brought the prisoner from the safe house. With a gesture, Vogel made clear that Shcharansky was now free to leave with Meehan in the ambassador's limousine, which would take them to the white border demarcation line that crossed the center of the bridge. As the two men got out of the Buick, Meehan pointed out the line, swept clear of snow by the East German guards that morning. As Shcharansky walked along in his outsize coat and floppy fur hat, Meehan thought he heard him say something about jumping, and to his surprise, the little man beside him then took a couple of short, quick steps and leaped over the line toward Burt and the rest of the American team on the other side.

So, on the banks of the Wannsee, where the Nazis had decided on the "final solution" forty-four years earlier, the most celebrated Jewish survivor of the Soviet gulag made his leap of faith to freedom, brought to this point by a German lawyer who had cooked eggs kosher for Ronnie Greenwald in a pail and sold his soul to the regime that had built the Wall. The United States had insisted all along that Shcharansky was not a spy, but had bargained for him as if he had been one for most of nine years. It had been behind-the-scenes bargaining in human flesh, belying Jimmy Carter's noble-sounding assurances that Americans would never stoop to such maneuvers, even in a good cause, but it had been the only way the Americans could see of obtaining Shcharansky's release. Vogel was not the only one at the bridge that day who had made a pact with the devil.

There was behind-the-scenes pushing and shoving for center stage at the bridge, too, this February day. Burt had insisted on greeting Shcharansky alone, and Ronnie Greenwald, who had done so much to get the negotiations going, was not invited to come. As Burt urged Shcharansky into his limousine to speed off to Tempelhof, Rehlinger realized that the ambassador was about to leave him behind, too, and he leaped into the front seat at the last minute to make sure the West Germans got their fair share of the public credit.[17]

In the West, the exchange of agents was treated as the United States intended, as a secondary scene. Little attention was paid to the Koechers and their comrades from the East, as they loaded an East German van full of Western consumer goods they had bought in prison, the last such goodies they would see until the collapse of Communism in Eastern Europe three and a half years later. For the Communist propaganda media, Shcharansky was of no interest at all, as the East German news agency, ADN, demonstrated by the play it gave to the events of the day. "On the basis of agreements between the USA and the Federal Republic of Germany as well as the USSR, the CSSR, the People's Republic of Poland and the GDR an exchange of persons who had been arrested by the respective countries took place on Tuesday, 11/2/1986. Among them were several agents," it reported.

In the limousine, Burt put Shcharansky on the telephone to President Reagan, a conversation about which Shcharansky would remember little later. There was a mishap at Tegel, where the Air Force executive jet taking them to Frankfurt malfunctioned—the brakes had frozen in the cold—and they had to take a backup turboprop plane instead. "You made your career so quickly," Shcharansky told Burt, who was thirty-nine years old. "Well, you're also very young and made a career quickly," the ambassador replied to Shcharansky, who jested that he had had help from the KGB and trusted that was not the case with Burt.[18] The ambassador took off his presidential cufflinks and gave them to Shcharansky on the spot, later cabling Reagan that he hoped the President would not be offended that he had done so. Shcharansky arrived in Israel the same evening.

Vogel still hoped he could obtain freedom for Andrei Sakharov as well. But before the end of the year, there would be no need to bargain for Sakharov's freedom, because Gorbachev summoned up the courage to invite the great human rights leader back to Moscow himself to help introduce the spirit of freedom in the Soviet Union. Moscow, Gorbachev was beginning to realize, needed the qualities of men like Sakharov far more than any Western democracy did.[19]

The human freedoms that men such as Shcharansky and Sakharov stood for were incompatible with the rule of Communism, in the Soviet Union no less than in Eastern Europe. Unwittingly, Leonid I. Brezhnev, Erich Honecker, and the other Communist leaders had signed its death warrant at Helsinki in 1975, at the Final Act of the Conference on Security and Cooperation in Europe.

While they had never intended to implement its pledges to ease travel across state borders for all citizens, to bring families together across ideological boundaries, or to guarantee freedom of the press and the right to free expression, courageous people, not only in the Soviet Union but in Eastern Europe, had insisted that they live up to their cynical promises, and braved prisons and labor camps until they did.

To the little men and women such as Shcharansky, persecuted and isolated in their "Helsinki Groups," the accords were a trumpet that did not give an uncertain sound at all. Amplified and made resonant by their courage and idealism, the clarion summons of human rights brought down Communism, the Berlin Wall, and finally the Soviet Union itself. The power of the human yearning for freedom, so long and successfully suppressed behind the Iron Curtain, became an insurmountable force, one that would preoccupy Vogel increasingly over the next three years. Soon it would put him out of business altogether.

PART FOUR

THE DEVIL'S ADVOCATE

CHAPTER ELEVEN

THE BEGINNING OF THE END

"Approved—E.H."

The day Shcharansky crossed the Glienicke Bridge to freedom, the handwriting was already on the Wall for the system that had held him prisoner, though few in the Soviet Union or in the rest of the Communist empire could yet see it. In East Germany, the real significance of Shcharansky's release was no clearer to Wolfgang Vogel: It was a symbol of the power of the idea of human rights, a force stronger than all the bombs and missiles and armies that held the Communist empire together. Vogel had thought of himself as the keeper of a safety valve that would relieve the rising pressure of discontent, driven up by the insistence of Shcharansky, Sakharov, and the people like them all over Eastern Europe that their Communist governments live up to ideals they had only cynically professed. In fact, the work Vogel had done had helped to undermine the repressive foundations of the East German regime. He would understand the full implications of his actions only later.

.   .   .

Perhaps the beginning of the end could be dated to the cold winter day of January 20, 1984, when six little-known East German dissidents entered the United States Embassy building on the Neustädtische Kirchstrasse in East Berlin and asked the librarian to help them send a letter to President Ronald Reagan in Washington.

"We ask for political asylum," their letter began, announcing that all six had been denied permission to leave East Germany and were now starting an unlimited hunger strike in the embassy that would not end until the Communists let them go. Within hours, the news was all over Germany, East and West, after the leader of the little group, a twenty-eight-year-old art student named Bernd Macke whose father was an employee of the Stasi, called a correspondent from the West German radio and television bureau to give him a copy of the text.

The Americans were caught off guard by this sudden occupation. The ambassador at the time, Rozanne Ridgway, was in the United States on consultations, and in her absence, the staff seemed uncertain about how to handle the invaders. They tried to explain that United States policy was not to offer asylum to political refugees in its foreign missions. The two most glaring exceptions, in the past, had been those of Cardinal Mindszenty, who had spent fifteen years in the U.S. Embassy in Budapest, and a Pentecostal family of Russians who had lived in the basement of the U.S. Embassy in Moscow for years after taking refuge there in 1978. At this point, the Embassy had still been unable to get permission for the Pentacostals to leave the Soviet Union. When people who forced their way into U.S. missions in Communist countries were told this story, usually they quietly agreed to leave.

But these six East Germans—Macke, two former East German political prisoners, the German son of an Italian worker whose Italian citizenship was not recognized by the East Germans, and a young couple who had been trying to leave the country for years to have a chance at a better life—did not listen to the pleas of the Embassy staffers. In particular, they rejected any suggestion that they should go up the street to the West German Permanent Mission and seek help there instead.

When the Americans asked the chief of this mission, Hans Otto Bräutigam, for advice, he told them he would call Wolfgang Vogel. Bräutigam reached him that night in a ski lodge in the Austrian Alps, and Vogel was on the first plane back to Berlin on Saturday morning.

The Americans had hardly welcomed their uninvited guests with open arms; indeed, the East Germans spent all night in the library with the lights on. Six Marine guards had hulked around ominously, as if ready to repel the boarders onto the street. When Vogel walked in, accompanied by Bräutigam and Ridgway, who had flown back early to cope with the emergency, the air was stale, for the visitors had been unable to wash or shave for two days. "You know Dr. Vogel represents the GDR," the Americans told the refugees; but both Bonn and Washington trusted his word, and they could rely on it as well.

Vogel knew Erich Honecker well enough by now to realize that his leader regarded the embassy occupation as a nuisance, and that he wanted it cleaned up just as soon as possible. Claude Cheysson, the French foreign minister, was due in on an official visit in a few days to inaugurate a French cultural institute on the Unter den Linden boulevard. Pierre Trudeau, the Canadian prime minister, was expected the following weekend. Honecker was not about to have these little diplomatic triumphs taken away from him by a band of ruffians.

It did not take Vogel long to get the six to agree to leave. Like practically everybody else in East Germany by now, they knew who he was, and trusted his assurances. Provided they left the Embassy and kept silent, he promised them, they would be allowed to submit new applications to emigrate, and he would see to it that these were approved within four weeks.

The Americans had expected a deal along these lines. Two years earlier, Vogel had secretly negotiated exit permission for Bernhard Marquardt, an East German Communist party member who had come in and demanded asylum. Marquardt had agreed to leave the building, and, not without difficulties with the Stasi, Vogel had gotten him permission to emigrate. But both Bonn and Washington had kept this case quiet, lest anybody else get the idea that charging into the U.S. embassy was a quick and easy way to get out when all else had failed.

This time, Vogel called Volpert late Sunday afternoon to report that he had succeeded in persuading the six troublemakers to go, giving Volpert plenty of advance notice to begin the complicated process of exit clearance. This would be handled by the Stasi's Central Coordination Group, and normally it took weeks. Volpert surprised him: "They are to leave for West Berlin tonight," he told Vogel—"out."

Vogel was not sure he could believe his ears. Perhaps Honecker had not thought about the consequences. In his office on the Reilerstrasse, Vogel had seen thousands of clients who had applied to leave for West Germany, and most of them had waited months or even years to go. There were tens of thousands more—perhaps even hundreds of thousands—waiting to apply. Honecker himself had put the fat in the fire earlier in the year, ordering a liberalization in the handling of applications for family reunifications, as a result of which thousands of people had been given permission to join relatives in West Germany. The word had gotten around and now others without family ties on the other side of the Wall were demanding the same basic right to travel wherever they wanted. Openness made the West more attractive. Once East Germans had been prosecuted for even watching West German television. Now, everybody watched the West German political talk shows; knew the West German brand names; saw the advertisements for dishwashers, refrigerators, sports cars, and luxury foods; saw the street scenes in Munich and Hamburg and Frankfurt on the evening news; and knew that life was better on the other side. The slight expansion in freedom that had been intended to relax the mood in the country had actually turned it sour. If spies could walk free across the border, why could not ordinary East Germans as well? If socialism was supposed to give them a better life, why did it look so dull and shabby compared to what they could see with their own eyes on their television screens, and confirm by talking with their West German relatives when they came on visits? In the East, the economy was going nowhere; the people were growing tired of empty promises.

To deliver on them, Honecker needed money, hard Western currency, and the only way to get it was through the West Germans, despite the heavy-caliber propaganda war that he had been waging at Moscow's insistence about the American plan to install medium-range nuclear missiles on West German soil to counter the Soviet SS-20s. One of the ways Honecker had used to get the West Germans to provide a long-term bank credit of a billion deutsche marks, all to be used on projects that benefited the ordinary people of the country, was to let 29,626 people move West in 1984, almost six times as many as the previous year. Honecker had also ordered the dismantling of the automatic shooting devices on the border, the infernal machines that had caused East Germany so much embarrassment in the 1970s. Border guards still had authorization to use deadly force to prevent escapes, however.

Yet the liberalization was having consequences that Honecker had not foreseen. An unsanctioned antiwar movement had sprouted in East Berlin despite the Stasi's best efforts to repress it and imprison its leader, a painter named Bärbel Bohley. She and others like her, given shelter and moral protection by the Lutheran Church, began to form the core of an increasingly daring and vocal East German democracy movement.

Vogel knew that in such a climate, the news—that six people without family ties to West Germany or any other qualification to emigrate under the normal rules had managed to get permission to leave simply by walking into the U.S. Embassy and demanding it—would spread like wildfire. He did not want to answer for the consequences.

He called the Central Committee and asked for permission to speak with Honecker. Within a few moments, he had the leader on the telephone. "This could set off a chain reaction," Vogel started to explain. "You don't understand," Honecker interrupted him. "I want them in West Berlin before midnight."

Hanging up, Vogel wondered if he ought to disregard the order, but quickly decided against it. Honecker was becoming increasingly autocratic and impulsive, making decisions on the spur of the moment, not always, Vogel thought, with sufficient regard for the consequences. But Vogel did want to make sure the West Germans knew what was about to happen. Driving to the Permanent Mission, Vogel went in to see Bräutigam. "We've got a solution," Vogel told him. "Good," Bräutigam smiled, but the blood drained from his face when he heard what it was: "We can drive them over right away. Our border guards have already been informed."

"For God's sake!" Bräutigam exclaimed. "Have you thought what could happen? I'll soon have a full house here!"[1]

A crucial watershed had been reached. The West Germans, like the Americans during both the Carter and Reagan administrations, had always supported the abstract principles of human rights, including the right to emigrate. Under American pressure, the Soviet Union had allowed hundreds of thousands of Soviet Jews to emigrate during the 1970s, and it had begun letting ethnic Germans leave for West Germany. But the Wall denied that right to most

East Germans. If millions of them suddenly realized that all they needed to claim it was to go to the West German embassy and refuse to leave until they got it, the result could be chaos.

Bräutigam's concern was justified. Not only he but his diplomatic colleagues in other capitals soon did have their houses full of East German refugees. In Prague, within only a few weeks, East Germans had begun forcing their way into the West German Embassy, the Lobkowitz Palace just below Prague Castle, demanding asylum. On the afternoon of February 24, 1984, a group of about twenty was joined by Ingrid Berg, the thirty-nine-year-old niece of the East German prime minister, Willi Stoph. She arrived with her husband, two children, and her mother-in-law, and announced she was not leaving until they, complete with Meissen porcelain and grandfather clock, got permission to go to West Germany. The news was a sensation for the anti-Communist Western tabloid press: Even the privileged families of the ruling Communist elite wanted out. Stoph's office issued an unusual statement, published in *Neues Deutschland,* the official East German party organ, denying that the prime minister knew what his niece had planned, or in fact that he had any sort of relationship with her. It also suggested that her husband was an unstable person who had been back and forth between West and East Germany for years, and had once tried to join the French Foreign Legion.

Anxious about the damage the case could do to East-West German relations, Rehlinger asked Vogel to help find a solution. After talking with the Bergs in Prague, Vogel decided not to call Honecker personally, though he knew that only the party chief could resolve the case. Instead, he wrote his recommendations to Streit. The Bergs would not give up trying to leave, he reported, and the publicity would burgeon—at the expense of relations between the two German states—until they got out. Better to get it all over with quickly and let them leave, saving face by making them come home and apply for permission first. So it was ordained, and the Bergs did as they were told, returned to East Berlin on March 1. Barely three weeks later, they turned up, with all their belongings, at a refugee camp in West Germany.[2]

By then, the nightmare Bräutigam feared had also begun to come true in the West German Permanent Mission in East Berlin. East Germans were beginning to pile into the building, refusing to leave unless they received permission to emigrate. At first, the West German staff tried to accommodate some of them in tiny rooms on the fifth floor, but as the numbers increased and it became obvious that there was no way to meet the demand, they had given up. By June 22, they had to close off the interior of the building and limit visitor access to the entryway. Even there, some of the East Germans insisted on camping out on the cold stone floor. There was only a pail to take care of sanitary needs.

Outside, the Stasi guards were getting tougher. On the 22nd, they brutally beat a man trying to enter the building and took him away. On the 26th, another man doused himself with gasoline and attempted to set himself on fire on the street. Only quick action by the West Germans saved him from serious injury.

The fifth floor came to look like a tenement. Those inside communicated with relatives and friends using messages on sheets and laundry hung outside the window. The West German television cameras picked up every hour of the drama. On the 27th, Bräutigam finally had to close the mission altogether.

"To our genuinely deep regret," the notice posted on the doors stated, "the mission is not able to receive visitors at this time." By then fifty-nine East German "guests" were inside.

Included among those were fifteen children. And children were always the fastest way to Wolfgang Vogel's heart. "The eyes always got to me," he said. "I would look into their frightened eyes and think that I had to do something, fast." He had looked into the eyes of two small twins, the children of an East German couple who had come into the office of the first West German ambassador to Prague in the mid-1970s and had refused to leave until they got permission to go to West Germany. The Germans had begged Vogel then to come to Prague and help, and he and Helga had driven down in the Mercedes. While Vogel was talking with the ambassador, the twins were crawling around beneath the desk and playing. Vogel had managed to convince the couple that even if the ambassador gave them the West German passports they were demanding, the Czech authorities would arrest them at the border because they would not be able to show how they had entered the country. He and Helga persuaded them to come back to East Germany with them in the Mercedes, with the twins. A few days later, they had driven the family to West Germany, in total secrecy, after the Stasi had cleared them for exit.[3]

This time, too, the West German civil servants at the Permanent Mission went out and bought toys and games to keep the children amused while their parents settled in for a long stay. But now the drama was taking place in the glare of full publicity, and mere promises by Vogel that the authorities would sympathetically consider their applications to emigrate were no longer enough. These people wanted to be driven directly to West Berlin, just like the six from the American Embassy.

The people occupying the mission had nothing in common but the desire to leave, the one thing that united so many East Germans. Now they could not understand why nothing seemed to be happening. The East German authorities had begun to recognize the mistake they had made in the American case, a fact that was evident from Vogel's first public statement. "I plead for a mutually acceptable and beneficial solution, above all in view of the children and the relations between both German states," he said, but then added: "Blackmail will not work. A way out as in the past will not be possible." With the intensive coverage of the drama in the West German media, politicians in Bonn were also getting into the act, declaring that the Permanent Mission was neither a hotel nor a travel bureau. But they insisted that East German citizens should have a right to go wherever they wanted, and that Bonn could not simply turn them out and leave them to the tender mercies of the Stasi.

Though Honecker still hoped to make his often-postponed visit to West Germany that summer—the trip that was to include a stop in his home town in the Saar—relations between the two German states began deteriorating rapidly under the pressure of these public events. What Honecker had intended as a safety valve had instead set off a hemorrhage. His leadership reacted in panic, showing annoyance over the West German government statements and threatening to stop family unifications altogether.

Vogel, in this situation, was performing a negotiator's high-wire act. His ability to get these people out depended on their agreeing to conditions that were acceptable to the regime they wanted to leave. Vogel had to find an acceptable formula, or make one acceptable to both sides, and only he had the necessary credibility in both camps to do it. The key to this credibility, now as always, was that he could represent the regime without being part of it—the crucial bit of distance that had enabled him to be the intermediary in the prisoner-release program and in the exchanges of spies as well.

Rehlinger and Vogel met with other West German officials in the building on the 27th. The atmosphere was tense; Vogel and Rehlinger both knew that the Stasi was listening to every word through the bugging devices in the walls. Rehlinger told Vogel the East German side would have to give the squatters a promise of freedom from prosecution and assurance of permission to emigrate, or they would stay in the building for months. Vogel reacted coolly, and emphasized that whatever the outcome with these 59, the West Germans would have to take steps to ensure that they were not replaced by another 59, or 159.

The next morning, again in Vogel's office, the two sides exchanged drafts of a statement resolving the impasse. Vogel, Rehlinger noticed, retreated to his private office several times for intense telephone conversations. Messengers bustled in and out, taking successive drafts off to higher authority. Finally they reached agreement: All the East Germans occupying the Permanent Mission could leave and apply for permission to emigrate; their applications would be decided quickly and favorably, and they would not be prosecuted for any crime connected with the occupation. Vogel would help all who wanted his assistance in making the necessary settlements of debts and property questions.

That the agreement would be carried out, Rehlinger had no doubt. For on Vogel's copy was a handwritten note from Honecker himself: "Approved—E.H."

There was still one important obstacle to be overcome—the skepticism and mistrust of the fifty-nine people inside the mission, one of them a twenty-one-year-old East German "National People's Army" deserter who feared for his life if the military should ever get hold of him again. The young soldier would need to be persuaded that he would come to no harm if he left the West German mission.[4]

On June 28, a hot, sticky day, Vogel and Rehlinger went up to the fifth floor to try to persuade him and the others that it was safe to leave. The scene resembled a campground, the West German civil servant thought. Some of the East Germans were dressed in sweatsuits. The air was oppressive with the sharp odor of human fear and anxiety. None of the members of the group trusted the others, and few were ready to trust Rehlinger or Vogel now. Rehlinger had come, he told them, as representative of the West German Ministry for Intra-German Relations, to help them. They all certainly knew Vogel; together, he and Rehlinger had negotiated what they hoped was an acceptable solution to the dilemma. Leaving directly for the border from the West German mission would be impossible. They would have to apply for permission from the East

German authorities first, but these authorities had promised to grant it and not to punish anyone for seeking asylum in the mission. Bonn would ensure that the East German government made good on these assurances, Rehlinger promised.

Again, the nature of Vogel's role was complex and contradictory. To the people in the room, he represented the Stasi; to Volpert and Mielke, Vogel represented the people in the room. Through Volpert, he could negotiate terms that the Stasi could accept. To Rehlinger, to the anxious refugees, to the Stasi, Vogel was a *passe-partout,* representing everyone and no one and useful precisely because of the ambiguousness of his situation. His usefulness would end the moment any one of the parties—refugees, West Germans, Communists—felt that he had betrayed them.

The talks had taken all afternoon, and Vogel had been in constant close touch with Volpert to make sure that the Stasi units outside the embassy and the field offices in the occupiers' home towns—the whole, all-encompassing, ubiquitous network of control, surveillance, and coercion, in fact—would respect the assurances he had given to these simple citizens inside. Vogel's credibility depended on the efficiency of Volpert's coordinating work, but Volpert knew his business, and the Stasi was nothing if not coordinated.

By the end of the day, Vogel's assurances were beginning to have an effect. Three of the fifty-nine inside the mission said they were ready to go home, agreeing to call the others upon arrival to report on what the East German authorities had done. Vogel was in constant touch with Volpert to make sure that all went smoothly. The three left that evening and called the next day, shortly before noon, to report that they had reached their destinations undisturbed, just as Vogel had promised. Now momentum began to build. First one, then two, then three, and finally twenty-three people decided to leave the building on the 29th, prompting Vogel to issue a press release calling attention to this success but emphasizing the need for "peace and calm." By Monday, July 2, only four were left, including the deserter, who was now insisting that he would only go if his fiancée, who knew nothing of what he had done, were allowed to go to West Germany with him. Rehlinger called in Vogel once more, and the lawyer arranged a tête-à-tête between the soldier and the girl in the garden behind his office, on the Reilerstrasse. She refused to leave home, and finally the soldier agreed to go West alone.

Vogel's office was busy over the next few weeks, making arrangements for the fifty-nine and their families to sell their property and their furniture, settle their debts, and make all the other myriad arrangements for departure, as East German law prescribed. But all were finally permitted to leave, even the soldier, without his bride. He would be back again, looking for another one, within a couple of years, crossing illegally over the border from Czechoslovakia and getting caught by the police. He was released again in an amnesty in the fall of 1987 and, this time as a West German citizen, was allowed to pass the border once more.[5]

In 1984, Vogel could not see where the fatal logic of these events was leading. But ordinary East Germans who wanted out could. One of the few countries East Germans could visit without visas was Czechoslovakia, whose regime, after 1968, was about as restrictive as their own. Needing only their identity cards, millions went every summer to the mountains and camping places of Bohemia and Slovakia, their two-cycle Trabants and Wartburgs choking the highways with clouds of acrid, blue smoke. This summer, the West German Embassy in Prague had suddenly become a popular destination. In the old center of the city, tucked away on a narrow, cobblestone street, the Lobkowitz Palace was easy to find. The Czechoslovak guards outside did not seem to pay too much attention to who was going in, and once in, many East Germans thought, they could stay until their government gave in to their demands, just as it had given in to Willi Stoph's niece.

By October 4, 140 people had managed to find shelter inside, camping out with mattresses on the floor of the eighteenth-century embassy building's fresco room, bringing all normal diplomatic activity to a halt, and leaving Ambassador Klaus Meyer no choice but to close the doors.

This new crisis put relations between the two German states under the greatest strain since the Guillaume case a decade earlier. Certainly this had not been Honecker's intention at the beginning of 1984; he had high hopes of making his trip to the Saar. But with U.S.-Soviet relations still frozen in confrontation over the medium-range missiles, his negotiating room was limited. Once again, on orders from Moscow, he postponed his travel plans.

He left it to Vogel to try to resolve the dispute over the East Germans in Bonn's embassy in Prague. But this time, Vogel was instructed, he was to handle things in such a way as to make such dramas impossible in the future.

Vogel chose to make the tougher conditions known to East Germans through the mass-circulation West German tabloid, the *Bild,* on October 19. He chose Axel Springer's most anti-Communist sheet deliberately, since it automatically had the greatest credibility with disaffected East Germans such as those who had taken refuge inside the embassy. "The promise given to State Secretary Rehlinger, that all concerned will not be punished if they return to their place of residence, is still valid," he said. "They can apply to their local authorities for exit permission. Beyond that there are and have been neither promises nor negotiations. There should still be grounds for a mutually acceptable and satisfactory solution to be found . . . I warn against asking too much."

Rehlinger made four visits to Prague to try to convince the East Germans to go home and do as Vogel had asked. He told them that Vogel had given assurances that he would continue to assist every one of them in their applications for permission to emigrate, but Rehlinger could point to no promise, written or oral, that guaranteed that they would get it.

The difficulty was that the would-be emigrants had burned all their bridges to the German Democratic Republic. As they saw it, they had nothing to lose by staying put. They could communicate with West German journalists and television crews in Prague over the fence surrounding the embassy's spacious garden grounds, and there were almost daily reports on the evening news. The publicity itself encouraged many to remain obstinate. The West German embassy staffers had evacuated their offices on the building's first floor to let the refugees bunk in, more than a score in every room, and the Foreign Ministry in Bonn had sent down one of its best cooks, a man named Martin who held culinary courses to distract them from their miseries—since there were only four showers, twelve toilets, and ten washbasins for the entire group, these were considerable.

The West German media played the drama for all it was worth, causing anger and embarrassment for Honecker and putting political pressure on Chancellor Kohl. Bonn would lose face if the embassy occupiers did not get permission to come to West Germany. But every attempt by a West German official to say that this would happen was immediately disavowed by Vogel. What Vogel had promised, "well-informed sources" told the West German press agency DPA on November 5, was "the limit of what G.D.R. officials can and will do in this matter." "Those who encourage these persons in any illusions" were urged to understand. Vogel was, indeed, pushing his limits: for the East German state, the question of control—of the state's ability to make its citizens follow its rules, by coercion, if necessary—was the foundation of its legitimacy. The East German leadership was counting on Vogel to solve the problem in Prague quickly, and in a way that made clear that more such incidents were out of the question.

By early December, a few people had begun leaving. But finally Rehlinger and Vogel agreed that only a personal visit by Vogel could convince the rest that staying on was pointless. On December 13, the two men appeared together before the assembled refugees in the fresco room. It was not easy for Vogel; passions among the refugees ran high, and some had hissed and booed him as he came in. Rehlinger, too, had to endure their jeers. "Dr. Vogel and I haven't come here for our personal pleasure," he told them. "There are other places where we can drink Pilsener Urquell together."

Vogel addressed the group for half an hour. It was a virtuoso performance, Rehlinger thought, reflecting the skills of argument and persuasion that made Vogel such a good lawyer. He acknowledged the fears and hopes of the refugees, but he had to tell them that there was only one way to get out to West Germany, and that was through the country on which they had turned their backs. He could make no promises, except to help get their applications approved.

As the Christmas holidays drew near, more and more decided to take him at his word. Only about seventy were left on the 20th of December, when Hans-Dietrich Genscher, the West German foreign minister, was due to visit, but of those about forty had decided on a hunger strike as a last desperate measure to force the East Germans to give in. "We can only tell you what the situation is as we see it," Genscher told the group, backing Vogel's and Rehlinger's appeals to them to leave. "What you do is your decision."

In early January, following instructions from Honecker, Vogel turned up the pressure.[6] "Time is running out," he warned. And on January 15, the last six refugees left the embassy. "After the 16th of January 1985 my negotiating authority . . . would no longer have been valid," Vogel told DPA. "And I will not be given such authority again. I warn therefore with all seriousness expressly against any similar attempt whatsoever in future."

The warning was mainly for public effect, to minimize the chances of repetition. Privately, Honecker and Mielke had given him continuing authority to settle similar cases in the future, and with more latitude than had been possible in the glare of publicity in Prague. In effect, the East Germans authorized Vogel to make the West German authorities their accomplices. Over the next four years, the West German mission could rid itself of unwanted East German "guests" by telling them that if they would go home and apply for permission to leave, their applications would be handled with "good will" by the East German authorities. The West Germans would then telex their names to Vogel's office, and he would quietly take care of the rest. For Honecker, getting rid of a few troublemakers before they could do much damage to East Germany's image was well worth the concession, and the West Germans could let their mission in East Berlin go back to its regularly assigned tasks. Once again, Dr. Vogel had been an agent of convenience for both sides.[7]

But all sides held a fatally flawed assumption—that the tide was stoppable. Later, Vogel realized that the events of 1984 had been the start of a chain reaction. "It was a vicious circle. Nobody saw the momentum that was building up. The Stasi thought that they were bleeding off excess pressure. The security people thought that letting 40,000 people go would take care of it. That there would be another 40,000—that, they couldn't foresee."[8]

Thus, it was not evident at the time to anyone in the aging and increasingly isolated East German leadership, or to Vogel, that the end had already begun. When, occasionally, Vogel discreetly alluded to the signs of a popular mood of growing discontent that he saw in his practice, Honecker always dismissed them. "Come up with me on the speaker's platform and tell me the people are discontented," Honecker would tell people who tried to tell him the way things really were; he, like all tyrants, was deluded by the sycophancy that surrounded him. Vogel was getting hundreds of letters and applications to emigrate from people whose descriptions of harrassment and persecution by the Stasi and other East German authorities made him physically disgusted. The rare occasions when he met with Mielke himself, usually in Honecker's office to discuss delicate questions like how to handle the embassy crisis, aroused a similar reaction. "We have an agreement with the Federal Republic," Vogel had said at one of these meetings, discussing family reunifications, only to hear Mielke interject, "Agreement? What do you mean, agreement? We can stop them anytime we like." Vogel left shaking his head.

He had become one of the system's most powerful men, but he was only an agent of the high and mighty; his influence depended not on himself but on them. Chance, as well as talent and inordinate hard work, had brought him to where he was—the friendship in the West of men such as Frank Meehan and Ludwig Rehlinger, and the association in the East with men such as Josef Streit, the prosecutor-general, and Heinz Volpert, who now sat at Mielke's right hand, the fixer at whose orders prison gates and border barriers were lifted, and without whom Vogel would have been just another lawyer. Through his associations with Wehner and Schmidt on the other side, through his ability to negotiate on spies and matters of state alike with Western governments, increasing East Germany's and Honecker's prestige in the eyes of his Soviet patrons, Vogel had earned Honecker's respect, and the freedom to exercise wide latitude. "You can do anything that enables you to carry out your mandate," Honecker had told him. Vogel never spoke, even in private, with anything but respect for the leader, but there was also a certain reserve between them. Even after a dozen years of close collaboration, Vogel had never been to the Honecker home in Wandlitz. The two men addressed each other formally with "*Sie,*" not "*Du*" as party comrades usually did. Mielke, who even so was jealous of Vogel's closeness to the head of state, would narrow his eyes and give him the feeling that he was watching him closely, and would often move to block his influence. Vogel told Klaus Bölling, then chief of the West German mission, of one occasion when he had suggested to Honecker that East Germany could earn more foreign currency by putting in additional snack bars and Intershops on the autobahn transit routes for foreigners. "Good idea," Honecker had said. But later he had told him that Mielke had vetoed the project because such places could be used as rendezvous for foreign spies.

Honecker was a man of no worldly sophistication, and quite unlike Vogel, was hampered by a massive inferiority complex vis-à-vis his West German opposite numbers. Son of a coalminer, as a boy in the Saar he had wanted to become a locomotive engineer but had been turned down, he said years later, because locomotive engineers were state officials, and workers were somehow seen as subversive; instead he had followed in the footsteps of an uncle who was a roofer. The idea that a roofer, a son of the working class, could consort on an equal level with great West German capitalists never ceased to amaze him. For Honecker, like most of his colleagues and like the rulers of the Soviet Union before Gorbachev, was a prisoner of the rigid class antagonisms of the early twentieth century, antagonisms that had given birth to the Bolshevik Revolution, the Nazi party, and to two world wars that had finally destroyed the world in which Marxism had lived and flourished.

The West had driven these people deeper into their defensive shells by the cold war policies of isolation. By the time these policies ended, in East Germany's case only at the end of the 1960s, diplomatic recognition had become a psychological obsession with the men in Honecker's Politburo. Having got it, they fell into the error of excessive pride. The goal of Communist politics now became not changing society, but preserving their own outdated illusions about what they had achieved. Honecker hardly had a chance to see how the working class lived under Communism, racing in his Volvo limousine through the forbidding and barren housing projects twice a day to and from the privileged cocoon of Wandlitz. Outwardly, Honecker could tell himself, the workers in Berlin lived a lot better than the coalminers of the Saar had lived, half a century earlier, and no socialist country was more prosperous than East Germany. Certainly there was no reason why he should change course.

In 1985, the end still seemed far off. Vogel still saw himself as part of a power structure that would be preserved no matter who the party's general secretary was. His own role, as he saw it, lay in helping to smooth the regime's rough edges and burnish its reputation, while helping the malcontents who did not fit in. He and Helga would enjoy their ski trips to Austria and Switzerland while they could, for after retirement they would be treated as members of the nomenklatura and their private travel would be restricted because they had been privy to so many government secrets. The prospect did not bother him. Vogel's strength had always lain in his ability to find the golden mean, the compromise, and he enjoyed being flattered for it.

Two years earlier, Honecker had added to Vogel's collection of medals the "Great Star of Friendship of the Peoples," for the contributions Vogel had made to extending and improving East Germany's foreign relations. Sweden had made Vogel an "Officer of the Royal Order of the North Star" for his humanitarian services over the years, and in 1984 the Austrian government had followed, with the "Great Medal for Service to the Republic of Austria" for his work as its embassy's lawyer in East Berlin. Vogel's reputation seemed secure on both sides of the Wall. He was seen as he had chosen to see himself: as a humanitarian, tirelessly shuttling around all of Central Europe and helping ordinary people in need. But he was also sparing his Western diplomatic clients the embarrassment that would have come if they had simply shoved East German squatters back out onto the streets.

Vogel's sixtieth birthday, on October 30, 1985, was a major social event in the claustrophobic diplomatic community of East Berlin. Limousines bearing the great and good from East and West passed up the narrow Reilerstrasse all day long, with a uniformed security policeman there to direct traffic. Bishop Gottfried Forck of the Lutheran Church came, as did Manfred Stolpe, the leading Lutheran layman of the Berlin-Brandenburg diocese, and Hermann Kunst, through whose church office in Bonn the political prisoner business had always run so discreetly; Schalck-Golodkowski, who booked the proceeds for CoCo, came to pay court, and Foreign Minister Fischer lent his patronage. From the West German side, Rehlinger came to show respect, as did the man who would be his successor, Walter Priesnitz, and Bräutigam, Bölling, and Gaus, present and former chiefs of the West German Permanent Mission. West German President Richard von Weizsäcker sent a handwritten letter attesting to Vogel's humanity and dedication. Even Lothar Loewe had been allowed in again, now that he was the official in charge of the Free Berlin television station.

But at the high water mark of Vogel's career, there were also storm signals. The first dark cloud along the horizon was the grave illness of Streit, his first and most constant protector, patron, and advocate with the East German party leadership. Streit was unable to come to the party, but his wife had brought a letter that Vogel proudly showed to Rehlinger, expressing his satisfaction that the trust and confidence he had placed in Vogel from the very beginning had been justified.[9] But poor health would soon force Streit to resign.[10] Honecker, busy with other duties, could not come, either; Honecker, too, would soon have other worries. Vogel would remain indispensable for only as long as his connection with Honecker, and Honecker's with the Kremlin, remained intact. And those days were already numbered.

Three months later, on February 15, 1986, Vogel suffered another personal loss, the sudden death of Heinz Volpert, as unexpected as it was unconvenient. Volpert, fifty-four years old, had attended a party conference at Stasi headquarters, a long and dutiful affair that took place over a weekend. When the delegates had been called upon to vote, Volpert had decided to go home early, before the vote count, to enjoy a couple of hours in the sauna that he had in his quarters; like so many Stasi officers, he emulated Russian habits even in his private life. Volpert, in the peak of physical health, an avid tennis player, and a jogging fanatic, had taken unusually long in the sauna this Saturday night, and at 2 A.M. his wife had gone looking for him there. She had found him slumped over on the wooden bench, a trickle of blood running down from the right corner of his mouth. The emergency ambulance crew had found him dead on the scene when they arrived. His wife, fearing foul play, had called Vogel and asked him to come to view the body.

By now Vogel considered the Stasi colonel and his family personal friends and was profoundly upset by the scene. He wondered, even, if Volpert had come to grief because he, like Vogel, had seen the inside of too many Stasi prisons, had seen too many busloads of prisoners cheer and cry with joy on being released at Herleshausen—had come to sympathize too much with the prisoners. Volpert's friends brushed off such suspicions. Perhaps he had had one or two drinks too many, fallen asleep, and suffered a heat stroke. Nobody ever knew. But Vogel knew that he had lost a valuable asset—that rare thing, a Stasi officer who, to him at least, also seemed to have a soul.[11]

Volpert's replacement was a slightly older man not cut from the same bolt of cloth at all, an orderly, heavyset Saxon with standard-issue East German military glasses, Lieutenant General Gerhard Niebling. He was head of the Stasi's Central Coordination Group, a 180-strong unit whose main assignment was keeping the lid on the growing popular desire to get out of the country and controlling the flow of prisoners and others the state was willing to get rid of. The prisoner exchanges and Vogel's embassy cases, Niebling was told by his minister, were to be his sole concern in working with the lawyer now. Niebling, too, continued the Stasi practice of referring to Vogel, in internal documents, as "Georg," the cover name he had used as a Stasi secret informant in the 1950s. Niebling, who had earlier been in the Stasi's investigations department, had occasionally stood in for Volpert before and knew who he was. Now, on his desk calendar, he would make dates to see "Georg" in his office. Vogel, who later claimed to be unaware that he was still known as "Georg," found Niebling a typical career Stasi officer, loyal and true but a bit dull. He was the kind of man who would spend his weekends drinking beer and watching the Stasi's soccer team, Dynamo—not like Volpert at all. Out of loyalty, Vogel took on Ingrid Volpert, his friend's widow, as a part-time secretary-translator in his office. She spoke a little English, and Vogel thought that a little work would be good for her morale, help to get her over the shock of her husband's sudden death.[12]

For Vogel himself, the work did not let up at all. The West Germans needed Vogel again in the summer, calling him to Bonn to help resolve a delicate diplomatic impasse with considerable complications. Professor Dr. Herbert Meissner, a Communist party member and general secretary of the East German Academy of Sciences, had been caught shoplifting a chrome shower hose connection worth DM29.50, the equivalent of less than $20, from the Wertheim department store in West Berlin. The matter quickly escalated into a tale of intrigue and espionage, and an affair of state. Caught red-handed by a house detective, Meissner had blurted out that he had high Stasi connections, asked to be put in contact with the BND, and been accommodated. But after spending three nights in the luxury Alpenhof Hotel near the West German intelligence service's headquarters outside Munich, he had disappeared sometime between July 13 and 14. On the 15th, the East German Permanent Mission in Bad Godesberg announced that Meissner had taken refuge there. The East Germans accused the Bonn authorities of detaining him under false pretenses, kidnapping him to Munich, drugging him, and forcing him to betray state secrets.

The West Germans issued an arrest warrant for Meissner and ringed the mission with police. The East Germans threatened to halt all travel between the two parts of the country in retaliation for this outrage against one of their citizens. To keep things from getting any further out of hand, both governments called on Vogel to help them save face and get them out of the mess.

He and Helga appeared in Rehlinger's office, a half mile or so down the Godesberger Allee from the East German mission, at 6:30 P.M. on the 19th, a Saturday evening. In three hours of talks, they worked out a compromise: The West Germans would lift the warrant, Vogel would bring Meissner to the office of the Federal Criminal Office in Meckenheim, and Rehlinger would talk with Meissner to decide whether he really did want to return to East Berlin of his own free will. Helga Vogel typed out the agreement on a piece of Rehlinger's office stationery, while the two men got the agreement of their respective higher authorities. In the Normannenstrasse, General Niebling had been much impressed. Vogel was imaginative, took the initiative, knew how to find his way to a solution that was acceptable to all sides, and he was well on the way to achieving what the Stasi wanted: to get Meissner safely back.[13]

On the 21st, all went as agreed, with a little twist: Rehlinger sneaked in a psychiatrist, without identifying him, to help him judge whether Meissner was *compos mentis*. All the man wanted was to have his red East German diplomatic passport back, a sign of status and privilege just like Vogel's, and to be assured that if he went back to West Germany he would not be prosecuted. About the chrome shower hose connection, not a word. Meissner returned to East Germany the same evening. There had been no quid pro quo, Rehlinger told the press later, but this was not strictly true. The East German threat to cut off travel between the two parts of the country had worked, and the government in Bonn asked the West German prosecutors to drop the case against Meissner in the national interest.[14]

Though Meissner may have been no agent, 1985 had been a vintage year for espionage scandals, and Vogel and Rehlinger both had plenty of cases in their files. Hans Joachim Tiedge, a top-ranking counterintelligence specialist in the Federal Office for the Protection of the Constitution, defected to East Germany on August 19, leaving behind in his home in Cologne piles of empty bottles, top-secret security documents strewn about the floor, and a heavy burden of debt. Two weeks later, Vogel hand-carried to Rehlinger's office a note from Tiedge, written on a piece of plain white paper, explaining that he had defected because of "a hopeless personal situation" and was "not ready to meet with official representatives of the Federal Republic or with representatives of the media."[15]

Tiedge's defection had been preceded by those of the private secretary of the West German economics minister and a secretary in Chancellor Kohl's office. A week later, Margarete Höke, a secretary in President Richard von Weizsäcker's office, was arrested in

Copenhagen after being seen with a German-speaking KGB agent who West German officials said was her lover. Markus Wolf's "Romeo" technique of sending agents to Bonn to woo the lonely single women who worked in the chanceries and ministries of Bonn had again succeeded brilliantly.

East Germans were not immune to tugs of the heartstrings, either. Rehlinger had been trying for years to negotiate the release of one of the most pathetic cases. This involved East German Christa-Karin Schumann, a doctor who had fallen in love with East German Rear Admiral Winfried Baumann. Baumann had headed the Defense Ministry's espionage operations in the Federal Republic before developing alcoholism and being fired in 1970. Through Schumann's brother, a professor of medicine who lived in Heidelberg, Baumann made contact with the West German BND intelligence agency, asking for help so that he and Schumann could escape to the West. The BND agreed, but the Stasi had intercepted and deciphered one of Schumann's coded letters to the West, and the couple had been arrested in June 1979.[16]

Rehlinger could not include Baumann's name on any of the lists he handed to Vogel, for the East Germans had executed the admiral after his trial, in June 1980. Christa-Karin Schumann had been luckier, receiving a prison sentence of fifteen years. Vogel had put Schumann on his list then, arguing with Mielke so vehemently year after year to let him try to arrange an exchange that the minister had complained to Niebling about it: "Why doesn't he drop Schumann? She isn't going to be exchanged."[17] Only in August 1987, after she had served half her time, did Mielke agree to release her, and only after Bonn had finally traded Lothar Erwin Lutze, the Romeo they had refused to trade for Shcharansky. The price for Schumann was an aeronautical expert the West Germans had caught passing high-technology information to the Soviets.

Honecker had thus managed to please both Bonn and Moscow and was finally granted permission to make his long-anticipated visit to West Germany, and revisit his homeland in the Saar, in September. By that time, the country Honecker ruled was already drifting away from its ideological and philosophical moorings. The long freeze of the cold war was coming to an end.

Helga Vogel, who had swum against the tide in 1969 in leaving West Germany to come and live under Communism with her husband, was beginning to ask herself where it was all going to end.

Fifteen years younger than he was, slight, blond, self-effacing, she was a tower of strength, and of all Vogel's assistants, surely one of the hardest working. Week after week for so many years, she had sat behind the wheel on the long and tiring journeys to Bautzen and to the border at Herleshausen. She had gone with him to all those prisons in the United States, to the embassy in Prague, and had worked with him in his office day and night, weekdays and weekends. When Vogel needed a file from his archive, at home or at the office, Helga was always willing, without a word, to find it, no matter how long it took. She was so shy and quiet that she was almost invisible; she was Vogel's alter ego, the purpose of whose life was solely to help him fulfill his own. She discussed politics with no one but her husband. Now they both could see that the system they lived in was entering a grave crisis.

For, though the occupations of Bonn's embassies in Prague and East Berlin faded from the headlines after early 1985, East Germans had kept coming—not in such large numbers as then, because of the conspiracy of silence between East and West, but steadily nevertheless. In 1987, 68 of the 628 East Germans—more than a tenth—who had managed to get past the Stasi guards on the street into the West German mission on Hannoversche Strasse had declined to leave until they received permission to go to West Germany; in 1988, it was 379, out of 6,608.[18]

As the pressure rose, the leadership dealt with dissidents ever more expediently. As fast as it could, it began to get rid of them, faster sometimes than suited Vogel. The most dramatic instance came on January 17, 1988. The burgeoning peace movement in East Berlin had turned a march in memory of the German Marxist revolutionaries Rosa Luxemburg and Karl Liebknecht into an annual pilgrimage on the anniversary of Luxemburg's assassination. This year, thousands of young people joined the parade, hoisting banners with one of her best-known quotations—"Freedom always means freedom for those who think differently." The Stasi, under orders to keep West German television crews from recording the event, had turned away the marchers in side streets and arrested more than a hundred of them, including some of the leading dissidents—Bärbel Bohley, the popular rock star Stephan Krawczyk, and his companion, the theater director Freya Klier.

Asked by church figures to do what he could to help, Vogel, accompanied by Lutheran Bishop Gottfried Forck, talked with

Krawczyk and Klier together, promising that he would try to negotiate their release from jail. One possibility, he knew, was to arrange for them to give up their East German citizenship and leave for West Germany; Niebling had come to him and told him that this was Mielke's preferred solution. "Go to the lawyer and ask him to talk Klier and Krawczyk into going to the Federal Republic or somewhere else," Mielke had asked his subordinate, who had gone to Vogel with the proposition and been brought up short by his refusal. "I'm not one of your troops," Vogel bristled, "I ought to throw you out of here."[19] The Stasi general had then gone back to the Normannenstrasse and reported the response to Mielke, who had listened calmly and responded, with a shrug, "He's the lawyer, he must know what he can and can't do."

But the Stasi interrogators kept up the pressure, and in the end all three gave up and agreed to emigrate against their better judgment. Klier laid most of the blame at Vogel's door, unaware of his resistance or unwilling to give it credence, for Vogel had also taken precautions and let West German press contacts he trusted know that he had objected in principle to giving the prisoners no alternative but to leave; this would have been coercion.

The repression of the Luxemburg demonstrations had set powerful forces in motion, driven by the increasing contradictions between the gathering force of change and reform in the Soviet Union under Gorbachev and the rigidity and stagnation at home. For Honecker, much of Gorbachev's *glasnost* went too far, and he ordered the East German authorities to ban one of the most free-wheeling Soviet monthly magazines, *Sputnik.*

So many clients were now crowding Vogel's office that it was beginning to resemble an assembly line. By early 1989, with Poland now halfway out of the Eastern bloc and Hungary headed out fast, Communism was crumbling fast, and in East Germany the first signs of panic had become evident, both in the populace and in the Politburo. By the end of July, a total of 47,000 people had been legally permitted to leave, but still 1,552 people had sought asylum in the West German Permanent Mission in East Berlin.[20] Only the unpublicized promise that if they left, their applications to emigrate would be considered "with good will" convinced them to leave. But Vogel, whose chugging ancient office telex was now clattering constantly into life with similar reports from Bonn's embassies in Warsaw, Budapest, and Prague, noticed that the demands were becoming steadily more insistent. Where a few years earlier people had been willing to accept assurances that they would get permission to emigrate within a few weeks, they now wanted it within a few days.

Belatedly, but sooner than it came to Honecker, Mielke, and the rest of the East German leadership, it began to dawn on Wolfgang Vogel that lowering the barriers all these years had eaten away at something that was not merely a regrettable aberration of Communist power, but was its essential foundation. The willingness to use brute force when necessary had put the old men in the East German leadership into power and kept them there these many years, but now they were beginning to be disoriented and confused. Gorbachev had ended the nerve-wracking tensions with the Western alliance, but he had turned the Communist world upside down with his *glasnost.* Soviet writers, historians, and politicians were openly denouncing Stalinism, but neo-Stalinism was the only thing keeping East Germany together.

The old men around Honecker reacted defensively. Just because your neighbor hangs new wallpaper doesn't mean you have to redecorate, said Kurt Hager, Honecker's ally in the putsch against Ulbricht and the Politburo member in charge of press and cultural affairs. *Neues Deutschland* kept publishing the same old Communist propaganda, building up Honecker's personality cult and once publishing forty-six pictures of him in a single issue.

Honecker felt personally offended by some of the rethinking that was going on in Moscow. That all of a sudden everything had been a mistake, that collectivization, for instance, was a historical error, was impossible for him to grasp.[21] Nevertheless, he invited Gorbachev, Nicolae Ceausescu, and most of the rest of the Communist world to come to East Berlin in the autumn for the German Democratic Republic's fortieth anniversary. He wanted them to see that he had things well in hand.

Honecker was closed to new ideas from almost any source. Vogel was beginning to see the state he served unraveling before his very eyes, in the West German embassies and chanceries in Eastern Europe. Since Honecker had built the Wall in 1961, as Vogel better than anyone else should have been in a position to see, its insuperable bounds had been the main thing keeping most of the sixteen and a half million East Germans from taking up their right of citizenship in West Germany. He had tried, as his West German negotiating partners in the Lutheran Church and successive governments in

Bonn had tried, to make the Wall less unbearable and had made passage through it possible for thousands of East Germans. In 1988, 2,730,000 East Germans had been allowed short visits to the West. In the first half of 1989 alone, Honecker allowed 50,000 East Germans to emigrate, more than had ever before been officially permitted to leave. But Honecker deluded himself into thinking that the safety valve would rid the country of all its malcontents, before the self-satisfied show he wanted to put on in October. What he did not know was that the real number of those who wanted out was not 50,000 but 500,000, and 5,000,000 were probably ready to follow. Bärbel Bohley, now a leader of the burgeoning East German civil rights movement, estimated it even higher, at half the total population.

On May 2, the Hungarian Communists, well on their way by now to introducing capitalism in their country, inadvertently revealed the depth and breadth of the crisis in East Germany to the entire world. Without consultations, they unilaterally opened their border with Austria and began taking down the barbed wire, much to the surprise and delight of thousands of East German vacationers and campers who, abandoning their Trabants, trailers, and tents, flocked across the border to what even a stung Erich Honecker would later describe as freedom.[22]

The Hungarians, by now embarked irreversibly on a course of change and reform, were not much concerned about what Honecker thought. Their own people were free to come and go, and besides they were irritated at the increasing frequency of critical attacks against their policies in the East German press, which seemed to be waging war against them, Foreign Minister Gyula Horn had complained to Egon Krenz, Honecker's heir apparent, in Bucharest. But they were still bound, the East Germans reminded them, by treaty commitments to their Warsaw Pact allies. Taken aback, the Hungarians attempted to stem the flow, sending back East Germans who tried to cross into Austria and stamping their passports. But this measure, too, proved ineffective.

Indeed, this measure set off a new storming of the barricades in front of Bonn's embassies, not only in Budapest but in Prague and Warsaw, in countries where millions of East Germans were spending their summer vacations, and at the Permanent Mission in East Berlin. Most of those who came in seeking asylum were happy to accept the terms of the five-year-old unspoken agreement Vogel had made, and go back home again with assurance that their applications for emigration would be handled with goodwill. Getting this assurance from Vogel usually took two days. The West German embassies all had his telex number, and would send daily the names, ages, and home addresses of the asylum-seekers who had turned up at their door. Vogel's telex, in the summer of 1989, was spewing out yards of paper every day, with a copy for a Stasi courier to pick up so that the names could be cleared. "A murderer might be among them," Niebling had explained, but the clearance was almost always routinely given. Helga, arriving in the morning, was happy when she found only one hundred names had come in overnight; usually there were many more. As soon as they had been cleared, Vogel would signal the embassy and, usually, this would be enough to get the occupiers to leave the embassy and go home. Two thousand East Germans had chosen to fight their way out this way in the first six months of the year.

By early August, East Germans were trying to desert their country in droves. More and more people were storming the West German embassies in Eastern Europe, refusing Vogel's usual informal guarantees, and demanding immediate permission to leave directly for the West. In East Berlin, the West Germans had to close the doors again, as in 1984, after 131 people had come in and refused to leave. Walter Priesnitz, who had succeeded Rehlinger in the Intra-German Ministry, had gone to East Berlin on August 7 to try to solve the problem through Vogel, as before. But publicly, Vogel told him, all he could assure the refugees was that they would not be punished if they left the building voluntarily and went home. Honecker was recuperating from a gall bladder attack he had suffered at the Warsaw Pact summit in Bucharest, and Krenz, who was in charge in his absence, was empowered to promise nothing more. "Herr Vogel," Priesnitz told him, "we're in 1989, not 1984. If that's the best you can do, it means the end of the GDR." Vogel made no attempt to contradict him.[23]

Wherever he turned, the problems were overwhelming. The West Germans needed his help in Budapest, where 187 East Germans were demanding asylum. "We do not ask, we demand that the German public do something to protect us from being expelled back into the Zone," thirty-three of them wrote in a letter to *Der Spiegel,* using the old word for Soviet-occupied Germany to describe what Honecker and his comrades called the first workers' and peasants' state on German soil.[24] In Prague there were twenty, in Warsaw ten; most were young people, twenty to thirty years old, people with a full working life ahead of them, people the old men in the Politburo could not afford to keep losing. The national mood was, in the words of *Der Spiegel,* "an explosive mixture of frustration, cynicism and an aggressive urge to emigrate."[25] Even some of the regime's fiercest critics, such as Bohley, whose ideals remained socialist at heart, formed a group called New Forum in September and urged compatriots not to give up, to stay at home and help build democratic socialism rather than be swallowed up by the capitalist West German state. East German church leaders, too, urged people not to flee.

Yet Krenz was not even able to reach Honecker to add the question of why so many people wanted out onto the agenda of a Politburo meeting that was scheduled for August 15. The old man, about to turn seventy-seven, thought that the embassy occupations were a West German problem. "What do you want to accomplish?" he asked Krenz. "Before the Wall, lots more than this were leaving." And he had taken the file Krenz had prepared, thrown it wordlessly into his safe, and told him to go take his vacation.[26] Vogel had obtained permission to assure the refugees in the Permanent Mission and in Prague, where their numbers had swollen to three hundred, to leave with assurances of his help in applying for emigration papers. But in the almost revolutionary atmosphere of the fall of 1989, mere promises were quickly losing their luster. On August 19, Otto von Habsburg, heir to the Austro-Hungarian throne and a visionary worker for European unity, organized a "peace picnic" on the border between Austria and Hungary, attracting hundreds of East German vacationers, who joined a throng that surged across the border. This time the Hungarian guards simply let them go through. Now Honecker turned his ire against the reform leadership in Hungary.

Tens of thousands of East Germans who had spent their summer vacations there began deciding not to return home, either to chance a crossing through the "green border" or to await a clearer signal that they could go West. Thousands of them streamed into camps set up by West German Catholic relief organizations in a churchyard in the suburb of Zugliget, and Hungarian officials opened up another camp at Lake Balaton, the vacation center southwest of the capital. The Hungarians allowed the Stasi liaison group in Budapest to open up a branch office there, but turned deaf ears to most of its requests to tell the assembled East Germans that they would never have a hope of going across unless they went home first and applied for permission. The Hungarian foreign minister shuttled between Budapest, East Berlin, and Bonn, trying to get the Germans to solve the problem for him, but neither side would budge. Bonn could not give up its promise of citizenship for all Germans, wherever they came from—the reason why the people had jammed into the tents and trailers on Lake Balaton—and East Berlin knew that once the Hungarians opened the border, it would be only a matter of time before the German Democratic Republic bled to death.

On September 10, the authorities in Budapest went ahead and announced that from midnight, all citizens of the German Democratic Republic who wished would be free to cross into Austria. The East Germans responded the only way they knew how, by imposing travel restrictions to Hungary. But by the time they slammed the door shut, an estimated twenty-three thousand people had already been able to slip across the Hungarian border to make their way to the West German embassy in Vienna, where they could pick up West German passports and travel on to start their new lives in the Federal Republic.

By mid-autumn East Germany was being consumed in a firestorm. Yet Honecker still appeared oblivious, with eyes only for the upcoming October 7 anniversary celebrations. Their fellow countrymen should shed no tears for those who had turned their backs on their country, *Neues Deutschland* told East Germans, in a phrase personally approved by the party chief, who neither knew nor cared that among those thousands were skilled workers, engineers, doctors, young parents, and students on whom the continued viability of the East German state depended. Now, with Poland and Czechoslovakia about the only places left to which they were free to go, thousands began pouring south from Dresden and Leipzig toward Prague. East Germans did not need visas to travel to Czechoslovakia, one country in the Warsaw Pact Honecker knew he could depend on not to let East Germans sneak across the border to the West. But so many flooded into the West German embassy in the Czechoslovak capital that once again, the West German diplomats had to close the gates. Even that did not keep the determined asylum-seekers out, for the Czech guards took no measures to try to prevent East Germans from going up the street and climbing the fence around the embassy's extensive grounds.

This time, the influx totally overwhelmed the West German staff, who abandoned their offices to entire families, and finally tens and even scores of people who crammed in with mattresses, blankets, suitcases, and the clothes on their backs, ready to give it all up in hopes of going West. The bathrooms were soon stopped up and flooded, raw sewage flowing down the palace's elegant corridors and fouling the carpets. The kitchen could not keep up with the demand, and the embassy's spacious grounds resembled a teeming refugee camp, with emergency tents to keep off the autumn rains. Still, the refugees came.

With thousands now jammed in, the situation was critical, so in the last week of September Priesnitz asked Vogel to come to Prague with him and two other West German officials and try to talk to the refugees. It was not an easy encounter for either Vogel or Priesnitz. "The mood was explosive," Priesnitz recalled later. "The people didn't trust anybody, and they were bitter because they thought not enough was being done to help them." Both men were spat upon as they walked through the crowd. Priesnitz remembered that this had happened to him here before, when, as a member of the Hitler Youth, he had left the city in August 1945. Vogel was deeply shaken after the crowd brutally jostled even Helga. "It has nothing to do with you personally," Priesnitz tried to reassure him. "It's the state they have contempt for."[27]

Vogel was overcome by the pathos of the scenes inside the embassy grounds. He was shocked, in particular, when the refugees had pushed a pair of small children up to him and said, "Here, show what you can do for them." The children's mother, Priesnitz told him, had already managed to get to West Germany through Hungary. Without identifying themselves, relatives had brought the children to Prague and handed them over the embassy fence to people in the crowd inside. Now, they challenged Vogel, he should show just what he was capable of.

"These children will be in West Berlin on Monday," he promised, angrily and impulsively. He had the weekend to make good on his word.

"My best wishes go with you," Priesnitz had said, and Vogel had minced no words with Niebling. "It'll take at least two weeks," the Stasi general told him. "If they aren't in West Berlin on Monday, I'm laying down my mandate," Vogel warned. The infants got to Berlin as promised, with West German television cameras to prove it to the refugees back in Prague.[28]

Vogel had told the other refugees that he could not promise that they would get out as fast as children whose parents had already emigrated. But, he said, he had already succeeded in getting exit permission for those who had left the same embassy a month earlier, and he would work just as hard on their behalf. At the most, even for young men facing the draft, Vogel assured them, getting permission would take six months. Priesnitz vouched for him, saying that they did not know of a single case in which Vogel had ever failed to keep his word. But with the prestigious October 7 anniversary less than two weeks away, most of the refugees were gambling on forcing Honecker into letting them go, just as their predecessors had done in 1984.[29]

With the West German embassy in Warsaw also under siege, Vogel asked Gregor Gysi, a widely respected young Communist lawyer who had defended Bärbel Bohley and had come with him to Prague, to go to Poland with him to defuse the crisis there. But the two lawyers had little more luck persuading the refugees in Warsaw than they had had in Prague. The Stasi had infiltrated agents among the refugees, the lawyers were told; how could Vogel guarantee that asylum-seekers would not be denounced and arrested if they took his advice and went home?

It would take greater powers than Vogel had to break the logjam. Bonn's Foreign Minister, Hans-Dietrich Genscher, was lobbying at the UN General Assembly in New York City with the Czechoslovaks, the Poles, and his Soviet counterpart, Eduard A. Shevardnadze, openly begging the latter for his "help and support." Finally, Genscher was able to persuade Honecker himself to yield. By Honecker's express orders, immediate permission to leave was granted to all 5,500 people in the embassy in Prague. Honecker insisted on only one condition—they could not leave directly, across the West German-Czechoslovak border, but had to be routed through East Germany. This, at least, would preserve the fiction that the decision to let them go had been a sovereign step taken by the German Democratic Republic.

On September 30, Genscher himself flew to Prague to break the news from the balcony of the embassy to the deliriously joyful crowd. It was, he said, "the most moving hour in my political career."

On specially sealed chartered trains, the refugees left on a ten-hour journey to Hof, south of the East German–Bavarian border, the next day. But, as Mielke's own Stasi field reports were telling him, the effect was the opposite of what Honecker had intended.

Thousands more East Germans flocked into the embassy in Prague right behind them. Honecker ordered East German authorities to ban travel to Czechoslovakia without a visa on October 3, thus effectively sealing off East Germany from the outside world. He did allow a new train to take the remaining refugees out from Prague on October 4th. This time, East Germans were lining the tracks and station platforms as the trains passed through, trying to sneak aboard. In Dresden, police moved in to clear the main station, setting off violent clashes that ranged through the streets of the bombed-out city for hours. Thousands of people were arrested.

Little noticed in all the rest of the turmoil, a smaller, similar drama was playing itself out at the U.S. embassy in East Berlin the same week. On the night of October 3, eighteen people, including five small children, had come into the embassy and refused to leave. Three people had even managed to break into the almost un-guarded grounds of Ambassador Richard Barkley's residence on the Nordendstrasse, in the diplomatic area a couple of miles to the north of the center of East Berlin. The residence, with a high wall and spacious garden, would have made an ideal spot for hundreds, even thousands of refugees to take shelter, and Barkley, with the television images of Bonn's embassy in Prague fresh in his mind, was gravely concerned. Picking up the telephone, he called Vogel to ask for help, and the lawyer quickly arrived on the scene.

"We were vulnerable," Barkley said later; the residence could easily have been overwhelmed by the human tide. "But Vogel did it all—he got them all out."[30] The Americans were also pleased that he had done it without the kind of publicity that could have led to larger crowds. Deputy Secretary of State Lawrence S. Eagleburger thanked Vogel in a letter a few weeks later for his "diplomatic skill and political sensitivity." The United States was "keenly aware of the positive role you have played in facilitating the emigration of large numbers of GDR citizens," Eagleburger wrote. "In a word, your help to others in difficult circumstances is both valued and respected here in Washington."[31]

With East Germany in turmoil, Gorbachev flew to East Berlin on October 6 before the anniversary. "Life punishes those who come too late," he told a meeting of the East German party Politburo that afternoon, in words Egon Krenz and others inside the crum-bling leadership belatedly took as a signal to move against Honecker. Gorbachev, Krenz thought, seemed to be waiting for a sign from Honecker that he recognized the gravity of the crisis. But he gave none. Instead, Honecker spoke "as if the country were an island of the blessed."[32] Even as Gorbachev was leaving, on the 7th, Mielke's security forces brutally repressed another massive demonstration on the Alexanderplatz, driving the mostly youthful protestors into the decaying Prenzlauer Berg residential neighborhoods, working-class sections of old Berlin where the bomb damage was still visible on every streetcorner forty-five years after it had happened. The police and the Stasi teargassed, clubbed, and arrested hundreds of young people demanding not an end to socialism but simply the same freedom to make demands on it that Gorbachev had long since given to his own people at home.

With Mielke secretly mobilizing Stasi forces and civilian workers' militia units for even tougher measures, Krenz and the other party leaders who had their ears to the ground began taking matters into their own hands. The immediate concern was what had become regular Monday-night demonstrations in Leipzig, the next ones scheduled for the 9th and 16th. Honecker and Mielke were insisting that all the trouble was simply the result of outside interference, not only by the class enemy but, now, by the betrayal of the Hungarians, whom Honecker had thought were on his side. Krenz, a pathetic figure whom Honecker had left in charge of the Free German Youth organization until he was forty-seven years old, so long that people joked that youth had become his profession, only now began sounding out the members of the Politburo about his replacing Honecker. Krenz quickly found that, each for his own reasons, even most of the older generation agreed that it was time for a change. Honecker had to go.

On the 13th, at Krenz's request, Honecker had signed a written pledge not to use force in Leipzig.

The East German Communists were losing their nerve, and their cohesiveness. But the Stasi, a state within a state, was carried along by its own cruel momentum. Vogel was receiving hundreds of letters, postmarked at Bautzen and Karl-Marx-Stadt and other East German prisons, from people reporting that they had been arrested trying to join fathers and husbands and wives who had made their way to the West German embassies in Warsaw and Prague and from there, through Vogel's services, to freedom. But their relatives, caught trying to wade across the Oder River, barely knee-deep at the end of a dry summer, or sneaking through the forest on the East German–Czechoslovak border, were still sitting in East German prisons.

For every emigration case Vogel negotiated, it now seemed to him, he was creating a family separation tragedy. And the West Germans had also let him know that they would no longer play the game of treating people such as these as political prisoners for whom they would pay a price.

As overwhelmed now as the regime he served by this succession of tragedies, Vogel hardly knew what to do. All the East German landmarks by which he had set his course since 1953 were being swept away, and the power structure that had made Vogel what he was was rushing rudderless downstream. Vogel had always found his moral bearings in the facts of his cases, and now he had a case that made him see red, the fate of a family of four who had decided to make for the West German Embassy in Warsaw. The father had crossed the Oder, made it, and been transported to freedom, to one of Bonn's refugee camps in Hessen. His wife had been too slow to escape the East German border guards, who had caught her and sent her to prison. But the real outrage, in Vogel's eyes, was what had happened to their two small children: they were now in an orphanage.

By now, Vogel could no longer even reach Honecker to discuss the problems piling in on him from every direction. Honecker was moving off into history. Mielke was moving off into paranoia. Vogel knew little about Krenz, and nothing about his political maneuvering. He did know that the few fragile constraints of legitimacy that the security colossus had were also being swept away. The frail foundations of East German law were crumbling, there was panic in the air, and with it the danger of mass violence and bloodshed. In such an atmosphere, the only protection against anarchy was to speak up for decent standards of civilized behavior.

There may also have been a shrewd calculation. Vogel knew, or suspected, that if the Wall fell, the state would fall with it, and unification would inevitably follow. His connections with the East German power structure would mean less in this new situation than his reputation as a pole of decency, in both parts of the country. It was everyone for himself now, and Vogel moved the only way he could to stake out a position of honor for himself if the regime did collapse: for almost the first time in his life, he resolved to denounce publicly the abuses of the system he had worked within for his entire professional career, in hopes of preventing even worse as the country descended into anarchy.

Two children in an orphanage had led him to this crossroads, but here he was, on Friday the 13th, the same day that Honecker made his fateful promise not to use force against the demonstrators in Leipzig, that Vogel showed Helga the statement he had drafted to send to DPA. "Type this telex," he asked her.

Helga Vogel turned pale when she read it. "Wolfgang, you can't do this," she whispered. "It'll be the end of us."

"No, I think they still need me," he told her, and insisted. As always, she did as he asked.

The statement caused a sensation in the West German media. "I see in the numerous criminal proceedings against unauthorized exit from the G.D.R. via Hungary, the CSSR or Poland a violation of the principle of equal treatment of citizens before the law," Vogel said. "It is impermissible, on the one hand, to allow special exit to West Germany and, on the other hand, to impose prison terms for similar conduct. The criminal prosecutions against demonstrators who have committed no acts of violence are also legally question-able." He felt himself "duty-bound as a lawyer" to demand that they be dropped, and that constitutional legal practice be followed. "The release of those concerned can brook no delay. For them, their families, and for society, every hour counts," he urged. "Everything should proceed calmly. We lawyers are challenged to live up to our responsibility to provide humane assistance and solutions. This applies to travel and exit procedures as well. We must accept bureaucratic delays no longer."

That he also rejected any right of "outsiders" to offer advice, and said that East Germany had adequate laws and legal procedures to ensure the just treatment of its own citizens, did nothing in Mielke's eyes to mitigate the offense of this unprecedented criticism of the regime by one of its own servants.

At 9 P.M. the telephone rang, just as Helga had feared. It was Mielke himself on the line. "The general secretary is deeply disappointed," the security minister, nearly eighty-two years old, told Vogel. He ordered: "Stay where you are in the office and be prepared to answer our questions."[33]

Their mouths dry with fear, the Vogels drove home to Teupitz anyway. The thought of being arrested struck them as almost too farfetched to contemplate. Vogel would not have to answer to

Mielke, or to Honecker. Soon these two men would have to answer to their party colleagues, and later to the East German people.

On Tuesday morning, October 18, with the entire Politburo assembled in the Central Committee headquarters, Willi Stoph, as prearranged, sprang a surprise agenda item on the outwardly calm party chief: "The replacement of Erich Honecker and the election of Egon Krenz as General Secretary." For the next two hours, Honecker himself presided over the discussion, calling on each of his Politburo colleagues in turn and listening to them say, some with regret, that he should retire for reasons of health. Honecker himself had been shocked to hear Günter Mittag, his closest ally and the man responsible for the East German economy, say that a change was long overdue. When Honecker called for a vote, every member had raised his hand, and finally Honecker had raised his own as well. In the Kafkaesque way of such Communist blood rituals, the decision had to be unanimous.

Honecker's resignation was accepted by the Central Committee that afternoon. Reaching his home that evening, he told Margot that he had been disappointed that no one had trusted him enough to warn him beforehand what they were about to do. "You know," he told her, "I am genuinely relieved. I couldn't go on any longer."[34]

The Wall would stand, Honecker had said, as long as the conditions lasted that had made it necessary—perhaps another hundred years. He was wrong by a century. Krenz lifted the ban on travel to Czechoslovakia on October 27, and announced an amnesty for all citizens who had fled or tried to flee the country, thus finally doing what Vogel had urged in his appeal. Between October 27 and November 9, more than 300,000 people had fled through the back door. On November 9, Krenz and his colleagues in the Politburo decided in panic to open the front door—to open the border to any East German citizen who desired to travel. Shortly before 7 P.M. on the 9th, Günter Schabowski, the Politburo official in charge of the media, told a press conference about the Politburo decision. Almost casually, in answer to a question, he said that from now on all the border crossing points would be open to anyone who wanted to come or go. Within a couple of hours, hundreds of thousands of East Berliners, scarcely believing their eyes, had descended on the border crossing points and flowed across in masses, the guards not even bothering to check their papers. Thus did the Wall, the symbol of Erich Honecker's work of the previous twenty-eight years, come down in a single evening.

Germans, east and west, could take pride in the first peaceful German revolution in history, "*die Wende*" as they called it, but it was much more than a turning point. In Leipzig and in Berlin, in Dresden and in Rostock, East Germans had gone onto the streets and demonstrated peacefully for their freedom, and freedom had fallen into their hands like a ripe fruit.

Markus Wolf, during a private trip to Moscow a few months earlier, had had an inkling of what this would mean to the state he and his spies had striven to protect. Valentin Falin had asked, in a conversation in his office in the Central Committee of the Communist Party of the Soviet Union, whether the East German leaders had given thought to the possible revival of Stalin's idea of a neutral German confederation. For nearly twenty years, Honecker's policy of "Delimitation" had been based on clear separation and had tried to establish a distinct East German national identity based on ideology. But if there was no clear ideological difference between the two halves of the country, the division would become entirely artificial, just as the West Germans had been saying all along.

Krenz promised a new, more democratic kind of socialism to correct the errors and abuses of the past. But Krenz was incapable of fundamentally rethinking the foundations of the East German state. He was a functionary, and he had made his move years too late. Even after Honecker's fall, he had not moved his family out of Wandlitz until the end of November.

The collapse of Communism produced an outpouring of anger, resentment, and revenge that played out on the streets of East Germany much as it did in Czechoslovakia and Bulgaria only a month later. There was rage, but there was also something else, a growing sentiment that was expressed in a verse of the 1949 East German national anthem, one that Honecker had dropped. It had not been sung for years, but now crowds were scanning the lines in the Alexanderplatz in East Berlin, and marching in front of the Central Committee building to the chant: "*Deutschland einig Vaterland,*" "Germany, one Fatherland."

"We are the people," the crowds in Leipzig had chanted before October; now this chant was being drowned out by a new call to the long-suppressed ideal of reunification: "We are one people."

"I can see the end coming," the new East German Communist prime minister, Hans Modrow, had told a friend before his selection on November 13.[35] For the next three weeks, he presided over the unraveling, as disclosure followed disclosure of how their Communist leaders had deceived the East German people. Deceit, corruption, exclusive privilege, and mass terror had all been imposed through the vast apparatus of the Stasi, with its 108,000 employees and hundreds of thousands more tipsters, spies, and stool-pigeons. The most insidious were the "Informal Collaborators," who reported to the Stasi, per contract and for money, on their friends, neighbors, clients, and colleagues, sometimes even on their husbands and wives.

With the Wall open, tens of thousands of people were walking away from all this just as fast as they could every month, going West with their families. By the end of November, it was obvious that Krenz's attempt to mollify the people's rage with promises of reform and gradual change were not going to work. Not even a belated decision to eliminate the SED's privileged constitutional position on December 1 held off the rising tide of discontent.

Krenz, Modrow, the party they represented, and the state that Communism had imposed on the sixteen and a half million East Germans were all politically doomed. An orgy of recrimination was about to begin, and it would be all the more bitter for the fact that, just like their parents and grandparents before them, most East Germans had not resisted or borne witness against the evils of a totalitarian state, but had gone along with them—often willingly—instead. Angry at themselves, they looked for others to blame. To his bitter disappointment, many of them now began to hold Wolfgang Vogel responsible for their hardships instead of thanking him, as thousands had done over the years, for trying to make the privations more bearable. Freedom had liberated them from gratitude, and now, in freedom, Vogel's own time of reckoning began.

CHAPTER TWELVE

FIGHTING TO PRESERVE A REPUTATION

"My conscience is clear."

The collapse of Communism in East Germany began an outpouring of frustration and anger that had been pent up for four decades. The revolution had passed peacefully—the first time in German history that such momentous change had occurred without bloodshed—but it had not cleared the air. Anyone who had held a position of power in the old regime was now reviled and discredited. But the vacuum of power was filled, for the most part, not by the grassroots reformers and human rights activists who had opposed Communism, but by more experienced West German politicians who arrived like a conquering army, contemptuous of Communists they had been only too happy to court while they had held sway.

In this new situation, history was turned on its head. Whatever good deeds Wolfgang Vogel had done over the years were to be weighed in the balance against whatever sins he had committed in collaborating with an evil regime. Vogel had needed close association with the East German rulers to carry out his mandates and had become rich from the power he derived from that association. Now, some of his clients began to claim that he had betrayed them and they wanted him to pay.

At first, he had been as slow to anticipate the consequences of change as Krenz and the others had been. Nevertheless, in the fall of 1989, he had been apprehensive. The first uneasy feelings had come upon him while he was negotiating with the asylum-seekers at the West German Embassy in Warsaw, where he had spoken with a Polish government official about the Solidarity revolution, already advanced far beyond what East Germans considered possible in their country. What about revenge, Vogel had wanted to know. How had Polish society coped with the pressure for revenge? What happened when a man became prime minister who had been in prison and had known his judges, jailers, and torturers by name. Would he insist on settling accounts? Poland was a Catholic country, came the answer. Catholics believed in forgiveness. The Protestant people of Prussia would not be so forgiving.[1]

In late 1989, Vogel's reputation was still intact. The West German government was considering him for a merit cross, its highest civilian award.[2] Western diplomats in East Berlin speculated that Vogel could become minister of justice in the first democratically elected East German government. But the idea did not lessen Vogel's apprehensions. For the elation that had followed the opening of the Wall had not lasted long. It was soon replaced by a darker and more menacing mood, one that he feared would mean nothing good for people such as himself who had long enjoyed positions of privilege.

The people had triumphed on the streets, and now the streets wanted revenge. What fueled the desire was the discovery that behind the walls that ringed the Politburo's elite settlement in Wandlitz, their Communist leaders had lived in the midst of Western luxuries denied to them in the name of their supposedly superior ideology. In Wandlitz, Honecker, Krenz, and twenty-one other families had each enjoyed two free maids, Western videos, champagne and cognac, and such simple Western pleasures as fresh strawberries out of season, all at bargain prices—things that were completely out of reach of ordinary East German citizens. Beyond the green-daubed walls of this ghetto of privilege, there were private estates, hunting preserves, even private planes. In the name of egalitarian Communism, the Communist leaders had been more equal than anybody else, living like feudal princes, earning for themselves salaries of thousands of marks, all the while preaching austerity and hard work for their subjects, who now agonized in self-pity. For these subjects, the German Democratic Republic had been nothing but one vast concentration camp, hemmed in by the Wall and run by overseers who had been worse than hypocritical—they had been sadistic on a grand scale.

Vogel had not been a member of the Politburo, but behind his own garden walls in Teupitz he had lived as well as any of them. He and Helga had kept the ordinary workers of the little village busy for years, making additions to the house, building the garage, adding the veranda behind the kitchen, the vitrines in the living room, the gazebo out on the little lake. He was a well-regarded figure in Teupitz. Unlike the men in the Politburo, Vogel had not lorded it over them; he had often gone out of his way to help his neighbors in their little battles with the bureaucracy and in their attempts to help relatives who wanted to get out. But for many other people around the country, gratitude for his mercies had lasted only as long as the Wall that had imposed their suffering. Freed from the evils of the distorted socialism the Stasi had imposed on them for forty years, East Germans emerged determined to find scapegoats, public figures who could not deny that they had gone along to get along. Vogel was a shining example.

What East Germans were least willing to forgive in the early days of the revolution was that they had been forcibly deprived of the benefits of West German consumer society. They could be shot at the border for trying to run across to get these things, persecuted and made miserable by the Stasi for saying that they were desirable. Now the Stasi files opened to reveal that the Stasi had been running a huge business in deutsche marks and Western consumer goods for the benefit of the leadership class. Revelation after revelation laid bare the Stasi's intimate involvement in a web of illegal and corrupt financial arrangements masterminded by the plump and prosperous Alexander Schalck-Golodkowski and his mysterious CoCo organization. CoCo was exposed as an intricate part of the security apparatus, and Schalck unmasked as a secret Stasi colonel who had run a business empire that had included arms sales to Middle Eastern terrorist groups and the governments that backed them, and a mysterious hoard of more than twenty tons of gold that was the main backing for the floundering East German currency. Under pressure from the streets, the State Prosecutor's Office now initiated an investigation, and the investigators were building a criminal case against Schalck.

Vogel's association with Schalck was undeniable. The Bonn government's payments from the prisoner-exchange business had all come to CoCo, and the two men knew each other well. Schalck's driver lived next door to the Vogels. In late November 1989, Schalck had suggested that Vogel fill in Krenz on the background of the program. Vogel complied with a memorandum for the record written, he said in a note to Krenz, "at Comrade Schalck's suggestion" on November 30.

The prisoner exchanges paid for by the West German government over the years, he wrote, had been

suggested by both churches in the FRG and also in the GDR in 1964, organized and agreed to by both governments through lawyers as intermediaries. It functioned until the beginning of November 89 and involved:

—Prisoners (compensation for damages)
—Emigration (training and education costs)
—Embassy cases (training and education costs)

The parenthetical explanations were Vogel's shorthand for the justifications that the West Germans had accepted for demands for payment to East Germany in return for letting prisoners go or trained workers emigrate.

"The churches remained involved to the end," Vogel wrote, with the Roman Catholic prelates in East Berlin and such Lutheran laymen as Manfred Stolpe, the head of the Lutheran church council in East Germany, all having played roles as "confidential mediators."

Vogel briefly explained how the church channels had been used to funnel the Bonn government payments to CoCo for twenty-five years, and then reported that the program was winding up by December 20 with a last payment of seventy-five million deutsche marks, on the condition that, except for spies, no further political arrests should be made.

Nothing in the tone or substance of the letter would have raised eyebrows in the church councils or the limited legislative oversight committees in Bonn that had dealt with the matter over the years. But what had seemed plausible morality through the distorting prism of the cold war would soon come to be seen as cynical Communist trickery, and throw Vogel's entire career into a new and harsher light.[3]

Three days after this letter was written, on December 2, Krenz was sweating in the cold night air outside the vast Central Committee headquarters on the Werdersche Markt square, as demonstrators jeered and whistled and demanded his resignation as party chief. The crowd got what it wanted the following day.

Both party and government continued to unravel. Vogel's lawyer colleague Gregor Gysi got a mandate to try to rebuild the party's credibility under a new name, the Party of Democratic Socialism, and Hans Modrow, who as party leader in Dresden had appeared to have relatively clean hands, took over the reins of government. But events were rapidly outrunning the ability of reform Communist leaders to control them.

December 1989 was indeed a time of chaos, on several levels. On the surface, the tumult appeared to be a joyous triumph of the forces of democracy, and it was celebrated that way in the Western media. But beneath the surface there was a vacuum of both power and authority. The old institutions—the party, the Stasi, the "socialist" way of life—were all crumbling, but it was not yet clear who or what would replace them. Desperately, the most heavily implicated leaders and functionaries of the old regime were trying to save themselves any way they could. Erich Mielke's ministry was soon partially dismantled, and the minister placed under lock and key, along with the carefully preserved files of his own involvement in the murder of two Weimar Republic policemen in Berlin in 1931. Also unearthed were the files on Erich Honecker's arrest by the Gestapo and his testimony, incriminating several fellow members of the Communist underground, from 1936. Mielke had presumably preserved these to protect himself and to use as blackmail in Communist power struggles. Stasi underlings now used thousands of documents like them to save themselves, taking or copying them from the files and later offering them for money to journalists.

December 2 was also Schalck's turn to sweat. Late that afternoon, the telephone rang at Vogel's home in Teupitz. The CoCo chief came on the line, begging Vogel to be his defense lawyer. The previous day, Schalck told Vogel, his voice shaking, he had been put under twenty-four-hour-a-day surveillance by the new East German state prosecutor, who had told him that he was acting under pressure from an inquiry by the suddenly renascent parliament. The outrage, Schalck said, had focused on an accusation that CoCo had arranged for East German party leaders to build homes in Wandlitz for their sons and daughters at the taxpayers' expense. Schalck was also under suspicion of having spirited millions of dollars' worth of gold away to Swiss banks. The walls were closing in on him, and he needed Vogel's help.

"You've got to represent me, or I don't know what I'm going to do," the voice at the other end of the line said. Vogel tried to calm him. It was already clear to him that Schalck would flee, but he and Helga arranged quickly to go to Schalck's office in the Wallstrasse. When they got there, they found Schalck in a desperate state. "If you don't take on my case, I'm going to shoot myself," he said. Vogel promised to do what he could. And Schalck said that his driver would bring over five suitcases full of material for the defense the following day.

As the Vogels drove back to Teupitz that night, they knew that Schalck was heading for the Invalidenstrasse checkpoint, on the way to West Berlin. "If he's arrested," Vogel told his wife in the car, "just you wait—he'll blame me for betraying him."

When they reached home, the telephone was already ringing. "I'm in Tegel," the airport in West Berlin, Schalck announced, without identifying himself. Vogel had the feeling he was farther away than that.

When the driver arrived on Sunday with the five suitcases, Vogel himself called Prosecutor-General Günter Wendland to report what had happened. The prosecutors would want to register the files as evidence, and Vogel would ask for the right to keep exculpatory material. But Wendland did not seem to be in much of a hurry, saying he would send a member of his staff the following Tuesday, December 5, at 10 A.M.

On this day, a team of prosecutors and bailiffs was waiting at the Reilerstrasse when the Vogels arrived. There, they got their first apprehension of the catastrophe that would throw the shadow of disgrace over Vogel's entire professional career and personal reputation.

"Dr. Vogel, I have a warrant for your arrest," he was told, "and we are going to make a complete search of your offices."

Vogel was dumbstruck. When he walked into the door, his secretary announced that the housekeeper in Teupitz was also on the line. "There are sixteen people outside who say they want to search the house," the woman told Helga when she came on the line.

"Don't let them in without a warrant," Helga urged her, but the prosecutors were threatening to kick the door in.[4]

"What is the meaning of this?" Vogel demanded of the magistrate. "Haven't you talked with the prosecutor-general?"

"He has resigned."

"Did he tell you that I had called him?"

"There was a note in his safe."

It made no difference; the search went on.

Vogel's office files contained thousands and thousands of dossiers involving the most sensitive and delicate negotiations over the years with a dozen governments, East and West: spy exchanges, prisoner exchanges—public and private matters he thought it would be in no one's interest to disclose. Vogel had kept the most delicate of these, such as the records of payment of nearly half a million dollars of East German state money for the defense of East German spies in the United States, in this locked file. Here, also, were his notes on Bonn's prisoner payments and on the handful of cases where the Stasi had allowed families to purchase freedom for their relatives at their own expense. In the basement were tens of thousands of dossiers, containing the most intimate private details on all the nearly quarter of a million people whose passage across the Iron Curtain Vogel had arranged, details that he, as a lawyer, was bound to keep private as long as his clients wished. As long as the Wall had stood, that privacy had been respected. Now, just as the Stasi was beginning to dissolve into the sands, he, Wolfgang Vogel, was being treated as cavalierly by the new regime as the Stasi had treated so many of his clients.

Vogel was bundled into a police car and taken to the main East Berlin police station in the Keibelstrasse, just off the Alexanderplatz, and brought into a locked and sealed room. At home, the Vogels' housekeeper watched disbelievingly as police opened the doors of a huge dark and carved eighteenth-century armoire from Potsdam worth thousands of marks, and peered inside as if expecting to find the corpulent Schalck hiding within. They found the five suitcases Schalck's driver had brought, and took those away. These later disappeared, as did Vogel's secret files from the bookcase in his office on the Reilerstrasse. It was, indeed, every man for himself.[5]

In Vogel's jail cell, the interrogators wanted to know where Schalck had gone, information Vogel crisply informed them that the attorney-client privilege would have barred him from divulging even if he had known. But there was also something else. Vogel was under investigation, he was told, for a crime unrelated to anything that might be in Schalck's suitcases: He was suspected of "criminal extortion" of former clients for whom he had helped to get permission to leave East Germany, on condition of giving up their property and their belongings.

This time, Vogel felt only a momentary fright, a mere twinge. The East German authorities were too weak and too confused to press the charge. In the chaos and their zeal to satisfy the public outrage, they had gone too far. The new East German minister of justice, Hans-Joachim Heusinger, apologized to Vogel in the prison and ordered his immediate release. Of course, Vogel was protected by the lawyer-client privilege, the minister explained to the press later, and trying to extort confidential information about a client from him from a jail cell had been impermissible.[6]

The news made headlines in both parts of Germany. In the West, press and politicians reacted, for the most part, with a superior air of disapproval. The forces of "democracy" in the East had run amok, confirming once again how little they understood about the normal rules that governed democratic political discourse, how they had reverted back to type.[7]

The weakened East German regime still needed him, and after contrite articles about his absolution appeared in the still-controlled press, Vogel called its bluff in a public statement in which he threatened to get out of law practice altogether. "I see myself exposed to a campaign that goes so far as to accuse me of blackmail," he said indignantly. "I have never had and still do not have any intention of leaving the G.D.R. After thirty-five years as a lawyer between the two German states I thank all who have placed their trust in me. I am through."[8]

Three days later, after a personal appeal from Hans Modrow to stay on and see to it that not a single political prisoner remained in an East German jail by the end of the year, Vogel backed down. For the moment, he had limited the damage. The East German prosecution had less credibility than he had.

But the system that had underpinned his work, and with it the foundations of his reputation, continued to crumble. Manfred Seidel, Schalck's deputy, was arrested the day after his boss; Honecker was now under house arrest in Wandlitz, after having been unceremoniously thrown out of the Communist party he had headed until two months earlier. The night Vogel had been released, a thousand angry people had broken into the Stasi headquarters in Dresden, vowing to prevent the destruction of the files that would document the secret police's wrongdoing. There was nothing noble or inspiring about this, Vogel thought darkly to himself. This was not democracy, it was mob rule, and the mob was driven by fury that Schalck and others like him might escape retribution for their deeds because they had gotten away before the files had been opened.[9] But the mob was also driven by its fatal fascination with what those files would show. A time was coming, Vogel knew, when everyone would fear being denounced by everyone else. And he could become one of the most exposed targets.

Modrow was just doing his best to try to keep East Germany from collapsing into the waiting arms of the government in Bonn. Chancellor Kohl was coming to see him in Dresden on December 19, and Modrow did not want to be on the defensive about political prisoners. Even after the second of two amnesties on December 6, there were still 130 of them, most of whom were held in the infamous Bautzen II prison.

With the Wall already coming down, and the country that had imprisoned them dissolving before their very eyes, the prisoners could not understand what they were doing still behind bars. Even their Stasi keepers, who insisted that they had committed real crimes, not political offenses, had begun to fear them. In Czechoslovakia, a former dissident was about to become the country's president. The same thing could happen here. The Stasi guards, low men on the totem pole of Communist power and privilege, were beginning to feel betrayed and abandoned by their superiors. Some of them were as angry as their charges. But with the situation in the prison outrunning their ability to control it, the authorities in East Berlin appealed to Vogel for help, and Vogel asked Walter Priesnitz, from the Ministry of Intra-German Relations in Bonn, to join him on a visit to the prison to try to convince the prisoners to stay calm. They went to Bautzen in mid-December.

Truly, the situation was absurd, and both men knew it. The Stasi had put these prisoners behind bars, and the West German government was prepared to buy their freedom. Priesnitz, as Bonn's representative, had come to ask these men to obey their Stasi guards just a little longer, while the two governments settled the paperwork that would free them. Some of the prisoners had been there fifteen years, serving life sentences on charges of having been West German agents, and they were bitter at both Vogel and Priesnitz for not having gotten them out earlier. The mood was hostile and mistrustful, more against Vogel than against himself, Priesnitz thought. To these prisoners, in this changed situation, Vogel was no longer the angel of deliverance he had seemed to the preceding generations of prisoners. Now he was a representative of the regime that had jailed them, stripped of the mask of mercy by the end of the cold war confrontation that had enabled him to play a double role for so many years. Vogel had put his heart into both roles, and now he had trouble understanding what had changed.[10]

Priesnitz and Vogel negotiated the release of the last of these prisoners, including one whom Bonn had been trying to get free for years—Bodo Strehlow, an East German sailor who had tried to hijack a patrol boat to the West in August 1979, had been shot by his comrades, and had been sentenced to life imprisonment. Rehlinger before him, and then Priesnitz, had failed to get Strehlow's name onto Bonn's list. Now there was no longer any point in refusing.

When Kohl arrived to talk with Modrow in Dresden on the 19th, one of the agreements ready for signature was an accord declaring the remaining political prisoners free. Strehlow and the rest of the 130 would go free by the end of the year.[11]

The crowds in Dresden were delirious. Chants of "Helmut! Helmut!" rang across the city squares, and Kohl sensed that a historical sea-change was in the making.

"My goal is the unity of our nation. I know we can reach this goal. God bless our German fatherland," he told them. They greeted him like a conquering hero. For by then, the German juggernaut was steaming at full speed toward unification.

But the knowledge that unification was coming only intensified the vengeful mood in the East. On December 5, criminal cases alleging state crimes were opened against Honecker, Mielke, Stoph, and three other members of the Politburo. Vogel felt no special pangs for Mielke when the Stasi chief was arrested on December 7. But about Erich Honecker, his feelings were more complex. Honecker, who had asked Vogel to help defend him, was to undergo a kidney operation in January, but no one knew where he and his wife were going to live after that; the compound at Wandlitz was being shut down, as a concession to the pressure from the streets, and their former party could find no room for them in any of the public housing it controlled. Meeting Markus Wolf, the spymaster for whom Vogel had negotiated freedom for so many agents over the years, on December 20, Vogel told him that he was trying to use his Lutheran Church connections to see if the Honeckers could be taken on as church charity cases.[12]

Honecker would have been spared much further indignity if he had died after his kidney operation. The Communist party wanted nothing more to do with him; it was trying to rid itself of all connections with its past to avoid complete annihilation in the democratic elections that would be held in the spring. Theoretically, the Honeckers were entitled to state housing just like all other East German citizens, but Vogel knew that in the current mood, the Honeckers would be torn apart before they ever got past the front door of one of the ugly concrete high-rises to which they had condemned so many East Germans over the previous two decades.

This was an unworthy spectacle, Vogel thought. Only a few weeks earlier, Honecker had been the most powerful man in the country, and most of the people over whom he ruled would have been happy to lick his boots. As malleable and imperfect as the law had always been in East Germany, Vogel thought it absurd that East German prosecutors were now trying to build a case of high treason against a man who had headed the state for nearly twenty years. According to the laws of the German Democratic Republic, high treason could mean only one thing: "attempting to eliminate the socialist state or the social order of the German Democratic Republic by force." Honecker's mistakes might well be blamed for the disappearance of the socialist state, but the law took no cognizance of irony. It seemed, to Vogel, patently ridiculous to accuse Honecker of having tried deliberately to undermine Communism in East Germany. The Nuremberg war trials after World War II had been held on the basis of legal principles respected by the rest of the world that the Nazis had deliberately trampled underfoot. The new East German authorities were not trying to bring Honecker to the bar of internationally recognized justice, Vogel felt; they were trying to twist Communist law ex post facto, to use it to achieve revenge. "What's happening here is chaos," he said at the end of January. "The anger of the streets does not make a wise judge."[13]

Honecker was released from the hospital on January 29 and

taken straight to Rummelsburg prison for further questioning by prosecutors intent on pressing the case. Vogel tried to reassure his client; he had lodged an appeal, he told Honecker, but the prosecutors had a court order prolonging his detention until the next afternoon.

When it expired, Vogel brought the Honeckers to the only shelter anyone had been willing to offer them. This was a refuge that was indeed rich in irony: the Lobetal religious settlement on the outskirts of Berlin. Here Uwe Holmer, a Lutheran pastor whose children had been denied a university education because of their religious affiliations, had a spare room on the second floor, and he was ready to offer it to his former persecutors as an act of Christian charity.

The Honeckers were not in a repentant mood. "Socialism has gone down the drain and we have landed in a capitalist Germany," Honecker told two East German interviewers in early 1990.[14] After enduring this awkward situation for a few weeks, with sensation-seeking photographers staking out the house the whole time, the Honeckers fled, finally, to a Soviet military hospital in Beelitz, southwest of Berlin. There Honecker's kidney complaints could be dealt with in private, and the press could be kept at bay.

But the unworthy spectacle of what was happening to the Honeckers sent chills through Vogel's spine. If the most powerful man in the country could be humiliated in this way, what would become of one of his closest confidants? Vogel, who had worked in the shadows all his life, had not developed the thick skin needed to come through such humiliation. And besides, he felt, he did not deserve it.

Revelation followed revelation of how the omnipresent police state had spied on citizens high and low, using informers to turn friend against friend, brother against brother, husband against wife. Not only Vogel, but church leaders such as Stolpe who had quietly worked with the Communists rather than defying them were now coming to be seen as suspect accomplices of the Stasi, rather than as respected intercessors.

The Stasi bore the brunt of the anger. Crowds of people who earlier had been afraid to go near the Normannenstrasse complex, bristling with security devices and antennae, now began converging outside the gates and chanting protests. The guards inside hung out sheets and placards with exculpatory messages that suggested that they were clean now: "We are only working for the security of all of us," they read. But such gestures had little effect against popular rage. On January 15, the crowd broke past the gates and invaded the three thousand rooms of the complex, breaking windows and furniture and scattering files, demanding that Modrow and the Round-Table opposition leaders meeting with him make changes faster.

Mielke and Honecker had not always seen eye to eye, as Vogel had often observed. What Mielke's minions were unwilling to concede, Honecker had often granted—the amnesties and sudden decisions to release prisoners held for years reflected that. Both Vogel and Honecker needed to remind the public of these acts of mercy; Vogel advised Honecker to issue a statement, which he helped to circulate quietly among Western journalists. But it was a document of self-justification more than of exculpation.

"It is known and can be proved," the four-page document, signed "E. Honecker," said, "that in my activities as head of the party and the state I paid great attention to humanitarian questions. This had significance for the establishment of good-neighborly relations with Western countries, as well. . . . In many meetings with statesmen of other countries lists with requests for examining humanitarian matters were given to me or my entourage, and all were decided positively. In resolving this questions, my agent Prof. Dr. Wolfgang Vogel often had to overcome resistance from our competent authorities. . . . Prof. Vogel had my complete trust and was always authorized to make full use of his mandate, his possibilities, and to turn to me if he should encounter resistance within the bureaucracy. Prof. Vogel won for himself undeniable recognition of his achievements in the exercise of his mandate in the interests of humanitarian relief."

Honecker claimed that he had eliminated one of the most fiendish anti-personnel devices, the SM-70 automatic bullet-firing mechanism, along the inner-German border, in 1984. He did not mention that these had been installed in 1971, after he had become party leader. Neither did he refer to the fact that he had agreed to take them and millions of landmines away, at least in part, after the Bavarian Christian Social Union leader Franz Josef Strauss had arranged a government-guaranteed line of credit of several billion deutsche marks for East Germany. "The closed borders between the G.D.R. and the F.R.G. were no longer suited to the times and created human difficulties," Honecker now wrote; he had made the decision, he said, over objections from within the apparat, and in 1987 he had also lifted the shoot-to-kill orders given to East German security guards.[15]

This claim had been accepted in West Germany in 1987, when Honecker had at last been able to visit the country as Kohl's guest. The West Germans had even passed a special law before his arrival to prevent his being arrested on West German soil to answer for the deaths of any of the 191 people killed trying to cross illegally into West Germany since 1961. Fewer than one hundred people had been killed at the Wall itself in Berlin, despite the fact that hundreds of people every year persisted in trying to breach it. Now there was talk of prosecuting him for issuing the shoot-to-kill order, which had become East German law in 1982. All Honecker had done in 1987, it was claimed, was to issue orders to the border guards to use deadly force only in exceptional circumstances.[16]

In January 1990, Honecker's exculpatory statement fell on deaf ears. As the two parts of the country swept along toward unification, their view of their own separate histories was changing. What need had there been to accommodate to Communism for all these years, people on both sides of the Wall were beginning to ask, when it could be so easily swept away? What need had there been of spies and counterspies, or of spyswappers, when the most efficient espionage and security system in the Communist world had been powerless to prevent the collapse of the country it was built up to defend? The people now wanted "democracy," they said, the right to decide their own future in freedom.

What East Germans understood by this was not so clear. All they knew was that they wanted to live like West Germans, to have as much money and material wealth as West Germans had. But of the free market mechanisms that made those things possible, of the free interplay of debate and ideas from which democracy sprung, they had little notion. "Democracy" for them had always been a sham, as it had been in every Stalinist system. The parliament was an empty shell, in which all deputies raised their hands to signal unanimous approval of whatever laws had been handed down from the Communist party Politburo. The Christian Democrats and the Liberal Democrats had been allowed to continue to function, in a political umbrella organization known as the National Front, but only on the condition of going along with the charade. Now, with contrite admissions of failure and responsibility for the past, they were pretending to be independent again, and to have rediscovered democracy.

The date of the first free East German elections was advanced from May to March, but the electorate was losing its moral bearings. All they knew was that they wanted to be rid of their sham legislature, rid of the Stasi, rid of the German Democratic Republic—and on March 18, that is essentially what they voted for, in the first and last democratic elections to the People's Chamber. Kohl's Christian Democratic Union won a majority of the seats in the new chamber and elected Lothar de Maizière prime minister, with a mandate of negotiating the terms for unification with West Germany. From then on nothing and no one could stand in its way.

The first thing the East Germans wanted was to unify the economy, so that they could have at least a little bit of the Western way of life, with Western clothes, Western stores, Western food, a Western standard of living—in a word, what they wanted was the West German deutsche mark. Kohl, not so much moving with the tide as trying to balance on top of a tidal wave, was forced to give it to them on exchange rate terms of 1:1 for wages, pensions, and savings of as much as a thousand marks, and 2:1 for higher amounts. Ordinary people were delighted, since the real value of the East German mark was far below that. But the exchange terms were a disaster for East German industries, which were far less efficient or competitive than the West German businesses with which, at these rates, they would now be set on equal terms. When economic union went into effect on July 1, 1990, most East German industry began, ineluctably, to sink into bankruptcy.

Once the Soviet Union had given its approval to unification—on terms allowing the united Germany to remain in the NATO alliance, terms that Kohl essentially bought with billions of deutsche marks—it remained only to negotiate the legal contract by which the Federal Republic of Germany would absorb the Eastern states on October 3. One of the main sticking points was the question of property rights. Wolfgang Vogel had helped nearly a quarter of a million people leave East Germany over the previous quarter century, and nearly all of them had had to give up the right to whatever property of value they had—house, land, and worldly goods. As long as Communism had held sway, people had willingly accepted the sacrifice, simply to get away from it. The state had nationalized nearly everything in any event.

It dawned on tens of thousands of former East Germans who lived in the West that the property they had given up or sold could once again acquire real value. The house in Prenzlauer Berg that had been crumbling away for forty years, the tarpaper shack on the Müggelsee, could suddenly be worth a fortune simply by virtue of where it was located, now that the free market had returned. Lawmakers, east and west, were determined that ordinary people whose properties had been confiscated by the Communist state should have the right to restitution or compensation. The arguments continued between Bonn and East Berlin until June, only two weeks before economic unification was to take place.

Crucially, the treaty, as finally negotiated, gave people who had been deprived of their property by confiscation or "unfair dealings" the right to reclaim it. "Unfair dealings" included the act of having been forced to sign over property in return for a permit to leave the country. Thus people who had long ago abandoned or sold property in the East and gone West to build new lives now had new reasons to come back and reclaim what they had lost. The relatively few East Germans who owned property would benefit, too. Hundreds of thousands of them did not own their homes or apartments, but rented them from the state at absurdly low rents. Now their "rightful" owners and their heirs could come back and evict them. Few East Germans earned salaries or had savings remotely comparable to what their West Germans cousins had, and many now began, bitterly, to feel that they were being sold out.

Vogel's conscience was clear; it had not been his idea that people who wanted to leave had been required to sell their property first. That had been the law of the land.

Yet here was one potential time bomb for any lawyer implicated in the implementation of the regulations, and particularly for Vogel, the lawyer to whom most people who wanted to leave had come. In this country where nobody dared trust his neighbor, people thought they could trust him. How could neighbor trust neighbor when the Stasi had secreted 109,000 informants among 16,500,000 people?[17] Now some East Germans were beginning to consider Vogel a collaborator.

Unification day, October 3, was a beautiful, brilliantly sunny, almost summerlike day, one that the entire nation took as a holiday. In the balmy evening there was a spectacular fireworks celebration at the Reichstag, where Hitler had destroyed the last all-German democracy in 1933. The festivities drew hundreds of thousands of people who reveled far past midnight, surging up Unter den Linden through the Brandenburg Gate in a lighthearted, joyful mood. But Wolfgang Vogel was not among them. He spent the day at home, in quiet and apprehensive meditation.[18]

His mood had not lightened by the time of his 65th birthday, at the end of October. Under the old regime, it would have been celebrated in festive dignity, accompanied by tributes from powerful and respected people from all over the world. Then the lines had been clearer, the distinctions simpler; people had found it easier to separate good from evil in those days. Now things were more complicated and ambiguous, and there would be no tributes to Dr. Vogel except from his family and a few close friends. And he was hardly in a mood to celebrate. He was under strain, and his health had begun to suffer. He was wracked by such severe stomach pain and heartburn that his doctors suspected serious illness. He had even spent his birthday, October 30, in a hospital in Spandau. The diagnosis finally gave him a clean bill of health, but Vogel withdrew from Honecker's defense team and in mid-1991 formally declared his retirement from law practice.

A malignancy was gnawing at the greatest source of Vogel's self-esteem, his reputation as a man who tried to do good in a system of terrible evil. People were beginning to demand that their persecutors be brought to justice. But who were the guilty, what was the real nature of their crimes? CoCo, the hunting preserves, the villas in Wandlitz, the orders to shoot at the Wall, the arrests in the Alexanderplatz the night of Gorbachev's departure, the threat to suppress the demonstrations in Leipzig—all these were state crimes for which the people on the streets were determined to hold Honecker, Mittag, Mielke, and the others accountable.

The government of the newly united Germany was just as determined, but disappointingly ineffective. Schalck had emerged from hiding, but investigators had been unable to build a case against him, though a special committee of the parliament in Bonn was taking testimony on CoCo and its machinations. Honecker, safely behind the walls of the Soviet Army compound in Beelitz, would not be immune once Soviet sovereignty formally expired by the terms of the unification treaty. But just before it did, in March 1991, he had been spirited away to safety in Moscow, where he and his wife took up residence in a KGB hospital. Erich Mielke was behind bars in Berlin, but the only criminal case prosecutors seemed able to bring against him was on the sixty-year-old charges of involvement in the murder of the Berlin policemen. Responsibility for the crimes that had been committed at the leadership's orders at the Wall was pushed onto the shoulders of two twenty-seven-year-old former Stasi border guards who were charged with fatally shooting the border's last victim, a twenty-year-old waiter, as he tried to swim to safety across the Teltow Canal in early 1989.[19]

Compounding the natural frustration that ordinary East Germans felt about their inability to bring their tormentors to justice was anger about being treated as second-class citizens by their Western neighbors. West Germany had not united with East Germany so much as it had absorbed it. Millions of East Germans had wanted to go to the West while the Wall had stood, but after unification, many of them felt the West had come to them, rather like a conquering army.

The huge disparity between living standards and values between East and West Berlin, had seemed, strangely, normal, while the East had been Communist. Now that Germans all belonged to one state, it seemed artificial and unjust. Some vented their frustration by lashing out at the growing numbers of "foreigners" in their midst, Vietnamese workers the Communists had brought in to do menial tasks in their factories, or the rapidly growing numbers of asylum-seekers, mainly from Eastern Europe, who began flocking to Germany because that was where the money seemed to be. Others sought scapegoats among their former rulers. Anyone who had been prominent or famous in the old days was fair game. East German politicians who had been regarded as heroes before unification were now denounced as collaborators and traitors. Lothar de Maizière had been elected to the all-German parliament after signing away the country he had led into unification, but in March 1991 he was forced to resign from Kohl's government after a drumbeat of charges in the press that he had been an informal collaborator of the Stasi, ratting on clients in political cases while working as their defense lawyer. In the climate of mounting hysteria about what was in the files, de Maizière's denials counted for little. The Stasi's legacy, some East German politicians even in Kohl's own party began to feel, was being used by their West German colleagues as a useful weapon of keeping them away from the levers of power in Bonn.

With most of the real leaders of the old regime now unreachable,

Wolfgang Vogel's premonitions came true: He had become a more attractive target for these resentments. He put the gold Mercedes in the garage and took to driving around in a more modest Renault coupe. He was retiring, he said, and all he wanted was peace and quiet, and the right to enjoy the rest of his life with Helga, and with his children and grandchildren in West Germany. He and Helga had bought a vacation home in the Alps, in Schliersee, near Munich, where he had hoped to go to enjoy his retirement and ski during the winter. They still hoped for the best, but it was a naïve hope.

For now the Vogels had been discovered by the new muckraking free press in Eastern Germany. Few East German papers managed to survive unification, and most of those that did were bought by Western publishers determined to feed their readers' appetites for stories about the corruption and misrule of their former Communist leaders. Everything in these publications was starkly black and white, where East German life had been gray. There was no room for examining ambiguity, compromise, or complexity; the sensationalist press told East Germans what it thought they wanted to hear, which was how they had been victimized, and who had done these terrible things to them.

Long ago, Axel Springer had kept news of Vogel's delicate negotiations on prisoner releases out of his papers, in the interest of those who would win their freedom, but now Vogel himself was fair game. By mid-1991, a few of his former clients had come to view him, too, as a victimizer, as the East German reading public discovered in *extra Magazin* that June, in an article titled "Exposed: The Human Trader."[20]

In this, the first of a series of similar articles in *extra* before it folded at the end of the year, and in other publications aimed at the East German market, all of Vogel's activities over the years were thrown into a harsh new light. The political prisoner releases negotiated over the years with Bonn were transformed, in this new view, into a cynical trade in human flesh. Seen in the light of oversimplification, the trade had been just a conspiracy between Vogel and the evil Schalck-Golodkowski, Vogel's "business partner," to make money and to fleece his clients; the memorandum for the record about the trades that Vogel had written to Krenz was evidence of the conspiracy, since Vogel had written it at Schalck's suggestion.

And the magazine had found former clients who claimed they

had been hard done by. Vogel had tricked them into committing political crimes as a way of getting out of the country, or he had forced them to sell their property for "laughable" sums, or he had made them pay large sums of money to the state as the price of escape. One of these, a woman named Helga Rothe, claimed that when she had asked Vogel to help her get to West Berlin in 1984, he had forced her to sell her house to one of his secretaries, for only fifty thousand worthless East German marks. "You want to go be with your grandmother?" Vogel had allegedly said. "Then let's help my secretary out. I won't collect a fee, but you take fifteen thousand marks off the assessed value, and I'll take care of registering the sale." Vogel had gotten her out to West Berlin without a hitch, Rothe admitted, but she had never received full payment and had sued after unification to recover the property. In the end, she settled out of court for sixty-four thousand West German marks, but she still thought she had been swindled.[21]

Vogel denied all accusations of having blackmailed or coerced anyone into selling property, and hired a spirited lawyer from West Berlin, Dr. Friederike Schulenburg, to take *extra* to court. Schulenburg was tenacious and she was fiercely protective of Vogel, who had taken her former husband's defense in an East German court in the 1970s when he had been convicted of smuggling East Germans across the Wall. In 1980, when the Frankfurt human rights group had accused Vogel of being a secret Stasi agent, Schulenburg pressed a libel action on Vogel's behalf in a West Berlin court, telling the judges in ringing tones, "I would not be a member of the same bar as an officer of the State Security Ministry." She and her client had won the day.[22]

But twelve years later, to a tiny fraction of his former clients Vogel seemed guilty of something far worse than complicity with the Communist state's blackmail; he was guilty of blackmail himself. There was self-interest in bringing such charges, of course. Properties that had been worth "laughable" amounts of money in 1984, when there was no free market in real estate, and East German marks that were worthless anywhere in the West, were worth real money, in deutsche marks now that capitalism was back. Any former owners who could prove that Vogel had used shady dealings ("unfair dealings," as the unification treaty specified) to coerce them into selling their property could establish legal grounds for reclaiming it.

Since unification, there was also a new team of prosecutors in

Berlin, many of them young lawyers from West Germany who had had little experience of life under Communism but were bent on discovering all evidence of its iniquities and bringing those responsible to book. They had no difficulty believing some of the claims against Vogel. Subpoenas from the Berlin prosecutor's office for documents from Vogel's files began to pile up by the end of 1991.

Professor Vogel was beginning to feel under siege, and he was bitter. The friends in the government in Bonn who had spoken up for him and protected his reputation over the years had fallen strangely silent. The leaders from whom he had derived all his influence were in jail. Honecker had just taken refuge in the Chilean Embassy in Moscow. Wolfgang Vogel, who had stayed right where he was, had not tried to evade his responsibilities, and had never denied what he had done, was now a prime target by default.

On January 11, 1992, the real siege began, with a telephone call from a reporter who announced that he was from the *Welt am Sonntag* newspaper's bureau in Berlin. Vogel's comment on a story that the newspaper was running in the next day's editions was urgently needed. The article would name several of Vogel's former clients who were now accusing him of having forced them to sell homes, properties, automobiles, and antiques at far below market value to get out of East Germany.

And the article would describe how these people had been coerced into selling their property—to him, to at least two high-ranking Stasi officers, and to a high-ranking officer of the East German Army. The Berlin prosecutors were investigating at least eighteen such charges against Vogel, the report said, and *Welt am Sonntag* wanted Vogel's reaction that afternoon. When Vogel protested that he needed time to check his files, and that these were all on the Reilerstrasse, an hour away in Berlin, the reporter said that he was on deadline. Protesting, Vogel told him that it was understandable that people who wanted to get their property back now put things in a different light, and that it was undeniable that many wrongs had been committed in the old days. "Lawyers didn't think up these things, the leadership of the GDR did. It was a hassle," he conceded. But, he explained, all these people who were bringing charges now had desperately wanted to leave East Germany then. The law required them to get rid of their property, and Vogel had only tried to help them, not to enrich himself at their expense; any other version of what had happened was a lie.[23]

The publication of this article on Sunday accelerated Vogel's downward spiral. At 9 P.M. that evening, a score of detectives roared up to his Reilerstrasse office with a search warrant authorizing them to seize the entire basement archive and more than one hundred thousand files, on the grounds that, now that the news of the charges against him had come out, Vogel might try to suppress evidence. Vogel offered no resistance, and detectives rummaged through the files in the basement and in Vogel's private office until the early morning hours of Monday, taking away an entire truckload of documents and sealing the basement storeroom. Vogel issued a statement to the press later that day, vowing to prove his innocence of all the charges being made against him, with material from his files and testimony from witnesses. He would defend his reputation with all the means at his disposal.

For years, whenever the charge had been made in the West that Vogel was a Stasi agent, a high-ranking Stasi officer, or had held any kind of formal association with the organization at all, he had consistently and vigorously denied it. He was still denying it now, both in public and in private. But as of January 1, 1992, a new law on the Stasi files had gone into effect, bringing together and organizing the files held by the secret police all over the country under a new federal agency headed by a clergyman named Joachim Gauck. The new law forbade the private circulation or sale of Stasi documents outside the framework of this new office, which would make them available for inspection by the Stasi's victims and by legal and judicial authorities investigating Communist misdeeds. The law had been passed over strenuous objections from *Der Spiegel* and other investigatory press organs, but it had been intended to protect the rights and sensitivities of hundreds of thousands of innocent people and to prevent unscrupulous blackmail by former Stasi officers or others tempted by the rich array of opportunities that uncontrolled access to the files would offer.

The Gauck office assembled what files remained after the frenzy of shredding and incineration that had taken place in the Stasi's death agonies in the winter of 1989–1990, in a building behind the old Soviet Embassy on Unter den Linden. Pastor Gauck himself was not altogether sure that looking into the files was a good idea for all the Stasi's victims, and urged people to think twice about whether they really wanted to know who had informed and spied on them all these years. In the "horror files," as *Der Spiegel* called them, lay lies as well as truth, provocations as well as revelations. But Germans were in no mood to let sleeping dogs lie.

The stories that began to emerge in the early days of January were indeed horrifying. Within the first ten days, Vera Wollenberger, a peace activist who had been jailed for six months and expelled from East Germany in 1988, discovered that the Stasi "informal collaborator" who had spied on her for nearly ten years under the code-name "Donald" had been her own husband. "I was not only the Stasi's informant on the peace movement," he tried to explain to her oldest child, "I was also the peace movement's informant on the Stasi."[24]

The files destroyed the reputations of many of Vogel's East German lawyer colleagues. Wolfgang Schnur, who had helped to build the new East German Christian Democratic Union party and had been active in the democratic movement before the collapse, was revealed to have been an *"inoffizieller Mitarbeiter,"* a secret informant, of the Stasi since 1964, under the codename "Torsten." Ibrahim Böhme, head of the reconstituted Social Democratic Party in East Germany, was soon revealed as another, who as "Paul Bonkarz" had furnished the Stasi with volumes of material denouncing dissident writers of the 1970s. Gregor Gysi, who had been chosen to rebuild the Party of Democratic Socialism on the strength of his reputation for integrity, was under suspicion of being an informal collaborator called "Notary" who had given reports to the Stasi on his dissident clients. Gysi strenuously denied that he had ever been an informal collaborator, read through the entire "Notary" file himself, and insisted that it was either based on information from somebody else in his office, or on electronic surveillance, but that he had always kept faith with his clients.

To forestall surprise attacks, Vogel's close friend Manfred Stolpe, who was now the governor of the state of Brandenburg, took the unusual step in late January of revealing that he had often conducted private negotiations on delicate matters, including the activities of dissidents and peace activists within the Lutheran Church, with the Stasi himself, often without the knowledge of his bishops. Stolpe's cooperative attitude had given him the same kind of influence Vogel had with the emigration authorities, and Stolpe, too, had often succeeded in getting permission for people to leave East Germany. Like Vogel, Stolpe had had his lists from the Interior Ministry of buyers for the real estate and other property the emigrants would have to leave behind, and had helped to arrange hush-hush financial cross-border transactions through the church's underground channels across the Wall, channels that no one ever thought would bear the harsh light of legal scrutiny they were coming under now. Stolpe, too, was accused of having betrayed to his Stasi contacts the confidences of the people he had tried to help, losing political credibility even as he denied the charges.

Disclosure after disclosure shocked a public that was already prepared to believe the worst, adding to the sense of demoralization and personal mistrust that was already beginning to shake East German society to its foundations. West Germans whose parents and grandparents had known such things under Nazi rule could indulge themselves in righteous moral outrage. Something like outrage may also have motivated the prosecutors working on the Vogel case, preparing them to assume the worst as they learned about the corrupt and corrupting milieu from which Vogel had drawn his authority.

Wolfgang Vogel had never concealed that he had an open relationship with the Stasi. No one who dealt with him on spies or political prisoners in Washington, Bonn, Jerusalem, or Pretoria could doubt that he had to be reporting on the negotiations to the organization that held the prisoners. A known confidant of Erich Honecker's could not possibly be a total stranger to Erich Mielke. Jürgen Stange, Vogel's West Berlin counterpart for so many years, knew Vogel's friend Heinz Volpert was a Stasi man, and no doubt the BND knew as well.[25]

Until early 1992, nobody besides Volpert and Vogel knew that Vogel, too, had been a Stasi secret informer in the early 1950s. Outside of the Stasi, nobody knew the precise nature of the continuing relationship since then. Volpert's knowledge had died with him six years earlier, and he had sealed the "Georg" file on Vogel back in 1957. Volpert and Niebling had kept referring to him as "Georg" in internal Stasi documents, but this did not mean he was still an informant. It was a common practice, but Vogel did not know that. He did not even know that his file had been sealed, or what it said about him or his work with Volpert and Niebling, he insisted—including whether all traces of it had been destroyed.

But perhaps Vogel had obtained and destroyed most of his Stasi file. One of the prosecution's star witnesses claimed that he had— Frank Michalak, a forty-four-year-old former military judge advocate-general corps prosecutor attached to the Stasi. Vogel knew

Michalak, but only distantly, as having been the Stasi officer in charge of political supervision of Mielke's ceremonial "Feliks Dzerzhinski Regiment" in the past. Michalak told the prosecutors that he had been in the team that had cleaned out Mielke's offices in December 1989. Among the materials that had been removed, Michalak said, was a plastic bag full of documents on Schalck-Golodkowski that he had sealed and taken for later examination. A month later, he testified, he had been ordered to look through the documents, which had contained not only information about Schalck-Golodkowski but about "Georg." Among the documents he had seen, Michalak said, were papers that showed that "Georg" had worked for the Stasi since 1953, and had received at least 2.5 million East German marks and 1.5 million deutsche marks for his services over the years. In the file, Michalak claimed, there had been a piece of paper identifying "Georg" by his real name—openly, as Wolfgang Vogel.[26]

It would have been an amateurish secret service indeed that allowed a covert agent to be revealed so easily by his own card, but the prosecutors found Michalak's testimony credible. They also believed Günter Seidel, the last prosecutor-general of the German Democratic Republic, when he told them that soon after Michalak had examined these files, Vogel had come begging for any that mentioned him, and had been given them. Indeed, all documentation of what Michalak claimed to have seen, all documentation on Vogel's relationship with the Stasi since 1957—whatever it might have been—had vanished without trace. For the prosecutors, there could be only one logical conclusion: Vogel had disposed of the evidence, which thus must be incriminating.[27] The only part of Vogel's "Georg" file that remained in the archive administered by Pastor Gauck was the one that had been opened in 1953 and closed, by Volpert's order, in 1957.[28] This the prosecutors promptly put under seal.

Vogel did not know how much the prosecutors knew in January 1992. But on the 16th, he received a call from the Berlin Bureau of *Der Spiegel.* Had he ever had dealings with the Stasi under the code name "Rubin?" the magazine asked. It was the first he had ever heard the name, Vogel insisted. *Bild* called an hour later, with the same question, and Vogel gave the same answer.

He was genuinely puzzled. Niebling, he thought, might be able to shed light on this mystery, but Vogel had never developed the bond of personal friendship with him that he had enjoyed with Heinz

Volpert. Niebling was a man more in the classic Stasi mold, all business and ideology. But they were in the same boat now. Niebling had been out of work since the end of March 1990, and few employers were offering jobs to ex-Stasi generals in their sixties. Vogel needed Niebling's help, and Niebling was willing to provide it.[29]

Yes, there was a "Rubin" file on Vogel, Niebling acknowledged after a pause. He had ordered the file opened in April 1986, shortly after Volpert's death, when he had discovered that the operational files on Vogel were nonexistent or missing. Mielke had worried that Vogel could be subject to blackmail by the "class enemy" or by terrorists, for that matter, Niebling said, and had ordered a complete background check run on Vogel and all who worked for him. This had been for Vogel's own security, Niebling told him. Why "Rubin?" Vogel asked. It had been a name plucked out of the air. Would Vogel have preferred "Blech?"[30]

The next day, Vogel went to the press with his story. On the widely viewed nightly *Tagesthemen* news magazine program on ARD television, he told the interviewer: "I found out yesterday, for the first time, that I am supposed to have been a man with the name of Rubin. I tell you first of all that it wasn't me."

"You had no official contacts to the Stasi, you signed no formal obligation, you were not an officer on special assignment for the Stasi?"

"That's right."

"Did you ever take money from the Stasi?"

"No."

"And besides the known contacts you had, you had no further contacts as a lawyer?"

"No. I had contacts as part of my mandate to help people . . . And I needed these connections for that . . . The only mistake that I ever made was that I was not in a position to tell my clients beforehand, be patient awhile, everything is going to change very soon."[31]

The same week, he told one of the new magazines for the Eastern German audience, "I did not betray a single one of my clients to the Stasi. You will find no tipster reports from me [in the Stasi files]."[32] He filed an application with the Gauck office to see what was in his file; like hundreds of thousands of others, his name was put on a long waiting list.

When the "Rubin" file became accessible, it revealed little more than Niebling had told Vogel it contained. The Stasi did its usual thorough job, reporting every bit of personal and political information or gossip it could assemble on each of Vogel's thirteen employees and any of their friends, relatives, or associates who had ever said a bad word or had a negative thought about East Germany. It reported who slept with whom, and who on Vogel's staff had ever had contact, knowingly or unknowingly, with the Stasi. It reported on the political views of Vogel's gardener, Herbert Hanuschek—he had once been reliable—and of his office janitor, Hanuschek's son, whom the Stasi found more suspect. It reported very little about Vogel himself, about all his contacts with West German and American intelligence over the years, or about Helga.[33]

The "Rubin" file was the least of the trials that Vogel was to face. Vaguely anticipating that the worst was yet to come, on March 12, he and Helga set off for the mountains of Bavaria. They had just reached the autobahn approaches to Nuremberg when Vogel switched on the radio to listen to the news. The lead item was the testimony of Mielke's chief of staff, Major General Hans Carlsohn, before the German parliamentary committee investigating Schalck-Golodkowski's machinations. Much of the testimony had concerned Heinz Volpert and his relationship to Schalck. Volpert had been, Carlsohn confirmed, Schalck's control officer. Now Ingrid Köppe, a member of Parliament who had been a dissident in the old days in East Germany, had put an unexpected question to him: "Was Heinz Volpert Wolfgang Vogel's control officer?"

"Control officer is not the right word," Carlsohn told her. "Volpert had contact with Vogel because his responsibilities required it."[34] But he described the close relationship that Vogel had had with Mielke, who, he said, had once given the lawyer a gold watch as a present.

Listening to the radio, Vogel realized that this could cause real trouble. From his car phone, Vogel called the editor of the *Bild* in Hamburg, and denied that he had any relationship of the sort with the Stasi. Then he looked darkly at Helga and said, "Let's go back to Berlin."

It happened that March 13 was a Friday, and this Friday the 13th lived up to its reputation. When the Vogels got back to their house on the Schwerinsee, the telephone was ringing incessantly. Friederike Schulenburg, Vogel's lawyer, reported that the prosecutors had been interviewing more witnesses. A reporter from *Der Spiegel* called to confront Vogel with the news that the magazine had obtained the Stasi list of the coded identification numbers of all "officers on special assignment," each beginning with the birth date of its owner, followed by his or her East German personal identification number. The magazine had one that began with Vogel's birthday, 30.10.1925. Would he give *Der Spiegel* his identification number? Vogel complied, reading off the figures: 301025430190. The number the *Der Spiegel* reporter had was not the one on the list.[35]

Toward afternoon, Vogel saw a car outside the metal gate at the end of the driveway. Two men in civilian clothes were in the car; the driver was communicating with someone by radio telephone. Now Vogel was infuriated. The neighbors across the street could see what was going on; this was deliberate humiliation. Vogel put on a jacket, went out the side door of the house, walked down through the garden to the gate, and approached the man with the telephone.

"Look, if this surveillance is supposed to be for me, you can make it easier on yourselves," Vogel told the man, figuring him to be a detective. "Come on into the house."

Almost in a replay of the brief nightmare of two years earlier, the police officer brusquely informed Vogel that he was under arrest.

"I want it made clear that I did not resist arrest—I came to you," Vogel protested. If he had wanted to flee, he could have gotten away through the back door.[36]

When they finally went into the house, Vogel was allowed to call Schulenburg. Then the telephone was cut off.

Schulenburg arrived at about 7:45 P.M. to find the house swarming with fifty detectives, supervised by a prosecutor whose superior was at that moment at Vogel's office on the Reilerstrasse in Berlin, with an equal number of detectives and assistants.

The detectives took Vogel away at about 9 P.M., bringing him later that evening to Moabit prison, the same jail where Erich Honecker had served much of his incarceration under the Nazis more than fifty years earlier. From Moabit, Vogel himself had delivered scores of imprisoned East German spies. This time, like countless numbers of his own hapless clients before him, Vogel had not even been able to take a toothbrush—only a rosary that Schulenburg had seen on his office wall and had slipped to him as the detectives were hustling him away.

The zeal and haste of the prosecutors probably resulted from their deep sense of frustration. Charged with bringing the former rulers of East Germany to justice for their misdeeds, they had so far had precious little success. Erich Honecker was still in the Chilean Embassy in Moscow, though they were preparing a case accusing him and five other members of the East German National Defense Council of manslaughter of forty-nine people killed trying to flee across the East German borders over the years. The only case the prosecutors had been able to bring against Erich Mielke had nothing at all to do with the Stasi's misdeeds. And Mielke's lawyer had fled the country ten days before Vogel's arrest and was suspected of having made off with seventeen million deutsche marks from CoCo's ill-gotten gains. Vogel had become a scapegoat once again, subjected to security rules as strict as if he, not Honecker, had been accused of the forty-nine cases of manslaughter at the Wall. Not even Helga Vogel was allowed to visit him in the prison. The Lutheran bishop of Berlin-Brandenburg, on his way to a church conference in Budapest, also was refused; the prosecutors apparently feared, Schulenburg joked sarcastically, that the bishop might help Vogel convert loot into Hungarian forints.[37]

Adding to his confusion and uncertainty were the vagaries of the German legal system. Investigations in complicated cases could take months, even years, and defendants could be imprisoned under "urgent suspicion" of committing crimes long before formal charges were brought. The arrest warrant under which Vogel had been imprisoned could also be amended; as soon as his lawyers dismissed one case, the prosecutors could bring another. The uncertainty preyed on him in his isolation, depressing him even more than his brief scare about his own health had done two years earlier. Vogel felt like a patient without a prognosis.[38]

The charge the prosecutors finally brought was blackmail. Vogel felt as though they had filtered the facts of his past life and career through a post-unification prism that distorted them completely.

The arrest warrant did, in fact, paint a picture of Vogel that made him resemble a villain in a trashy spy novel. For it had gone back all the way to the unhappy episode of Rudolf Reinartz's defection from the East German Justice Ministry in 1953. As the prosecutors saw it nearly forty years later, Vogel had not been victimized then by the Stasi's suspicions; he had betrayed his mentor to become a secret Stasi agent.

In the stark legalese of the indictment, this convoluted story of multiple betrayals had no complexity. It was only a two-dimensional Stasi plot: "The accused was since Nov. 10, 1953 an em-

ployee of the Ministry for State Security, which decisively contrib-
uted to his obtaining a license to practice law in Berlin [West]."
From then on, in the prosecution's view, Vogel's powers seemed to
have no limits. Sometime in the 1960s, according to the charges,
Vogel had conspired with the Stasi to rewrite East German law to
require people who wanted to leave the country to give up their
valuables and real property, so that it could be taken over by other
Stasi officers or members of the East German politically privileged
classes, or cashed in by CoCo.

This charge seemed to ignore virtually the entire history of the
German Democratic Republic, which could and did nationalize
and sequester private property at will and had never needed to hide
behind the figleaf of conspiracy described in the arrest warrant. But
in the revisionist climate of 1992, these facts availed Vogel little.
"To give the said confiscation the appearance of legality, the accused took on a legal mandate for the complainants," the arrest
warrant charged; he had told his clients that they would get permission to leave only if they sold property to buyers he suggested and
transferred the payments thus received to accounts he controlled, or
paid him cash. Vogel's legal exertions on behalf of such clients,
then, had been simply a scam that he and the Stasi used to fleece his
clients of all they had.

Thirty-two individual cases were alleged, most of them from the
1980s, one going back to 1975. Among them were the family that
had paid 250,000 deutsche marks in cash to get out in 1981; this was
now portrayed as an extortionate plot foisted on them by Vogel,
rather than as a response to a request by their lawyer to see if money
might be a way to get them out. Some other cases concerned people
who had tried unsuccessfully after the Wall had come down to
retrieve the property they had been forced to sell in order to get out;
prominent among these was the Zapff family, whose island property Helga Vogel had bought as a favor and whose house had gone
to a Stasi officer Vogel claimed he did not know though he had been
Niebling's deputy.

The prosecutors charged a systematic pattern of deception. In all
these cases, according to the arrest warrant, Vogel had been duplici-
tous, pretending to represent his clients but actually representing
the East German state. And he had received secret payments from
the Stasi every six months, at first 15,000 East German marks, plus
5,000 West German deutsche marks, but leading up to 150,000 East
marks and 80,000 deutsche marks in 1989. Over the years, the

prosecution charged, he had received 2.5 million East German marks and 1.5 million deutsche marks, altogether, the same sums Michalak had told the prosecution about. Coming on top of the annual fee Vogel had collected from the West German government (given in the arrest warrant as 320,000 deutsche marks, though it had actually been 360,000 by the end), and with the individual fees of many of his clients, the prosecution charged extortion on a grand scale. Vogel had to be arrested before he could try to flee abroad, where he was suspected of having stashed away all this money. The prosecution ascertained that Vogel had a 600,000-mark certificate of deposit with the Deutsche Bank in Berlin, but there could be more in Switzerland, according to the charge.

To prove all this, the prosecution said, it had documentation from Vogel's files, testimony from witnesses, and evidence from Vogel's "Georg" file. He had already done away with some evidence, the prosecutors charged, and he would suppress more unless he was promptly jailed. For the moment, a judge was persuaded that they were right, and Vogel stayed behind bars.

Vogel's arrest was shocking news. But on the face of it, the main grounds of the arrest warrant were absurd. Vogel was not about to try to flee; he had turned the car around himself to drive to Berlin when he had heard Carlsohn's testimony, and had gone back to answer these new charges. His reputation was worth a great deal to him, as the prosecutors suggested, and he was the only one who could answer the charges and put the facts into proper perspective.

From his jail cell, with Schulenburg working feverishly from her offices in West Berlin without benefit of any of the thousands of files that now sat in the prosecutors' offices, Vogel did his best to summon a defense from memory.

First, the matter of the Stasi money. Vogel had indeed received vast sums, not directly from the Stasi, but from the State Bank of the German Democratic Republic. The money had been not for him, but to pay his expenses and the legal bills of the captured spies whose freedom he had later negotiated. Where had the ten thousand dollars James Donovan had received for Rudolf Abel's defense come from, in July and September 1959? From Vogel, who had indeed gotten it as a result of his connections with Heinz Volpert in the Stasi, but not as his "control officer." The same was true of the $360,407.50 that Harvey Silverglate in Boston had charged for the defense of Alfred Zehe in 1984 and 1985, and the additional $150,000 that Leonard Boudin in New York City had been paid for Alice Michelson's defense. These honoraria alone, at the exchange rate prevailing in the mid-1980s, could account for the 1.5 million deutsche marks Michalak claimed to have seen in the missing file. Silverglate, informed by Schulenburg of the charges, was happy to confirm the amount and wired that he hoped that Vogel would be released forthwith. Silverglate even offered to testify in his defense, as did Rabbi Ronnie Greenwald, who had carried some of the money to New York, in cash, during the years of negotiation on the Shcharansky case.

Much of the rest had been money Vogel had had to lay out as expenses, during the thousands of trips to Karl-Marx-Stadt, Bautzen, and the border crossing at Herleshausen, as well as the flights to Bonn, Hamburg, London, Washington, New York, and Miami all through the years; the reimbursements had been made partly in East German marks and partly in Western currency, because the regime had given Vogel special tax and foreign-currency advantages, as he conceded himself.

Second, Stasi membership. The arrest warrant charged Vogel with being an "employee" of the Stasi, not an "unofficial collaborator." Over the previous twenty years, Vogel had always denied any kind of formal association with the secret police. If he had been a Stasi officer since 1953, he would have been the first one not to have been required to have been a Communist party member, for Vogel had only joined the party in 1981, after Chancellor Helmut Schmidt had unwittingly drawn Honecker's attention to the lapse at the German summit that December. Vogel did not dispute having worked closely with the Stasi for many years. How else, indeed, could he have achieved the release of convicted spies and brought tens of thousands of political prisoners to freedom from Stasi jails?

Third, the plot to rewrite East German law to make it possible to fleece émigrés of their property. This seemed illogical, as well as implausible. The Communists had not built the Wall to encourage people to leave. The entire purpose of the punitive laws was to force East Germans to stay where they were, not to make them give up their property. The Communist state did not need to resort to cumbersome stratagems involving Vogel to confiscate private property. Ever since the Red Army had marched into eastern Germany in 1945, confiscation had been a regular, even routine, occurrence, and it had taken place on a vast scale. Besides, what property was "desirable" in East Germany under Communism? No free property market existed then; property was worth only what the state said it was worth, and that was very little. Vogel's clients had come to him begging him to help them get rid of houses and valuables that they had to sell before they would be allowed to leave.

Vogel's friends who had been brought low from their high places in East Germany took his arrest as a humiliation, as one more symbol of the attempt by the new masters of the country to discredit everything and everybody associated with the old regime. The Berlin prosecutors clearly did not come from a world that understood how things had worked in the old East Germany. The few good deeds that those in power, or close to it, had tried to do under Communist rule would not be allowed to go unpunished.

But Vogel was not completely under siege. Schulenburg's office was soon overwhelmed with letters from hundreds of Vogel's former clients coming to his defense, protesting against the oversimplifications and accusations being made against him. More than one wrote that if Vogel had been a Stasi officer, he had had a curious attitude toward his own institution. More than one, such as Frederic Pryor back in 1962, had been struck by his warnings to be careful what they said in their jail cells in his presence because Stasi bugs were in the ceiling. Others credited Vogel with having helped them to avoid being drawn into the Stasi's traps, or even to escape. Three former West German permanent mission chiefs in East Berlin wrote saying that it had always been clear to them that Vogel had worked closely with the Stasi to solve the many delicate and difficult humanitarian cases when they had called him in, and that he had often had to overcome considerable resistance in dealing with it. Lothar Loewe, the television correspondent Honecker had expelled for accusing him of allowing people to be shot at the Wall "like rabbits" in the 1970s, wrote, after examining his own voluminous Stasi file, that he had had almost daily contact with Vogel in those days, but nowhere had he come across any mention that would indicate betrayal by a secret agent code-named "Georg" or "Rubin."[39]

In his jail cell, Vogel did his best to reconstruct the trips to the West and payments to lawyers and law firms for the past thirty years, from 1959 down to the last year of his own law practice, and to remember what he could of the real estate transactions.

Finally, on the 30th of March, the Tiergarten District Court ruled that Vogel's attestations of good faith and willingness to face the charges against him were credible, and freed him, setting a "symbolic" bail of one hundred thousand deutsche marks. Also symbolically, the money was provided by Vogel's friends in the Roman Catholic Church. "By their fruits ye shall know them," Georg Cardinal Sterzinsky said in justifying the contribution; the church and Vogel had stood together for a quarter century in the humanitarian cause, and they would stand together now.[40] Vogel was required to sign in with the mayor of Teupitz once a week, but otherwise he was free to go about preparing his defense.

Free again, after his second taste of a jail cell, Vogel was a deeply shaken man. He hired another lawyer, Wolfgang Schomburg, a former prosecutor, to help with the defense. He kept a satchel packed with a toothbrush, a razor, and a change of underwear. "My conscience is clear," he said in May. "I am not going to do anyone the favor of evading responsibility. Only I can clear up these charges, and with God's help I will."[41]

Partial vindication came on July 14, when the Berlin District Court dismissed many of the charges in the warrant and lifted the arrest order. Neither the testimony of the prosecution's witnesses nor what it had seen of the "Georg" file, the court decided, was evidence of a crime grave enough to warrant Vogel's pretrial imprisonment, let alone a charge of blackmail. Material collected in a Stasi file could not be taken, uncorroborated, as bona fide evidence, given the Stasi's methods and morals. It was even possible, the court observed, that the file might be a complete falsification (though even Vogel did not dispute most of it). The credibility of the Stasi witnesses, and of their claims about Vogel's links to the Stasi and the Honecker leadership, would become clear only after examination and cross-examination at trial. These witnesses, as well as the other East German officials whose testimony the prosecution had cited in support of the arrest order, were all closely tied to that leadership, so their testimony against Vogel was inherently suspect.

In any case, the court noted, Vogel's close contacts with the party leaders and to the Stasi, had been in the nature of things. It was "self-evident," in the court's judgment, that in acting as East Germany's special representative in emigration matters, Vogel could hardly have been acting against their interests.

As for the charge that he had knowingly sought to acquire properties for the benefit of East German officials or Stasi members, the court said, further investigation would provide the answer to whether Vogel was guilty, if not of blackmail then of coercion. But there seemed no compelling reason to put him behind bars while it continued.

"The accused, now 66 years old and previously unconvicted, is threatened with the loss of his undoubtedly considerable reputation, since his disappearance would be taken by the public as a confession of guilt," the court ruled. This, not any amount of bail, was the best guarantee that he would stay and defend himself.[42]

Two weeks later to the day, the man who had made Vogel what he was flew into Berlin from Moscow to face the charges against him. Erich Honecker, finally expelled from the Chilean Embassy, arrived just as the sun was going down. He, too, was driven to Moabit prison, passing through the gates amid jeers and derisive whistles, completing a journey he had begun with his first imprisonment in the very same jail in 1935.

For a few months, it seemed as if they would share a common time of trial: Honecker, who had built the Wall, and Vogel, who had unwittingly helped to undermine it. There had been little ambiguity in Honecker's life and career, but illness cut short his trial in January 1993. Vogel's life had been replete with ambiguity, and when Honecker flew off to Chile to spend his remaining days, Vogel was still under investigation by the prosecutors. Vogel's reputation, his freedom, and ultimately his place in history would depend on how they, and his fellow Germans on both sides of the Wall, finally judged which side he had really been on—the Stasi's, his clients', or simply his own.[43]

EPILOGUE

"Whether I should reproach myself, history will have to judge."

I n the sweep of European history, the country whose two faces Wolfgang Vogel and Erich Honecker represented was a fleeting illusion. The East German economy, supposedly one of the ten most powerful in the world, collapsed almost totally within a year of unification. The Stasi, supposedly one of the most ruthlessly efficient intelligence services anywhere, had lost its nerve. A little more than a year after East Germany disappeared, the Soviet Union, a superpower feared and long treated as an equal by the United States, disintegrated in turn.

Wolfgang Vogel had lived the Communist myth for forty years and built his reputation on it. As long as the cold war lasted, few in the West had reason to doubt his integrity. He had performed his good deeds in the shadows. And as long as the Wall stood, nobody on either side asked whether he had taken moral shortcuts with clients who were at a disadvantage and depended wholly on him to help them get out.

Vogel accepted the Communist rules, and, implicitly, so did the Western officials who welcomed his services as a mediator. If the

East Germans required people to sell or leave their property behind before giving them permission to emigrate to the West, there was little reason to see anything sinister in Vogel's offers of help. It hardly mattered. All that mattered to most of his clients then was that Vogel could get them out.

The main practical rule of survival under Communism had been "to get along, go along." Western governments, resigned to the survival of the Communist world well into the twenty-first century, often followed a similar rule in their dealings with it. To help people in need in East Germany, West German governments had been willing to enter into all kinds of shady arrangements over the years with their Communist rulers—agreements that they were not eager to expose to public scrutiny at home. Curiously, while both sides had been furiously spying on one another over the years, they had also been doing their best to keep many of one another's secrets.

Light began to flood in after the Wall fell. In East Germany, people who had been kept in the dark for forty years did not like the look of much of what they saw. Having lived in circumstances of frustrating complexity, they began demanding clear, simple explanations for their deprivation. The questions they posed were hard, but the answers they were willing to settle for were often far too easy and simplistic.

Vogel was also a convenient scapegoat for the Germans who thought they had won the cold war. The moral complexity of his career did not fit easily into an analytical framework that reduced everything to a confrontation between good and evil, the Stasi on one side and the ordinary people of East Germany on the other. Yet this seemed to be the view taken by the prosecutors who were investigating Vogel in 1992 and early 1993.

By then, the archivists combing through the Stasi's surviving files had found thousands of documents: Vogel's original "Georg" file, the "Rubin" file with everything the Stasi knew about his employees and their contacts, and hundreds and hundreds of documents produced by Volpert and Niebling and their subordinates over the years.

The files showed in chilling detail how the Stasi had used every means at its disposal—blackmail, coercion, fear, bribery, and subversion—to try to keep East Germans from being seduced by the West. They made it perfectly clear that not a single East German ever got official permission to leave without Stasi approval, documenting this truth down to every jot and tittle, with the cover names of all the secret informants and traitors who had helped the secret police do the work they thought would save the East German Communist state from its enemies. But nobody really needed the Stasi files to know that this was true. What the prosecutors appeared to be looking for in the files was evidence that Vogel had been either a paid Stasi operative, or one of the architects of its master plan of repression and control. By the spring of 1993, they had taken testimony from witnesses in more than two hundred cases where Vogel had allegedly swindled people of their properties and from former Stasi officers, and combing through the Stasi files, as if the documents in them would finally provide the answer to who Vogel really was. As this book went to press, the prosecutors had not yet completed their investigation. Vogel's lawyers fully expected them to bring charges in the Berlin courts by mid-1993.

All of Vogel's difficulties had a common cause. He had tried to be too many things to too many people and had convinced himself that in a state where the law was whatever those in power wanted it to be, he could do no wrong. If he was ultimately disgraced, it seemed more likely to be for using his Stasi connections to take ethical, moral, and legal shortcuts, than for having those connections in the first place.

His powers had always been derivative, from the moment when Heinz Volpert and the KGB's liaison officers had asked him to defend "Frau Abel" in the Abel-Powers case. Vogel had taken the mandate that the Stasi had given him and gone far with it, but only as far as East Germany's Soviet connections had allowed him to go. As soon as those connections had been cut off, he had no power at all. It did not flatter Vogel's view of himself to be portrayed this way, as a sort of Wizard of Oz, a little man behind the curtains pulling levers and blowing smoke. But in a sense, this is what he had been.

Without the Soviets, not only Vogel, but Honecker and the East German Communist party as well were nothing. Over the years, Vogel had seen more than 150 agents go back and forth across the Glienicke Bridge and the border crossing at Herleshausen, spies from fifteen different countries. But it was no accident that most of the countries from which he could "deliver" were those where the Stasi had liaison offices: Bulgaria, Czechoslovakia, Poland, and Hungary, Angola, Cuba, and Mozambique, for example, and the Soviet Union, through the vast KGB liaison office in Karlshorst.[1]

Vogel had never been able to free spies or political prisoners from any country that lay beyond the pale of Soviet influence for the simple reason that Honecker—like Walter Ulbricht before him—had no pull beyond Moscow. Vogel could never bring any influence to bear in China. By the time he appeared on the scene, the Sino-Soviet split had made that impossible, as he learned after Anthony Grey, a Reuters correspondent Vogel had known from his earlier posting to Berlin, was arrested in mid-1967 in Beijing. "I hope I won't be needing your services," Grey had joked with Vogel before leaving for China. As Grey's imprisonment dragged on—it lasted for 806 days, to the end of 1969—Vogel made one attempt to intercede on his behalf, going to the Chinese ambassador in East Berlin to ask whether he could fly to Beijing to try to help. "One way, yes," the ambassador had told him. "Round trip, not so sure." Vogel wisely stayed at home.[2]

Nor did Vogel ever have much influence in Romania, for the simple reason that Nicolae Ceausescu and the Securitate paid little attention to what Moscow or the KGB wanted and saw East Germany as Moscow's surrogate. Ceausescu did not even allow the Stasi to have a liaison office in Bucharest.

Even Moscow had used Vogel's services only when it had not wanted to bargain directly. Often the Kremlin had preferred to keep matters in its own hands. It had shouldered Vogel out of the Abel case at the dénouement in 1962, leaving him to the sideshow with Frederic Pryor, and it had told him to keep his nose out of the Shadrin case, fifteen years later. When the Kremlin decided to exchange the dissident Vladimir Bukowski for Luis Corvalan, the Chilean Communist party chief, in 1976, it had dispensed with Vogel's services entirely.

Some Western governments, Britain's for instance, were consistently reluctant to let Vogel in on their espionage games. When ambiguity had been an asset, as during the long negotiations on the Shcharansky case, it had suited the United States to use Vogel's services. But as soon as the East German Communist regime collapsed, East Berlin's leverage with Moscow was gone, and Vogel's spy-trading days were over.[3]

Up to that moment, the question of Vogel's relationship to the Communist intelligence services had seldom been raised, perhaps because it seemed so obvious: He had been, in the literal and open sense, an agent of the KGB and of the Stasi in every spy swap he had brokered, and for every one of the 33,755 political prisoners he had "sold" to the West Germans.[4] When assertions were occasionally made that Vogel was in the employ of the Stasi, Vogel's vigorous denials seemed convincing. As long as the Stasi files were safely locked away in the Normannenstrasse, nobody could prove him wrong.

Vogel has always insisted that between 1959, when he entered the Abel-Powers case, and 1989, he visited Moscow just twice. He had never had any direct liaison with the Soviet agency, he said; he had always gone through the Stasi's liaison with the KGB.

The KGB dissolved, along with the Soviet Union, at the end of 1991, but before it did, I visited its forbidding headquarters in the Lubyanka and asked one of its spokesmen, Colonel Oleg I. Tsarev, to accept a formal request to see whatever information the files might contain on Wolfgang Vogel. Such a search would cost money, Tsarev warned, and he asked for a cash deposit of one hundred U.S. dollars to cover the cost of file searches and duplication of materials.

Three months later, I saw Tsarev again in the office that Yuri V. Andropov had used when he had run the KGB. Tsarev returned my hundred-dollar bill, and waved a letter, stamped secret and signed by a general, attesting that the KGB files contained "no information" at all on Dr. Vogel. All exchanges of KGB agents in which Vogel had played a role, the letter said, had been carried out through the Berlin liaison office with the East German Ministry for State Security. It was exactly as Vogel had insisted.

To me, a room away from where Vogel himself had been sitting at the end of 1966 when he came to pick up the *Frankfurter Rundschau* journalist Martina Kischke, it hardly seemed possible that the Soviets had "no information." Perhaps the KGB files in Karlshorst and the Communist Party Central Committee International Department's archives in Moscow contained more. But it seems unlikely that they will show that Vogel was a secret Soviet agent.

"He was very highly qualified and precise, as a lawyer and as a man, exact and scrupulous in carrying out his assignments, and was viewed as a reliable, trustworthy partner by everybody who dealt with him," Valentin Falin, the last Central Committee official in charge of Soviet foreign policy, said in his office in Moscow in the summer of 1991. "I would say everybody should be thankful to Vogel for his services, which tempered the pain of many ordinary people, and maybe saved the lives of some. I am sure that as long as special operations continue we will need such middlemen, and if they are as decent, professional, and dedicated as he, then a middleman role will remain justified."[5]

But the key reason why the Soviets had found Vogel so useful in the Shcharansky case, Falin said, was that Vogel was known around the world as the lawyer who arranged spy swaps. The Soviets were insisting that Shcharansky was a spy, and by letting Vogel handle the negotiations for his release, they had succeeded in getting the West to admit implicitly that he had been one.

In other words, Vogel was useful to the Soviets and to the East Germans not because he was a secret Communist agent, but because he was openly one. For this same reason, he was important to the Americans and the West Germans. No Western power would have found Vogel a worthwhile negotiating partner, on Shcharansky or any of the thousands of other political prisoners and spies whom Vogel had freed over the years, if he had not been, in the literal sense, an agent for the Communist intelligence services.

But in the reexamination of past assumptions that followed unification, many Germans were not satisfied by Vogel's claim that this was as far as his relationship with the Stasi had gone. The discovery of his Stasi "Georg" file seemed to prove him a liar.

When Heinz Volpert had sealed the file on March 14, 1957, he had not ended Vogel's formal relationship with the Stasi. If Vogel had continued as a Stasi "informal collaborator"—or, like Schalck, a "secret officer on special assignment," the most closely guarded of all clandestine employee categories—he would not have been the first to resort to outright lies to deny it. In their arrest order against him in March 1992, the German prosecutors charged that Vogel had been emboldened to lie because of assurances that all his Stasi files had been destroyed. But having processed a quarter of a million individual cases through the Stasi apparatus for permission to leave for West Germany, Vogel would have been naïve indeed to think that he could obliterate all traces of his cooperation with the secret police by destroying just his own personnel file. If "Georg" had been betraying the confidences of his clients, he would have been cross-referenced in hundreds, perhaps thousands, of the files on the Stasi's victims whom he represented as counsel, and starting in January 1992, all of them were free to apply to the authorities to see these files.

Vogel's role required him to be in contact with security agencies and government ministries on both sides of the Wall in a way that was clearly incompatible with the Stasi's usual rules for clandestine collaborators. "It was no secret within the ministry or within my unit that Vogel was an official contact," General Niebling said. "It was a quite official business. People from the Interior Ministry, the Justice Ministry and the Foreign Ministry knew that I was working with Vogel on releases of prisoners and agents. If he had had the status of an unofficial collaborator, then I never could have indicated to someone from another ministry that he was my contact."

Finally, Niebling said, "If he had been an unofficial collaborator, I would have destroyed his file."[6]

Niebling would hardly be the first Stasi officer to lie outright to protect the confidentiality of a clandestine relationship, if Vogel in fact did have one. But neither could Stasi files be taken as repositories of unadulterated truth, as the Berlin court understood when it lifted the arrest warrant against Vogel in July 1992.

"The observations in this file were all collected at a time when a legal system that cannot be described as constitutional . . . was in effect in the G.D.R.," the court ruled. "It cannot be determined to what extent MfS [Stasi] workers were bound by law and legal procedure, or how the observations were collected and put into the files. It would be contradictory to regard the Ministry for State Security—rightly—on the one hand as a quasi-criminal administrative structure, and on the other hand to take at face value observations it collected and use them as the basis for an arrest order. . . ."[7]

Poking around in the dark of the Stasi archives for proof that Vogel had collaborated secretly, the prosecutors could not see what Heinz Volpert and Josef Streit must have seen: As an open agent of influence, moving freely across bureaucratic lines on both sides of the Wall, with a special relationship to the Stasi and the state it served, Vogel was worth a hundred times more than any ordinary secret informant.

Unlike some other East German lawyers, Vogel defended few political dissidents. He was the attorney East Germans went to see when they wanted to get out of the country. But no one could leave unless the Stasi approved, and everyone in East Germany knew this. Clients, like foreign intelligence services, sought him out because of his open Stasi connections, and because he had proved time and again that he could use those connections to help them.

The Stasi did not need Vogel to tell it what the clients wanted; it already knew what most of them had had in mind. They wanted to leave "socialism." When the Stasi was through with such people, it could still control how and when they left, through Vogel. But this had been obvious before the Stasi files were ever opened.

For those who mistrusted him, Vogel would always be the devil's advocate. In his own eagerness to justify himself, Vogel pointed out that in everything he did, he had had the blessing of the churches, both Protestant and Catholic. But the Church, too, was compromised, infiltrated, and exploited. The prisoner-release system had run through the Church's finance channels, but both Vogel and the Church had undeniably helped to weave some of the strands of Schalck-Golodkowski's web of corruption. If Vogel did not know that some of the thousands of dissidents and divided families he had helped get to the West had been referred to him by Church leaders who were cooperating with the Stasi, he should have known it.

Under Honecker, the Stasi saw the Church as a buffer, a force that, kept under close control, could guide the opposition into constructive channels. The most cooperative men of the cloth were carried on the books as collaborators with cover names; whether this was done with or without their knowledge was not clear. After the files spilled open, it was revealed that Vogel's friend Manfred Stolpe, the Lutheran Church lawyer who had worked so closely with him on the prisoner releases, had been an unofficial collaborator code-named "Secretary," who had reported on internal church activities to the Stasi for about twenty years. After some of his senior wardens confirmed the charges, the files disclosed that a majority of the wardens, too, had signed unofficial collaborator contracts.[8]

The core moral question—for Stolpe, for the other churchmen, for Vogel, for every East German citizen who had lived under the unique stresses and strains of Communism—was not whether they had gone along with repression. It was a more troubling question: could even collaborators behave morally? It had been asked in Germany before, after the Nazi defeat. Vogel had hundreds, if not thousands, of former clients who would willingly testify that he had not only done his duty, but he had gone far beyond it in their eyes and had earned their lasting respect and gratitude.

"Were you a scoundrel or a hero?" one of the new scandal sheets had asked Vogel. "I was knowingly mixed up with 'class justice,'" he had answered. "I have to answer for that." If he had anything to regret, it was that he had become involved in the human trade business with Bonn at all, despite the trade's good intentions. "It couldn't have been done any other way," he said. "Whether I should reproach myself for this, history will have to judge."[9]

There was a self-righteous undertone in much of the West German press reporting about Vogel's troubles in 1991 and 1992 that seemed incongruous with what the same newspapers and magazines had reported only a few years earlier. Then, Vogel had sat with the high and mighty at tables in Bonn, Munich, and Hamburg, not only in East Berlin. He had carried messages from Helmut Schmidt to Erich Honecker, not just from Honecker to Schmidt, and he had earned huge fees from the Bonn government for prying prisoners free from the Stasi. Now he was a nobody, carrying messages nowhere, his reputation being systematically dismantled by people who seemed either to know little of the past or to be deliberately ignoring it and trying to discredit everything and everybody connected with the East German regime.

There was a certain self-interest in this revisionist view. If Vogel had been a secret Stasi agent all along, if all the prisoner-release arrangements with Bonn had been just a Stasi trick to swindle Bonn out of billions of deutsche marks and deprive helpless East Germans of their property, then West German politicians and officials who had gone along with the scheme could heave a huge sigh of exasperation, say they had been swindled, and consider themselves absolved.

The cold war had had its own peculiar morality, and those who had acted in accordance with it could not now simply wish it away. Vogel had not tricked his Western negotiating partners; they had made agreements with him with open eyes. Nothing in the Stasi files on Schalck-Golodkowski could change the fact that both the church and the government in Bonn had found money an acceptable way of propitiating Communist evil while it lasted. Indeed, at the end, Chancellor Kohl and his government bought Soviet assent to unification as well, with billions of deutsche marks.

Not all of Vogel's former partners in the West turned their backs on him. "The 'special efforts' helped to alleviate manifold sufferings and terrible afflictions in Germany," Ludwig Rehlinger wrote. "They had far-reaching social effects in the G.D.R., and one can certainly add without exaggeration that they prepared the ground for the change in 1989."[10] The former West German permanent representative in East Berlin, Hans Otto Bräutigam, now serving under governor Manfred Stolpe as justice minister of the state of Brandenburg, had come to Vogel's support while he was still in jail. "He never let me down in a single case," he said, "and I had extraordinarily difficult cases to discuss and negotiate with him. Just think of the people who had sought refuge in the Permanent Mission. He had extraordinary difficulties. He had many enemies. I will not now withdraw the trust I had in him then."[11]

The trade in human souls that Vogel, Bishop Kunst, and his successors had conducted with each other for decades had not been transformed from good to evil overnight. It had always been gray, a slithering creature of the cold war shadows, a necessary evil. "War and historical upheavals awaken various forces, good and bad, both sometimes powerfully. Life sends both to us on our journey," the bishop had written to Vogel, before his brief imprisonment.[12]

What life would send to Wolfgang Vogel as he approached the end of his sixties was not clear. "I am not proud of what I did then," he said of his work as a Stasi secret informant in the 1950s. Whatever he had done, it was too late to change.[13]

If Vogel had somehow wrested freedom for a quarter of a million of his countrymen by self-sacrifice—if he had followed some of his clients into jail under Communism and suffered as they had suffered—he would have been hailed as a hero. But he had done it, instead, through the Stasi, and had become rich and prosperous. For that, it seemed, he would have to pay.

Taking responsibility for their past actions has never come easily to Germans, on either side of the Iron Curtain. In the eyes of their neighbors, all Germans will always carry the burden of the Nazi past with them, though few understand why. Germans from what were called the "old Federal states" (West Germany) thought after unification that their exemplary democratic conduct over the previous four decades had earned them the right to be considered free of responsibility. Kohl often reminded Americans that he had been a schoolboy when the Nazis had committed their crimes. But even the German schoolchildren of the twenty-first century will grow up with the historical responsibility of atoning for what the generation of their grandparents and great-grandparents did. Germans from the "new Federal states" (East Germany) had grown up listening to their Communist masters assure them and the rest of the world that fascism and all its root causes had been pulled up and discarded forever in their part of Germany. But as riots against foreigners by skinheads and neo-Nazi radicals and other outbreaks of xenophobia in the crumbling inner cities of Rostock, Leipzig, Halle, and Chemnitz proved after Communism fell, the past had only been buried, not overcome. East Germans faced a double burden of simultaneously overcoming two horrendous legacies—Nazism and Communism—and they felt increased resentment and frustration for being treated so differently from their West German cousins.

"I regard the campaign being led against people like de Maizière, Stolpe, Vogel and others with great skepticism and concern," Helmut Schmidt wrote in the spring of 1992. "Since I myself grew up under a dictatorship, fourteen years old when Hitler seized power in 1933, I know better than most young people who have lived their whole lives in freedom that even under a total dictatorship, it was possible to carry out tasks that serve the causes of human compassion and peace (if chance and professional position provided the opportunity), and certainly to preserve one's personal integrity as well, assuming the necessary caution and tact. Vogel and Stolpe tried to achieve the best they could for people for whom they felt responsible, in overall conditions that were evil. In doing so they may have made mistakes or done things that could be seen later as inappropriate; but it is no different for anyone who holds political office."[14]

Unification did not solve the German problem; it only cast it in a new light. There is still a Wall dividing Germans, the one inside their heads. Almost certainly, it will outlive Wolfgang Vogel.

APPENDIX

PAYMENTS BY THE WEST GERMAN GOVERNMENT THROUGH LUTHERAN CHURCH CHANNELS

Year	Political Prisoner Releases	Family Reunifications	Payments
1964	884	—	DM37,918,901.16
1965	1,555	762	67,667,898.52
1966	407	393	24,805,316.38
1967	554	438	31,482,433.19
1968	693	405	28,435,444.15
1969	880	408	44,873,875.05
1970	888	595	50,589,774.55
1971	1,375	911	84,223,481.52
1972	731	1,219	69,457,704.26
	2,087 in amnesty		
1973	631	1,124	54,028,288.39
1974	1,053	2,450	88,147,719.74
1975	1,158	5,635	104,012,504.93
1976	1,439	4,734	130,003,535.00
1977	1,475	2,886	143,997,942.27
1978	1,452	3,979	168,363,141.86

PAYMENTS BY THE WEST GERMAN GOVERNMENT THROUGH
LUTHERAN CHURCH CHANNELS *(Continued)*

Year	Political Prisoner Releases	Family Reunifications	Payments
1979	890	4,205	106,986,866.24
1980	1,036	3,931	130,015,131.77
1981	1,584	7,571	178,987,210.84
1982	1,491	6,304	176,999,590.94
1983	1,105	5,487	102,811,953.50
1984	2,236	29,626	387,997,305.12
1985	2,669	17,315	301,995,568.10
1986	1,450	15,767	195,009,307.73
1987	1,209	8,225	162,997,921.59
1988	1,048	21,202	232,096,191.43
1989	1,775	69,447	267,895,657.76
1990	—	—	65,000,089.13
Totals:	33,755	215,019	DM3,436,900,755.12

SOURCES: Vogel, office archives; Ludwig Geissler, *Unterhändler der Menschlichkeit* (Stuttgart: Quell Verlag, 1991), p. 475.

BIBLIOGRAPHY

Andert, Reinhold, and Wolfgang Herzberg. *Der Sturz: Erich Honecker im Kreuzverhör*. Berlin/Weimar: Aufbau Verlag, 1991. The only post-collapse extended interview with the Honeckers, in their own words, in Q & A form.

Andrew, Christopher, and Oleg Gordievsky. *KGB: The Inside Story*. New York: HarperCollins Publishers, 1990.

Battle, Hellen. *Every Wall Shall Fall*. Old Tappan, N.J.: Spire Books/ Fleming H. Revell Company, 1972. A personal account of her arrest, imprisonment, and liberation by one of Vogel's early American clients.

Bernikow, Louise. *Abel*. New York: Trident Press, Simon & Schuster, 1970.

Beschloss, Michael R. *The Crisis Years: Kennedy and Khrushchev, 1960–1963*. New York: Edward R. Burlingame/HarperCollins, 1991.

———. *Mayday: Eisenhower, Khrushchev and the U-2 Affair*. New York, Harper and Row, 1986. The most thorough and readable historical accounts of both incidents available.

Binder, David. *The Other German: Willy Brandt's Life & Times.* Washington, D.C.: The New Republic Book Company, Inc., 1975.

Bölling, Klaus. *Die fernen Nachbarn: Erfahrungen in der DDR.* Hamburg, Stern/Gruner + Jahr AG & Co., 1983. Like that of Günter Gaus, see infra, a thoughtful memoir from inside East Germany before the Wall went down by a former journalist who served as Bonn's envoy to East Berlin.

Brandt, Willy. *Erinnerungen.* Frankfurt, Propyläen Verlag, 1989.

Donovan, James B. *Strangers on a Bridge: The Case of Colonel Abel.* New York: Atheneum House, Inc., 1964. The definitive insider's account of the American side of the negotiations that led to the Abel-Powers exchange.

Felfe, Heinz. *Im Dienst des Gegners.* Berlin: Verlag der Nation, 1988. A partisan memoir by the former East German Communist spy.

Filmer, Werner, and Heribert Schwan. *Wolfgang Schäuble: Politik als Lebensaufgabe.* Munich: C. Bertelsmann Verlag GmbH, 1992.

Gaus, Günter. *Wo Deutschland liegt: eine Ortsbestimmung.* Hamburg, Hoffmann und Campe, 1983. An interpretation of East German society and politics by the first West German "ambassador" to East Berlin.

Geissel, Ludwig. *Unterhändler der Menschlichkeit, Erinnerungen.* Stuttgart: Quell Verlag, 1991. Secret dealings with the Communists, recalled by the West German Lutheran Church's principal negotiator over many years.

Gill, David, and Ulrich Schröter. *Das Ministerium für Staatssicherheit: Anatomie des Mielke-Imperiums.* Berlin: Rowohlt-Berlin Verlag, 1991. An introductory explanation of how the Stasi worked, by two East Germans who helped make sure its archives were preserved and opened to the public.

Gwertzman, Bernard, and Michael T. Kaufman, eds. *The Collapse of Communism.* New York: Times Books, 1990.

Hurt, Henry. *Shadrin: The Spy Who Never Came Back.* New York: McGraw-Hill Book Company/Reader's Digest Press, 1981.

Kessler, Ronald. *Escape from the CIA.* New York: Pocket Books, 1991. An account focused mainly on the Vitaly S. Yurchenko defection/redefection.

Koch, Peter-Ferdinand. *Das Schalck-Imperium: Deutschland wird gekauft.* Munich: R. Piper GmbH, 1992. A polemical pamphlet denouncing both Alexander Schalck-Golodkowski and Wolfgang Vogel as creations of the Stasi.

Krenz, Egon. *Wenn Mauern Fallen.* Vienna: Paul Neff Verlag, 1990. Honecker's short-lived successor's self-justifying account of how he tried and failed to save Communism in East Germany.

Mangold, Tom. *Cold Warrior.* New York: Simon & Schuster, 1991. A provocative exposition of James Jesus Angleton's obsession with penetration of the CIA by Communist agents.

McElvoy, Anne. *The Saddled Cow: East Germany's Life and Legacy.* London: Faber and Faber, Ltd., 1992. An excellent and readable retrospective by a British journalist who studied and lived in East Germany.

Mende, Erich, *Von Wende zu Wende, Zeuge der Zeit 1962–1982.* Bergisch Gladbach, Bastei-Lübbe Taschenbücher, 1988.

Meyer, Michel. *Des hommes contres des marks.* Paris: Editions Stock, 1977. An early, imaginative, and partly imaginary French treatment of Vogel and "Freikauf."

Powers, Francis Gary, with Curt Gentry. *Operation Overflight.* New York: Holt, Rinehart and Winston, 1970.

Przybylski, Peter. *Tatort Politbüro, Die Akte Honecker.* Berlin: Rowohlt-Berlin Verlag, 1991. Documents from Stasi files on Honecker, some of them collected by Erich Mielke over the years, written in an intelligent narrative by a former spokesman for the old East German prosecutor-general's office.

———. *Tatort Politbüro Band 2: Honecker, Mittag und Schalck-Golodkowski.* Berlin. Rowohlt-Berlin Verlag, 1992. A continuation by the same author with important archival information on Schalck, the evil genius who ran the Stasi's hard-currency operations over the years.

Reese, Mary Ellen. *General Reinhard Gehlen: The CIA Connection.* Fairfax, Va: George Mason University Press, 1990. See Rositzke.

Rehlinger, Ludwig A. *Freikauf: Die Geschäfte der DDR mit politisch Verfolgten, 1963–1989.* Berlin/Frankfurt, Verlag Ullstein, 1991. The most complete West German account of negotiations over three decades with Vogel on political prisoners as well as spies.

Rositzke, Harry. *The K.G.B.: The Eyes of Russia.* Garden City: Doubleday & Company, Inc., 1981. Polemical but well-informed cold war account of the opposition's spy service, as the CIA saw it.

Runge, Irene, and Uwe Stelbrink. *Markus Wolf: "Ich bin kein Spion."* Berlin: Dietz Verlag, 1990. An extended informal interview in which the East German spymaster rambles about his life and times, with two East German socialists as interlocutors.

Schell, Manfred, and Werner Kalinka. *Stasi und kein Ende, Die Personen und Fakten.* Bonn: Die Welt; Frankfurt/Berlin, Verlag Ullstein, 1991. Documentation seized from the Stasi after the Wall fell in 1989.

Schmidt, Helmut. *Menschen und Mächte.* Berlin: Siedler Verlag, 1987. Published in the United States as *Men and Powers, a Political Perspective.* New York: Random House, 1989.

———. *Die Deutschen und ihre Nachbarn: Menschen und Mächte II.* Berlin: Siedler, 1990.

Schmidthammer, Jens. *Rechtsanwalt Wolfgang Vogel, Mittler zwischen Ost und West.* Hamburg: Hoffmann und Campe, 1987. A skillful but mostly uncritical German-language biography of Vogel, written before the fall of Communism and thus without the benefit of later documentation.

Seiffert, Wolfgang, and Norbert Treutwein. *Die Schalck Papiere: DDR-Mafia zwischen Ost und West, Die Beweise.* Vienna: Zsolnay Verlag, 1991. Another polemic exposition of Schalck-Golodkowski's doings.

Sharansky, Natan. *Fear No Evil.* New York: Random House, 1988.

Talbott, Strobe. *Khrushchev Remembers: The Last Testament.* Boston: Little, Brown & Co., 1974.

Van Altena, John, Jr. *A Guest of the State.* Chicago: Henry Regnery Company, 1967. Another personal account by one of Vogel's earliest jailed American clients.

Von Lang, Jochen. *Erich Mielke: Eine deutsche Karriere.* Berlin: Rowohlt-Berlin Verlag, 1991.

Wolf, Markus, *In eigenem Auftrag, Bekenntnisse und Einsichten.* Munich: Franz Schneekluth Verlag, 1991. Wolf's own description of his failed attempts to save "socialism" in East Germany by encouraging reforms in the late 1980s.

Wright, Peter. *Spycatcher: The Candid Autobiography of a Senior Intelligence Officer.* New York: Viking Penguin Inc., 1987.

Wyden, Peter. *Wall: The Inside Story of Divided Berlin.* New York: Simon and Schuster, 1989. A thorough history of the Wall with much information about Vogel's activities up to the point of publication, just before the Wall finally came down.

———. *Children of the Cold War.* London: The Independent Magazine, Oct. 6, 1990, following up on the case of the Grübel children, one of the focal points of Wyden's earlier book.

NEWSPAPERS AND PERIODICALS

The weekly German newsmagazine *Der Spiegel,* the weekly newspaper *Die Zeit,* the weekly *Stern Magazin,* and dailies such as the *Frankfurter All-*

gemeine Zeitung, Berliner Morgenpost, Berliner Tagesspiegel, Frankfurter Rundschau, The New York Times, The Washington Post, and *Newsday* have all published numerous articles on Wolfgang Vogel during the course of his career. Detailed references are given in the chapter notes. Readers seeking special insight into Vogel's views and attitudes at various periods in his career might start with the following:

Freeman, Simon. "Profile: A human bridge who spans the world of spies." *The Sunday Times,* London, Feb. 16, 1986.

Laudor, Richard. "Gilman's Rabbi." *Gannett Westchester Rockland Newspapers, Suburbia Today,* June 26, 1983.

Levitt, Leonard. "Swap." *Newsday,* Part II, June 1, 1978. "The Man in the Middle." *Newsday,* Part II, Feb. 12, 1986.

Pragal, Peter. "Ein ehrlicher Makler." *Stern Magazin,* March 5, 1987.

Der Spiegel, "Ich hätte mit dem Teufel paktiert." Interview with Vogel by Ulrich Schwarz and Georg Bönisch, Vol. 15, 1990.

Super Illu, "Der Fall Vogel." Interview with Vogel, Jan. 30, 1992.

Whitney, Craig R. "The Fixer." *The New York Times Magazine,* March 20, 1977.

Witter, Ben. "Ich gehe stille Wege." *Die Zeit,* June 20, 1986.

INTERVIEWS BY AUTHOR

Backlund, Sven, Bonn

Barkley, Richard C., Berlin

Bölling, Klaus, Berlin

Copaken, Richard D., Washington, D.C.

Falin, Valentin M., Moscow

Felfe, Heinz, Berlin

Frucht, Adolf-Henning, Berlin

Gordievsky, Oleg, London

Greenwald, Ronnie, New York City

Heidemann, Arnold, Berlin

Heinz, Volker G., London

Hirt, Edgar, Zurich

Kalugin, Oleg D., Moscow

Kunst, Dr. Hermann, Bonn

Loewe, Lothar, Berlin

Lush, Christopher, London

Koblitz, Donald, Washington, D.C.

Mapother, John, Washington, D.C.

Meehan, Francis J., Helensburgh, Scotland

New, Ricey S., Jr., Washington, D.C.

New, Justin, Washington, D.C.

Niebling, Gerhard, Berlin

Priesnitz, Walter, Bonn

Pryor, Frederic L., by telephone from Swarthmore, Pa.

Rehlinger, Ludwig A., Bonn

Silverglate, Harvey A., Boston, Mass.

Smith, Jeffrey H., Washington, D.C.

Svingel, Carl-Gustaf, Berlin

Thiel, Heinz Dietrich, Berlin

Tsarev, Oleg I., Moscow

Vogel, Wolfgang, Berlin and Teupitz

Vogel, Helga, Berlin and Teupitz

von Wedel, Reymar, Berlin

Wolf, Markus, Berlin and Klosterfelde

DOCUMENTATION

Many of the documents excerpted or quoted from in the book come from Vogel's vast office files, some of which were seized by prosecutors in Berlin in January 1992. The author has had only the most fragmentary access to them.

Bundesbeauftragte für die Unterlagen des Staatssicherheitsdienstes der ehemaligen Deutschen Demokratischen Republik, file 2088/57 Zentralarchiv, Vogel's Stasi file from 1952 to 1957. The author has seen most of the content of this file but not all of it. The author has also seen the file called "Rubin" maintained by the same ministry and now held by this, the so-called "Gauck office," whose title translates as Federal Office for the Materials of the State Security Service of the former German Democratic Republic.

Bundesministerium für gesamtdeutsche Fragen, "Unrecht als System, Dokumente über planmässige Rechtsverletzungen im SBZ." Bonn, 1955.

Bundesministerium für innerdeutsche Beziehungen, "Der Aufstand vom 17. Juni 1953." Bonn, 1988. Publications by the West German ministry responsible for relations with the eastern part of the country on conditions there in the early 1950s.

Deutscher Bundestag, "Erste Beschlussempfehlung und erster Teilbericht des 1. Untersuchungsausschusses nach Artikel 44 des Grundgesetzes," Bonn, Oct. 14, 1992, Drucksache no. 12/3462. A preliminary report by the Bundestag committee investigating Schalck-Golodkowski's activities, in the form of 242 documents from former East German files.

Fricke, Karl Wilhelm, "Politik und Justiz in der DDR: Zur Geschichte der politischen Verfolgung 1945–68, Bericht und Dokumentation." Cologne: Verlag Wissenschaft und Politik, Berend von Nottbeck, 1979.

Internationale Gesellschaft für Menschenrechte, "Dokumentation: Internationale Anhörung über die Menschenrechtssituation in der DDR, 6–7 Dezember 1984." Frankfurt, 1985, transcripts of a hearing on human rights held in 1984.

Senator für Justiz, Berlin, "Personalakten über den Rechtsanwalt Dr. h. c. Vogel, Wolfgang," Vogel's East German Justice Ministry files, now held by the Berlin city authorities.

NOTES

INTRODUCTION

1. As first pointed out by Peter Schneider, *The German Comedy; Scenes of Life After the Wall.* (New York: Farrar, Straus and Giroux, Inc., 1991).

2. Wolfgang Vogel, interview with author, Teupitz, Germany, June 22, 1991; and Helmut Schmidt, letter to author, May 11, 1992.

3. Helmut Schmidt, *Die Deutschen und ihre Nachbarn: Menschen und Mächte II.* (Berlin: Siedler Verlag, 1990), p. 32.

4. Peter Wyden, *Wall, The Inside Story of Divided Berlin.* (New York: Simon and Schuster, 1989); and Michael R. Beschloss, *Mayday: Eisenhower, Khrushchev and the U-2 Affair.* (New York: Harper & Row, 1986).

5. Willy Brandt, *Erinnerungen.* (Frankfurt: Propyläen, 1989), p. 233.

6. Armin Volze, "Kirchliche Transferleistungen in die DDR," *Deutschland Archiv,* 1/91, p. 64. Also Vogel and Peter-Michael Diestel, former interior minister of the German Democratic Republic, interviews with author, Teupitz, June 22, 1991.

7. For the sake of clarity for American readers, though at the cost of complete accuracy, I have used the terms "Lutheran" and "Protestant" interchangeably in referring to what Germans call the "Evangelical" Church, in both parts of the country.

8. Vogel's copy is in his office; the text is also given in Jens Schmidthammer, *Rechtsanwalt Wolfgang Vogel, Mittler zwischen Ost und West* (Hamburg: Hoffmann und Campe, 1987), p. 133.

9. Vogel, interview with author, Berlin, May 7, 1992.

CHAPTER 1

1. Wolfgang Vogel, interview with author, Teupitz, June 22, 1991. This story was also confirmed by Heinz-Joachim Lomosik, a childhood friend of Vogel's from Glatz, in a telephone conversation with the author on June 14, 1992.
2. Vogel, interview, Teupitz, June 22, 1991.
3. Ibid.; and Wolfgang Vogel, "Mein Lebenslauf," a handwritten curriculum vitae prepared in April 1949 and kept in his personal file in the East German Justice Ministry.
4. Vogel, interview with author, Teupitz, June 22, 1991, and Heinz-Joachim Lomosik and Josef Schiller, classmates of Vogel, telephone conversations with author on June 14, 1992.
5. Vogel, c.v., op. cit.
6. The discovery of the mixup was made in 1985. Both then and later, there was much speculation in the German press about whether the Stasi had given Vogel the identity of a dead soldier, the better to construct a cover legend for his activities, just the way the KGB often did for its secret agents. See Peter-Ferdinand Koch, *Das Schalck-Imperium* (R. Piper GmbH & Co. Kg, Munich, 1992). This thesis disregards testimony by such German officials as Ludwig Rehlinger, who helped Vogel establish that there had been a mixup in 1985. Vogel had kept what he thought was "his" dogtag and with it the West German authorities were able to explain the mystery. Lomosik and other childhood schoolmates of Vogel's from Glatz have also independently assured the author that Vogel is the same man they knew as a schoolboy.
7. Vogel's "Lebenslauf," op. cit.
8. Carl Gustaf Svingel, interview with author, Berlin, June 27, 1991; and Vogel, interviews with author, Teupitz, June 22, 1991, and Dec. 12, 1991.
9. Supervisor's report, Waldheim district court, Dec. 29, 1949, in Vogel's East German Justice Ministry file, now in the Berlin city government justice archives.
10. Documents from Vogel's office files.
11. From a publication on the uprising of June 17, 1953, by the West German ministry for intra-German relations: *Der Aufstand vom 17. Juni 1953,* (Bundesministerium für innerdeutsche Beziehungen, Bonn 1988), pp. 29–39.
12. From documentation on violations of law in the Soviet occupation zone published by the West German ministry for all-German questions: *Unrecht als System, Dokumente über planmässige Rechtsverletzungen im SBZ,* (Bundesministerium für gesamtdeutsche Fragen, Bonn 1955), pp. 257–59.
13. Reymar von Wedel, notes, from the file on Reinartz kept by the West German legal defense office, West Berlin.
14. *Unrecht als System,* op. cit., p. 78.
15. Vogel, interviews with author, Teupitz, June 22, 1991; May 7 and Aug. 11, 1992.
16. Vogel, interviews with author, Teupitz, June 22, 1991, and Aug. 11, 1992; and testimony before the CoCo investigating committee of the German Parliament, Bonn, Oct. 8, 1992.
17. Vogel, interviews with author, Teupitz. Aug. 11, 1992, and Berlin, Oct. 14, 1992. According to Wyden, op. cit., footnote p. 94, police records in West Berlin documented 229 successful and 348 attempted Communist kidnappings between 1945 and August 1961.

18. "Recruitment Report," Vogel's Stasi file, No. 2088/57, Nov. 11, 1953. Berlin, Federal Agency for the materials of the State Security Service of the former German Democratic Republic.
19. "Personnel form," Sept. 19, 1952; "Proposal for Recruitment," Aug. 31, 1953; and other documents in Vogel's Stasi file, op. cit.
20. The handwritten "Final Report" in Vogel's Stasi file, on March 3, 1957, says that he was "recruited as a secret informant on Oct. 19, 1953, for the security of the objective, in the 'Justice' line."
21. "Recruitment Report," op. cit.
22. "Certificate," Jan. 29, 1954, from the Cadre Department of the East German Justice Ministry, in Vogel's East German Justice Ministry file, op. cit. Also, sworn affidavit by Vogel's lawyer, Dr. Friederike Schulenburg, given to the Berlin District Court on May 21, 1992.
23. Vogel, interview with author, Teupitz, June 22, 1991.
24. Schulenburg affidavit, op. cit.
25. Vogel, interview with author, Teupitz, June 22, 1991.
26. Original document from Vogel's personal archives.
27. Vogel, interview with author, Berlin, Oct. 14, 1992.
28. Vogel's Stasi file. On a few occasions, Vogel was given gasoline coupons, lubricating oil, flowers, and small amounts of cash.
29. "Evaluation," Jan. 1, 1955, Berlin, signed by Johde, in Vogel's Stasi file.
30. On June 1, 1954, for instance, Johde reported that "Eva" had called the secret Stasi telephone contact number he had been given and asked for a talk. Vogel told the Stasi officer in his law office that one of his former clients, a man who had been accused of violating economic regulations, had offered to provide film that would be of interest to East German intelligence, identifying Western agents operating out of West Berlin. Vogel's client had visited him the day before and told him he wanted to work for the Stasi. Vogel was told, the file says, not to accept the man's invitation to come to West Berlin for dinner.
31. "Meeting report," Feb. 15, 1955, in Vogel's Stasi file—two weeks after Reinartz's arrest.
32. Carl Gustaf Svingel, affidavit to the Berlin District Court, Apr. 15, 1992.
33. Reinartz's Stasi file, MfS AU 386/55.
34. German prosecutors investigating Vogel's activities in early 1992 were apparently working on the suspicion that Vogel had helped the Stasi find Reinartz and kidnap him, a charge Vogel heatedly denied.
35. Reinartz Stasi file, o.p. cit., and Vogel, Svingel, and von Wedel, interviews with author, Teupitz and Berlin, June and Dec. 1991. Later, Reinartz's sentence was commuted to 15 years.
36. Report signed "Georg," March 17, 1955, in Vogel's Stasi file.
37. On Apr. 7, 1955, for instance, "Georg" made such an assertion about an East German colleague named Gerhard Weyer. Vogel's Stasi file.
38. Report by "Georg" on June 11, 1955, in Vogel's Stasi file.
39. "Eva" report to the Stasi, Mar. 9, 1955, in Vogel's Stasi file.
40. "Eva" report dated Apr. 16, 1955, in Vogel's Stasi file.
41. "Memo for the Record," in Vogel's handwriting, signed "Eva," in his Stasi file.
42. Ibid.
43. "Eva" report, June 12, 1955, in Vogel's Stasi file. At a public hearing of a Bundestag investigating committee in Bonn on Oct. 8, 1992, Vogel also said that a West German government lawyer named Behling had tried to recruit him as a BND agent.
44. Vogel, letter to the Executive Board of the West Berlin bar, from his

personal archive. A report in Vogel's Stasi file, Oct. 17, 1955, notes that the application was submitted "at our instructions."
45. Report, "concerning Commichau," Jan. 15, 1956, in Vogel's Stasi file.
46. Letter from the Berlin Supreme Court chief judge to Vogel, Nov. 13, 1957, in Vogel's Justice files.
47. Schulenburg deposition, May 21, 1992.
48. Vogel interview, Berlin, May 7, 1992.
49. Vogel and Jürgen Stange, interviews with author, Berlin, June 12, 1992.
50. Document in Vogel's Stasi files.
51. Vogel insists that he never signed any Stasi contract as a secret informant or as a secret collaborator and that after 1957 he had no formal relationship with the Stasi. Some of what follows in this book supports this view; some does not. The relationship often seemed ambiguous. In late 1959, for instance, Vogel was one of two lawyers defending a Dr. Gottfried Matthes, who was accused of having assisted in killing twenty-six mental patients in a hospital in Upper Silesia in 1945 rather than letting them fall into the hands of the invading Red Army. The trial took place in West Berlin. It is not clear from the files kept on Vogel by the East German Justice Ministry after he became a lawyer how or why he had taken on the case, but the trial became a newspaper sensation, something the East Germans had apparently not expected. An entry in Vogel's Justice Ministry file dated Dec. 1 recounts that Hilde Benjamin took violent exception to his participation. "The minister, comrade Benjamin, consulted Col. Richter of the MfS [Stasi]," the file notes. "A determination is to be made of whether the MfS has an interest in lawyer Vogel's continuing the defense. . . . If there is no such interest on the part of the MfS, lawyer Vogel should drop it." The file further records that if it was decided that he should drop the case, Vogel was to explain himself publicly by saying that he could no longer square defending Matthes with his conscience, and that he should "be forced to identify himself openly with our policies." Vogel did withdraw from the case, on Dec. 6. But he gave no political grounds for doing so. Instead he let his old stomach problem flare up, and checked into an East Berlin hospital. See "Unbekannter bedroht das Gericht," *Berliner Zeitung,* Dec. 8, 1959.

CHAPTER 2

1. James B. Donovan, *Strangers on a Bridge: The Case of Colonel Abel* (New York: Atheneum House, Inc., 1964) p. 253. Donovan gives a reasonably full though one-sided account of the case from the time of his own involvement. For more details of Abel's and Hayhanen's lives and activities, see Louise Bernikow, *Abel* (New York: Trident Press, Simon & Schuster, 1970). For contemporary and later background on Abel, refer to Harry Rositzke, *The K.G.B., The Eyes of Russia* (Garden City: Doubleday & Company, Inc., 1981), pp. 54–58 and elsewhere.
2. Oleg D. Kalugin and other Soviet intelligence officials, interviews with author, Moscow, June and September 1991. These confirm the modus operandi and many of the details given by Vogel; Markus Wolf, the head of the Stasi's foreign intelligence service for many years, believes that Shishkin was sent in specifically for this purpose.
3. Vogel, interview with author, Teupitz, June 22, 1991.
4. Vogel, interviews with author, Teupitz, June 1991–June 1992.
5. Vogel, interview, Teupitz, June 22, 1991. Stasi documents displayed in the Leipzig headquarters of the secret police after the collapse of Communism in

1989 showed a Stasi conspiratorial address on Eisenacherstrasse in the same neighborhood.

6. Ibid.

7. Letters in Donovan, op. cit., p. 314, and infra.

8. Donovan, op. cit., p. 323, some of the correspondence about the money, and the details about receipt of the installments, are given in the preceding 25 pages. That the Stasi was the source of the money was conceded by Vogel's attorney Dr. Friederike Schulenburg in court papers filed to Amtsgericht Tiergarten in Berlin on March 25, 1992, and Volpert's role was confirmed by Vogel in a later interview with the author.

9. The details of Powers's flight and captivity are recounted in Francis Gary Powers with Curt Gentry, *Operation Overflight* (New York: Holt, Rinehart, and Winston, 1970). His interrogations and encounter with Rudenko are on pp. 100–102. The diplomacy of the U-2 incident is definitively recounted in Michael R. Beschloss, *Mayday; Eisenhower, Khrushchev and the U-2 Affair* (New York: Harper & Row, 1986; see, in particular, pp. 265–66).

10. Vogel, interview with author, Teupitz, February 1992.

11. Strobe Talbott, ed. and trans., *Khrushchev Remembers: The Last Testament* (Boston: Little, Brown & Co., 1974), p. 490.

12. Vogel, interview with author, Berlin, June 1992. Shishkin later served as head of counterintelligence in London from 1966 to 1970, and as head of counterintelligence at the KGB's higher school in Moscow until the early 1980s, according to the author's conversations with two former KGB officers, the defector Oleg Gordievsky (in London in 1990) and Oleg D. Kalugin, a former chief of foreign counterintelligence (in Moscow in June, 1991). Also see Christopher Andrew and Oleg Gordievsky, *KGB: The Inside Story* (New York: HarperCollins Publishers, 1990), pp. 7, 523, and 614.

13. Vogel's reconstruction from memory of financial records after his arrest in March 1992 listed the $10,000 transferred to Donovan in payment of his fee, and another $3,000, which was apparently the fine. It is unclear whether an additional $5,000 Donovan asked for was ever transferred to New York.

14. Donovan, op. cit., p. 363.

15. Ibid., p. 365.

16. Ibid., p. 367.

17. Vogel, interview with author, Teupitz, June 22, 1991; Millard H. Pryor, telephone conversation with author, Aug. 15, 1991; Frederic L. Pryor, letters to author, Aug. 26, 1991, and March 15, 1992; Pryor letter to Vogel, received May 9, 1962, from Vogel's personal archive.

18. Vogel, interview with author, Teupitz, June 22, 1991.

19. Donovan, op. cit., p. 374.

20. Ibid., p. 381.

21. Ibid., p. 393.

22. Ibid., p. 395.

23. Ibid.

24. Vogel, interview with author, Teupitz, June 22, 1991.

25. Donovan, op. cit., pp. 401–403.

26. Ibid., p. 403.

27. Donovan, op. cit., p. 408.

28. Donovan, op. cit., pp. 411–17.

29. Lt. Gen. Gerhard Niebling, interview with author, Berlin, May 7, 1992.

30. Frederic L. Pryor, letter, Aug. 26, 1991.

31. Pryor, letter to author, Aug. 26, 1991; and telephone conversation with the author, May 17, 1992.

32. Donovan, op. cit., p. 418.
33. Oleg Gordievsky, interview with author, London, Oct. 13, 1990.
34. Donovan, op. cit., p. 419.
35. Meehan, interview with author, Helensburgh, Scotland, Sept. 13, 1990.
36. Donovan, op. cit., p. 419.
37. Powers was cleared of treason or dereliction of duty and granted back pay, but the CIA didn't want him back. Eventually, as a helicopter pilot for KNBC-TV in Los Angeles, he fell out of the sky again, on Aug. 1, 1977, this time to his death. The police found that he had let his Bell Jet Ranger run out of fuel after flying a television crew to cover a brush fire in the mountains.

Abel was welcomed back to Moscow and awarded the Order of Lenin and many other medals. Two weeks after his release, *Izvestia* published a letter from Yelena ("Hellen") and Lydia Abel expressing gratitude for the "humane magnanimity" shown by Khrushchev and the Soviet government in obtaining his release from imprisonment, which they blamed on "denunciation by an adventurer and provocateur." Abel, too, had trouble reintegrating with his spy service, which found him fit only for lecturing young illegals in the KGB's "Higher School." After he died in November 1971, he was buried under the name with which he had been born in 1903 in Britain, William H. Fisher, the son of Russian émigrés who had gone back to help build Communism in 1921.

Makinen was freed, finally, on Oct. 11, 1963, a year after the Cuban Missile Crisis.

Donovan, a Democrat who later became president of the Board of Education and of the Pratt Institute in New York City, tried and failed to unseat Sen. Jacob K. Javits in 1962, and undertook more hostage diplomacy for President Kennedy in Havana after the missile crisis. He died of a heart attack at the age of 53 in 1970.

Pryor's interrogator had warned him, before his release, not to try to publish his dissertation, but Pryor proudly let M.I.T. Press publish it in 1963. Later he taught at the University of Michigan and Yale University before settling down and becoming a professor of economics at Swarthmore College. He did not return to East Germany until April 1990, when Vogel told him he would have spent ten years in prison if his case had ever come to trial. His most recent book is *The Red and the Green: The Rise and Fall of Collectivized Agriculture in Marxist Regimes* (Princeton: Princeton University Press, 1992).
38. Lothar Loewe, conversation with author, Berlin, June 24, 1991, and Pierre Salinger, conversation with author, London, May 1992.
39. Pryor, undated letter to Vogel received in East Berlin May 9, 1962, from Vogel's office archive.
40. Vogel flew to London in the summer of 1963 to try to obtain the release of two Soviet spies—Peter and Helen Kroger, whose photographs had been among the belongings of Col. Abel that the FBI had seized. The Krogers had been identified in America by their real names, Morris and Leontina Cohen, and implicated in the case of Julius and Ethel Rosenberg, executed in 1953 after being convicted of passing American nuclear secrets to the Soviets. The British had convicted the Krogers of being agents of Gordon A. Lonsdale's so-called Portland spy ring, which had penetrated the British Admiralty's Underwater Weapons Research Center in Portland, England, and sentenced them both to twenty-year terms. The Soviets were also interested in having Vogel negotiate a swap of Lonsdale (whose real name was Konon Trofimovich Molody) for Greville Wynne, the British agent who had been the contact man for the legendary Colonel Oleg Penkovsky in Moscow.

Despite Vogel's lack of English, the Soviets carefully orchestrated his trip to generate maximum publicity in the spy-hungry British press. He visited Amnesty International's London headquarters to complain that while Wynne had received an eight-year sentence in Moscow, Lonsdale was doing twenty-five years in Britain. Vogel also engaged Derek H. Sinclair, a member of a distinguished London law firm who had tried to represent Wynne at his trial in Moscow, to negotiate with British authorities for the release of the Krogers.

Vogel got absolutely nowhere with the British, he told me in February 1992. Her Majesty's Government was interested in the idea of swapping Lonsdale for Wynne, but it would not deal with Vogel. The British conducted their own negotiations with the Soviet Union in London and Moscow, according to Vogel, and Wynne and Lonsdale were in fact exchanged in Berlin on April 22, 1964.

But Vogel returned to London in July and again in September 1965 to deal with Sinclair again on the Krogers. Here again, the Soviets invented a fictitious relative to bring him into the case, but this time at second remove: "Maria Petka," from Lublin, who had announced that the Krogers were her cousins and asked a Polish lawyer named Jerzy Pogonowski to write to Vogel.

Vogel claims to have paid Sinclair fees totaling DM30,000; after Sinclair's death, his former partners claimed they had no knowledge whatever of any of his dealings with Vogel. Vogel also floated the idea of swapping the Krogers for Gerald Brooke, a British lecturer who had been caught smuggling in anti-Soviet materials for an émigré group in Russia and been arrested on April 25.

On Sept. 9, this time representing a twenty-seven-year-old British man arrested in Berlin two weeks earlier for helping East Germans escape through the Wall, Vogel returned to London, but once again failed to make any headway at getting the British government to deal with him on the Krogers.

In January of 1966, the United States handed him a new bargaining tool: a list of eleven U.S. Navy and Air Force pilots shot down in Indochina, handed by Frank Meehan to Jürgen Stange with a request to ask Vogel if the Soviets were willing to pressure their North Vietnamese allies into releasing them as part of an agent swap.

The men on the list were: Lt. (j.g.) Everett Alvarez, Jr., shot down on Aug. 5, 1964; Lt. Phillip N. Butler, April 20, 1965; Cdr. Jeremiah A. Denton, Jr., July 18, 1965; Lt. Cdr. Robert H. Shumaker, Feb. 11, 1965; Lt. (j.g.) William M. Tschudy, July 18, 1965, all of the Navy; Capt. Robert N. Daughtrey, Aug. 2, 1965; Maj. Lawrence N. Guarino, June 14, 1965; Capt. Carlyle S. Harris, Apr. 4, 1965; Capt. Richard P. Keirn, July 24, 1965; 1st Lt. Hayden J. Lockhart, Jr., Mar. 2, 1965; and 1st Lt. Robert D. Peel, May 31, 1965, all of the Air Force. (Vogel, office archives)

Vogel's recollection years later was that the American authorities may have been testing intelligence reports that the men were being held or treated in hospitals in East Germany. In any case, he passed on the list to Streit and Volpert, but by the middle of 1966 it was clear that those of the pilots who were alive must be in Indochina, not in East Germany, and that the Vietnamese were not interested in letting the Soviets have any of them. Denton, for instance, was held prisoner until the United States pulled out of the war in 1973. Vogel told the Americans that he had been unable to accomplish anything for any of those on the list, and he was not asked to try again. (Meehan, telephone conversation with author, Jan. 15, 1993, and Vogel, interview with author, Teupitz, Jan. 18, 1993.)

Again with no help from Vogel, the British finally negotiated Brooke's release from Moscow on July 24, 1969, and allowed the Krogers to fly off to

Warsaw airport three months later, in exchange for the release of two British subjects arrested on drug smuggling charges in the Soviet Union. The Krogers later lived as honored guests of the KGB outside Moscow. "Helen Kroger" died there on Dec. 30, 1992.

41. Dr. Crosta, letter to Dr. Friederike Schulenburg, Berlin, April 1992, and conversation with the author on June 6, 1992. Crosta's recollection in the letter had been that Vogel had told him he had received the information from the "chief of Soviet intelligence in Berlin." Vogel also sent his fourteen-year-old son, Manfred, to visit the Crostas in Merseburg to give them a plausible reason to travel to Berlin the following Saturday to bring the boy back home. After dropping Manfred off at his father's house, they continued across the border to the West, Dr. Crosta said.

42. Vogel, interview with author, Berlin, June 12, 1992. See also Wyden, op. cit., pp. 151–52.

CHAPTER 3

1. The Eastern Bureau was the "Ostbüro," long under the direction of Stephan Thomas.

2. Under Berlin's occupation statutes, West Berliners did not have West German citizenship or passports.

3. John Mapother, interview with author, Washington, D.C., Aug. 5, 1991.

4. Arnold Heidemann, interview with author, Berlin, Dec. 16, 1991.

5. Vogel, conversations with author; and Nelle, telephone conversation with author, July 18, 1992. Nelle became a member of the West German Bundestag in 1980.

6. See Ludwig Geissel, *Unterhändler der Menschlichkeit, Erinnerungen* (Stuttgart: Quell-Verlag, 1991), pp. 253–63.

7. Ibid., pp. 277 and 471.

8. Von Wedel, *Im Auftrag des Bischofs,* a privately printed testimonial written for Kurt Scharf's 85th birthday.

9. Vogel, interviews with author, Teupitz, June 21, 1991, and Berlin, May 7, 1992; von Wedel, interview with author, Berlin, Dec. 1991; Heinz D. Thiel, interview with author, Berlin, May 6, 1992; and Bishop Hermann Kunst, interview with author, Bonn, Oct. 20, 1992. Von Wedel said the idea of using money had seemed natural, not at all a cynical and brutal East German proposition dreamed up by the Stasi and forced upon the church officials by Vogel. This latter thesis was advanced in some lurid post-unification accounts (by, for example, Peter-Ferdinand Koch, op. cit., pp. 122–23). Thiel, a Roman Catholic charities director who was also involved in the political prisoner trade, told the author that he shared von Wedel's view that the idea of money for prisoners came from the Western side and was not imposed on the Western churchmen by East German trickery or moral blackmail. And finally, Bishop Hermann Kunst said: "Who knows who made the suggestion first. It arose naturally from the conversation, because both men knew the church had paid money in individual cases before."

10. Vogel, interviews with author, Teupitz, June 22 and Dec. 12, 1991.

11. Kunst, interview with the author in Bonn, Oct. 20, 1992.

12. Von Wedel, testimonial, op. cit., p. 18.

13. Geissel, op. cit., p. 329.

14. Von Wedel, testimonial, op. cit. 18–19. In the Oct. 20, 1992, interview with the author, Bishop Kunst said he could not recall the exact amount but thought it was possible that the government in Bonn had provided the ransom.

15. Wyden, op. cit., pp. 317–18.
16. Ludwig A. Rehlinger, *Freikauf: Die Geschäfte der DDR mit politisch Verfolgten,* 1963–1989. Berlin/Frankfurt, Verlag Ullstein, 1991, p. 15.
17. An account of the meeting, apparently based on interviews with Fritzen, is given in Wyden, op. cit., pp. 319–21. The account was confirmed in a separate recollection by Carmen Greifenhagen, Fritzen's longtime assistant, in a letter to Vogel's lawyer, Friederike Schulenburg, April 10, 1992.
18. Greifenhagen, letter to Schulenburg, April 10, 1992.
19. Rehlinger, op. cit., p. 23.
20. Ibid, pp. 25–27.
21. Vogel, interview with the author, Berlin, May 7, 1992.
22. Vogel, interview with the author, East Berlin, November 1975.
23. Rehlinger, op. cit., p. 33.
24. Ibid., pp. 28–31.
25. Ibid., pp. 30–32.
26. Rehlinger, op. cit., p. 35. See also Michel Meyer, *Des hommes contre des marks* (Paris: Editions Stock, 1977), and Martin Höllen, "Der innerdeutsche Freikauf," *Der Monat,* Vol. 2 (1980), pp. 64–65.
27. Rehlinger, op. cit., p. 35.
28. Vogel, interview with author, Berlin, May 7, 1992.
29. Rehlinger, op. cit., p. 38.
30. Rehlinger, op. cit., p. 56, and Vogel, testimony before the Bundestag CoCo committee, Bonn, Oct. 8, 1992.
31. Geissel, op. cit., pp. 331–32.
32. Ibid., p. 332.
33. Ibid., pp. 333–34.
34. Rehlinger, op. cit., pp. 62–63.
35. Ample documentation for this assertion is contained in "Erste Beschlussempfehlung und erster Teilbericht des 1. Untersuchungsausschusses nach Artikel 44 des Grundgesetzes" ("First decision recommendation and first partial report of the first investigating committee under Article 44 of the Constitution"), the Bundestag CoCo committee's documentation report, Oct. 14, 1992.
36. Rehlinger, op. cit., p. 47.
37. Rehlinger, interview with author, Bonn, July 22, 1991.
38. Niebling (Volpert's successor), interview with author, Berlin, May 7, 1992.
39. Rehlinger, op. cit., p. 58.
40. Ibid., p. 59.
41. Ibid., p. 61.
42. Ibid., p. 60.
43. "Zu viele Worte," *Berliner Morgenpost,* Aug. 27, 1964.
44. Wyden, op. cit., pp. 299–300.
45. Geissel, op. cit., pp. 333–34; and Vogel files; see table in appendix.
46. This is as Stange recollected the incident in an interview with the author in November 1975.
47. Geissel, op. cit., p. 358.
48. Original document is in the Bundestag CoCo Committee documentation report cited above, pp. 48–50. See also the book by Peter Przybylski, *Tatort Politbüro Band 2: Honecker, Mittag, and Schalck-Golodkowski* (Berlin: Rowohlt-Berlin Verlag GmbH, 1992), p. 381 (hereafter *Tatort Politbüro 2*).
49. As determined by the Bundestag's CoCo committee. See Przybylski, op. cit., p. 241.
50. See the earlier volume by Peter Przybylski, *Tatort Politburo, die Akte*

Honecker (Berlin: Rowohlt-Berlin Verlag, 1991), pp. 126–30 (hereafter *Tatort Politbüro*).

51. Table, in appendix.

52. Przybylski, *Tatort Politbüro 2*, p. 247.

53. Vogel, interview with author, Teupitz, June 21, 1991; and Rehlinger, interview with author, Bonn, July 22, 1991. Rehlinger had no recollection of Reinartz's name or of the case at all.

54. Svingel, quoting Vogel, in an interview with author, Berlin, June 27, 1991.

55. Ibid.

56. Svingel, affidavit to Dr. Friederike Schulenburg, Berlin, April 15, 1992.

57. Svingel, affidavit; Eberhard Zachmann was the West German official.

58. Svingel, interview with author, Berlin, June 27, 1991.

CHAPTER 4

1. Vogel, testimony before the Bundestag investigating committee on CoCo, Bonn, Oct. 8, 1992.

2. Excerpt from the charge sheet of the prosecutor-general. "Trial of the West Berlin student Gottfried Steglich in the Supreme Court of the German Democratic Republic," in Vogel's office archives.

3. The German word is *Menschenhandel,* the same word often applied derogatorily to the prisoner-release trade.

4. Vogel, closing argument, from his office archives.

5. Vogel, interview with author, Berlin, May 7, 1992.

6. Fuchs's story is in Wyden, op. cit., pp. 294–96.

7. Volker G. Heinz, interview with author, London, March 12, 1991.

8. Ibid.

9. Ibid. Agent exchanges were later negotiated in a separate framework.

10. Ibid. Heinz worked for Wilmer, Cutler & Pickering in London, Brussels, and Berlin when I met him in March 1991. Nearly a year of East German prison left him with the lifelong habit of sleeping with his arm over his face. "They'd put the light on in the cell every three minutes all night long, and you weren't allowed to put a blanket over your head," he told me. "I never got out of the habit."

11. Vogel, testimony, op. cit.

12. Vogel's plea before the first criminal chamber of the Supreme Court of the GDR, from Vogel's office archives. The other case was the trial in Magdeburg in June 1966 of Dr. Kurt Heissmeyer, another doctor accused of having performed experiments on inmates of the Nazi concentration camp at Neuengamme. The prosecution demanded life imprisonment, and Vogel pleaded unsuccessfully for a lesser sentence.

13. "Tulsan Claims Plot Made Him 'Fall Guy,'" *Tulsa World,* Aug. 29, 1965; and Ricey S. New, interview with author, Washington, D.C., Aug. 5, 1991.

14. New, interview, op. cit.

15. Van Altena's story and his observations of Vogel from John Van Altena, Jr., *A Guest of the State* (Chicago: Henry Regnery Company, 1967), pp. 234–36 and passim.

16. New, interview, op. cit.

17. "Trial of American citizen Peter Feinauer at the first criminal part of the city court of Greater Berlin," from Vogel's office archive.

18. Ibid.

19. Ibid.

20. Ibid.
21. He was later freed in an exchange arranged by the West Germans, according to Vogel.
22. New, interview, op. cit.

CHAPTER 5

1. Vogel, interviews with author, Berlin, May 7, 1992, and Teupitz, Jan. 18, 1993; and testimony before the Bundestag CoCo committee in Bonn, Oct. 8, 1992.
2. Michel Meyer, *Des hommes contre des marks* (Paris: Editions Stock, 1977), pp. 159–61.
3. Rehlinger, op. cit., p. 66.
4. Ibid.
5. Ibid., p. 64.
6. Ibid., p. 64.
7. Ibid., p. 74, and Rehlinger interview with author, Bonn, July 22, 1991.
8. Rehlinger, interview with author, July 22, 1991; the figures are in Geissel, op. cit., p. 475.
9. Heinz Felfe, interview with author, Berlin, June 28, 1991.
10. Ibid.
11. Petty later turned up as a major figure in the U.S. Iran-Contra scandal in the late 1980s.
12. Mary Ellen Reese, *General Reinhard Gehlen: The CIA Connection* (Fairfax, Va.: George Mason University Press, 1990), pp. 155–59.
13. Ibid., pp. 161–62.
14. See also Felfe's own memoirs, *Im Dienst des Gegners* (Berlin: Verlag der Nation, 1988).
15. "Sowjets verhaften FR-Redakteurin," *Frankfurter Rundschau,* Sept. 27, 1966; "Sowjets erheben Spionage-Vorwurf," *Frankfurter Allgemeine Zeitung,* Sept. 8, 1966.
16. Martina Kischke, interview with author, Frankfurt, Jan. 16, 1992.
17. Vogel, interview with author, Teupitz, Dec. 12, 1991.
18. Ibid.
19. Kischke, interview with author, Frankfurt, Jan. 16, 1992.
20. Ibid.
21. See also "Frenzel in die CSSR entlassen," *Frankfurter Rundschau,* Dec. 28, 1966, and "Frenzel war dem Ostblock vier Gefangene wert," *Frankfurter Allgemeine Zeitung,* Dec. 28, 1966. Kischke resumed her work as women's editor of the *Frankfurter Rundschau,* where she remained for many years. She never made another trip to the Soviet Union, and never heard again from Boris Petrenko, who she assumed had been assigned all along by the KGB to entrap her.
22. Rehlinger, op. cit., pp. 78–79, and Vogel, interview with author, Teupitz, June 22, 1991. Mielke often looked at the agent-swap lists and complained, when the Communist side gave up more people than it got in return, that Vogel had not negotiated hard enough, but usually calmed down and accepted that he had probably done the best he could, according to Lt. Gen. Gerhard Niebling, who succeeded Volpert after his death as Vogel's liaison with the Stasi. Niebling, interview with author, Berlin, May 7, 1992.
23. Vogel, interview with author, Teupitz, June 22, 1991.
24. Felfe, interview with author, Berlin, June 28, 1991.

25. "Bonn Trades Top Soviet Agent for 3 Students Jailed as Spies," *The New York Times,* Feb. 15, 1969.

26. Felfe, interview with author, Berlin, June 28, 1991.

27. Ibid, and Felfe, op. cit., pp. 398–407.

28. The Soviets treated Felfe like a returning hero, taking him off to a KGB sanatorium in the Crimea for a couple of months of relaxation and recovery. But the following March, at a celebration of Felfe's 52d birthday, in the presence of the chief Soviet liaison officer with the Staatssicherheit, the old spy was shocked to hear a toast raised in his honor wishing him all happiness in his retirement. "You've earned it," his comrades told him, and Felfe burst out in anger. "But I'm only just over 50," he protested. "I need to work." If the East Germans wouldn't let him, he said, he'd go back to the West. He finally landed in the criminal science section of the Humboldt University in East Berlin, in an office reached through the hearse entrance used to bring in cadavers.

29. "Vermerk," Vogel's East German Justice Ministry file, April 29, 1967.

30. Vogel, interviews with author, Teupitz, June 21–22 and Dec. 12, 1991; Berlin, May 7, 1992, and June 12, 1992.

31. Ibid.

32. Ibid.

33. The document is also given in Schmidthammer, op. cit., p. 133.

CHAPTER 6

1. From the title of a book by Peter Bender, a political writer who influenced Brandt and Bahr.

2. Party documents published in Peter Przybylski, *Tatort Politburo,* pp. 280–88.

3. Ibid., pp. 54–55.

4. Reinhold Andert and Wolfgang Herzberg, *Der Sturz: Erich Honecker im Kreuzverhör* (Berlin and Weimar: Aufbau-Verlag, 1991), p. 272.

5. Przybylski, op. cit., pp. 114–15.

6. Ibid., p. 287.

7. *Abgrenzung* in German.

8. Vogel, testimony before the Bundestag CoCo committee in Bonn, Oct. 8, 1992.

9. Vogel, interview with author, Teupitz, June 22, 1991. In early 1992, *Die Welt* obtained a transcript purporting to be a report of one of Vogel's meetings with Wehner, on June 11, 1968, in Wehner's apartment in Bad Godesberg. The report identifies Wehner's conversation partner as "Georg," and the clear implication—not accepted by the newspaper, which decided "Georg" could be somebody else—was that the Stasi still carried Vogel on its books as a secret collaborator. Vogel, who provided the transcript to the author, disputed having such status in 1968, but acknowledged that the Stasi may have continued to use his old code name internally then.

10. Andert and Herzberg, op. cit., pp. 344–50.

11. Vogel, submission to Amtsgericht Tiergarten, Mar. 25, 1992.

12. Vogel, interview with author, Teupitz, June 22, 1991; Svingel, interview with author, Berlin, June 27, 1991.

13. *Neues Deutschland,* June 1, 1973, p. 1.

14. Vogel, interview with author, Teupitz, June 22, 1991, and testimony to CoCo investigating committee, Oct. 8, 1992.
15. Markus Wolf, conversation with author, Berlin, Aug. 12, 1992.

CHAPTER 7

1. Willy Brandt, op. cit., p. 329.
2. Ibid., p. 335.
3. Quoted in the *Frankfurter Allgemeine Zeitung,* June 15, 1990.
4. David Binder, *The Other German: Willy Brandt's Life & Times* (Washington, D.C.: The New Republic Book Company, Inc., 1975), p. 313.
5. Brandt, op. cit., p. 332–33.
6. Markus Wolf, *In eigenem Auftrag; Bekenntnisse und Einsichten* (Munich: Franz Schneekluth Verlag, 1991), pp. 266 and 267.
7. Ibid., pp. 266–68.
8. Ibid., and Irene Runge and Uwe Stelbrink, *Markus Wolf: "Ich bin kein Spion"* (Berlin: Dietz Verlag, 1990), p. 51.
9. Brandt, op. cit., p. 318.
10. Ibid., pp. 338 and 339.
11. Despite the rumors about Brandt's private life, the letter took Bonn by surprise. Only an article in *Der Spiegel* that Monday had suggested, in passing and deep down in the story, that Brandt had become so depressed that he was even considering resignation. I was *The New York Times* correspondent in Bonn at the time and, wondering whether it was true, decided to call upon Sven Backlund, the Swedish ambassador and a close friend of Brandt's and Wehner's. "I'm getting married on Saturday. Should I postpone the ceremony?" I asked. "No," Backlund laughed. "But if I were you, I'd keep a short-wave radio close by tonight."
12. Brandt, op. cit., pp. 324–25.
13. Ibid., op. cit., p. 219, confirmed by Vogel to the author.
14. Valentin M. Falin, interview with author, Moscow, June 11, 1991.
15. Ibid.
16. Honecker's true feelings may be guessed from the fact that after both Guillaumes were released, in 1981, Honecker decorated them, personally and in secret, with East Germany's highest military order. Markus Wolf, conversation with author, Berlin, Feb. 1992.
17. Wolf, op. cit., p. 269.
18. Klaus Bölling, *Die fernen Nachbarn: Erfahrungen in der DDR* (Hamburg: Stern/Gruner + Jahr AG & Co., 1983), p. 227.
19. Helmut Schmidt, *Die Deutschen und ihre Nachbarn: Menschen und Mächte II* (Berlin: Siedler Verlag, 1990), pp. 32–33; and Schmidt, letter to the author, May 11, 1992.
20. Schmidt, op. cit., p. 36, and "Lieber im verborgenen," *Der Spiegel,* No. 36, 1975.
21. Schmidt, op. cit., p. 32.
22. Vogel, interview with author, Teupitz, Dec. 12, 1991.
23. Details of the case from Henry Hurt, "Shadrin: the spy who never came back." New York: McGraw-Hill Book Company, Reader's Digest Press, 1981; *Literaturnaya Gazeta,* Aug. 17, 1977; Ronald Kessler, *Escape from the CIA* (New York: Pocket Books, 1991), pp. 134–38; "Wife of Soviet Defector Says the C.I.A. May Have Caused His Death," *The New York Times,* May 25, 1978; and Richard D. Copaken, interview with author, Washington, D.C., Aug. 28, 1991.
24. Meehan, interview with author, Helensburgh, Scotland, Sept. 13, 1990.

25. Copaken, interviews with author, Washington, D.C., Aug. 28, 1991; and Vogel, interview with author, Teupitz, Dec. 12, 1991.
26. Copaken, interview with author, Washington, D.C., Aug. 28, 1991; the document in Copaken's files.
27. Copaken, interview with and letter to the author, Nov. 6, 1992.
28. Vogel, interview with author, Teupitz, Dec. 14, 1991.
29. William Hyland, letter to the author, Feb. 4, 1992.
30. Copaken, interview with author.
31. Copaken, letter to the author, Nov. 10, 1992.
32. Copaken remained suspicious of Kissinger's motives in apparently deliberately violating Vogel's "cardinal rule," not once but twice, despite the risks to Shadrin. Copaken, in any case, did not give up. He returned to Berlin on April 15, 1977, to see Vogel again. "The Shadrin case does not exist for the Soviets," Vogel warned him. When Copaken asked Vogel whether the Soviets had forbidden him even to discuss the case, he bristled. "I am not a soldier," he objected. "They can't give me orders." Copaken insisted on meeting him one more time, during a visit by Vogel to Washington to discuss another case in April 1978. Vogel agreed to the meeting in Congressman Benjamin Gilman's office with Copaken and Ewa Shadrin, only on condition that all parties concerned would deny that it had ever taken place, but again he had no news to report.

In an article in the Soviet weekly *Literaturnaya Gazeta* on Aug. 17, 1977, the writer Genrikh Borovik claimed that Shadrin had approached "Igor" in Washington, not the other way around; Shadrin had repented of his defection and wanted to find a way to earn his way back home, according to this account. At the first of the last two meetings in Vienna, he had evaded his American minders, confessed his weariness, and pressed for permission to come back home to Moscow. But he had never shown up for his second meeting, on Dec. 20. Perhaps the CIA, learning of the defector's wish to go back to the motherland, had "removed" him to avoid embarrassment, Borovik insinuated. Stansfield Turner, then director of the CIA, vigorously rejected the charge.

Before he, too, changed his mind and returned home in late 1985, another Soviet defector, Vitaly S. Yurchenko, told the CIA that the Soviets had abducted Shadrin in Vienna, subduing him with an accidentally fatal dose of chloroform that killed him before the car reached the Czech border. Perhaps the files of the former KGB in Moscow will one day reveal the truth; attempts by the author to obtain them in 1991 were unsuccessful. (Yurchenko's account was reported contemporaneously in American newspapers, e.g., *The Washington Post,* Oct. 30, 1985, and as described in Kessler, op. cit., p. 141.)
33. Frucht, interview with author, Berlin, June 25, 1991. See also *Der Spiegel* series "Der Spionagefall Frucht," by Gwynne Roberts/Clive Freeman, in *Der Spiegel,* Nos. 24–28, 1978.
34. Frucht, interview with author, Berlin, June 25, 1991.
35. "Giftwolken—dort wäre die Hölle los," *Der Spiegel,* No. 26, 1978; Vogel, interview with author, Teupitz, June 21–22, 1991.
36. Honecker's daughter, Sonja, had married an exiled Chilean student and become personally involved in trying to free Montes. Vogel also tried to arrange a swap for a prisoner held in Cuba, but having little leverage with Pinochet, he had gotten nowhere until Wehner offered to ask Schmidt's specialist in such secret missions, Hans-Jürgen Wischnewski, "Ben-Wisch," as the German press dubbed him, to go to Chile secretly on Vogel's behalf. Wischnewski, a jovial, back-slapping political Social Democratic Party operator, also became a close friend of Vogel. Frucht and ten other East

German prisoners were released in exchange for Montes. Only after the Germans made the deal did the Americans finally show signs of interest in their old agent, picking him up from Vogel at the border at Herleshausen, and leaving him to fly by himself back to West Berlin. Later, Frucht told the author, they compensated him for his imprisonment with several hundred thousand deutsche marks that Frucht used to build a home on a secluded, tree-shaded street in a quiet corner of West Berlin.

37. Schmidt, op. cit, 58–63.
38. Edgar D. Hirt, interview with author, Zurich, Dec. 14, 1991.
39. The list was not made public but is in Vogel's office archives.
40. Hirt, interview, op. cit.
41. Vogel, interview with author, Teupitz, June 21, 1991.
42. Bölling, op. cit., p. 160.
43. Documents unearthed in early 1993 showed that Honecker had been pressing for Warsaw Pact intervention in Poland since late 1980. See "Noch war Polen nicht verloren," *Der Tagesspiegel,* Berlin, Jan. 9, 1993.
44. Schmidt, op. cit., pp. 72–73, and Bölling, op. cit., pp. 160–62.

CHAPTER 8

1. Wyden, op. cit., pp. 464–65.
2. "Meine Eltern sind nicht meine Eltern," *Der Spiegel,* No. 49, 1976.
3. Wyden, a German-born American journalist, wrote to Vogel in September 1988, asking if there wasn't something he could do to help the Grübels find their children after so many years, but got no positive answer until 1990, after the Wall had fallen. Then Vogel supplied him with the address of the children's adoptive father, Ulrich Klewin, in Frankfurt an der Oder. Bärbel and Ota Grübel were then reunited with their children. Klewin's wife had died in 1982. The young adults their children had become had no memory of the Grübels. (Peter Wyden, *Children of the Cold War* [London: *The Independent Magazine,* Oct. 6, 1990].)
4. Vogel, interview with author, Teupitz, Feb. 16, 1992.
5. Bundestag CoCo committee documentation report, op. cit., Document 100, pp. 709–19.
6. "Nur wenige Übersiedler Kamen in den Genuss Kirchlichen Entgegenkommens," *Frankfurter Allgemeine Zeitung,* Feb. 28, 1992.
7. Przybylski, *Tatort Politbüro 2,* pp. 313–14.
8. "Alte Puppen für den Westen," *Der Spiegel,* no. 50, 1978. In a letter to Vogel on May 13, 1976, Kath also wrote that he had given up the rights to his property on Vogel's advice, expressing thanks to him for making possible his emigration to West Germany and getting the case against him dropped.
9. Von Wedel interview with author, Berlin, Dec. 16, 1991.
10. Vogel's office files contain documentation of the case, including a letter from Kath to Vogel dated May 13, 1976, complaining about the lawyer's demand for an honorarium but emphasizing that rumors that he had complained about the quality of Vogel's legal advice were false. "I emphasize expressly once again that you represented my and my wife's interests completely acceptably," he wrote. Kath offered to pay Vogel a 10 percent commission on the value of his seized property if Vogel could arrange to get it back; nothing came of this request, because CoCo had sold it to Western buyers. But, unusually, Kath was set up in business in West Germany with the

help of a DM20,000 loan from Seidel in 1976, and was later even able to return and do business in East Berlin.

Horst Schuster fled to West Germany in the spring of 1983 and became an informant for the BND, according to members of the Bundestag's CoCo investigating committee, who were unable to get the intelligence agency to release any of its secret files on the information he provided. (Press release issued by Alliance 90/The Greens, Nov. 4, 1992. See also Przybylski, *Tatort Politbüro 2*, pp. 313–16.)

11. See Przybylski, *Tatort Politbüro 2*, pp. 292–93, and Die Zeit, op. cit., Aug. 28, 1992, pp. 11–14.

12. Vogel testimony before the Bundestag CoCo investigating committee, Oct. 8, 1992.

13. "Ich hätte mit dem Teufel paktiert," *Der Spiegel*, No. 15, 1990.

14. Edgar Hirt, interview with author, Zurich, Dec. 14, 1991.

15. Dr. Hoene, letter to the prosecution in the Berlin supreme court, Jan. 26, 1992; and Vogel arrest warrant, Mar. 1992.

16. Vogel made this estimate in an interview with *Der Spiegel*, "Ich hätte mit dem Teufel paktiert," cited above.

17. Vogel, testimony to the Bundestag CoCo investigating committee, Oct. 8, 1992, and in a memorandum prepared for Dr. Friederike Schulenburg dated Jan. 9, 1993. In this memorandum and in an interview with the author, Teupitz, Jan. 18, 1993, Vogel said he had never been anything but an intermediary in cash payment arrangements, that the initiative had often come from people in the West, not from the Stasi, and that he had refused to have anything to do with such private deals after 1986. Vogel vigorously denied all suggestions that he had pocketed some of the money from such cash payments himself, saying he had always passed on the money to Volpert, who he assumed gave them to Schalck-Golodkowski. After Volpert's sudden death in February, 1986, Vogel said, two of the Stasi captain's secretaries—Ursula Drasdo and Ursula Beyer—reported that a large sum of money had been found in his office safe in the Normannenstrasse when it was opened in the presence of Mielke's chief of staff, Maj. Gen. Hans Carlsohn. "When Hans Carlson [sic] opened the safe in his office," Mrs. Drasdo said in a signed statement to Vogel dated Aug. 1, 1990, "inside were fairly large envelopes with return addresses from lawyers Stange, von Wedel and Vogel. In them were, in large bills, sums of money totalling over 2 million [deutsche marks], which were noted and on Hans Carlson's instructions paid by me to the finance department. . . ." Drasdo, statement, Aug. 1, 1990, from Vogel's office archives.

18. Vogel, interview with author, Teupitz, Dec. 12, 1991. The Gabin film was distributed in Germany as "No Room in the Clink."

19. Gerhard Strunk, letter to Dr. Friederike Schulenburg, June 8, 1992. "Herr Dr. Vogel, although a 'GDR lawyer,' fought against the espionage and sabotage charges of the Stasi with every means available to him, and without regard to the possible negative consequences for himself," Strunk wrote.

20. Quoted in *Rheinischer Merkur/Christ und Welt*, Oct. 26, 1979.

21. Wolfgang Seiffert, and Norbert Treutwein, *Die Schalck Papiere: DDR-Mafia zwischen Ost und West, Die Beweise* (Vienna, Zsolnay, 1991), pp. 331–33.

22. Rehlinger, op. cit., p. 114.

23. Winkler, Karl, "Auf dem Käse krabbelten die Maden," in *Der Spiegel*, No. 12, 1983.

24. Vogel, interview with author, Teupitz, June 22, 1991.

25. "Dokumentation," international hearing on the human rights situation in

the GDR, Bonn–Bad Godesberg, Dec. 6–7, 1984. Frankfurt, Internationale Gesellschaft für Menschenrechte (IGFM), Feb. 1985.
26. Dr. Rothenbächer, open letter, Jan. 14, 1992.
27. Ibid.
28. Schulenburg, submission to the Berlin District Court, Apr. 29, 1992, and "Der Fall Vogel," *Super-Illu,* Jan. 30, 1992, p. 6. The property had an interesting pedigree. It was confiscated by the state in 1954 after its owner fled to West Germany, and given to Helene Weigel, the longtime companion of Bertolt Brecht. Weigel, in turn, gave it to a friend who was Vera Zapff's mother. Thus Vera Zapff had come by the property, and in 1980 she told Brecht's daughter that she was selling it again. Barbara Brecht-Schall offered immediately to buy it back, but the offer was refused. Vera Zapff wanted "that nice Dr. Vogel" to have it, she said, because he had done so much to help.
29. Vogel, written statement on the purchase, Sept. 9, 1991, and documents in Stasi files. After unification, Vogel lost the property. The state's confiscation in 1954 was illegal, according to the all-German property law adopted before unification, and the courts decided that it should revert to the heiress of the original owner, a woman named Ursula Wesch from Essen. "Herr Professor Vogel was quite understanding," she later told the tabloid *Bild Zeitung.*
30. Henning, letter, May 4, 1990, to the committee liquidating the former Stasi, sent to Dr. Schulenburg. He did not tell Vogel what his Stasi connection was, Henning wrote, until Feb. 2, 1990, when the Pietzsches were trying to reclaim the property.
31. Edgar Hirt, interview with author, Zurich, Dec. 14, 1991.
32. Ibid.
33. Ibid.; and Heinz Thiel, interview with author, Berlin, May 6, 1992.
34. Ibid.
35. Hirt, interview with author, Zurich, Dec. 14, 1991.
36. "Via Caritas," *Der Spiegel,* No. 12, 1984.
37. Hirt, interview with author, Zurich, Dec. 14, 1991. Wolfgang Vogel had represented the Soviet side on this occasion, concerning the release of a high-ranking agent code-named "Swenson" whose real name was Kozlov. He had been caught two years earlier and offered by the South Africans to the United States and every major Western European country as a possible object of exchange. Lt. Col. Kozlov had coordinated the KGB's aid to all the resistance and liberation movements of southern Africa, from Angola, Namibia, and Mozambique to South Africa. Foolishly, he had risked flying into South Africa, posing as a West German tourist, for an inspection trip. The South Africans were eager to use every opportunity to break down the international isolation that revulsion against apartheid had imposed on them, and they knew that in Bonn they had allies—particularly in the BND, which was eager to keep tabs on the extensive East German intelligence activities in southern Africa and had been helpful in exposing Kozlov's real identity. They offered Kozlov to the British, the Americans, and the West Germans, and finally decided to favor Bonn with the release. They flew Kozlov to Frankfurt on a special chartered Lufthansa plane, going on by helicopter to Herleshausen for an exchange that was to include a South African soldier taken prisoner in Angola as well as eight captured BND agents held in East German prisons, a package Vogel had worked out with Hirt. Hirt seemed to be preoccupied, Vogel noticed. The Soviet representative who was to meet Kozlov had not shown up, and the South Africans were getting cold feet. Hirt argued strenuously with the South Africans to let the exchange go ahead anyway, but they said they would take the prisoner back to Pretoria. They changed their

minds, Hirt said, after he offered to pay them DM468,000. This money, too, Hirt claimed, came from the church funds. Vogel, in an interview with the author in Teupitz on Feb. 16, 1992, claimed to know nothing about any payment. See "Punkt und Komma," *Der Spiegel,* No. 8, 1983, "Via Caritas," No. 12, 1984, and "Wa is Boris?", No. 47, 1992.
38. Rehlinger, op. cit., pp. 91–94, confirmed by Thiel, interview with author, Berlin, May 6, 1992.
39. Full text quoted in Rehlinger, op. cit., p. 99. In effect, Franke's argument was one that both Vogel and his negotiating partners in the church often used. In late 1982, the church had paid DM250,000 directly to the Stasi, in recompense for damage allegedly done to the East German state by a patently illegal currency-exchange operation that had gone on for six years. The church had needed East marks and, unwilling to change deutsche marks at the exorbitant official rate of 1:1, had bought Communist currency from people it could trust at an exchange of 3.50:1, thus obtaining three and a half times as many East marks to spend on its charity activities in the East as it would have through the official rate. Karl-Heinz Barthel, an East German worker who played a role in the scheme, had been arrested and charged with crimes carrying an eight-year penalty. The church had called on Vogel to do what he could for Barthel, and after the restitution payment had been made, he had succeeded in arranging his release. Vogel had also arranged the sale of his house, to Jürgen Wetzenstein-Ollenschläger, chief judge of the Lichtenburg District Court, a notorious zealot widely known for his tough sentences against dissidents. See "Weiss der Teufel," *Der Spiegel,* No. 22, 1992, and arrest order against Vogel by the Tiergarten District Court, March 30, 1992.
40. Both Thiel and Vogel insist that Vogel was never told.
41. Vogel, interview with author, Teupitz, Feb. 16, 1992.
42. "Da ist mir fast die Mokkatasse aus der Hand gefallen," Bonner General-Anzeiger, July 22, 1986.
43. Stange, interview with author, Berlin, June 11, 1992.
44. Hirt, interview with author, Zurich, Dec. 14, 1991.
45. Ibid.
46. After appeals and intercessions for mercy from Vogel and most of Germany's leading churchmen, Hirt actually spent only five weeks behind bars, and was pardoned in April 1991. Shambling around Zurich trying to drum up business as a consultant at the end of that year, he cut a sad figure, keeping a man he identified as the Turkish ambassador to Switzerland waiting for two hours while we talked. The "Turkish ambassador" and a swarthy assistant had left by the time we finished, and Hirt ended our interview by asking me if I could help him out by paying his $100 hotel bill. Wolfgang Vogel's possible involvement in the case was also investigated by the Stasi. "They tell me you're in the clear," Honecker told him, a few months after the trial. Vogel, interview with author, Teupitz, Feb. 16, 1992.

CHAPTER 9

1. Shcharansky changed his name to Natan Sharansky after being freed and flying to Israel in 1986. Where it is historically accurate I use the transliterated Russian spelling of his original name.
2. Vogel, interview with author, Teupitz, Dec. 12, 1991.
3. Vogel, interview with author, Teupitz, June 22, 1991.
4. Vogel office archives.

5. "L.I. Spy Tells of Serving Soviet," *The New York Times,* Mar. 9, 1965. The oil company was called Best Fuel Oil Service, and years later, Thompson claimed that Gregor Alexander Best had been his real name all along. He had been born in Germany and taken by his Russian father to the Soviet Union before World War II, he said. There, he had served as a tank commander in the Red Army before signing up with the Stasi to be infiltrated, like Col. Abel, into the United States through Canada under a false name. See Nigel West, *The Perfect Spy* (London: *The Mail on Sunday,* July 28, 1991). Whoever "Thompson" really was, he asked Vogel after his release to send a monthly check of $200 to an address in Howell, Michigan, and Vogel did so until Jan. 1990.

6. Vogel, interview with author, Dec. 16, 1991.

7. Meehan, interview with author, Helensburgh, Scotland, Sept. 13, 1990.

8. Greenwald, interview with author, New York, Aug. 27, 1991.

9. Greenwald office files in New York.

10. Ibid.

11. Meehan diary entry, Apr. 11, 1978.

12. Greenwald office files.

13. Meehan, interview with author, Helensburgh, Scotland, Sept. 13, 1990.

14. Greenwald, interview with author, New York, Aug. 27, 1991; Gilman, interview with author, Moscow, Sept. 9, 1991.

15. Copaken, interview with author, Washington, D.C., Aug. 28, 1991.

16. Smith, interview with author, Chatham, Mass., Aug. 9, 1991.

17. Thirteen years later, not far away, in a café in downtown East Berlin, Rupert Allason, the British MP who writes under the pseudonym of Nigel West, found Thompson. Allason had been told by British intelligence that the convicted spy had been suspected of having worked for the East Germans as a "false flag" recruiter of agents before the Communist regime collapsed, posing as an undercover CIA officer. At least one Western diplomat fell for the ploy, Allason later wrote. But in their meeting, Thompson claimed to have been head of the Stasi's American intelligence department in Markus Wolf's foreign espionage service. "He was never the head of a department," Wolf scoffed in a conversation with the author in December 1991, then and later professing himself unable to recall precisely what function Thompson had performed, and for whom.

18. Meehan and Smith interviews.

19. Greenwald, interview with author, New York, Aug. 27, 1991.

20. Agence France Press, June 5, 1978.

21. Vogel initially thought he might have found the bargaining counterweight he needed for Shcharansky, when the FBI trapped three Soviet spies in a sting operation in Woodbridge, N.J., on May 20, 1978. Vladimir P. Zinyakin, an attaché at the Soviet Mission to the United Nations, had diplomatic immunity and was promptly shipped back home, but Valdik A. Enger and Rudolf P. Chernyayev, as civilian employees of the U.N. Secretariat, did not, and were charged with espionage and with paying a U.S. Navy informant more than $20,000 to obtain "secrets" that American counterintelligence had selected to entrap them. Bail was set at $2 million each. (For the background of the case, see Harry Rositzke, *The K.G.B.: The Eyes of Russia* [Garden City, N.Y.: Doubleday, 1981].)

Shcharansky had not been tried, either, and Vogel believed that if he moved quickly, he might be able to arrange a swap of the two Soviets for him before things went any further. He called Greenwald in New York and told him he could try to strike a deal for their release in exchange for Shcharansky, if

Greenwald could get Gilman to use his influence to convince the Carter administration to agree. (Greenwald interview, New York, Aug. 27, 1991.)

Vogel was operating entirely on his own, but he was closer to a possible deal than he knew. Separately, the Soviet ambassador, Anatoly F. Dobrynin, was making a similar pitch, directly to Carter's National Security Adviser Zbiegniew K. Brzezinski, in the White House. But the United States government had now hardened its stance. Chernyayev and Enger were spies who had been caught red-handed, even if they had been lured into a trap, and the American intelligence community, feeling its oats after the successful defection of Arkady N. Shevchenko, the UN's Under Secretary General for Political and Security Council Affairs a few weeks earlier, wanted to move ahead with prosecution, as Ben Gilman found when he pressed Secretary of State Cyrus R. Vance a few weeks later.

Gilman, impressed by Vogel's assurances that he could negotiate a deal, could not understand why the Carter administration wasn't interested. "I know I can get Shcharansky for Chernyayev and Enger," Gilman insisted in Vance's small private office on the State Department's top floor. Vance replied that the United States appreciated Gilman's loyalty and his attempts to help get Shcharansky free, as the administration was also trying to do, but that this wasn't the way. "Why?" the congressman persisted. Vance leaned forward in his chair, took off his glasses, and said, "Because the President wants it that way." (Jeffrey Smith, interview with author, Chatham, Mass., Aug. 9, 1991.) Valdik and Enger were sentenced to 50-year terms at their trial in October, and were finally swapped for Aleksandr Ginzburg and four other imprisoned Soviet dissidents in April 1979.

22. Greenwald, interview with author, New York, Aug. 27, 1991.

23. The verdict against Shcharansky was punctuated by another one, on the same day. Anatoly N. Filatov's trial also began on July 10, before a closed military collegium of the Soviet supreme court, but it had gone almost unnoticed. Filatov was also accused of treason, as the agent of a "foreign intelligence service" that had recruited him on diplomatic service in Algeria in 1974. Little was revealed about the case publicly in the sketchy accounts published by the official Soviet government news agency, Tass. But on July 14, the same day Shcharansky was found guilty, Tass reported that Filatov had been sentenced to death by firing squad.

The report did not reveal which intelligence service Filatov had allegedly worked for. But on the first night of September, a Soviet woman who did not give her name called the Moscow Bureau of *The New York Times* and said she had urgent information that could not be imparted by telephone. You must send a correspondent to meet me, she implored. She would be nearby, at Red Army Park, promptly at 9 P.M., she said, before abruptly hanging up.

Red Army Park was just down Sadovaya Samotechnaya Street from the building that housed *The Times*'s bureau. The compound, "Sad Sam" to its denizens, was home to many Western and Japanese news correspondents and British military attachés, and it was guarded by uniformed police from a special KGB detachment 24 hours a day. Often, there were plainclothes agents in unmarked cars outside the building, and at least once a KGB officer appeared in a window across the street with a pair of binoculars. The telephones and even the walls had more bugs than the garbage chutes had cockroaches.

The Times was closed by a strike in New York most of that summer, but its news service was operating, and the reporter who had taken the call—the author—decided to go hear what the woman had to tell. But just in case, he also decided it would be wise to bring along a colleague from the Reuters news agency, which was just upstairs. The KGB might have had a frameup in mind, as it had framed Robert Toth to get at Shcharansky the year before. Darkness had fallen as Chris Catlin and I approached the park from the underpass that goes by Sad Sam, but there, waiting for us, was a young woman, her dark blond hair blown by the cold wind. She identified herself, with a Soviet passport, as Tamara Filatova, wife of Anatoly Nikolayevich Filatov, and she had a message for us. She spoke it, urgently, in Russian:

"My husband worked for the Americans as an agent. He did his job loyally. Now he is counting on the mercy of President Carter to save him," she said. She had met her husband twice after his trial, at which he had pled guilty, and she said that he told her that he had twice tried to appeal directly to the president in letters that evidently never arrived. "If the American public finds out," she said, "then there's a chance of saving him. The people at the top would probably come to some agreement." Imploring us to send this message to the West, she then disappeared into the shadows of the ash and poplar trees, already shedding yellow leaves into the blustery wind of the early Russian autumn.

Surely, Chris and I agreed, this little meeting in the park could not have been by chance. Enger and Chernyayev (see note above) were still hostage to fate in the United States. Filatov's lawyer, Leonid M. Popov, was the same Soviet attorney who was representing Jay Crawford, an American businessman who had been arrested in Moscow on a flimsy pretext.

It didn't take much knowledge of how these things worked to figure the KGB wanted to use Catlin and me to float a suggestion that even if the Americans weren't quite ready to make a deal for Shcharansky, then Filatov and Crawford might go free in exchange for the Soviets who had been arrested in New York. But time was running short. Filatov's execution could come at any moment, his wife warned.

We reported the meeting just as it had happened. My account went out over *The New York Times* News Service on Sept. 1. But Filatov's case sank back into the mysterious depths from which his wife had brought it to us in Red Army Park. Neither in Washington nor in Moscow, as far as we could tell at the time, did it seem to have any effect, either on the case against Chernyayev and Enger or on the case against Shcharansky.

In the immediate aftermath, Shcharansky was not a subject of negotiation, and Vogel was cut out of the bargaining. Moscow, which had not yet given Vogel a mandate for Shcharansky in any case, dealt directly with Washington on Chernyayev and Enger, who were found guilty in their trial in Newark in October and sentenced to 50 years' imprisonment each. Less than a year later, after talks between Brzezinski and Ambassador Dobrynin in Washington, both Soviet agents were swapped in a trade for five imprisoned Soviet dissidents. The Soviets had learned of American interest in most of them through a handwritten list Meehan had given Vogel during his soundings, but when they finally released the five—Aleksandr Ginzburg, Mark Dymshits, Eduard S. Kuznetsov, Valentin Moroz, and Georgi P. Vins—they had not used Vogel's services at all. The men were flown to New York City on a special Soviet plane that flew back to Moscow carrying Chernyayev and Enger.

According to Smith, the Carter administration had asked him at around this time to give Filatov's name to Vogel, who after a few weeks had come back with a puzzled smile. "I understand from Moscow that you already have a deal," he said; "Dobrynin and Brzezinski worked it out as part of the deal for Enger and Chernyayev." he reported.

What the United States did for Filatov has never been acknowledged publicly. A hint came out in September 1980, during a political controversy in Washington about whether a Soviet CIA agent code-named "Trigon" had been inadvertently compromised by one of Brzezinski's aides, David L. Aaron, or some other Carter administration official. The cost of the blunder was supposed to have cost "Trigon" his life. The investigation by the Senate Select Committee on Intelligence seemed based on the assumption that "Trigon's" true identity had been Filatov. None of my colleagues at *The Times* had asked the Moscow Bureau to check the story, but I was still assigned there, and reading the reports on *The Times*'s News Service wire to Moscow, I asked Boris Zakharov, one of the translators, to call Filatov's lawyer and see when Filatov had been executed. "The sentence was never carried out," Boris reported, "it was commuted to 15 years." Years later, Smith discovered that Brzezinski had tried to include Filatov in the package for Enger and Chernyayev, and had obtained agreement to commute his sentence.

24. Vogel, interview, Teupitz, June 22, 1991, confirmed by Loewe, interview with author, Berlin, June 22, 1991. Loewe gave the list to Thomas M. T. Niles, the State Department's ranking official on German affairs at the time; to friends in the White House; and to John Mapother, a retired CIA official in Washington, and a major interagency review of the handling of such cases ensued.

25. Smith, telephone conversation with author, Sept. 23, 1991. The fee slip is in Vogel's office files.

26. Markus Wolf, interview with author, East Berlin, June 13, 1992.

27. Smith, interview with author, Chatham, Mass., Aug. 9, 1991.

28. Greenwald, interview with author, New York, Aug. 27, 1991.

29. Silverglate, interview with author, Boston, Mass., Aug. 21, 1991, and letter to author, Feb. 27, 1992.

30. Ibid.

31. Smith, interview with author, Chatham, Mass., Aug. 9, 1991.

32. Silverglate, interview with author, Boston, Mass., Aug. 21, 1991.

33. Vogel, interview with author, Teupitz, Dec. 12, 1991.

34. Smith, interview with author, Chatham, Mass., Aug. 9, 1991.

35. Ibid.

36. Ibid.

37. Ibid.

38. Ibid.

39. Wolf, interview with author, Feb. 16, 1992.

40. Vogel, interview with author, Teupitz, Dec. 12, 1991.

41. Ibid., and submission of Dr. Friederike Schulenburg to Tiergarten district court, Berlin, Mar. 25, 1992.

42. "Ex-CIA Employee Held as Czech Spy," *The New York Times,* Nov. 28, 1984; "Friend Says Spy Suspect 'Hated Communists,' " *The New York Times,* Nov. 29, 1984.

43. Silverglate, interview with author, Boston, Mass., Aug. 21, 1991.

44. Greenwald, letter to Dr. Friederike Schulenburg, Mar. 18, 1992; Silverglate, letter to Schulenburg, March 19, 1992; and Vogel, interview with author, Berlin, May 7, 1992.

45. Telephone conversation with Jeanne Baker, cocounsel with Silverglate, in Miami, Fla., Sept. 23, 1991. The U.S. attorney was William F. Weld, who later became governor of Massachusetts.

46. Greenwald, interview with author, New York, Aug. 27, 1991.

47. Silverglate, interview with author, Boston, Mass., Aug. 21, 1991.

48. Vogel, interview with author, Teupitz, Feb. 16, 1992, and Wolf, interview with author, Berlin, Feb. 16, 1992.
49. "East German Enters Guilty Plea To Buying Secret U.S. Documents," *The New York Times,* Feb. 22, 1985.
50. Silverglate, interview with author, Boston, Mass., Aug. 21, 1991.
51. Vogel, interview with author, Teupitz, Feb. 16, 1992.
52. Lt. Gen. Gerhard Niebling, interview with author, Berlin, May 7, 1992.
53. Vogel, interview with author, Teupitz, Dec. 12, 1991.
54. Ibid.
55. Vogel office archives.
56. Ibid.

CHAPTER 10

1. Valentin M. Falin, and Oleg D. Kalugin, interviews with author, Moscow, June 10, 1991; and Wolfgang Vogel, interview with author, Teupitz, Dec. 12, 1991.
2. Rehlinger, op. cit., and Rehlinger, interview with author, Bonn, July 22, 1991.
3. Rehlinger, op. cit., p. 199.
4. Lt. Gen. Gerhard Niebling, interview with author, Berlin, May 7, 1992.
5. Vogel, interview with author, Teupitz, June 23, 1991.
6. Lutze was released a year after Shcharansky, in another exchange arranged by Vogel.
7. Ambassador Richard C. Barkley, interview with author, Berlin, Oct. 4, 1990; and Niebling, interview with author, Berlin, May 7, 1992; see also Per Egil Hegge, "The Spy Oslo Sent to School," *International Herald Tribune,* June 27, 1985. Treholt, in failing health, was released on compassionate grounds on July 3, 1992.
8. Vogel, interview with author, Berlin, May 7, 1992.
9. Details on those exchanged from Rehlinger, op. cit., pp. 204–5; "Shcharansky Wins Freedom in Berlin in Prisoner Trade," *The New York Times,* Feb. 12, 1986; and Schmidthammer, op. cit., pp. 164–65.
10. Rehlinger, op. cit., p. 206; Schmidthammer, op. cit., p. 166; and Meehan, recollections to author, Jan. 11, 1992. The protocol is in Vogel's office archives.
11. "U.S. Weighs Moves In Czech Spy Case," *The New York Times,* Dec. 2, 1984; "Wife is Held in Contempt of Court for Refusing to Testify in Spy Inquiry," *The New York Times,* Dec. 5, 1984; "Intrigue and Countercharges Mark Case of Purported Spies," *The New York Times,* Jan. 13, 1985.
12. Vogel, interview with author, Teupitz, June 23, 1991; and Meehan, recollections to author, Jan. 11, 1992.
13. Ibid.
14. Meehan, unpublished personal memoir, from his personal files.
15. Ibid; Vogel, interview with author, Teupitz, June 23, 1991.
16. Rehlinger, op. cit., p. 213.
17. Ibid., p. 214; and Schmidthammer, op. cit., p. 170.
18. Natan Sharansky, *Fear No Evil* (New York: Random House, 1988), p. 414.
19. On Jan. 31, President P. W. Botha had publicly proposed a three-way exchange involving Shcharansky, Sakharov, and a South African captain who had been captured during a cross-border operation in Angola. Most people dismissed the gesture as a cheap publicity stunt. But after Shcharansky's release, Shabtai Kalmanovich, frequently in touch with South African officials

while he wheeled and dealed with the authorities in Bophuthatswana—bilking them out of millions of dollars, some of them would charge later—pushed Vogel to make a trip. He could arrange for him to see Mandela in prison, Kalmanovich promised. Ronnie Greenwald was skeptical. "How do you know Sakharov would agree to leave the Soviet Union?" he kept asking. Sakharov's wife, Yelena Bonner, had made it clear on several occasions during the visits to her family in the United States that she was allowed to make that her husband wanted freedom, not exile. But publicly, Soviet officials were also saying that Sakharov knew too many secrets to be trusted abroad, in exile or on his own. Greenwald himself had discussed the prospects of getting Mandela free with his own contacts in South Africa, and thought the possibility unlikely. When Vogel told him he was going to see for himself, Greenwald told him, "Don't go."

Vogel had gone anyway, secretly, in March. The temptation was too great to resist: Mandela and Shcharansky in the same year would certainly bring him the Nobel Peace Prize. The South Africans were interested in whatever he could accomplish, and he had several hours of talks with a member of Parliament and some security officials, trying to put together another package of spies—the captured captain, a Soviet spy couple nabbed by the South Africans, perhaps some German cases, East and West, as well.

But the South Africans insisted that Mandela would only be released if he went into exile in Sierra Leone. And the African National Congress let it be known that this was totally unacceptable to Mandela. Vogel had wanted to approach Richard Barkley, who had become deputy chief of mission at the U.S. Embassy in South Africa, for help, explaining that he had known him in Berlin, but the South Africans would not hear of it. He flew back to Berlin empty-handed. Don't worry, Greenwald consoled him. Shabtai often plays a game of mirrors and shadows. Greenwald, interview with author, New York, Aug. 27, 1991, and Vogel, interview with author, Teupitz, June 22, 1991.

CHAPTER 11

1. Vogel, interview with author, Teupitz, Dec. 12, 1991.
2. Ibid., and "Erich, mach das Licht aus," *Der Spiegel,* No. 10, 1984.
3. Vogel, interview with author, Teupitz, Dec. 12, 1991.
4. Rehlinger, op. cit., p. 145.
5. Rehlinger, op. cit. pp. 148–53.
6. Honecker also instructed Schalck-Golodkowski to tell his official West German contact in Chancellor Kohl's office that henceforth the West Germans should quietly pass on the names of East German citizens seeking to leave the country through Bonn's embassies abroad, and advise them that they would get permission to leave if they applied at home through official channels. See Werner Filmer, and Heribert Schwan, *Wolfgang Schäuble, Politik als Lebensaufgabe* (Munich: C. Bertelsmann Verlag, 1992), p. 139.
7. The events in the embassy in Prague are described extensively in Rehlinger, op. cit., pp. 154–93.
8. Vogel, interview with author, Teupitz, Dec. 12, 1991.
9. Rehlinger, interview with author, Bonn, July 22, 1991.
10. Streit was replaced by Günter Wendland at the end of 1986, and died on July 3, 1987, at the age of 76.
11. Vogel, Niebling, interviews with author, Berlin, May 7, 1992, and Wolf, Klosterfelde, June 13, 1992.

12. Niebling and Vogel, interviews with author, Berlin, May 7, 1992, and Teupitz, Jan. 18, 1993.
13. Niebling, interview with author, Berlin, May 7, 1992.
14. Rehlinger, op. cit., pp. 220–37.
15. "Bonn Spy Case: 'Hopeless Personal Situation,' " *The New York Times,* Sept. 3, 1985.
16. For details of the Baumann case see "Der Tod des Roten Admirals," *Stern Magazin,* Oct. 8, 1992, pp. 88–97.
17. Niebling, interview with author, Berlin, May 7, 1992.
18. "Bitte, bitte machen," *Der Spiegel,* No. 34, 1989.
19. Niebling, interview with author, Berlin, May 7, 1992.
20. *Der Spiegel,* op. cit., No. 34, 1989.
21. Andert and Herzberg, op. cit., pp. 65–66.
22. Ibid., p. 66.
23. Priesnitz, interview with author, Bonn, July 1990.
24. "Das droht die DDR zu vernichten," *Der Spiegel,* No. 33, 1989.
25. Ibid.
26. Egon Krenz, *Wenn Mauern fallen* (Vienna: Paul Neff Verlag, 1990), p. 28.
27. Priesnitz, interview with author, Bonn, July 1990.
28. Vogel, interview with author, Teupitz, Dec. 12, 1991.
29. "Wer konnte das ahnen?," *Der Spiegel,* No. 40, 1989.
30. Barkley, interview with author, Berlin, Oct. 5, 1990.
31. Vogel office archives.
32. Krenz, op. cit., p. 88.
33. Vogel interview, Berlin, Dec. 12, 1991.
34. Andert and Herzberg, op. cit., p. 33.
35. "A Contrite Government: Contrite Deputies Say Party Failed the East Germans," *The New York Times,* Nov. 14, 1989.

CHAPTER 12

1. Vogel, interview with author, Teupitz, June 22, 1991.
2. "Bundesverdienstkreuz für DDR-Anwalt Vogel?" *Bild,* Dec. 5, 1989.
3. Vogel office archives. A partial text of the letter appeared in "Enthüllung, Der Menschenhändler," *extra Magazin,* No. 24, 1991,
4. Vogel, interview with author, Teupitz, June 22, 1991.
5. Vogel, submission to the Amtsgericht Tiergarten district court, through Dr. Friederike Schulenburg, Mar. 25, 1992.
6. Text in ADN and *Neue Zeit,* Dec. 7, 1989.
7. See, for example, the account in "Der Vermittler wirft das Handtuch," *Süddeutsche Zeitung,* Dec. 7, 1989.
8. Ibid.
9. The suitcases Schalck's driver had brought to Vogel's home were taken after the search to the East German prosecutor-general's headquarters on Hermann-Matern-Strasse. There, they were rifled—by whom was never clear—and all the incriminating materials they had contained on party funds, income, and ownership of the party firms that CoCo controlled were removed, as were the files on the secret CoCo bank account that had been kept in Honecker's name. After unification, German prosecutors apparently found that they could prove nothing against Schalck with what was left in the suitcases. He had turned himself in, but emerged after investigative arrest to run an antiques business on the Tegernsee, a fashionable Bavarian alpine resort near

Munich. See "Gezielt entfernt und 'gesäubert,' " *Frankfurter Allgemeine Zeitung,* Oct. 16, 1991.

10. Priesnitz, interview with author, Bonn, July 1990.

11. Rehlinger, op. cit., pp. 246–47.

12. Wolf, op. cit., p. 319.

13. "Honecker Finds Strange Bedfellows," *The New York Times,* Feb. 2, 1990.

14. Andert and Herzberg, op. cit., p. 52.

15. A copy of the document is in the author's possession.

16. Przybylski, op. cit., p. 188.

17. David Gill, and Ulrich Schröter, *Das Ministerium für Staatssicherheit: Anatomie des Mielke-Imperiums* (Berlin: Rowohlt-Verlag, 1991), pp. 95–96.

18. Vogel, interview with author, Teupitz, Dec. 12, 1991.

19. The Stasi guards were convicted in January 1992.

20. "Enthüllung: Der Menschenhändler. Milliardengeschäft des Rechtsanwalts Dr. Wolfgang Vogel," *extra magazin,* No. 24, 1991, June 6, 1991.

21. Ibid.

22. Vogel, interview with author, Teupitz, Feb. 16, 1992; and Schmidthammer, op. cit., p. 187.

23. See "Dann bleiben Sie eben in der DDR," *Welt am Sonntag,* Jan. 12, 1992.

24. "Sie hat nichts merken können," *Der Spiegel,* No. 3, 1992.

25. Stange, interviews with author, Berlin, June 16, 1992, and Bonn, Oct. 8, 1992.

26. See "Unterlagen, die den Weltfrieden gefährden," *Der Spiegel,* No. 13, 1992.

27. Court order against Vogel, Mar. 30, 1992.

28. See chapter 1.

29. Niebling, interview with author, Berlin, May 7, 1992.

30. Ibid.

31. From transcript of the "Bericht aus Bonn" program, ARD television, Jan. 1, 1992.

32. "Held oder Schurke? Der Fall Vogel," *Super Illu,* Jan. 1, 1992.

33. Documents signed by Niebling in Vogel's Stasi files.

34. "Makler im Zwielicht," *Die Zeit,* Mar. 20, 1992.

35. Vogel, interview with author, Berlin, May 7, 1992.

36. Ibid.

37. "Sore in Forint," *Der Spiegel,* No. 15, 1992.

38. Vogel, interview with author, Berlin, May 7, 1992.

39. Loewe's letter and others in Vogel's office files were submitted to the court by Dr. Schulenburg in aid of an application for relief from the arrest warrant.

40. Thiel, interview with author, Berlin, May 6, 1992. Vogel repaid the money out of his own funds after his release.

41. Vogel, interview with author, Berlin, May 7, 1992.

42. The court decision is "Landgericht Berlin Beschluss No. 511 Qs 35 and 36/92," July 14, 1992.

43. Honecker's trial began Nov. 12, 1992, with him, Mielke, former Prime Minister Willi Stoph, and three other former high East German officials charged with the manslaughter of 13 people killed at the border, as those ultimately responsible for giving the border guards orders to shoot to kill. The proceedings gradually disintegrated as the defendants became more feeble. The Berlin Constitutional Court ruled on Jan. 11, 1993, that Honecker, suffering from liver cancer and not expected to live to the end of the proceedings, should not be tried, and he was released the next day.

EPILOGUE

1. For the complete list of Stasi liaison offices abroad, see Gill and Schröter, op. cit. pp. 78–79.

2. Vogel, interview with author, Teupitz, June 22, 1991.

3. Vogel's ability to get things done had begun to diminish even before the Wall collapsed. Kalmanovich, who had been moldering in an Israeli prison since his arrest at the end of 1987 on charges of spying for the Soviets, was one of the first to find this out. Kalmanovich turned to Vogel immediately after his arrest, asking his wife to pass a message to Ronnie Greenwald in New York: "Talk to Vogel and get me out," he said, before the Israelis sentenced him to nine years in prison in 1989. Kalmanovich's plea intrigued both Vogel and Honecker, for it turned out that there was someone the Soviets wanted very badly to get out of Israel, one of their best and most trusted agents: Prof. Avraham Marcus Klingberg, a Russian Jew who had gone to Israel in 1948. The KGB had lost contact with him there in 1983. Klingberg suddenly vanished from sight under mysterious circumstances, apparently while working at a top-secret Israeli research station in the field of germs and epidemology. Later, it was learned that the Israelis had convicted him, too, of being an undercover Soviet agent. (See "Holds Scientist for Spying," *The Guardian,* Feb. 26, 1988.)

Honecker hoped that Vogel could bring off an exchange of agents and prisoners that would give East Germany a diplomatic foothold in Israel, and sent Vogel off to try at the end of May 1989. Wolfgang and Helga flew to Tel Aviv, where Vogel called on both Kalmanovich and Klingberg in their jails. The Israeli authorities provided him with a negotiating partner, a lawyer named Amnon Zichroni who had the same kind of shadowy connections to the government in Jerusalem as Vogel had in East Berlin. (Vogel and Niebling interviews; confirmation of Vogel's mission also appeared in secret East German files obtained by the *Frankfurter Rundschau* newspaper, which published details on July 17, 1992.) They sketched the outlines of a possible deal. The Israelis wanted Air Force Capt. Ron Arad, a navigator who had been shot down and taken prisoner near the Syrian border in Lebanon in October 1986. Capt. Arad, 28 years old when he was captured, had been seized by the Lebanese Amal guerrilla group and later turned over, apparently for $300,000 in cash, to the Hezbollah party, the Iranian-controlled Muslim extremist organization then holding Terry Waite, Terry Anderson, and other Western hostages in the Bekaa Valley. For a few weeks, both Vogel and the Israelis had high hopes for what he could accomplish through the KGB's connections in Syria, and the Stasi's in South Yemen. There was even talk of a comprehensive East-West exchange that would free all the Western hostages, Waite and Anderson included. Vogel drew up a package that was to include Capt. Arad, seven other Israeli prisoners of war, Kalmanovich and Klingberg. He also hoped to include Arne Treholt, a Norwegian diplomat convicted of providing NATO secrets to Moscow, as well as a pair of East German agents imprisoned in Britain. And he was still hoping to free Nelson Mandela from jail in South Africa.

On May 30, Vogel and Zichroni negotiated a written agreement for a swap of Capt. Arad for Klingberg. Vogel was at the point of going to Lebanon to try to talk with the Hezbollah himself when, fortunately for him perhaps, the deal fell through because Hezbollah was demanding weapons—fast boats they could use for guerrilla raids on Israel from the Mediterranean. They had no interest in Marcus Klingberg, and the East Germans had no desire to follow in the footsteps of Oliver North with an arms-for-hostages deal. (Vogel interview.) Flying to Vienna to see Vogel again in September 1989, Zichroni told him the Israelis were very disappointed in the meager results. (See *Frankfurter Rundschau,* op. cit.) Waite, Anderson, and the other Western hostages in the Middle East all eventually came free in 1992, but not through Vogel's efforts; Capt. Arad and Klingberg were still held prisoner as this book went to press; Kalmanovich was freed on March 10, 1993.

4. How self-evident this was to American policymakers in Washington—and yet how little they understood about how things had actually worked behind the scenes—can be seen from a letter written to Vogel on Jan. 26, 1990, by Deputy Secretary of State Lawrence S. Eagleburger. More than three months after Honecker's fall, and more than two months after the Wall had come down, the United States asked if Vogel could arrange a swap of one of the most important Soviet agents the Americans had ever had in Moscow, for two KGB agents held in the United States.

This was Dmitri F. Polyakov, a legendary agent known to American intelligence as "Top Hat." He had walked into the FBI offices in New York City in 1960 as a junior officer and had worked for the Americans for a quarter century, rising to the rank of lieutenant general in the Soviet Army Air Defense Command, his last known job in the mid-1980s.

Twelve days before Eagleburger's letter to Vogel, *Pravda* had published an unusual article announcing that a former Soviet diplomat identified as "Donald F." had been sentenced to death for working for the United States since 1961. "Donald F.," it soon became clear, was Polyakov, but the *Pravda* article left it unclear whether the death sentence had actually been carried out; hence Eagleburger's letter to Vogel, who was by then unable to accomplish anything in response.

Even if he had tried, it would have been too late, for eventually the Soviets revealed that Polyakov had been executed on March 15, 1988. Some experts suspected that he had been tracked down from leaks authorized by James Jesus Angleton of the CIA, who had long suspected "Top Hat" of being a KGB deception. See Tom Mangold, *Cold Warrior—James Jesus Angleton: The CIA's Master Spy Hunter* (New York: Simon & Schuster, 1991), pp. 233–36. The Eagleburger letter is in Vogel's office archives.

5. Falin, interview with author, Moscow, June 11, 1991.

6. Niebling, interview with author, Berlin, May 7, 1992. The German office in charge of preserving Stasi files wrote to the author, on Feb. 18, 1992, that it had "no indications" that Vogel had been any kind of employee of the Stasi. "Access to Herr Prof. Dr. Vogel's files, since this is clearly a case of a victim in the meaning of the statute StUG section 32, Paragraph 2, is possible only with his agreement. An exception is permissible only in the case of former members of the State Security. In Herr Prof. Dr. Vogel's case there is no such indication," the letter said.

Vogel acknowledges that he did receive documents from the files that East German prosecutors seized from Mielke's office in late 1989. The protocol prepared by the East German prosecutor-general's office, dated June 20, 1990, listed 6 expired passports, 5 photographs, 3 personal contract forms, 5 identity papers, 6 "discrediting press articles," 10 personal letters, and 4 private drawings. The reports Vogel had made of his conversations with Wehner over the years were also among Mielke's papers, but according to Vogel, listed on a separate protocol. All these papers were examined by the German prosecutors again after unification, but Vogel got only some of them back, he told the author on Nov. 13, 1992.

7. Landgericht Berlin decision, July 14, 1992.

8. "Verbindungen abends über den Privatanschluss," *Frankfurter Allgemeine Zeitung,* Apr. 13, 1992, p. 3.

9. *Super Illu,* Jan. 30, 1992, p. 64.

10. Rehlinger, op. cit., pp. 247–248.

11. "Bräutigam bezeugt Vogel Vertrauen und Respekt," *Frankfurter Allgemeine Zeitung,* March 30, 1992.

12. Kunst, letter in Vogel's office files.

13. Vogel, interview with author, Berlin, Oct. 14, 1992.

14. Helmut Schmidt, letter to author, May 11, 1992.

INDEX

ABOUT THE AUTHOR

CRAIG R. WHITNEY, European diplomatic correspondent of *The New York Times,* was born in Massachusetts in 1943 and educated there in the Westborough public schools, at Phillips Academy, Andover, and at Harvard College. He was James Reston's assistant in the Washington bureau of *The New York Times* from 1965 to 1966, and served as a public affairs officer with the U.S. Navy in Washington and Saigon, Vietnam, from 1966 to 1969. He has worked as reporter, foreign editor, and assistant managing editor for *The Times* in New York, and as bureau chief in Saigon, Bonn, Moscow, Washington, and London. He and his wife, Heidi, live in Bonn–Bad Godesberg and have two children, Alexandra and Stefan.